VINTAGE TIMECHARTS

IN MEMORY OF JLG

Jancis Robinson

VINTAGE TIMECHARTS

The Pedigree and Performance of
Fine Wines to the Year 2000

WEIDENFELD & NICOLSON
NEW YORK

VINTAGE TIMECHARTS

Published by Weidenfeld & Nicolson, New York
A Division of Wheatland Corporation
841 Broadway
New York, New York 10003-4793

Published in Canada by General Publishing Company, Ltd.

Edited and designed by
Mitchell Beazley International Ltd
Artists House, 14/15 Manette Street, London W1V 5LB

Library of Congress Cataloging-in-Publication Data

Robinson, Jancis.
    Vintage timecharts: the pedigree and performance of fine
wine to the year 2000 / Jancis Robinson. — 1st ed.
        p.   cm.
    Includes index.
    ISBN 1-55584-440-5 (elk. paper)
    1. Wine and wine making. I.   Title.
TP548.R646   1989
641.2′2—dc20   89-9053
                                                                  CIP

Senior Art Editor Tim Foster
Editor Diane Pengelly
Designers Rupert Chappell and Joan Curtis
Research Simon Ryder
Translation Cathy Rigby
Production Ted Timberlake

Senior Executive Editor Chris Foulkes

Typeset in Bembo and Gill by Servis Filmsetting Ltd,
Manchester, England
Origination by Scantrans (Singapore)
Printed and bound in Spain by Printer Industria Gráfica SA,
Barcelona

First American Edition

10 9 8 7 6 5 4 3 2 1

CONTENTS

ACKNOWLEDGEMENTS:

As well as to all the wine producers acknowledged on the opposite page, I owe enormous thanks for the apparently infinite patience of the Mitchell Beazley team and to numerous wine people who were far more helpful than they need have been, especially Lisa Barnard, Jean-François Bazin, G Belloni & Co, Joseph Berkmann, William Bolter, James Burgis, Ellen Catsonis, Cordier Wines, Bipin Desai, Direct Wines, Anthony Hanson MW, João Henriques, David Hodges, Justerini & Brooks, O W Loeb & Co, Maisons, Marques et Domaines, Jean-Paul Médard, Paul Merritt, Hazel Murphy, David Pinchard, Stuart Pigott, Belle and Bernard Rhodes, Professor Pascal Ribéreau-Gayon, Peter Shamash, Peter A Sichel, Kerry Stewart, Professor Vernon Singleton, Simon Taylor-Gill, Renato Trestini and Jeremy Watson. And most of all I thank Nick Lander and the rest of my family for so gallantly putting up with me and my manuscript.

PREFACE

I am not naturally audacious, but this is a very audacious book. Many readers will be amazed by my effrontery in trying to answer so many supposedly unanswerable questions, in giving concrete form to something as apparently unpredictable as a wine's evolution.

They may also be shocked that I have based such a book on a single brain and palate. Although I was lucky enough to taste most of these wines with their makers, and to benefit from their comments and accumulated wisdom, I must take responsibility for the judgements that follow – even if they comprise an attempt to objectify one of the world's more subjective areas.

What gave me the strength to risk such a bold approach was my determination to highlight just how little is known about what happens to wine once it is in bottle, the period in its life cycle that is surely most important for the consumer. Some wine drinkers have access to the somewhat haphazard experiences of themselves and others in working out when to open a treasured bottle, but many of us who spend money on wine nowadays do not. If *Vintage Timecharts* does something to encourage more research in this direction, then that will give me some comfort when errors of judgement are pointed out and my lack of proper humility chided.

I have already been immensely cheered by the enthusiastic response from fellow wine drinkers when I have outlined the point of this book, but encouragement has come most of all from the wine producers themselves – the people who have cared for the vines, picked the grapes, nursed the fermentation process, racked, fined and decided when to bottle, yet who perhaps have least opportunity to monitor the development of the wines themselves.

Without exception, even at *premier grand cru* level, they seemed to leap at the chance of opening up perfectly-kept bottles going back to the seventies and beyond (to the 1880s in the case of Louis Jadot) and seeing how they had developed. Without their generosity, and their willingness to share their knowledge and their wines with me, the research involved in creating this book would have been impossible. Nothing has been too much trouble, no question too mundane.

Throughout the time I was researching this book, I was aware that no researcher had ever had a better lot. Which of us would not gladly have dedicated eight months to tasting some of the world's finest wines *in situ*? For that I must particularly thank Dan Green in New York who prompted the ideas that gave rise to this book.

INTRODUCTION

Prediction is a difficult business. Particularly, as they say, with regard to the future. *Vintage Timecharts* attempts to answer the question most often and most justifiably put by wine drinkers: "When is this wine ready to drink?" It is difficult to give precise advice about wine's evolution, but that is no excuse for evading the issue entirely, particularly since so many of the wines bought by the current wave of relative newcomers to wine have long but varying lifespans. (And as these charts demonstrate, even old hands at wine collecting can be surprised by the disparity between the reputation and the actual performance of some vintages.) This book is addressed not just to those who have started their own cellar by investing in wine by the case. It is also designed to inform those who want to buy wine of some quality on a more impulsive – or perhaps less financially demanding – basis, by the bottle.

From the eighteenth century when we worked out how to conserve wine in an effectively stoppered bottle, the question "when?" has been relevant – but never so pressing. The great cellars of the nineteenth and early twentieth centuries were maintained by relatively few well-heeled individuals, who had often inherited bottles laid down by their fathers. They bought and drank on a long-term, strictly chronological basis so that they could, in turn, hand on a cellar of mature wine to the next generation. Bottles were opened because they had reached a certain age rather than because the individual characteristics of different vintages were necessarily fully monitored or understood.

Today however there is less excuse for such a broad brush approach. There are millions rather than hundreds of consumers who could make good use of comprehensible information on different wines' maturity patterns. And just when there are so many more people asking "When should I open this bottle?", the cost of that bottle has escalated enormously. A fine wine worth ageing can now constitute a major investment, but unlike so many other tempting investments, the return on a fine wine is neither swift nor certain.

The bottles offered on many restaurant wine lists and by most wine retailers bear little relation to what is actually ready to drink (although this fact is not widely advertised). The great majority of fine wines on sale today are years and often decades away from a state of pleasure-giving maturity. Yet the consumer is given little guidance as to how to address these expensive but still embryonic treasures.

Why have wine producers, wine retailers and even wine writers been loath to provide an answer to this crucial question? Die-hard cynics, of which I am not one, might suggest that is because it is in the interests of distributors and retailers not to encourage the new wine drinker to garner his collection of expensive wines waiting for them to mature, but to keep on drinking, buying and reading about the latest (and most commercially available) wines.

There is also the inescapable fact that definitive single answers to the question "When should I open this bottle?" are maddeningly elusive. Any answer must be couched in conditionals. If the wine has been shipped and stored correctly, if your taste is more English than French, if you plan to drink the wine with food and at the right temperature, and so on. One further frustrating aspect is that, in a sense, one never knows for sure when a wine has reached its peak until that peak is past and the wine begins to show signs of decline. (All these factors will be covered in some detail later in this book. See Wine and Time, beginning on page 10.)

It is usually no good turning to the wine producers themselves for guidance. They are often too preoccupied with the current vintage (and have much too empty a cellar) to address fully the consumer's concern with middle-aged bottles. In fact when asked how long a good vintage will last, some producers use the exasperatingly portentous phrase "It will outlive us both" – and tend to rebuff criticisms of less successful vintages with the unanswerable defence that they have been opened years too early.

But I know at least one much more fundamental reason why so little information is given about what happens to individual wines in bottle: because so little is known.

For scientific knowledge of wine we look to the great faculties of viticulture and oenology, two disciplines that are increasingly seen as symbiotic halves of one. It is producers and not consumers who direct and subsidise the academics in their choice of research work. It is hardly surprising then that almost all the research work achieved by wine academics and the more academically minded wine producers concerns vine and wine at some point during the production process, rather than once it has left the producer and is heading for its ultimate consumer.

The end of the bottling line effectively constitutes the end of quantifiable knowledge of wine. If it is clonal selection, vine trellising methods, different yeast cultures, barrel ageing and bottling techniques you're after, then you will find volumes of information covering every nuance. But the body of knowledge concerning what happens to wine once it is in bottle and, especially, once it is the responsibility of us consumers, is minimal – even though this phase usually accounts for much the longest epoch in a wine's life.

The Champenois have probably done more work than most on the evolution of wine in bottle, at least partly because their wine spends practically all its life in bottle and, once there, is peculiarly prey to the ravages of light and heat. As we shall learn, however, their work sheds little light on the ageing of still wines in bottle.

The Bordelais on the other hand, whose wines are indisputably the prime candidates for any cellar, have discovered surprisingly little about what actually happens there. In Professor Emile Peynaud's classic 350-page *Connaissance et Travail du Vin*, the subject of bottle ageing is dealt with in just over half a page. And when I wrote to the estimable Professor Pascal Ribéreau-Gayon, head of Bordeaux's Institute of Oenology, asking for a digest of current research work on the subject he disarmingly replied: "The question you raise is very interesting, but it has rarely been studied in an academic way, bearing in mind the difficulty of the subject and the complexity of the chemical phenomena set in train."

(To the same request for information Professor Vernon Singleton, his Californian counterpart at UC Davis, replied "Because our research and that of others is diverse and voluminous, it is difficult to answer your very general request . . . " but it transpired that much of this New World research focused on the more sterile subject of how to accelerate artificially the process of ageing.)

Professor Ribéreau-Gayon is of course right. It is an extremely intricate subject, and one that will take a great deal of time (decades) and money (all those control bottles of classed growth Bordeaux) to accomplish. I am sure that one of these days – perhaps when commercial pressures shift slightly – academe will give wine consumers a clearer idea of just what happens to wine in bottle, and show producers and consumers how to get the most from that process.

In the meantime however, as a consumer and writer dedicated to maximising the pleasure that wine can give, I can see more reasons than ever before to tackle this difficult subject even if my answers must necessarily be given more on the basis of experience than analysis. When bottles of even infant wine can be outrageously expensive, it is no longer good enough to advise customers to trust their own judgement – a judgement which is all too often impossible to make until the cork has been so expensively and irreversibly pulled.

The following offering is based on the judgements of just one palate, my own, informed in almost all cases by the opinions of the man at my elbow, the wine-maker himself. It is written in full cognizance of just how mutable a thing wine is, and in humble admiration of that fact.

WINE AND TIME

Wine is the most extraordinary thing. It is easy but carelessly insulting to take it for granted. It not only offers a wider range of sensations than any other single food or drink, it is also one of the few things we buy that is capable not just of changing but of changing for the better.

Other foodstuffs and organic matter are also in a state of constant flux, but they are usually bought at or near their optimum maturity. Changes in them over days, let alone months or years, tend to be observably for the worse as they are attacked and degraded by bacteria. Although much of modern wine-making is designed specifically to ward off predatory bacteria, wine has always risen above the process of rapid deterioration that threatens most other victuals, not just because of its alcohol content but also because the fruit of the vine family has such a high level of tartaric acid, a notable inhibitor of the microbe. This means that wine is capable of lasting for decades, in some cases centuries, and can therefore put us in a unique sort of direct, tactile contact with the past.

The products of other art forms such as sculpture and painting are just as tangible so can give us the thrill of sharing some common experience with our predecessors. But in a much more fundamental way than any other product designed by man for the long term, wine is constantly evolving and, in many significant cases, improving. All of the very finest wines improve with age. Indeed what distinguishes a noble wine from the merely pleasant is this ability to evolve.

One of the most exciting and challenging aspects of wine appreciation is monitoring this evolution. The most obvious and objective way in which a wine changes is in its colour. Wine's maturation cycle is most dramatic in red wines. A red wine runs out of the fermentation vat as a deep blackish purple liquid with brilliant shocking-pink foam. In most cases this will be the deepest colour the wine will ever be. If it is given a stint in a storage vessel that is not absolutely airtight, such as an oak cask, then it becomes perceptibly paler, browner and less blue. Since a wine in cask is exposed to small but significant amounts of oxygen, it is subject to some **oxidation** – the browning effect that exposure to

The colour just after fermentation is the deepest and bluest it ever gets – from now on it will gently fade and brown.

oxygen can be seen to have on, for example, a cut apple (although this is just one of a maelstrom of complex reactions that take place in a wine in cask).

Once the wine is bottled, it undergoes a much slower version of this visible ageing process that lightens and browns the wine from purple through crimson, ruby, mid-red, fox red and brick red to tawny. Because the process looks so similar to oxidation, it is tempting to think that it is a sort of slow in-bottle oxidation. Pasteur advanced the theory more than century ago that wine maturation was the result of the slow oxidising effect of a small amount of oxygen that was allowed into a bottle by the cork, and this theory is so attractively simple that many people continue to believe it.

But this stately ageing process, observable over the years that a wine spends in bottle, is much more complicated. More recent scientific work has shown that any decent cork offers complete protection against oxidation to a wine cellared on its side, and that the amount of oxygen entering a properly corked bottle is negligible. In fact the process of ageing in bottle, as outlined below, owes less to oxidation than to its exact opposite, reduction.

The ageing rate of a wine in bottle varies enormously from wine to wine and from vintage to vintage, but it is helpful to the wine drinker to note

The visible effect of time on wine. The two-year-old wine on the left is deep red, still with purple tints and great depth of colour. The wine on the right is a 12-year-old sample of the same wine.

that the colour at the rim of a glassful of wine is the most revealing indicator of the wine's maturity. Two glasses of wine can seem to be exactly the same colour when the main mass of the wine is examined from directly above, but when they are tilted away against a light background, the two different colour patterns often seen at the rim can provide major clues in establishing the maturity of each wine.

Two wines from the same property from the vintages 1978 and 1979 in Bordeaux, for example, can provide an illuminating contrast in this respect. The main mass of the wines is usually much the same mid-ruby colour, but once the glasses are tilted away so that the rim can be examined, more often than not the 1978 has a completely clear rim of colourless liquid shading into a ring of tawny which itself shades into the mid-ruby mass. The mid-ruby of the 1979 on the other hand goes right out to the rim and still has, in some cases, even a hint of youthful purple. This provides a clear indication (although not incontrovertible proof, wine being a capricious thing) that in this case the 1978 is maturing more rapidly than the 1979. Lightening and browning are the two great indicators of red wine maturity.

The initial deep purple colour in young red wine comes from **anthocyanins** (the "cyan" owing its origins to the Greek word for dark blue), the same sort of colouring matter that tints vegetables and flowers. It is found just under a grape's skin and is leached out by alcohol during fermentation. Within limits, the longer and warmer the fermentation, the more anthocyanins are leached into the wine, but a major key to the potential longevity of a wine is the concentration of anthocyanins in the grape. Some grape varieties such as Cabernet Sauvignon, Syrah, Nebbiolo and many of the port varieties of the Douro are naturally high in colouring matter and therefore particularly well suited to producing wines for the long term.

Monsieur Rougier at Château Simone of Palette (see page 91) studying the colour of his wine with particular care.

The choice of grape variety or varieties has an enormous influence on the wine's life cycle and ageability. Relatively small grapes with thick skins and high pip-to-juice ratios are most likely to produce wines which develop and last.

In general the smaller the yield of grapes from a vineyard, the more concentrated the anthocyanins, and the deeper and bluer the colour of a red wine, the longer future it has ahead of it. The colour and ageability of a red wine are also determined by the strength of the wine's acidity, its "pH". The pH of water is exactly seven, and somewhere between seven and 14 for any alkaline substance; for wine, it usually varies between three and four. The higher it is, the less lively and concentrated the colour will be and the sooner the wine browns. In recent years, much of the research work in warmer wine-producing regions where pHs can easily be higher than four has been concentrated on achieving grape musts with lower pHs.

The amount of sulphur, the wine-maker's antiseptic, used also influences the initial colour and ageing rate of a wine, sulphur having a bleaching effect on colouring matter in young wines.

Tannins are also closely linked to anthocyanins as a determinant of longevity. Like anthocyanins, tannins are **phenols**, phenolics or polyphenols, and are also found in grape-skins as well as in grape pips and stalks. Different sorts of tannins are also present in the oak used for wine casks and play a major role during red wine ageing.

Everyone who has ever tasted cold tea has experienced the mouth-puckering sensation of tannin. Any red wine destined for a long life needs a high tannin level at the outset. It acts as a preservative and wards off harmful excess oxidation. Many "serious" red wines have such a high tannin level in their first year or two that they can be almost painful to taste. The tannins that come from the grape are often complemented by further tannins from the oak in which the wine is initially stored: up to 0.2 gm/litre a year from new oak according to some studies. Tannins exist in varied, if poorly understood forms and much of the focus of modern research is on trying to make young wines higher in softer, riper, less aggressive tannins that are no less useful than the harsher tannins that were traditionally extracted from the grape.

During maturation these phenolics, both anthocyanins and tannins, have a tendency to aggregate, to form much larger chemical entities or "polymerise". The larger the aggregation, the less pronounced the dark blue elements and the paler and browner the colour. And the larger the aggregation the softer and less painfully, spikily tannic is the impression on the palate. The result of this increasing aggregation is a progressively paler, browner, softer wine in which, eventually, the large aggregates become too heavy to remain in solution and are precipitated as sediment. These processes are susceptible to temperature so that the aggregation is encouraged by heat (during the summer) and the precipitation by cold (during the winter).

At the end of its effective life a red wine will be pale, probably distinctly brown and it will start to taste more acid, higher in the lemon juice-like substance that tends to crinkle up the edges of the tongue. Such a wine is often described as "drying out", an expression that, confusingly, has nothing to do with the sweetness level in the wine (which will have remained constant and in reds is negligible in all but the most nakedly commercial wines anyway). A wine is said to be drying out when it is difficult to perceive the flavour of ripe fruit on the palate and the acidity becomes more and more dominant. In fact during a wine's life the acid level remains more or less constant, if anything diminishing slightly, as alcohols combine with acids to form esters (esterification, along with oxidation, was for a long time erroneously thought to be a measure of a wine's quality and maturity). What happens as a wine "dries out" and appears more acid is that the phenolics are precipitated and no longer add their softening, flattering influence to what is perceived on the palate, which allows the acid in the wine to become more evident.

An apparent excess of acidity rarely poses a problem in a white wine, young or old, however. Indeed acidity is often cited as the white wine equivalent of tannin, the life preserver. But if little is known about the precise ageing process of red wines, even less is understood about exactly what happens as a white wine matures (partly because the majority of long-living wines are red, partly because it must be quite different from what happens in red wines with their much higher level of phenolics). What is clear is that white wines also become progressively brown with age, although at a much slower rate than most reds. Instead of getting paler with age they deepen in colour. It can happen therefore that a great old Sauternes can actually end up looking remarkably like a great red Bordeaux of about the same age: both of them mid-tawny.

What is also known is that excessive oxygen is even more inimical to a white, or rosé, wine than a red because its browning effect is more obviously distasteful and because the fresh, untainted fruit flavours of youth usually form a higher proportion of a white or pink wine's allure than they do in reds – although an increasing number of modern white wines seem to be made simply in order to broadcast significant investment in new oak barrels even at the expense of the wine's intrinsic fresh fruit flavours.

The other major way in which we wine drinkers can monitor a wine's maturity is of course with our noses rather than our eyes. Odour development may be less easy for scientists to observe and quantify but it is probably more important to consumers than

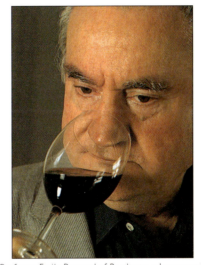

Professor Emile Peynaud of Bordeaux, whose nose has influenced the life cycle of thousands of wines.

colour, particularly since it is in this way that we derive such a high proportion of our sensory pleasure from wine. The difference, put crudely, between a young, simple wine and a mature, great one is in the range of sensation available to the sense of taste, which effectively means the sense of smell.

The predominant smell of a young wine, as distinct from the carbon dioxide gas given off during fermentation, is vibrantly fresh and fruity in a direct, unadorned and uncomplicated way. These sort of grape-derived smells are often stronger in wine than in the actual grape because the process of maceration has made the flavour elements of the grape, also situated just under the skin of the grape, more volatile. These are called **primary aromas** which come straight from the grape.

The more complicated smells that derive from the processes of wine-making are called **secondary**

aromas. These can take time to manifest themselves but tend to be more intense the more fermentable sugar there is.

It is only after a wine has been in bottle for at least a year and often for several years that **tertiary aromas** start to assert themselves, a very much more nuanced, complex and many-layered amalgam of flavour elements that is probably derived from compounds formed by the interaction of the sources of primary aromas, secondary aromas and other compounds that have formed in the wine. Such an amalgam of tertiary aromas is called, much more attractively, the wine's **bouquet**. But no-one should be bamboozled by the apparent neatness of this nomenclature into thinking that the process of bouquet or flavour formation is understood with any precision.

Generally speaking the more primary aromas a wine has the more intense will be its bouquet. And since the bottle in which the bouquet is formed is hermetically sealed so that the wine is protected from oxygen, this bouquet is regarded by chemists as reductive, the opposite of oxidative.

Scientific detail is useful in understanding the roles played by various youthful ingredients in the course of a wine's life, but it still cannot explain fully the way in which wines mature. Let us consider the practical example of a typical fine red wine.

Just after fermentation the red wine will be deep, deep purple and stink of carbon dioxide and simple primary aromas. If tasted during the initial months in cask, the effect it has on the insides of the cheeks will show that it has probably become even more uncompromisingly tannic, especially if the cask is new oak. The secondary aromas also start to be perceptible now – although the wine's flavours will be heavily influenced by cellar treatments such as fining and racking, when the sulphur is added.

Immediately after bottling the aromas will sometimes be muted but at some point during the wine's first year or two in bottle any good wine will usually exhibit the most gloriously youthful array of primary and secondary aromas, a wonderfully attract-ive if simple array of fresh fruit flavours overlaid with scents of oak. Nothing is knit together; it is clear that this is a wine worth waiting for, but it is also very tempting to enjoy the young wine without giving it a chance to mature.

Few ever taste century-old wines but it's a waste to drink them in callow youth if they are built to last.

There is nothing wrong with deriving this sort of straightforward pleasure from a young wine – in fact developing wines are much more attractive than those that are fading – but it is waste of money and potential. There are other wines designed specifically not to be aged and their lower price reflects this. Drinking a classed growth Bordeaux from a good vintage in its fourth year is to deny yourself a high proportion of the pleasure you have paid for.

At some point over the next 10 years or so, depending on the wine and the vintage but often at about four years after the grapes were picked for burgundies and eight to 10 years for Bordeaux, some wines seem to hibernate. The aromas seem to disappear into the deep dark tannic mass of the wine, which in all probability tastes more unattractive than at any other point in its life. This can be a worrying time for the wine collector who has paid more than he or she cares to admit for the other eleven bottles in the case, but there is no need to lose your nerve. Many very good vintages and several great wines go through a sullen phase before emerging as much more splendidly gorgeous liquids afterwards. Many 1966 red Bordeaux tasted quite charmless in their early teens for example, and the successful 1975s are just starting to blossom after a period of tasting very hard and unyielding. To be even more specific, Château Margaux 1978 suddenly drew in its horns in 1988 but now seems to be opening out again and will undoubtedly become one of the greatest wines of the vintage.

French *tonneliers* are working harder than ever to meet worldwide demand from wine-makers who wish to add another element promoting longevity in their wines: new oak casks for ageing.

This phenomenon is thought to be due to the action of certain tannins on the wine's more aromatic components at this point in their interaction with the colouring matter. There is no need to worry about the apparent disappearance or muting of bouquet in a maturing wine so long as the colour is healthy and there seems to be good concentration and balance of body, tannin and acidity on the palate.

The general maturity pattern of a top quality wine designed for ageing can therefore be charted as a continuing rise in quality and in the range and complexity of sensations that it offers the taster, with perhaps a hiccup during that rise. The wine then reaches its maturity, the period during which it does make sense to open the bottle. The bouquet is fully formed and alluring, the initial tannins are softened so that the mature wine's complex layers and nuances of flavour can be enjoyed and the wine seems a harmonious whole. One would call this stage the wine's plateau of drinkability, were it not for the fact that the wine is not necessarily identical throughout this state of maturity, as many of the Timecharts illustrate. Depending on the fragility of the wine, it may even evolve quite considerably during this time, but it should be lively, fully formed and satisfying throughout.

There then comes a point at which the bouquet becomes less intense and the concentration of extract and alcohol on the palate seems to wane, the colour browning all the while. This signals the start of a decline which can take many years but which ends in an acid, thin-tasting, tawny liquid offering only a hint of the rich, fruity pleasures of the past. Some wine collectors treasure these poignant manifestations of senility and find that the impact of a wine at any earlier stage is just too brutally forceful, but the maturity of a wine charted in this book starts when the wine has developed a perceptible bouquet and lasts until that starts to fade.

White wines tend to go through a similar, though less dramatic and often shorter, cycle. In youth the acidity seems pronounced because the softening process of age has only just begun – and a white wine can also taste quite astringent at this stage because of tannins that have been absorbed into the wine from grape skins or pips. The bouquet develops as in a red wine and the wine reaches a similar, though often shorter, period of maturity. Towards the end of a white wine's life however the wine not only browns but the bouquet fades in intensity and also loses its freshness to take on a stronger smell of oxidation. A white wine on its last legs is deeply tinted with brown and smells more like oloroso sherry (made by controlled oxidation) than like freshly picked grapes.

The white wines with the greatest longevity tend to be either the very best sweet wines, those in which the curious *Botrytis cinerea* concentrating fungus has played a part, such as the great Sauternes or finest sweet German wines, and/or those with extremely high levels of acidity, possibly accentuated as in Germany and the middle Loire by suppression of the softening second, malolactic fermentation. This

Pickers waiting to bring in the new vintage of Château Lynch-Bages. The date of harvest, and the state of the grapes when they are picked, play a vital role in determining the cellar potential of the resulting wine.

transforms harsh malic acid into softer lactic acid, adding a few extra flavours along the way. This is now *de rigueur* for red wines and for many whites.

"*Le malo*" or "MLF" is seen as a vital ingredient in most Chardonnay-based dry whites – even the greatest white burgundies and their counterparts – but such wines tend to reach maturity within the first or at most second decade, markedly earlier than top quality non-malo whites or great red wines.

Malolactic fermentation is a wine-making tool that has been available for use only relatively recently. Even in Bordeaux it was only in the sixties and early seventies that most wine-makers began to understand it. It is worth remembering that this may well have an effect on modern wines' ageability. The combined results of extensive use of malolactic fermentation, later picking dates, riper grapes, softer tannins and much more circumspect use of sulphur dioxide, is to make the wines drinkable much younger – to make them reach maturity earlier. This is understandable in an era of inflation and of frenetic enjoyment of life's pleasures, but it is not yet proven whether such wines will last as well as their antecedents. In *Le Vin et Ses Jours* Professor Peynaud provides an illuminating analysis of the main differ-

ences between modern red Bordeaux and those of the last century and first half of this. Modern wines are in general a good degree more alcoholic, distinctly lower in fixed acidity (2.8 to 3 gm/litre rather than 3.5 gm/litre in the fifties) and much, much lower in volatile acidity, and therefore more stable. The most interesting comparison is in levels of tannin which, although difficult to measure in mature wines since a large part of the original tannin has already been deposited as sediment, seems to have been "excessively high" until 1950 (although this high level has presumably helped preserve older vintages so that we could enjoy them); well balanced between 1950 and 1966; rather too low between 1967 and 1974 and well judged, partly thanks to a run of good vintages, since 1975. There has also been an increase in the extent to which all but the very finest wines have been filtered, possibly denying them a significant proportion of that potential. In the light of these observations it seems reasonable to chart the development of modern wines assuming that they will decline as well as ripen rather sooner than their counterparts in the first half of this century, but no wine drinker would be more delighted than this one to be proved wrong.

FACTORS AFFECTING MATURITY

Personal Taste Wine appreciation is, happily, nothing if not subjective. And like so many other subjective judgements wine appreciation seems to be heavily influenced by local conditioning. The French for example like to drink their wines notably younger than most other nations. The oldest vintage to be offered in 1989 by the Bistrot de Bordeaux, arguably the most important wine-dedicated bistro in the French provinces, was a 1979. Britain on the other hand probably harbours the greatest number of wine necrophiliacs. collectors who are still looking forward to opening their white burgundies from the twenties and thirties and listening to their death-bed whispers. And Scandinavia, with its famously cold and therefore slow-maturing cellars, has its fair share of those who believe that wines should preferably be older than those who consume them. There are also wine-drinking masochists who confuse future possibility with present pleasure and positively delight in an eye-watering combination of youthful characteristics.

For the record I think my taste lies somewhere between typically French and typically British (and is probably therefore typically American). I do like wine to exhibit some of the fruit of its youth, the primary aromas to be more than a faded memory, and I see opening a bottle too late as a far greater waste than opening one too soon.

Those who know they side with the average Frenchman, and Italian, in liking the piercing zest of youthful acid in their whites and the strong bite of still harsh tannin in their reds should head for the first half of the maturity periods indicated on the Timecharts. Those whose taste is more traditionally British should concentrate on the second half.

Storage and Shipping Wine is a relatively sensitive commodity. The two worst things to which a bottle of wine can be subjected are being warmed to above 70°F (21°C) or so when it starts to taste burnt and its volatile flavour elements begin to boil off, and being stored so that air enters the bottle and the wine begins to oxidise. This can happen surprisingly fast – if bottles are kept dry or upright for more than a few weeks and the cork dries out – which is why wine bottles are increasingly stored horizontally.

It is in the interests of the wine producer, merchant or individual buyer to be careful to store bottles at the right temperature. Shipping agents and freight forwarders find it less easy to see what all the fuss is about however and a wine is almost certainly most at risk whenever it travels (from breakage of course as well as from overheating). A stevedores' strike or an unexpected heat-wave can ruin a wine shipment, although no-one can tell until the bottles are actually opened. Only recently have wine importers realised the importance of paying the premium for specially insulated, temperature-controlled containers. This is why the most prized bottles of all are those which have lain for years undisturbed at the property on which they were produced, and why those about which there are most doubts are those known to have crossed an ocean or two.

All the wines tasted for this book were tasted direct from the property's own stocks (although in many cases, particularly in Burgundy, these can be far more depleted than those of a distant importer or enthusiastic collector). The warmer a wine has been kept, as outlined on page 13, the faster it evolves and vice versa. It is well known that bottles stored in the chilly cellars of the Swedish liquor monopoly mature particularly slowly while those kept in a Manhattan apartment evolve perceptibly more rapidly than those kept at the traditional cellar temperature in the high forties or low fifties. Those who have drunk fine wines in places as warm and humid as the Caribbean know how much faster and less satisfactorily many bottles seem to mature there.

How your bottles have been stored will therefore have an effect on when they reach maturity but, so long as they are not allowed to get hotter than 70°F (21°C) the quality should not be adversely affected. It may indeed be that in times of high interest rates it seems sensible to hasten the maturing process. A few months in a warm cupboard is not so intuitively appealing as decades in a damp cobweb-strewn cellar however, and it has been shown to hasten the physical decline of a wine. For the moment, what is known about storing wine is that it is preferable to keep bottles at a reasonably even temperature, preferably below 70°F (21°C), out of direct light, free from vibration and in an atmosphere that is not so dry that it will start to dry out the corks. Wine is almost as susceptible to humidity as to temperature.

Few operators own such smart decanting apparatus as this, but decanting makes sense for robust wines that have thrown a sediment. This can happen from about six years onwards.

Serving Wine Wines can actually be made to taste slightly older or younger than they really are by the way in which they are served. The cooler a wine the more marked is its tannin and acid content, and vice versa. This means that the aggressive youthfulness of a wine opened slightly too early can be masked if the wine is served a degree or two warmer than usual.

It is a bit more difficult to add spurious youth to a slightly faded wine but not impossible. Serving any wine cool accentuates the tannin and acid but diminishes the intensity of the bouquet. An ancient red wine served slightly cooler than usual will have any residual tannin enhanced but will also accentuate the increasing acidity (the "drying out" phenomenon) and the decreasing intensity of the bouquet. Better to serve an old red very, very slightly warm to enhance the bouquet and mute the acidity. The slightly oxidised smell and apparently declining acidity of an old white can be diminished by serving the wine a little cooler than usual.

One useful distraction from an intrusively high tannin level is food, preferably food which provides distraction of an equally tactile nature as tannin – chewy meat, for example. Thoughtful matching of food to wine makes far more difference to its apparent maturity than is generally realised.

Size of Bottle One final factor affecting maturity is the size of bottle in which the wine has been stored. Half bottles mature much more rapidly than magnums. For a half bottle, accelerate the relevant Timechart by a year. For a magnum or larger bottle, retard it by two years.

EVERYDAY WINES

Study of the evolution of a fine wine shows quite clearly why it is important to open a bottle of wine neither too soon nor too late, and why it is worth trying to consume a wine during its period of maturity, as outlined in How to Use the Timecharts.

However, although these Timecharts apply to the sort of wines that preoccupy wine writers and connoisseurs, far more wine is made for immediate or early consumption than is designed for ageing, in strictly numerical terms at least. And it is as much of a waste to drink a simple wine too old as it is to rush to open one that is designed for a complex old age.

The wines that are most obviously designed to be drunk young, in some cases straight off the bottling line, are those called "table wines" in Europe and "jug wines" in America: usually the cheapest available. Such wines – whether red, white or pink – have usually been produced from vines from which the maximum weight of grapes has been culled, so they tend to be short on fruit flavours, extract, anthocyanins and tannins and generally, perhaps significantly, to taste more like water than any other wine. A skilled wine-maker, employed by a company where quality is a recognised attribute, can do his or her best to turn out a wine in which the elements of acidity, residual sugar, alcohol and tannin are in reasonable harmony and, provided the winery is well equipped, can make a wine that is not only clean-tasting (a fairly recent bonus in the majority of such wines) but makes the most of the wine's only real attribute: youth.

The quality of such wines varies only marginally from year to year. The quantity produced can be quite substantially affected by the weather during the vines' flowering but the character of a table wine is liable to far more variation as a result of a change in wine-making equipment or policy (as we have seen in recent years in the white table wines of Chile and La Mancha in Spain, for example) than of individual vintage characteristics. This is partly because such wines come mainly from hotter areas where vintage variation is slight in any case, and partly because the fairly industrial methods employed by the maker of everyday wine allow him to compensate for any deficiencies – by adding acid, sugar, water and chalk (to deacidify) or even tannin – in the winery.

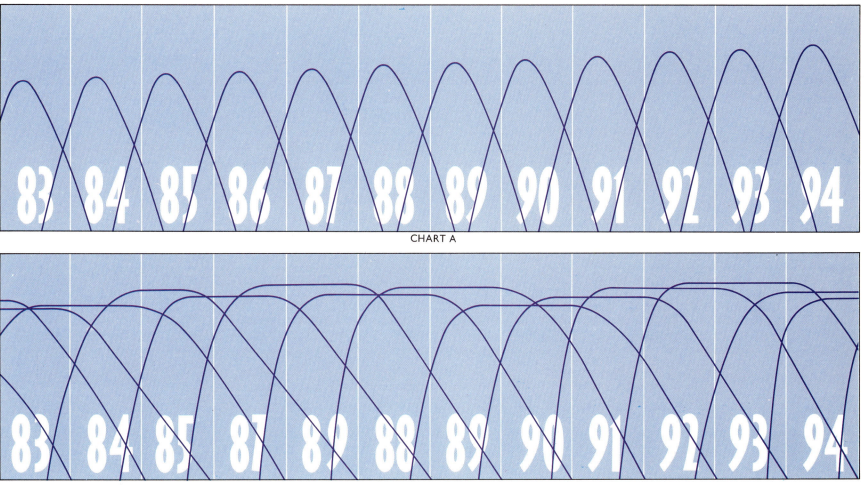

CHART A

CHART B

Chart A above shows the sort of pattern that would emerge from charting succeeding "vintages" of table wines or jug wines on one of the timecharts specially designed for this book. Such wines are rarely vintage dated, but even more rarely made from grapes produced in more than one year. Since the short peak in the year following the vintage (assuming this is a wine produced in the northern hemisphere) is at about the time when the wine reaches the marketplace, it seems sensible to try to drink these wines as young as possible. The slight rise in quality over succeeding years is meant to illustrate reality – that the quality of everyday wine has risen perceptibly, albeit from a low base.

In between these basic wines and the finest, long-term bottles produced, there are of course gradations of quality and potential for longevity. The regional commentaries and the Wine Cross Reference Index give guidance on how to relate relevant wines to the Timecharts in this book. In very general terms, a mid-quality wine such as a simple Beaujolais, Sancerre or superior rosé or *gris* wine which is a distinct step up from those charted in Chart A, will retain its fruitiness considerably longer and may exhibit slightly more variation. Chart B outlines maturity patterns from a typical example of such a wine, although it should be read in conjunction with the relevant Timechart.

HOW TO USE THE TIMECHARTS

This book charts in detail 46 paradigm wines of the types that deserve a place in our cellars. These are generally the best and therefore longest-lasting examples of each type. Thus Burgundy is represented by three classic Côte d'Or wines and by top examples from Beaujolais, Chablis and the Mâconnais. The choice of representatives from the newer wine regions, Australia and California for example, has been governed in part by which wines have any established track record for ageability. Another factor in all choices has been the extent to which the wines are exported.

The underlying premise is that understanding the life-cycle of a paradigm wine greatly enhances understanding of the pattern of evolution of a wine of the same sort. Much of the book is devoted to

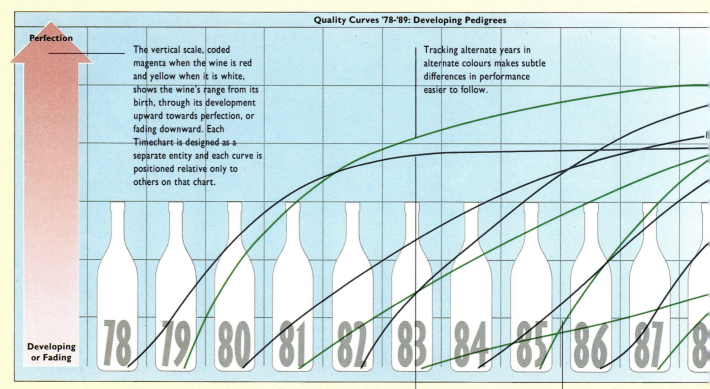

Quality Curves '78-'89: Developing Pedigrees

Perfection

The vertical scale, coded magenta when the wine is red and yellow when it is white, shows the wine's range from its birth, through its development upward towards perfection, or fading downward. Each Timechart is designed as a separate entity and each curve is positioned relative only to others on that chart.

Tracking alternate years in alternate colours makes subtle differences in performance easier to follow.

Developing or Fading

78 79 80 81 82 83 84 85 86 87 8

The text gives an introduction to the property, tasting notes for each vintage from a decade of consecutive years, notes on fine older vintages and background information such as weather patterns, the size and date of the harvest and the original price of the wine. Events that affect the property, the district and the market are also recorded.

The bottle shapes show the vintages for which full notes are given in the text above. Lines appear on the chart only for those wines which have been tasted by the author. Gaps usually indicate that the wine was not made in that vintage, often the sign of a truly quality-conscious producer.

Compare the 78 and 79: the 79 reaches a plateau of maturity relatively quickly and sustains it, but the 78 has a long period of static development in the late eighties before overtaking the 79 in the late nineties.

Wines reach maturity at different rates. Those with the steepest initial incline are most drinkable in youth.

giving clues as to how best to relate other wines to those detailed on the Timecharts.

Each chart shows in graphic form the rise, maturity and decline of a run of vintages of the same wine. Of course during its period of maturity a wine does not necessarily stop evolving. The complex chain of reactions that constitute ageing continues, and during this state of maturity a wine will change slightly in quality and even style. While the maturity period represents the years I believe to be the optimum time for drinking the wine, I am keenly aware that in practice, probably most bottles of fine wine are opened at some point on the upward curve towards maturity. Although this represents a certain

degree of waste – of what the purchaser has paid for and of the potential the producer has packed into the bottle – I personally find it much less sad than opening a bottle too late, on the slope towards disintegration, although connoisseurs of this stage – wine necrophiliacs? – certainly exist.

The Timecharts are grouped in geographic chapters. Each chapter has an introduction which explains how the particular Timecharts can be used to illustrate the development of other wines from the same region. Those of us unable to drink great wines every day can use the charts, and the text that accompanies them, as guides to the degree of maturity of a wide range of lesser wines – though the

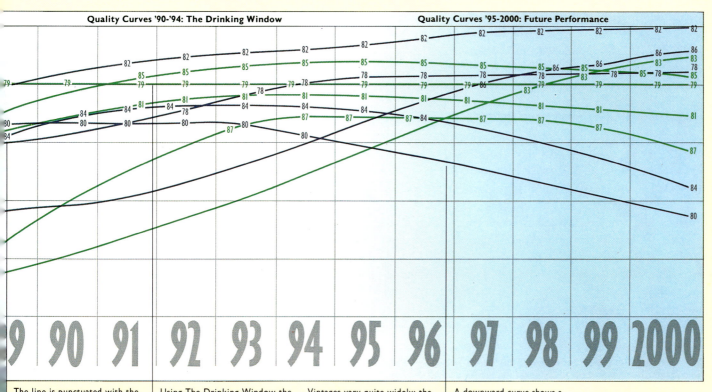

Quality Curves '90-'94: The Drinking Window   **Quality Curves '95-2000: Future Performance**

The line is punctuated with the year of the vintage only when the wine reaches its plateau of drinkability: this is, ideally, when it should be drunk. So track upwards on any Timechart from the current year to see which vintages of that wine are ready to drink.

Using The Drinking Window the reader can judge which wines are at their best during the currency of this book, which are worth investing in and – occasionally – which should be avoided unless they are at knock-down prices.

Vintages vary quite widely: the 80 is the least good, the 82 the best. The 82 is expected to reach perfection (in Margaux terms) by the turn of the century, when the 80 will be steadily declining after its brief peak of maturity between 1988 and 1994.

A downward curve shows a vintage declining from its peak. This doesn't imply that it is undrinkable, just that it is no longer at its best.

Future performance to the year 2000. These speculative assessments by the author are based on tastings.

actual shape, especially the height, of the curves will inevitably differ.

Above the charts are my tasting notes on the wines and background information on weather, the vital statistics of the vintage and other factors which influenced each particular wine.

The tasting notes themselves refer to how the wines tasted in late 1988 or early 1989 and have been written with the consumer rather than the scientist in mind. I apologise in advance for those occasions on which I have allowed my enthusiasm to sweep me off Dr Ann Noble's famous "aroma wheel" of descriptions recommended at UC Davis.

To relate the maturation of the bottle in your hand to one of the Timecharts:

1 Establish which is the appropriate category. Do this by looking up the appellation or wine description on the label of your wine in the Wine Cross-Reference Index. This will direct you to the relevant Timechart and/or introduction. For less grand bottles, see the section on Everday Wines (page 18).

2 The relevant regional introduction will give guidance on how to relate your bottle to the ones charted. It will tell you either to accelerate or, occasionally, to retard the relevant Timechart by a certain number of years to find the likely maturity pattern of your wine. Suppose your bottle was a Château Giscours 1981, a wine from the commune of Margaux like Château Margaux, but a third growth rather than a first growth. The introduction to the Médoc and Graves region on page 28 indicates that to find the maturity of a typical Margaux classed growth relative to its first growth you should accelerate the Château Margaux Timechart by two years. The Château Margaux Timechart suggests 1991 to 1999 as the maturity span of Château Margaux 1981. This means that the recommended maturity span of Château Giscours 1981 is two years earlier than this – that is 1989 to 1997. And to find out which other vintages of Château Giscours can be broached in, say, 1991, project forwards two years and track upwards from 1993 on the Château Margaux chart to see the vintages tagged as recommended.

3 In some cases, usually of lesser wines, the reference section will direct you not to a specific Timechart but to a more general section which outlines the likely development of your wine.

4 If the wine is notable and was made before 1978 (1975 in the case of several wines which reach the marketplace particularly slowly) the information will not be represented on the Timechart itself but should appear in the text above it, under the heading "Earlier vintages".

5 If the wine was made very recently, or is not yet at a stage when it can be tasted, it may be possible to project the information you need on the basis of past performance. Try to match the weather pattern of the young vintage to that of an older vintage on the Timechart. The weather notes for past vintages should be helpful in deciding how an uncharted vintage may perform.

6 When interpreting any Timechart, bear in mind the most important factors affecting maturation that are outlined on page 17.

7 For quick reference to which wines are at their best in a given year, see the Maturity Index.

There are several more ways in which the Timecharts can be used to help the wine-lover get the best from his or her cellar. For instance, comparison of the maturity patterns of wines based on a certain grape variety in differing parts of the world – Cabernet profiles in the Médoc, California and Spain, for instance, indicate the different life expectancies of wines made in those regions. And comparison with Timecharts of Pinot Noir-based wines such as Saintsbury show how much earlier they mature than the Cabernets from the same region.

It is also instructive, even for experienced connoisseurs, to note the extent to which current performance can be at variance with vintage reputation. Many California Cabernets of 1980 now seem as inconveniently top-heavy in tannins as 1983 burgundies, for example. In the southern Rhône meanwhile 1981, and even 1984, are far better years than is generally realised. And 1982 is by no means invariably the best vintage between 1978 and 1987 for Bordeaux.

A more detailed reappraisal of your cellar than is available from a simple vintage chart can dramatically increase the pleasure it gives you. These Timecharts try to project known facts and impressions into future performance. They are thus fallible, but if thoughtfully used can be, I hope, helpful to those of us who are concerned to get the most from the exasperating but magical drink that is wine.

BORDEAUX

Storm-clouds over the vineyards of St-Emilion may make Bordeaux a less-than-perfect tourist region, but they help make the climate ideal for fine wine production by slowing ripening, thereby producing a more complex, longer-living wine.

No wine repays understanding of its maturity pattern more handsomely than red Bordeaux. A bottle can provide the most wonderful array of sensations and cerebral stimulation if opened during its period of maturity but the same bottle, if opened too early, can be no more enjoyable than ink stew. Open that bottle too late, and the scent of decay has completely ousted that of the fruit.

So many pages of this book are devoted to ageworthy red Bordeaux because so much of it is produced: about five million cases a year of very serious wine. A flourishing market in red Bordeaux of all ages exists, thanks largely to the auction houses, so that in theory at least a collector can completely refit his cellar if he decides that its contents are maturing at an inconvenient pace.

What makes red Bordeaux a rewarding wine to cellar in the first place is that it is made from Cabernet and Merlot varieties, whose high tannin and anthocyanin content marks them out as slow developers and long lasters. Many wine-makers nowadays are realising that it is worth investing in cellar techniques – carefully judged maceration and fine oak cooperage most obviously – that will maximise this exciting possibility.

What makes red Bordeaux such a fascinating subject for study however is that it is shaped so decisively by the different characteristics of each vintage. Bordeaux is, from the wine drinker's point

Château Margaux (page 38) heads for winter. The canes have yielded fruit of exceptional concentration thanks not only to severe winter pruning, but also to strict crop-thinning in July – an increasingly common practice in Bordeaux.

of view, ideally situated on the cusp of territories warm enough to ripen its red vines almost every year (unlike Burgundy) but sufficiently subject to the vagaries of climate that the year leaves its tasteable mark on the wines – even after decades in bottle.

The Bordeaux grower's main aims are to get his Cabernet grapes to ripeness, or even nowadays slight overripeness, before the autumn rains and to avoid rot in his (earlier ripening) Merlot. The ideal annual cycle for top quality red Bordeaux therefore begins with a winter that is cold enough to harden the wood and kill off any vine bugs but not so cold as to freeze and kill vine roots. Another danger is that an unseasonably warm spell is followed by a dangerously cold one that freezes the sap and splits the vine. Spring frosts can also damage early vegetation and therefore the quantity of wine produced, but the crucial time for determining the size of the vintage comes during the two-week flowering period in early to mid-June for Merlot followed by Cabernet Franc and then Cabernet Sauvignon. If the flowering is late there is a risk of the grapes' not ripening until the advent of autumn rains and rot. If the weather is cool, unsettled or windy the vines suffer *coulure* (the flowers drop off, ruining any

chance of the grapes' developing) or *millerandage* (uneven fruit set, which can be followed by uneven ripening and produce unripe flavours in the resulting wine). And even perfect weather is not enough for a successful flowering. The Merlot flowering in 1984, for example, was disastrously hit because the vines had not yet recovered from a particularly harsh May, whereas the sap had risen in time to support the Cabernet Sauvignon flowers. All 1984 red Bordeaux is therefore heavily dominated by Cabernet.

During the Bordeaux summer the crucial factor is sufficient heat to ripen the fruit and sufficient sunlight, particularly in September, to encourage the internal transformations necessary to ripen the grapes. Even if the flowering is late and the year cool until the end of August, a warm, dry September, such as ripened the 1978 and then 1983 crops so late in the day, can rescue a vintage's reputation.

Although the rule is by no means infallible, as 1976 showed, generally speaking the hotter and drier the summer the better the Bordeaux vintage, as for example in 1961, 1982 and 1985. It is almost impossible in Bordeaux for the summer to be too dry for the best vines, most of which have a root system well driven into the damp subsoil anyway. An early

Autumn sunshine at Château Cos d'Estournel (page 32), an oriental fantasy of a building housing some of the most distinctive wine-making in the Médoc, thanks to proprietor Bruno Prats' dedication to making wines that are more drinkable in youth.

vintage, itself a function of an early flowering, usually bodes well. Hot days tend to result in high alcohol levels; hot nights lower the acidity of the grapes and therefore of the wine.

A little rain in June, July and even August does no harm but a combination of warmth and prolonged humidity encourages pests and diseases. Too much rain when the grapes are ripe and unprotected by anti-rot sprays leads to rot which punctures the skins and destroys much of the wine's potential quality.

But poring over the records at the meteorological office at Villenave d'Ornon just south of Bordeaux is not enough to predict the characteristics of a vintage. Bordeaux's broad weather patterns for 1978 and 1979 were remarkably similar and yet the wines are quite different. The pattern of rainfall from June to mid-October was almost identical for 1982 and 1980, arguably the best and the worst vintages of the decade respectively. What made the difference was that the 1982 flowering was particularly early and successful, thanks to fine weather in early June, and ripe grapes could be picked before the October rains.

Knowing the overall characteristics of a vintage, even in a given commune, (as outlined on pages 28/9 and 42/3) does not always tell the whole story. Styles of vinification and *élevage* differ in ways which can influence ageing capacity – notably length and temperature of maceration, proportion of new oak casks used and, an often overlooked factor, the amount of press wine incorporated.

THE GREAT CHATEAUX OF BORDEAUX COMPARED

These pages compare the seven star châteaux of Bordeaux, setting out their contrasting characters and showing how the Timechart concept can help the wine drinker get to know a wine. The individual charts that follow go into detail on three of the châteaux.

The star châteaux of Bordeaux – the *premiers grands crus classés*, or first growths, of the Médoc, Graves and St-Emilion together with the king-pin of Pomerol, Château Petrus – are sometimes seen as more of homogeneous group than they really are.

Those lucky enough to have regular opportunities to make the comparison know that they mature at very different rates, demonstrate widely varying success rates over the years (more often due to man than to nature) and illustrate the distinction between the left and right banks of the Gironde, the Atlantic influence tempering the climate of the Médoc.

The charts opposite show how the great châteaux (with the exception of tiny Château Ausone) typically mature in the years after a good vintage such as 1978, 1982 and 1985 and after a lesser vintage such as 1980 or 1984. In the good vintage each line rises to the same notional level of perfect maturity for that property. (The wines' styles vary enormously, of course, with Lafite's more delicate, ethereal charms for example being less obvious than the chunky might of Latour.) The interest is in how much cellaring time the different wines require before being broachable. Those impatient to experience the fruits of the great estates before these charts suggest could try their "second wines": Pavillon Rouge du Château Margaux, Les Forts de Latour, Moulin des Carruades (Lafite), Bahans Haut-Brion and Le Petit Cheval. Petrus and Mouton sit this game out.

Château Margaux wines are most attractive in youth and yet manage to attain great heights. In lesser years they often make the best, or one of the best wines of the vintage, though in these cases the wines tend to be for early consumption.

Latour still makes wines for very long keeping, although this policy has been less in evidence in recent years. This property is usually particularly good at producing wines in lesser years which are so reticent that they are almost unattractive at first, but which eventually come round.

Mouton-Rothschild has begun to produce wines with more and more Margaux-like early opulence, but their high proportion of Cabernet Sauvignon keeps them going longer. Mouton has less of a record than some the others for producing successful wines in "off" years.

Lafite is the lightest, and takes longest of the non-Latours to resolve itself into a liquid of great, scented finesse. Typically, patience is needed while waiting for the bouquet of this wine to come together. Like its cousin Mouton, its record in off years is by no means distinguished.

Haut-Brion is always the bridesmaid, never the bride. It makes some lovely characterful wines which are certainly different – often more easily approachable – with their lower tannin and intensity. Haut-Brion, a property underestimated by many, evolves more rapidly than its peers.

Petrus makes wines that are delightfully easy to drink in youth: so much so that many bottles are opened far too young. The wines can last extremely well because they have such great concentration. Even in off years they can be very tempting: selection in the vineyard and among the *cuvées* is particularly strict.

Cheval Blanc is, like Haut-Brion, an exceptionally long-lived wine and is, uniquely, based on Cabernet Franc. The Merlot that constitutes a third of the *encépagement* gives it a beguiling youth, but the Cabernet Franc then sweeps in to bear it off in good vintages to a majestic and prolonged old age.

BORDEAUX 1855 CLASSIFICATION

The first of the many rankings of Bordeaux châteaux dates from the 17th century, but the 1855 attempt is the most influential. It was drawn up by the Bordeaux trade and based on the price the wine commanded. By 1855 the best land in the Médoc was under vines, and under the ownership of sophisticated and able proprietors. The techniques and the ability has fluctuated, but the land is still the best.

The venerable but evolving ranking of the Médoc Châteaux continues to be useful. They are listed here by class. The page numbers listed alongside refer to the Timechart or introduction which, with appropriate modifications, deals with that classed growth's probable maturity curve.

PREMIERS CRUS
Ch Lafite-Rothschild, Pau *28*
Ch Latour, Pau *28*
Ch Margaux, Mar *38*
Ch Haut-Brion, Pessac, Gra *40*
Ch Mouton Rothschild, Pau *28*

DEUXIEMES CRUS
Ch Rausan-Ségla, Mar *38*
Ch Rauzan-Gassies, Mar *38*
Ch Léoville-Las Cases, St-J *34*
Ch Léoville-Poyferré, St-J *34*
Ch Léoville-Barton, St-J *34*
Ch Durfort-Vivens, Mar *38*
Ch Lascombes, Mar *38*
Ch Gruaud-Larose, St-J *36*
Ch Brane-Cantenac, Cantenac-Mar *38*
Ch Pichon-Longueville Baron, Pau *34*
Ch Pichon-Longueville Comtesse de Lalande, Pau *34*
Ch Ducru-Beaucaillou, St-J *36*
Ch Cos d'Estournel, St-Es *32*
Ch Montrose, St-Es *32*

TROISIEMES CRUS
Ch Giscours, Labarde-Mar *28*
Ch Kirwan, Cantenac-Mar *28*
Ch d'Issan, Cantenac-Mar *28*
Ch Lagrange, St-J *36*
Ch Langoa-Barton, St-J *36*
Ch Malescot St-Exupéry, Mar *38*
Ch Cantenac Brown, Cantenac-Mar *38*
Ch Palmer, Cantenac-Mar *28*
Ch La Lagune, Ludon, Mar *34*
Ch Desmirail, Mar *38*
Ch Calon-Ségur, St-Es *32*
Ch Ferrière, Mar *38*
Ch Marquis d'Alesme Becker, Mar *38*
Ch Boyd-Cantenac, Cantenac-Mar *28*

QUATRIEMES CRUS
Ch St-Pierre, St-J *36*
Ch Branaire-Ducru, St-J *36*
Ch Talbot, St-J *36*
Ch Duhart-Milon-Rothschild, Pau *34*
Ch Pouget, Cantenac-Mar *38*
Ch La Tour Carnet, St-La *34*
Ch Lafon-Rochet, St-Es *32*
Ch Beychevelle, St-J *36*
Ch Prieuré-Lichine, Cantenac-Mar *38*
Ch Marquis-de-Terme, Mar *38*

CINQIEMES CRUS
Ch Pontet-Canet, Pau *34*
Ch Batailley, Pau *34*
Ch Grand-Puy-Lacoste, Pau *34*
Ch Grand-Puy-Ducasse, Pau *34*
Ch Haut-Batailley, Pau *34*
Ch Lynch-Bages, Pau *34*
Ch Lynch-Moussas, Pau *34*
Ch Dauzac, Labarde-Mar *38*
Ch Mouton Baronne Philippe, Pau *34*
Ch du Tertre, Arsac-Mar *38*
Ch Haut-Bages Libéral, Pau *34*
Ch Pédesclaux, Pau *34*
Ch Belgrave, St-La *36*
Ch de Camensac, St-La *36*
Ch Cos Labory, St-Es *32*
Ch Clerc Milon, Pau *34*
Ch Croizet-Bages, Pau *34*
Ch Cantemerle, Macau *36*

KEY
Pau = Pauillac
Mar = Margaux
Gra = Graves
St-J = St-Julien
St-Es = St-Estèphe
St-La = St Laurent

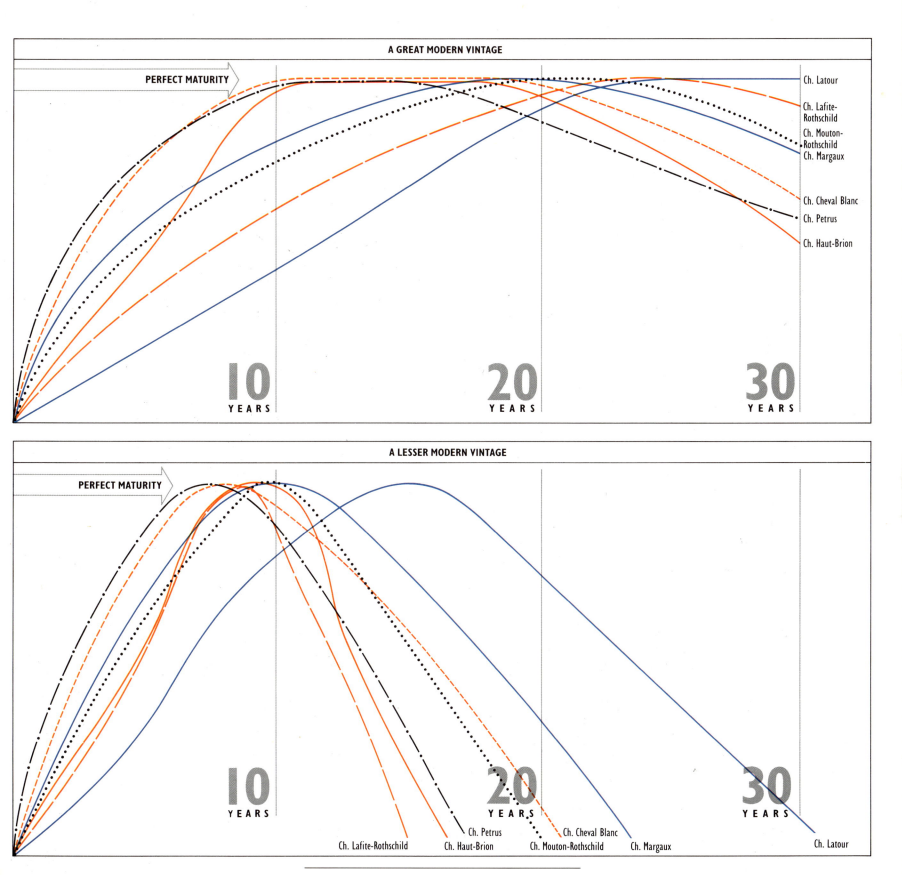

A GREAT MODERN VINTAGE

PERFECT MATURITY

Ch. Latour

Ch. Lafite-
Rothschild

Ch. Mouton-
Rothschild

Ch. Margaux

Ch. Cheval Blanc

Ch. Petrus

Ch. Haut-Brion

10 YEARS

20 YEARS

30 YEARS

A LESSER MODERN VINTAGE

PERFECT MATURITY

10 YEARS

20 YEARS

30 YEARS

Ch. Lafite-Rothschild

Ch. Petrus

Ch. Haut-Brion

Ch. Mouton-Rothschild

Ch. Cheval Blanc

Ch. Margaux

Ch. Latour

MEDOC & GRAVES

The emergence of second wines such as Lynch-Bages' Château Haut-Bages-Averous (page 34) has been a vital component in elevating the average quality of the Médoc's *grands vins*.

Since the Médoc and Graves provide so many of the bottles worth cellaring, six properties have been chosen to represent the different quality levels and different provenances of red Bordeaux on this left bank of the Gironde. They appear not in the conventional order of the famous 1855 classification (see page 26), with first growths to the fore and lowly bourgeois growths skulking at the back, but in geographical order from north to south. Weather after all is the chief determinant of vintage characteristic, and weather varies with geography rather than official ranking.

Château Potensac represents climatologically the whole of the region to the north of the Haut-Médoc. It also shows the maturity pattern of an exceptional *Cru Bourgeois* whose wines are built for as long a life as any other *Cru Bourgeois* (and have an even longer life than some *Crus Classés* that are still neglected and lacklustre). To calculate the maturity of another wine worth ageing with the simple appellation Médoc, that is an unclassified château-bottled wine (a so-called "*petit château*") from the Bas-Médoc, accelerate the Potensac chart by two years. Wines bottled as generic Médocs are usually ready to drink three years after the vintage.

There follow Timecharts for each of the Haut-Médoc's four most important wine-producing communes: Château Cos d'Estournel represents a top second growth and St-Estèphe; Château Lynch-Bages represents the concentration of wine-making talent in Pauillac, meriting a ranking considerably above its fifth growth status; Château Gruaud Larose represents the five St Julien second growths; and the Château Margaux Timechart exhibits the maturity cycles of a modern, well-run first growth.

The Cos d'Estournel Timechart (page 32/3) reflects the long life-cycle of wines from St-Estèphe. To work out the maturity of another St-Estèphe, assume a similar pattern to Cos for Château Montrose, accelerate two years for any other classed growth, four years for a *Cru Bourgeois* and five years for any other château bottled wine.

Lynch-Bages made a 1985 and a 1980 that were exceptionally good for Pauillac, and Pauillac generally produced better wines in 1986 and 1981 than did Lynch-Bages. Bear this in mind when comparing vintage performance, but otherwise the classed growths of Pauillac follow a remarkably similar ageing pattern, although from 1986 Pichon-Lalande and Pichon-Longueville can last up to 10 years longer than Lynch-Bages in good vintages.

The three Pauillac first growths: Château Mouton-Rothschild, Lafite-Rothschild and Latour provide an exception to this, however. Page 26 gives some guidance as to how they perform relative to each other and to Châteaux Margaux, Haut-Brion and Petrus, which are charted on pages 38/9, 40/1 and 44/5. Unusually, the Timechart for Lynch-Bages (page 34/5) has to be retarded rather than accelerated for these three Pauillac first growths, by three years for Châteaux Mouton-Rothschild and Lafite-Rothschild and by four years (five years in a very good year) for Château Latour. For unclassified Pauillac wines, advance the Lynch-Bages chart by two years.

In St Julien the other second growths should follow the same pattern as Château Gruaud Larose (although Château Léoville-Barton was particularly successful in 1980, Château Léoville-Las Cases in 1982 and the wines of these two properties can take

Scudding clouds – here above the Médoc's largest property Château Larose-Trintaudon of nearly 400 acres (160 hectares) – are as much part of the typical Bordeaux summer as the blue tinge to the leaves. The "Bordeaux mixture" of copper sulphate helps ward off mildew.

longer than Gruaud Larose to soften in particularly tannic years). Vintages of renovated third growth Château Lagrange from 1985 should have the staying power of these seconds while for pre-1985 Lagranges and other classed growth St Juliens, accelerate the Gruaud Larose Timechart (page 36/7) by a year. Accelerate by two years for a St Julien *Cru Bourgeois* and three for a petit château.

The Margaux notes (page 38/9) indicate the conditions for the southern Médoc. The 1983 vintage was notably successful here but the likely evolution of Château Margaux 1983 is so slow that this is hard to tell from the chart. Accelerate the Margaux Timechart by two years for other classified growths, by three years for *Cru Bourgeois* and by four years (five for 1983) for other properties.

Although the Haut-Brion properties are geographically separated from most of the rest of the Graves, Jean Delmas insists that they can be taken as representative of their performance. In 1986 for example the Graves was particularly badly hit by a heavy rainstorm on September 23 when more than 4″ (100mm) fell, and the 1985 Graves are in general more successful. Château La Mission-Haut-Brion and Domaine de Chevalier mature at about the same rate as (and sometimes even a year or so behind) Château Haut-Brion while the Haut-Brion chart should be accelerated by two years for other classified growth reds and three years for unclassified properties.

The very general rule for classed growth red Bordeaux is that is should not be drunk younger than 10 years – although vintages such as 1980, 1984 and 1987 provide many exceptions. For sweet white Bordeaux see page 50 and for dry white and other Bordeaux reds see page 54.

Château Potensac

Potensac is one of the best-known ambassadors of the Bourgeoisie Médocaine, thanks to its famous big brother Château Léoville-Las Cases. This is not just because this admirably disciplined St Julien second growth provides Potensac with an entrée to the hearts and cellars of wine collectors on both sides of the Atlantic, but also because the family relationship means that paterfamilias Michel Delon can employ the same meticulous policies, and some of the same equipment, at both properties.

Potensac benefits noticeably, for example, from being next in line for the top quality casks used at Las Cases although even at Potensac about a fifth of the casks used each year are brand new. And no concessions are made to Potensac's lower status when it comes to bottling or packing. Fining is by egg whites only and in the vineyard natural fertilisers and equally animate picking methods are used. The vineyards are unusually densely planted for this area: as many as 3,200 plants per acre (8,000 per hectare) with about 60 per cent Cabernet Sauvignon, 15 per cent Cabernet Franc and 25 per cent Merlot.

Château Potensac's recently much extended vineyards lie in the Bas Médoc to the north of St-Estèphe in the commune of Ordonnac, about three miles inland of Gilbey's Château Loudenne on the Gironde. Michel Delon and his father Paul gradually expanded Potensac from under 20 acres (8 hectares) to more than 120 (48) of clay and gravel on the same slightly

raised ground as its neighbour Château La Cardonne, now part of the Lafite-Rothschild holdings. The most important result of this expansion is that Michel Delon has also acquired the properties and the right to use the names of Châteaux Gallais-Bellevue, Lassalle and Goudy-La-Cardonne, in descending order of wine quality.

Another result is that the *cuvier*, *chais* and cellars at Potensac have become increasingly crowded. Like any seriously run Médoc property, Potensac has benefitted from a completely revamped (and gleaming) *cuvier*, but it has the distinction of having commandeered the deconsecrated church of the hamlet of Potensac for cellar storage, where Potensac is stacked in its uncompromisingly top-drawer wooden cases underneath the stained glass.

Château Potensac is the undoubted current star of the appellation Médoc, but, as has been outlined, it is by no means the only *Cru Bourgeois* designed so ambitiously for a long life. While Potensac reflects most directly the weather patterns for the Bas Médoc, it indicates the maximum lifespan that can be expected from any *Cru Bourgeois*. While it fails to shine in off vintages, unlike some of its grander châteaux in this book, its peaks in good years are relatively long. Potensac owes some of its rigour to the quality of its *élevage*, but also to a bracing dose of press wine that it is given in most years. Michel Delon is one of the few proprietors of a *Cru Bourgeois* who is still proud to exhibit the château's 1966 and 1970 vintages.

Earlier vintages

In 1989 the **1966** could still seduce with its alluring perfume which, to many palates, is only enhanced by the very slightest whiff of decay. Drink soon. The **1970** still has a way to go with its lively acidity and perceptible tannin. The **1970** is for traditionalists. The **1975** and **1976** are extremely creditable examples from two difficult vintages. The **1975** is built like the **1970** but has a little less stuffing, while the **1976** is still very much alive with far more fruit concentration than most 1976s and still some oak on the nose.

1978 A highly successful wine with a well-constructed, open and developed bouquet of blackcurrant and plump dried fruit flavours. A gentle, neatly built wine that is alluringly in its prime.

Weather and timing

Very good vintage, below average crop. Cold spring, late flowering. Cool summer. Dry Aug. Warm, dry Sept and Oct. Ideal conditions for harvest which began early Oct.

Quantity produced

20,000-25,000 cases released at Fr f226 a case. Médoc regional production: 3,800,000 cases.

1979 Less generous than the 1978 although with markedly more youthful colour. High in extract and therefore a little dull on the nose. The fruit, much scrawnier than that of 1978, is somewhat submerged by the acid and tannin. May be worth waiting.

Weather and timing

Very good vintage, large crop. Wet winter and spring. Excellent June; good set. Average July followed by cold Aug and Sept. Showers during Oct harvest.

Quantity produced

20,000-25,000 cases released at Fr f211 a case. Médoc: 5,150,000 cases.

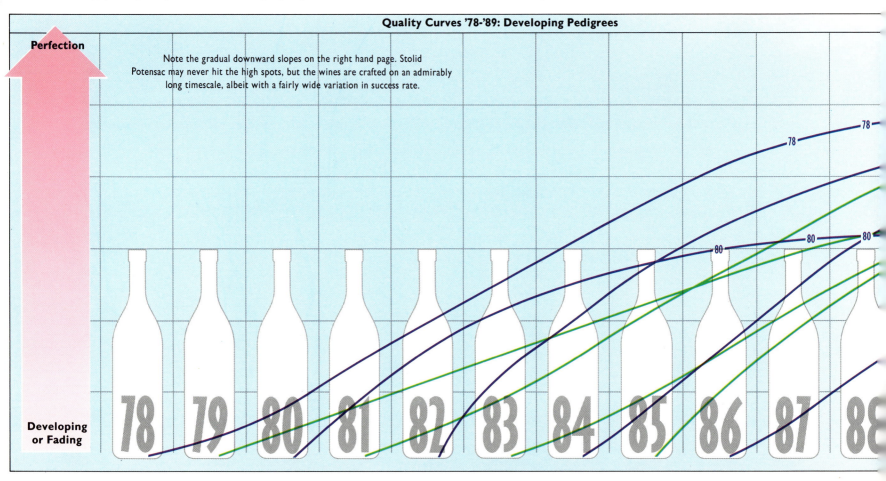

Quality Curves '78-'89: Developing Pedigrees

Perfection

Note the gradual downward slopes on the right hand page. Stolid Potensac may never hit the high spots, but the wines are crafted on an admirably long timescale, albeit with a fairly wide variation in success rate.

Developing or Fading

78 79 80 81 82 83 84 85 86 87 88

1980 Very light, simple colour, matched by light, simple flavours. The wine is ageing fast, as can be seen from its orange rim and fading fruit. Some pleasant enough blackcurrant flavour and much more acid than tannin.

Weather and timing
Fair vintage, small crop. Cold, wet June affected flowering. Dullest Sept for a decade. Rain before harvest which began mid-Oct.

Quantity produced
20,000-25,000 cases released at Fr f214 a case. Médoc: 3,250,000.

1981 A great success for Potensac. Good dark crimson colour similar to that of the 1982. An intriguing bouquet of integrated oak and fruit – toasted coconut and warm, ripe red fruits – has already evolved. Some complexity and layers of sensation. Perfectly proportioned if on a slightly smaller scale than the 1982. Long and already very pleasurable.

Weather and timing
Very good vintage, very large crop. Average spring. Hot and dry July 28 to Sept 20 then some rain. Harvest began end Sept.

Quantity produced
20,000-25,000 cases released at Fr f240 a case. Médoc: 6,050,000 cases.

1982 Wonderful deep colour right out to the rim and (like both the 1983 and 1981) markedly viscous. Dark, spicy and rich (not a word used often for Potensac) although very juvenile. Autumnal truffley flavours and great fruit impact covers the remarkably soft tannins. A laster.

Weather and timing
Great vintage, large crop. Fine, dry June ideal for flowering. Heatwave Sept 1–20; excellent maturation. Harvest late Sept before Oct rains.

Quantity produced
20,000-25,000 cases released at Fr f256 a case. Médoc: 5,250,000.

1983 Some development already visible, and smellable in its smoky, mineral-scented bouquet. Not enormously concentrated but the impact of press wine can be tasted – possibly marginally too much for the attractive but not particularly powerful fruit. An agreeable but not great bottle.

Weather and timing
Good vintage, above average crop. Good flowering. Exceptionally hot July. Warm, wet Aug encouraged disease. Indian summer; good harvest.

Quantity produced
20,000-25,000 cases released at Fr f259 a case. Médoc: 4,800,000 cases.

1984 A low-key wine in every respect, but then the current price reflects that. Diluted Cabernet impression with soft, slightly inky cassis flavours and very little tannin.

Weather and timing
Average vintage, very small crop. Warm Apr encouraged growth: wet, cold May stopped it. Perfect for flowering but severe *coulure*. Hurricane Hortense (Oct 4) brought driving rain and gale-force winds. Harvest early Oct.

Quantity produced
20,000-25,000 cases released at Fr f280 a case. Médoc: 1,850,000.

1985 A hugely successful wine that looks much more concentrated than the 1986. Wonderful blackened crimson with the spice of Merlot and an aromatic cocktail of dried fruits. Some good oak flavours are still perceptible in this intense and already complex wine that can already give pleasure. Shows every sign of proceeding towards something much grander. Moderate tannins and good acid and with more than a trace of Léoville-Las Cases build about it.

1986 Very attractive and correct Cabernet-styled wine. Too light to suggest long-term cellaring but is excitingly, nervily aromatic and can show lots of classic claret characteristics. In 1989 the slightly skinny fruit was fighting against considerable acid and tannin but will probably flesh out a little in bottle.

Weather and timing
Very good vintage, small crop. Arctic winter killed some vines. Good spring. Very dry July 4 to end Oct. Excellent harvest.

Quantity produced
20,000-25,000 cases released at Fr f351 a case. Médoc: 3,250,000.

Weather and timing
Exceptional vintage, large crop. Excellent start to season. Perfect flowering. Hot and dry July-Aug. Storms mid-Sept. Fine for harvest.

Quantity produced
20,000-25,000 cases released at Fr f337 a case. Médoc: 5,700,000.

1987 (Not tasted) M Delon reports that this wine is quite light in colour and complexity for a 1987, marked by Cabernet Sauvignon on the palate and Cabernet Franc in its aroma. For the early nineties.

Weather and timing
Average vintage, small crop. Wet June, warm July, hot Aug and Sept. Wet for harvest early Oct.

Quantity produced
20,000-25,000 cases. Médoc: 3,950,000 cases.

1988 (Not tasted) M Delon sees similarities with the 1985 in this classically-styled, still firm and closed, wine.

Weather and timing
Excellent vintage, below average crop. Wet winter and spring necessitated spraying May-June. Dry July-Sept. Rain early Oct then Indian summer. Good harvest.

Quantity produced
20,000-25,000 cases.

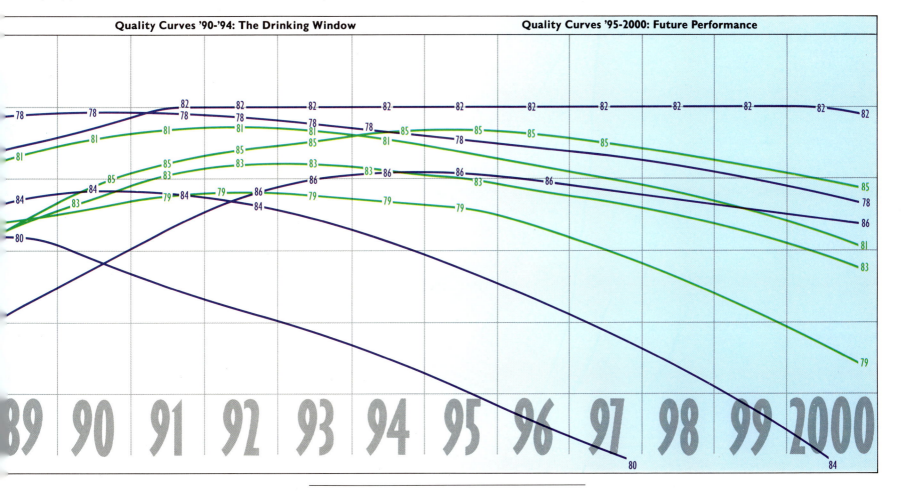

Quality Curves '90-'94: The Drinking Window

Quality Curves '95-2000: Future Performance

Château Cos d'Estournel

The wines of St Estèphe have historically been famous for their longevity, but at the price of a relatively austere and prolonged youth.

Bruno Prats is the enlightened current incumbent at second growth Château Cos d'Estournel. This is now the indisputable star of the appellation, and M Prats has put considerable effort into providing increasingly dazzling wines that are brazen in their youthful fruitiness and yet seem to have forfeited nothing of St-Estèphe's traditional long-term potential. The typical young Cos (which rhymes, disconcertingly, with "loss" rather than "low") is headily scented and seduces the palate with its initial bodyweight of lush, opulent fruit. In cases such as the 1985 and 1982 this manages to remain the dominant impression, but in many others it simply provides temporary distraction from tannin levels which are as high as one would expect of a top St Estèphe property.

Working closely with the University of Bordeaux, Bruno Prats is still designing wines to peak at 15 to 20 years, but he has tried to add to the wine's attractive, youthful flesh by implementing a number of carefully monitored techniques throughout the wine-making process. These include waiting for the optimum ripeness for each individual parcel of vines, paying more attention to their exposition and age, for example; trying to extract only the softest tannins through what he calls the "espresso method", tirelessly pumping over

for two to three weeks rather than allowing inert maceration; and trying to balance fruit tannins with oak tannins through giving the wine a year in much thicker casks than normal and its final six months' ageing not in small oak barrels but in vats.

The youthful fruit may be partly a reflection of Cos's exceptionally high proportion of Merlot for the Médoc: 40 per cent. A sixth of the Cabernet vines are Cabernet Franc and Bruno Prats points out that on Cos soil it can be difficult to distinguish healthy Merlot fruit from fully ripe Cabernet (the respective problems of the two vines being rot and low sugar levels).

The 150 acres (60 hectares) of limestone-based Guntz gravel vineyard stretch round the exotically oriental château building which sits on a small hill at the south of the appellation and makes such a striking neighbour for Château Lafite-Rothschild.

Although much that goes on in the vineyards and cellars of Cos closely follows tradition, Prats is a modernist. He is happy to use agro-chemicals rather than philosophy or more wholemeal methods to counter vineyard pests and disease, and is an unashamed exponent of filtration.

Only about two-thirds of each year's crop goes into the *grand vin*. Fruit from vines less than 12 years old and from the less successful vats goes into the wine called Château de Marbuzet, made at Cos and named after the home of Bruno Prats and his family.

Earlier vintages
The very fine 1961 is in its prime. The 1966 was still a meaty, powerful, well coloured wine in the late eighties while the 1970 was still tough and unyielding. The 1971 was more mature and accessible. The 1976 is opulent if light, as was the slightly menthol-scented 1977. Both should be drunk.

1978 Traditional Bordeaux. Lighter, more developed and a more classical structure than the 1979. Subtle and chewy with tannin on the finish. Complex enough to provide real interest.

Weather and timing
Excellent vintage, small crop. Late season saved by excellent Oct. Flowering June 26. Normal harvest: Merlot picked first (Oct 6-13) then Cabernet (Oct 14-19).

Quantity produced
15,300 cases released at Fr f384 a case. St-Estèphe: 530,000 cases.

Other details
33% new oak.

1979 One of the Médoc's most concentrated; deep, youthful colour. Aromatic and leafy; hints of underripe Cabernet in the bouquet but substantial on the palate. Big, brawny, tarry and very long. Tannin still in evidence.

Weather and timing
Very good vintage, small crop. Rain during flowering. Fine summer. Harvest Oct 1-7, 8-15.

Quantity produced
18,000 cases released at Fr f372 a case. St-Estèphe: 660,000 cases.

Other details
55% Merlot, 45% Cabernet Sauvignon. 33% in new wood. Began drainage work.

1980 Stylish for the vintage. Lightish, evolved colour, scent of tea leaves and soaked sultanas. A loose-textured lightweight but classically sculpted for a long life. Fruit flavours before the tannin.

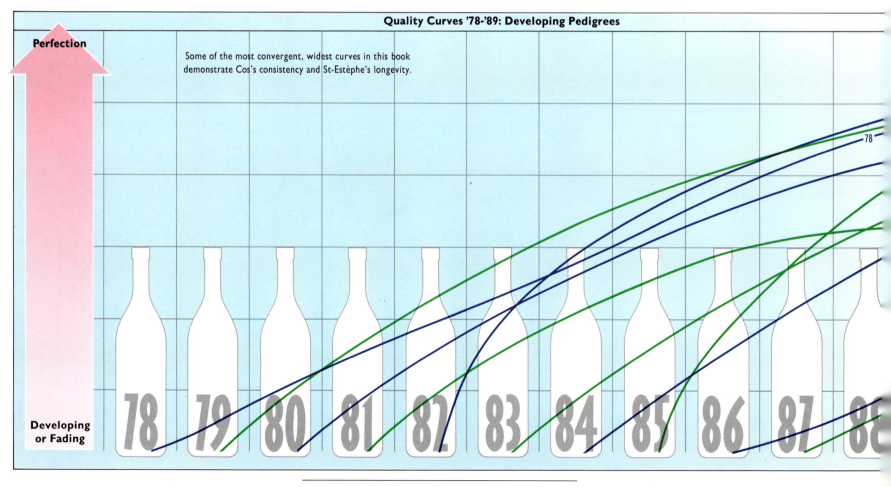

Quality Curves '78-'89: Developing Pedigrees

Perfection

Some of the most convergent, widest curves in this book demonstrate Cos's consistency and St-Estèphe's longevity.

Developing or Fading

78 79 80 81 82 83 84 85 86 87 88

Weather and timing

Light vintage, very small crop. Mediocre start to year. Flowering June 25. Fine Sept: late ripening. Good Oct: harvest 8-14, 15-24.

Quantity produced

15,500 cases released at Fr f390 a case. St-Estèphe: 455,000 cases.

Other details

40% Merlot. New planting of 25 acres/10 ha of AOC land. *Chef de culture* Jacques Pélissié returned.

1981 A big, exotic wine that seems seriously built for a long life. By 1989 it showed little charm because of its pronounced tannin and acidity. Needs time.

Weather and timing

Average vintage, small crop. Early flowering June 12. Long growing season. Lovely Aug. Violent storms interrupted harvest Sept 28 to Oct 4 and Oct 5-13.

Quantity produced

19,000 cases released at Fr f540 a case. St-Estèphe: 560,000 cases.

Other details

30% Merlot. 30% in new wood. Jean-Baptiste Irrigaray succeeded René Sementery as *maître de chai*.

1982 Rich and heady with initial sweetness. Dark: only a narrow ruby rim to its blackened crimson distinguishes it from the 1987. Intense, too concentrated to release much aroma after it closed up at about five years old but there are glorious spicy flavours on the finish. Soft tannins.

Weather and timing

Great vintage, large crop. Early flowering, ripening and harvest (Sept 15-21, 22-Oct 1).

Quantity produced

24,100 cases released at Fr f720 a case. St-Estèphe: 645,000 cases.

Other details

40% Merlot. 70% in new wood. Bruno Prats directed the winemaking from his sick-bed.

1983 More open than most Cos wines at this stage. Looks older than the 1982. Leafy, spicy well-knit bouquet with a range of fully ripe secondary flavours. Ripe fruit dominates the tannins.

Weather and timing

Good vintage, above average crop. Flowering June 13. Tropical Aug: vines required careful management. Fine for harvest Sept 26-Oct 4 and Oct 5-11.

Quantity produced

23,400 cases released at Fr f720 a case. St-Estèphe: 670,000 cases. Sold quickly: underpriced compared with other second growths.

Other details

65% Merlot. 60% in new wood.

1984 Excellent colour, very correct, appetising bouquet suggesting the warm fruitiness of currants and the leafiness of a currant bush. Lovely smooth fruit on top of a tannic grip.

Weather and timing

Average vintage, below average crop. Rain in June caused incomplete flowering, especially of Merlot. Harvest Oct 2-5, 5-15.

Quantity produced

19,500 cases released at Fr f1,020 a case. St-Estèphe: 435,000 cases.

Other details

60% in new wood. 20% Merlot. US$ strong: hyped Bordeaux market. New steel *cuvier* installed.

1985 An opulent wine full of ripe mulberry Merlot flavours, glycerol and purple highlights. The exotic nose suggests molasses, chestnuts and game. The tannins are well hidden.

Weather and timing

Good vintage, large crop. Almost perfect season. Humid spring. Flowering June 15. Dry, warm summer. Fine for harvest Sept 26-Oct 3 and Oct 4-11.

Quantity produced

25,000 cases released at Fr f1,020 a case. St-Estèphe: 795,000 cases.

Other details

100% in new wood. 40% Merlot.

1986 Classic. Healthy deep crimson right out to rim and great rich, concentrated, intense nervy Cabernet flavours with layers of prunes and even orchids. Glowing aftertaste: slightly inky grip on the finish recalls St-Estèphe austerity.

Weather and timing

Exceptional vintage, large crop. Dry summer. Good maturation. Storm before perfect harvest Sept 29-Oct 4 and Oct 6-14.

Quantity produced

34,000 cases released at Fr f984 a case. St-Estèphe: 790,000 cases.

Other details

90% new wood. 30% Merlot. 2% Cabernet Franc introduced. US$ weakened.

1987 (Cask sample) Crimson but less concentrated than the 1986. Exuberant silky young fruit and new oak. Aromatic but lightish weight. Marked by tannins now: exciting medium-term drinking.

Weather and timing

Unexceptional vintage, average crop. Flowering June 15. Wet during harvest so old vines harvested first: Oct 1-6 (Merlot) and 7-13 (Cabernet).

Quantity produced

20,000 cases released at Fr f780 a case. St-Estèphe: 595,000 cases.

Other details

33% in new wood. 50% Merlot.

1988 (Not tasted) Traditional St-Estèphe, according to Bruno Prats. Intense colour, huge tannins and a long finish.

Weather and timing

Excellent vintage, normal crop. Mild spring. Mildew controlled. Very dry summer. Harvest Sept 27 to Oct 3 and Oct 5-12.

Quantity produced

About 30,000 cases for the whole Domaine. Estimated release price: Fr f1,560 a case.

Other details

Francis Carle new *maître de chai*.

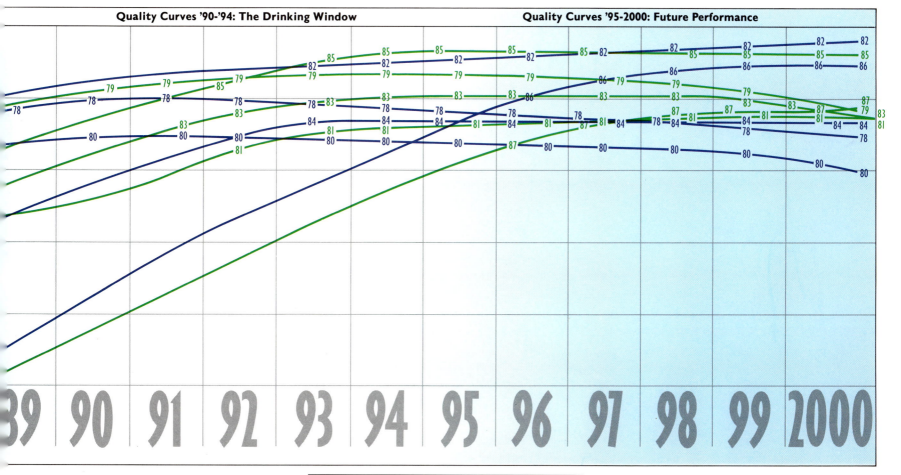

Château Lynch-Bages

This famous Pauillac estate provokes strong reactions, which is a healthy state of affairs in a landscape dotted with châteaux – all of which are trying to carve out an identity and reputation for themselves and their wines. There are those whose eyes light up at the mention of a wine with such opulent spice as well as the robust cassis structure of any decent Pauillac; then there are those, a minority as well they might be, who disapprove of such a sensual, lush, almost suspect interpretation of a theme which, played elsewhere, can be so rigorous and spare.

I remember just before a visit there in the late seventies being urged by a Master of Wine to "ask them what they put in the wine that makes it taste so different". There is of course no magic ingredient, but the wine-making facilities themselves have been transformed over the last two decades.

As is so often the case in the Médoc, Lynch-Bages must owe its distinction to the core of its terrain, nearly 175 acres (70 hectares) between the Bages plateau and the town of Pauillac. Lynch-Bages' domination by about 70 per cent Cabernet Sauvignon is obvious in the blackcurrant or cassis scent of most vintages, and has earned it the soubriquet "poor man's Mouton-Rothschild".

The wine rarely shows the polish of this first-growth, but it certainly deserves higher than fifth growth ranking, a point conceded even in the official bible of Bordeaux properties, *Cocks et Feret*.

The property has been in the Cazes family for three generations and the present incumbent Jean-Michel Cazes, who now also manages Château Pichon-Longueville, has overseen one of the Médoc's radical wine-making modernisations. Jean-Michel joined in 1973 and took on the impressive Daniel Llose as wine-maker during the difficult 1976 vintage which was, he said, "the last year there was any serious rot at Lynch-Bages".

The replacement of old wooden fermentation vats by stainless steel began in 1975 and this improvement alone resulted in an exceptionally fine wine. But it was not until 1980 when they had 25 new, temperature-controlled vats that they finally had enough space to make the sort of wine necessary to stay afloat in the quality-driven wine market of the late twentieth century. Certainly the 1980 is a handsome reward for all this investment, the 1982 a distinct step up from the era of the late seventies, and the 1985 and 1986 are quite exceptional.

Settled geographically mid-way between the Mouton and Lafite high ground at the north of the commune and the cluster of Pichons and Latour at the south, Château Lynch-Bages provides a Pauillac truly representative of this much-renovated appellation.

Château Haut-Bages-Averous is to Lynch-Bages what Château de Marbuzet is to Cos d'Estournel and both mature about three years ahead of the *grand vin*.

Earlier vintages

There is enormous pleasure to be had from the still meaty 1952, the dense and heady 1953, the delicate 1955 and the surprisingly youthful 1959, the slightly rustic 1960 and the overpoweringly cassis 1961. The 1966 also shows strong cassis and is holding well while the attractive 1962 and 1967 are fading. The disappointing 1971 and 1973 are fading fast, as is the somewhat coarse 1976, but the 1975 should continue to charm until 1993. The 1977 is a bit skinny but still alive while the 1970 is for the nineties.

1978 An attractively meaty wine with autumnal scents of mushrooms and woodsmoke. Lighter than one would expect. Particularly dry and "masculine" Lynch-Bages. Aggressive tannins without the voluptuous fruit.

Weather and timing

Very good vintage, small crop.

Long, late flowering. Sunny Aug then fine Sept; ripened well. Fine but cool for harvest.

Quantity produced

33,000 cases released at Fr f420 a case. Pauillac: 380,000 cases.

Other details

23% in new oak. Replanting increased vineyard by 25 acres/10 ha. Roger Mau, *maître de chai et culture*, was succeeded by Guy Bergey and Daniel Llose.

1979 Young, concentrated crimson. No sign of ageing. Muted bouquet for Lynch-Bages without extravagant spice or gaminess but with lots of ripe fruit. Relatively simple.

Weather and timing

Very good vintage, normal crop. Warm, dry June. Good flowering. Humid July and Aug. Cold, dry Sept. Harvest began Oct 4.

Quantity produced

37,500 cases released at Fr f348 a case. Pauillac: 540,000 cases.

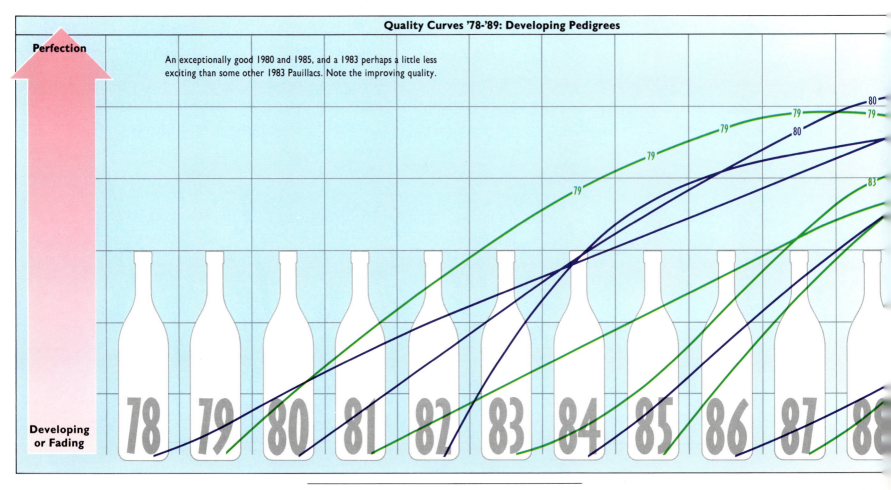

Quality Curves '78–'89: Developing Pedigrees

Perfection

An exceptionally good 1980 and 1985, and a 1983 perhaps a little less exciting than some other 1983 Pauillacs. Note the improving quality.

Developing or Fading

78 79 80 81 82 83 84 85 86 87 88

Other details

20% in new oak.

1980 A real success for this vintage. Healthy, evolved crimson. Lovely well-knit bouquet of ripe fruit; floral top notes and a good spike of acidity. Definitely drinkable but with soft tannins perceptible in 1988.

Weather and timing

Average vintage, very small crop. Cool May and June. Long, uneven flowering. Dry, cool summer. Very late harvest began Oct 13.

Quantity produced

24,000 cases released at Fr f348 a case. Pauillac: 360,000 cases.

Other details

31% in new oak.

1981 Crimson shading to a ruby rim. Dense cocktail of savoury aromas with real meat in the middle. The acidity starting to fade in 1988. Good value.

Weather and timing

Excellent vintage, small crop. Good start to season. Average summer. Ripened well. Fine Sept. Harvest began Oct 2.

Quantity produced

31,000 cases released at Fr f480 a case. Pauillac: 390,000 cases.

Other details

24% in new oak.

1982 This is a big, beefy wine that could do with more discipline. There is almost unbridled ripe fruit and notable tannins. In the late eighties the wine was engulfed in its own flab, from which it will doubtless eventually emerge to astound us.

Weather and timing

Great vintage, above average crop. Early flowering. Balmy June and July. Dull Aug. Hot Sept. Harvest began Sept 20.

Quantity produced

43,000 cases released at Fr f660 a case. Pauillac: 490,000 cases.

Other details

23% in new oak. Fermenting room too small: picking had to be slowed. Favourable exchange rate increased demand 1982-1986.

1983 A successful wine with all the spice, game and mineral notes of a fully ripe Pauillac. Good balance of acidity, soft tannins and a silky texture.

Weather and timing

Good vintage, very large crop. Very wet Mar-May. Excellent for flowering. Good summer. Fine for harvest Sept 29 to Oct 15.

Quantity produced

48,500 cases released at Fr f720 a case. Pauillac: 540,000 cases.

Other details

21% in new oak.

1984 This somewhat dry and dusty wine can still give pleasure. Mid-crimson without much colour density. The light bouquet offers a cocktail of mineral elements but there is sufficient fruit, tannin and acidity for it to continue to mature for a few years.

Weather and timing

Mediocre vintage, below average crop. Cold, humid May delayed flowering. Hurricane Hortense Oct 4, then fine for harvest.

Quantity produced

28,000 cases released at Fr f1,020 a case. Pauillac: 420,000 cases.

Other details

45% in new oak.

1985 The star. Jean-Michel Cazes is convinced this wine will continue to eclipse even the 1982 simply because of its balance. It is stunning in its combination of concentration, allure and promise. The scale is massive, the colour still a brilliant purple. Again there is the merest suggestion of mineral dust on the base of super-ripe fruit, laced with exciting spice. The wine could be drunk with enormous pleasure already but it would be a great pity.

Weather and timing

Great vintage, very large crop. Warm spring; good flowering. Exceptional Sept; good ripening. Harvest began Sept 28.

Quantity produced

45,000 cases released at Fr f1,020 a case. Pauillac: 680,000 cases.

Other details

44% in new oak.

1986 Massive, impenetrable. A super block-buster.

Weather and timing

Exceptional vintage, large crop. Cold, wet Apr; late, uneven bud break. Cool, dry summer. Wet Sept 15-23. Sunny for harvest which began Oct 1.

Quantity produced

45,500 cases released at Fr f936 a case. Pauillac: 660,000 cases.

Other details

47% in new oak. Weakened American demand: significant European buyers including Switzerland, Denmark and Germany.

1987 Excellent colour; herbaceous nose. Rigorous.

Weather and timing

Average vintage and crop. Cool, humid June; uneven flowering. Warm, showery July; good ripening. Sept 1 very wet then sunny. Dull and wet during harvest which began Oct 5.

Quantity produced

30,000 cases released at Fr f660 a case. Pauillac: 580,000 cases.

Other details

58% new oak. Stagnant market: concentrated on French sales.

1988 *(Not tasted)* A complex wine rich in tannins, according to J M Cazes, comparable to the 1966 and 1970. One to keep.

Weather and timing

Excellent vintage, average crop. Mild, wet start to year. Dry from mid-July. Slow, uneven ripening. Harvest Oct 3-16.

Quantity produced

38,000 cases.

Other details

62% new oak.

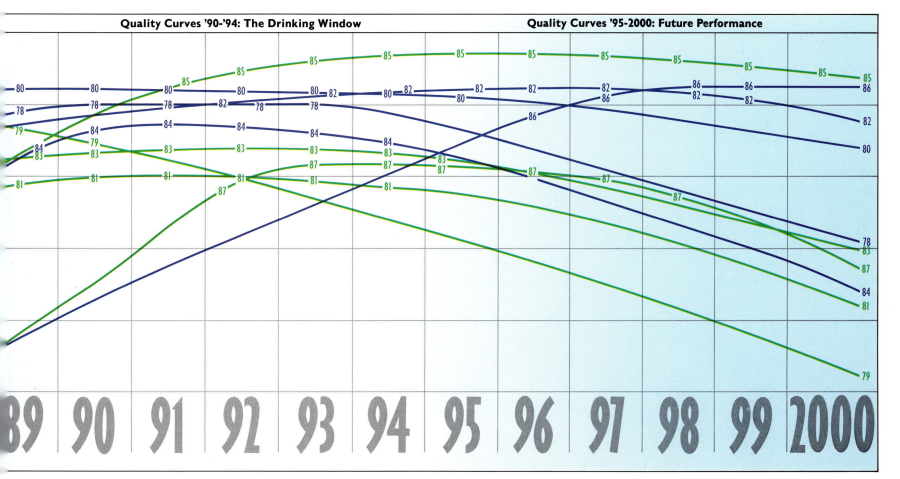

Quality Curves '90-'94: The Drinking Window — Quality Curves '95-2000: Future Performance

Château Gruaud Larose

St Julien, with its trio of Léovilles and Château Ducru-Beaucaillou, is the second-growth capital of the Médoc. It is logical therefore to analyze a St Julien example of a second growth, of which Château Gruaud Larose is the largest and therefore most widely available. The vines are the furthest from the Gironde and the most southerly of the St Julien seconds, at the centre of a triangle formed by the equally well managed Châteaux Lagrange, Lanessan and Beychevelle. The soil is a mixture of sand and gravel on iron-rich red sandstone, which doubtless adds vigour to the wines. The vineyards, which surround the grandiose château, are planted with an *encépagement* that is fairly standard for the Médoc: about two-thirds Cabernet Sauvignon supplemented by two to three per cent Petit Verdot, less than 10 per cent Cabernet Franc and therefore a rather higher proportion of Merlot than Ducru-Beaucaillou, Léoville-Las Cases or Léoville-Barton.

This shows in the style of wine produced, which is almost invariably plumper and earlier maturing than any other St Julien of this stature. It also manages to develop the structure and stuffing necessary for considerable longevity. The large and growing merchant house of Cordier, that can boast this property as their flagship, have persistently maintained prices at a relatively reasonable level.

In some years Léoville-Las Cases exhibits more concentration (and certainly more tannins), and in others there is more finesse apparent in Ducru-Beaucaillou, but the wines of

Château Gruaud Larose maintain a consistent level of quality and, despite their deceptively bumptious youth, can truly be taken as benchmark St Julien. The property is big, even by Médoc standards, with about 200 acres (80 hectares) planted, and it is managed with unusual vigour and care by Cordier's technical director Georges Pauly. He instituted a system of summer leaf plucking some time ago in order to maximise each bunch's exposure to light, and has no qualms about crop-thinning in particularly prolific years.

The enthusiasm and thoroughness with which all this is carried out make it clear to even the most casual visitor how cherished are the vineyards of Gruaud Larose, along with those of its neighbour and stable-mate fourth growth Château Talbot.

In most vintages Châteaux Talbot and Gruaud Larose show something of a Cordier house style in their accessibility and stuffing while maintaining the qualitative distance that is seemly between a second and fourth growth. Just occasionally however Talbot, an even bigger property than Gruaud Larose, manages to close the gap. The 1978 Talbot was particularly successful.

Monsieur Larose was so successful in boosting Gruaud Larose's reputation among the French aristocracy at the end of the last century that he felt emboldened to add to the label a (now slightly hackneyed) line which remains there to this day "*Le Roi des Vins, Le Vin des Rois*".

Earlier vintages

An 1870 Gruaud Larose tasted in 1985 was a vibrant demonstration of the keeping potential of this property's wines. The 1955, 1961, 1970 and possibly (eventually) the 1975 are all great wines.

1978 A classic wine that has shed puppy fat since its somewhat chunky, dense youth to become leaner and more aristocratic. It looks older than the 1979, especially at the rim. A mature bouquet with definite mineral notes. Dry, balanced and ultra-digestible, relatively restrained.

Weather and timing

Excellent vintage, average crop. Month-long flowering. Dry, sunny June-Aug. Beautiful Sept and Oct. Harvest Oct 9-24.

Quantity produced

31,400 cases released at Fr f435 a case. St Julien production: 290,000 cases.

1979 Full-bodied, alluring and enticing wine that has achieved full maturity. Could do with slightly more acid to preserve it to the turn of the century. Floral top notes on a fully ripe, flatteringly plummy base.

Weather and timing

Very good vintage, large crop. Flowering mid-June. Fine autumn. Fine for harvest Oct 1-20.

Quantity produced

40,200 cases released at Fr f393 a case. St Julien: 405,000 cases.

Other details

Second label introduced: Sarget de Gruaud Larose. Cordier replaced its period bottle with the classic Bordeaux bottle.

1980 One of Gruaud Larose's less successful vintages although there is some bottle variation. Pale with tawny hints, the wine is unusually acid for this vintage. Seems half a wine, with green underripe bits on the nose and

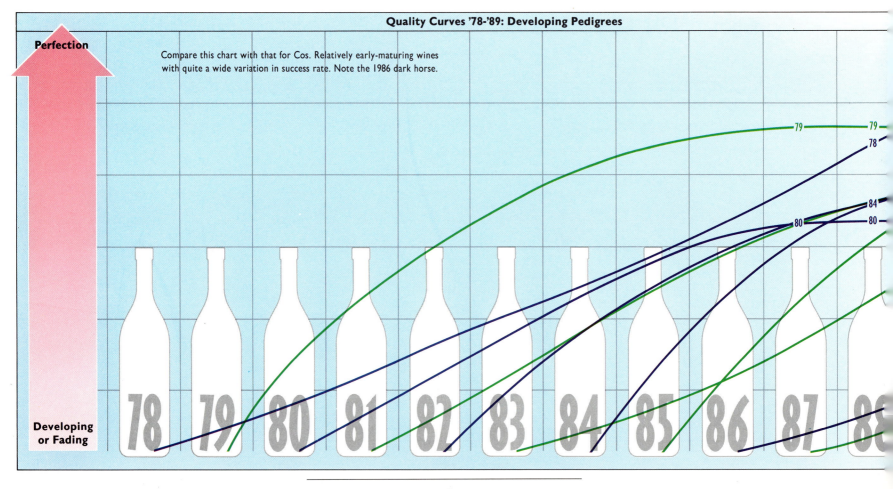

Quality Curves '78-'89: Developing Pedigrees

Perfection

Compare this chart with that for Cos. Relatively early-maturing wines with quite a wide variation in success rate. Note the 1986 dark horse.

Developing or Fading

78 79 80 81 82 83 84 85 86 87 88

palate. It is difficult to see how it can improve.

Weather and timing

Good vintage, small crop (down by 30% on 1979). Sunny season. Late harvest Oct 9-24.

Quantity produced

26,880 cases released at Fr f428 a case. St Julien: 260,000 cases.

1981 A serviceable rather than exciting wine: a "good lunchtime claret" to those who recognise the category. Some shading at the rim. Aromatic, with some herbaceousness. Smoky bouquet of secondary flavour elements. A relatively lightweight, well-mannered claret.

Weather and timing

Very good vintage, average crop. Quick flowering. Dry summer. Sept hot and dry then rain. Good maturation. Harvest Oct 1-15.

Quantity produced

32,000 cases released at Fr f534 a case. St Julien: 325,000 cases.

1982 An exciting wine that seems to have so much of everything it is hard to distinguish the individual elements. More concentrated than the 1983 with lively purple out to the rim. Very ripe fruit flavours. Beneath lurks the acid and, particularly, tannin sufficient to support its weight in years to come. Full, spicy, but so far unintegrated. For some years this one will be for admiring rather than drinking.

Weather and timing

Exceptional vintage, very large crop. Flowering early June. Hot, stormy July. Ripened well. Hot and sunny from Sept 6. Fine for harvest Sept 14 to Oct 6.

Quantity produced

45,340 cases released at Fr f674 a case. St Julien: 450,000 cases.

1983 Another impressive, if quite different, specimen. Good concentration of colour although the nose was relatively dumb in 1989. Some oak in evidence and explosive, though raw, flavour elements. Quite obtrusive tannins add texture to this medium-weight wine. Wait.

Weather and timing

Very good vintage, large crop. Poor start to season. Hot and dry for flowering. Tropical Aug. Warm from Sept 20. Slight overripening. Harvest Sept 26 to Oct 22.

Quantity produced

53,730 cases released at Fr f716 a case. St Julien: 510,000 cases.

1984 A charming wine for current drinking. Good youthful crimson but without great concentration. Far from intense, this wine is attractively balanced. It was well evolved at four years old and can offer the straightforward pleasures of a fairly soft, classically styled Bordeaux.

Weather and timing

Fair vintage, small crop. Variable spring. Warm Apr then cold, wet May. Uneven flowering. Early Oct wet (hurricane Hortense Oct 4) then dry and hot for harvest Oct 1-17.

Quantity produced

30,570 cases released at Fr f1,193 a case. St Julien: 270,000 cases.

1985 Soft, attractive, plummy wine that is more forward and insubstantial than its immediate successor. With some ruby already in evidence at the rim, this wine shows relatively simple fruit flavours and very little evidence of oak. Hugely enjoyable: not a wine for the masochist school of Bordeaux classicists.

Weather and timing

Exceptional vintage, large crop. First half of season slightly hotter and more humid than usual. Early flowering. Hot, dry Sept and Oct. Harvest Sept 26 to Oct 14.

Quantity produced

44,420 cases released at Fr f1,292 a case. St Julien: 470,000 cases.

1986 A stunning concentrated wine with all the rich fruit flavours of the 1982 but more rigour. Exceptional colour: crimson right out to rim. Notes of chocolate and coconut in the richness of the oak, and fruit cocktail as well as masses of acidity and rigorous dryness on the palate. Medium weight, strongly tannic classic build with great life.

Weather and timing

Great vintage, average crop. Quick, even flowering. Good July and Aug. Heavy rain mid-Sept then warm and dry for mature harvest Sept 29 to Oct 17.

Quantity produced

47,640 cases released at Fr f1,348 a case. St Julien: 465,000 cases.

Other details

M Carmagnac succeeded M Moreau as *maître de chai*.

1987 (Cask sample) Relatively pale with low-key aromas, some of them rather stalky but others pleasantly scented. Marked acidity and perceptible tannin so that the wine tasted quite classy in early 1989.

Weather and timing

Fine vintage, small crop. Cold Jan. Cool June; slow, uneven flowering. Warm July and Aug. Fine Sept but wet Oct. Harvest Oct 2-18.

Quantity produced

36,050 cases released at Fr f1,074 a case. St Julien: 420,000 cases.

1988 (Not tasted) Reported as round, smooth, comparable to the 1982, with strong tannins.

Weather and timing

Excellent vintage, average crop. Warm and humid Apr-July. Warm, sunny Aug. Hot early Sept; good maturation. Fine for harvest Oct 3-19.

Quantity produced

47,220 cases.

Other details

Crushing and de-stemming machines improved.

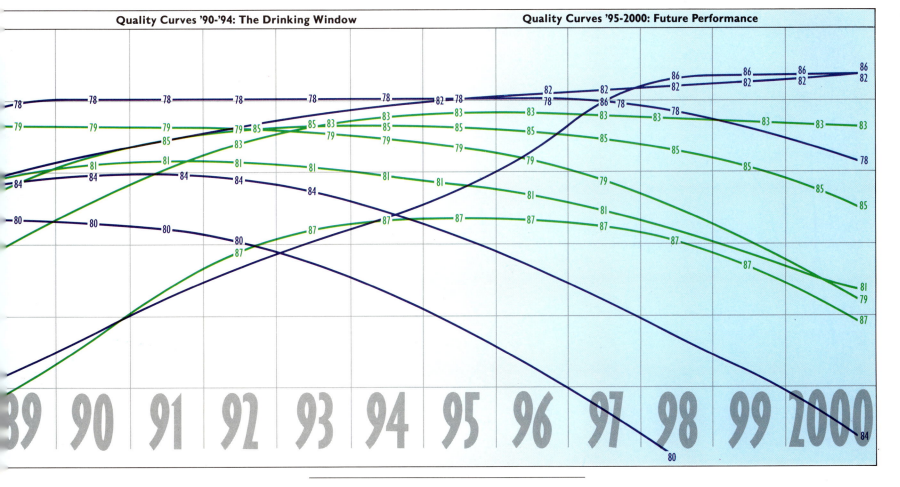

Château Margaux

No other Médoc first growth, perhaps no other Bordeaux property, is as tailor-made for vintage analysis since 1978 as Château Margaux. One of Bordeaux's favourite fairy stories, a favourite with consumers if not invariably with fellow producers, begins with the 1978 offering from the Médoc's most spectacularly beautiful château. With this single wine the new Mentzelopoulos regime showed just how dramatically they had managed to reverse the fortunes of their run-down property. But their 1979 seemed if anything to be even better, and the 1980 showed what a carefully chosen team could do with an off vintage. Their 1981 managed again to trump the entire region.

In 1982 the inevitable happened. Long before anyone had tasted a drop of the relevant wine, rumours spread throughout the trade of a disaster at Château Margaux during the 1982 harvest. When the wine eventually made its debut on the tasting tables, the rumours could only evaporate. And so, miraculously, the quality of Château Margaux, and even of its second wine Pavillon Rouge du Château Margaux, continues to astound with each new vintage.

The wine-making team is directed by the youthful and dedicated Corinne Mentzelopoulos, advised by the world-famous Professor Emile Peynaud and led by the personable director Paul Pontallier. Links with the old regime are retained through *maître de chai* Jean Grangerou and *régisseur* Philippe Barré, recently retired but still on hand.

Constantly renovating and improving, they manage just over 175 acres (70 hectares) of planted red wine vines. Just 30 acres (12 hectares) of Sauvignon Blanc yield the lauded Pavillon Blanc du Château Margaux. The policy is to leave 32 acres (13 hectares) fallow for a financially indulgent six years before replanting. Today the split is a high 75 per cent of Cabernet Sauvignon together with 20 per cent Merlot, three per cent Petit Verdot and very little, just two per cent, Cabernet Franc. The current success rate of Château Margaux suggests that Cabernet Franc may not be such an essential ingredient in the Médoc *encépagement*. Petit Verdot is certainly particularly successful on Margaux soil, and was probably even more widely planted in the past.

The current style of Château Margaux certainly seems quintessentially modern Médoc rather than recalling the scented delicacy of great Margaux vintages of old. It has great concentration, a high level of soft tannins, verve and polish with enormously luscious, silky, often mulberry fruit. The pronounced bouquet and softer tannins help to distinguish it from other Médoc first growths in blind comparisons.

So far we have seen the new Château Margaux output as wine to taste rather than to drink but it would be strange indeed if the team which had charmed so many tasters, and so many cost-conscious drinkers with Pavillon Rouge, did not fulfil such a fabulous succession of early promises with the *grand vin*.

Earlier vintages
The California collector Bipin Desai organised a lunch in 1988 and served: the gloriously subtle and still youthful 1961; the ripe, succulent and deservedly legendary 1953; the delicate yet lively and complete 1945; the sweet, chunky 1928; an overwhelmingly complex and gorgeous 1900; the succulently Margaux 1893; and a full, rich relic from the 1870 vintage. Generally, immediate pre-Mentzelopoulos vintages are not the most exciting. The only wine produced since 1961 with any real life in it is the 1966.

1978
The first knock-out vintage seemed disturbingly to have knocked itself out for a few months around its tenth birthday but by late 1988 was opening out again. One of the few examples in which the 1978 is deeper and more purple than the 1979. It is also much more concentrated, powerful and backward. Should charm us into the next millenium.

Weather and timing
Remarkable vintage, small crop. Mediocre first half of year. Late flowering June 25. Hot and dry from Aug. Harvest began Oct 9.

Quantity produced
15,300 cases. Margaux production: 385,000 cases.

Other details
Extensive overhaul of vineyard, winery and cellar continued.

1979
Most approachable. Ripe mulberry fruit flavours with excellent structure and seductive silkiness. A rigorous backbone that has maintained the wine's perfect balance. Opulently long.

Weather and timing
Very good vintage, average crop. Cool spring. Hot, dry Sept. Harvest began Oct 4.

Quantity produced
17,400 cases. Margaux: 520,000.

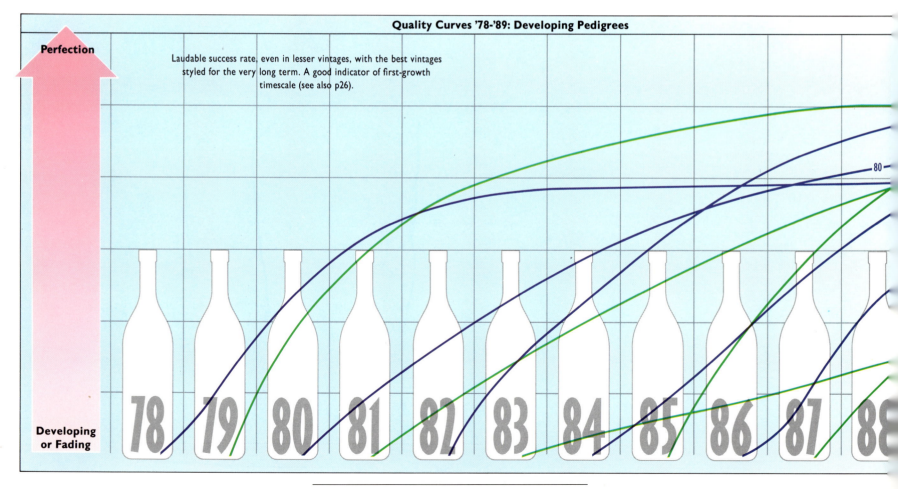

Quality Curves '78-'89: Developing Pedigrees

Perfection

Laudable success rate, even in lesser vintages, with the best vintages styled for the very long term. A good indicator of first-growth timescale (see also p26).

Developing or Fading

78 79 80 81 82 83 84 85 86 87 88

1980 Impressively dark for the vintage although a watery rim. Strongly perfumed with the oak just perceptible. Lightweight with marked acidity but respectable ripe fruit flavours.

Weather and timing
Fair vintage, very small crop. Cool spring; late flowering June 25. Cool early Oct delayed harvest but allowed full maturation. Harvest began Oct 17.

Quantity produced
16,200 cases. Margaux: 380,000.

1981 Very deep crimson and admirable complexity for this serviceable vintage. Evolved and excitingly well-knit bouquet. An appetizing cocktail of ripe red fruits and oak. Toastiness and warmth in the scent arguably makes the 1981 more typically Margaux than the 1978 or 1979. Medium-weight with some underlying toughness that will preserve the wine.

Weather and timing
Very good vintage, average crop. Rapid, even flowering. Fine for harvest which began Oct 1.

Quantity produced
20,000 cases. Margaux: 430,000 cases.

1982 Extraordinary wine but difficult to say when it should be drunk. Exceptionally deep colour and the bouquet includes spice, voluptuousness and layers of exotic fruits. Almost Petrus-like in aroma. Supple and melting, this wine's flavour elements soar enticingly above the sheer size that bedevils so many 1982s.

Weather and timing
Great vintage, large crop. Late frosts. Hot summer; early maturation. Harvest began Sept 20.

Quantity produced
29,300 cases. Margaux: 565,000 cases.

Other details
New underground barrel cellar.

1983 A more seriously built specimen but with just as impressive a colour if markedly less fragrance by the late eighties. For the very long term, with marked tannin and an austerity unusual for this range. Cassis and oak flavour elements were still unintegrated after five years. Wait.

Weather and timing
Classic vintage, large crop. Sunny year. Excellent flowering. Hot July-Aug. Hot and sunny from Sept 10; harvest began Sept 30.

Quantity produced
29,200 cases. Margaux: 645,000.

Other details
New manager, Paul Pontallier. Replanting programme begun.

1984 Great selection ensured this triumph for a somewhat mean, Cabernet-dominated vintage. Much more concentration than the 1980, although lightweight. Good, attractive aromas should provide respectable, classic drinking that has more polish and class than practically any other 1984.

Weather and timing
Good vintage, normal crop. Cold Feb and Mar. Hot, dry Apr; cold, humid May; hot, dry June (disrupted flowering); warm July and Aug; cold, humid Sept. Harvest began Sept 29. Early Oct wet due to hurricane Hortense.

Quantity produced
15,500 cases. Margaux: 380,000 cases.

1985 Another very successful wine that is the opulent, broad counterpoint to 1986's taut rigour. Spicy bouquet with velvety texture: a wine for hedonists. Cassis and truffles on the nose and gorgeously soft tannins with a dry finish.

Weather and timing
Exceptional vintage, large crop. Good flowering. Fine summer. Excellent Sept and Oct; good maturation. Harvest began Sept 26.

Quantity produced
25,500 cases. Margaux: 590,000 cases.

Other details
Large production of second wine, Pavillon Rouge.

1986 (Cask sample) A classic. Wonderful crimson right out to rim. Gorgeous if back-straightening silky, inky, aromatic intensity and vibrancy. Should close up after bottling.

Weather and timing
Exceptional vintage, large crop. Cool, wet Apr; late bud break. Hot, dry May and June; good flowering. Dry summer. Fine for harvest which began Sept 27.

Quantity produced
25,400 cases. Margaux: 705,000 cases.

Other details
Cuvier enlargement completed. Stainless steel vats introduced. Crop thinned for first time.

1987 (Cask sample) Exciting for the vintage. A wine with real nerve and fruit.

Weather and timing
Good vintage, normal crop. Severe winter followed by irregular flowering. Aug and Sept very hot and dry; excellent maturation. Wet during harvest which began Oct 5.

Quantity produced
13,700 cases. Margaux: 630,000 cases.

Other details
Strict selection: only 40% used for first wine.

1988 (Not tasted) Similar tannin levels to 1986 and perhaps best colour ever.

Weather and timing
Excellent vintage, normal crop. Mild winter. Hail storm at end June thinned crop. Early July wet then hot and very dry until harvest. Showers at beginning of harvest (Oct 3) then fine.

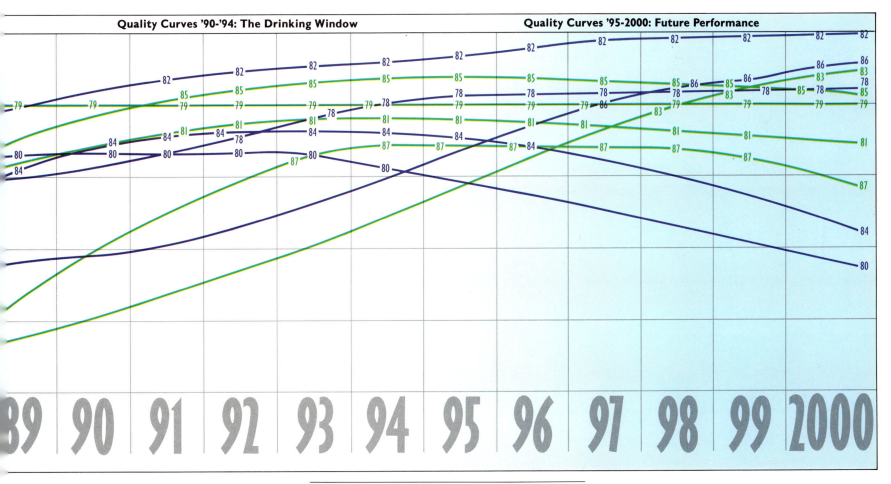

Quality Curves '90-'94: The Drinking Window   Quality Curves '95-2000: Future Performance

89 90 91 92 93 94 95 96 97 98 99 2000

Château Haut-Brion

It is perhaps not surprising that Jean Delmas, Château Haut-Brion's exceptionally able steward, is one of the most vociferous critics of the current vogue for blind comparative tastings of the "Cabernets from around the World" genre. Haut-Brion's style and intentions are possibly unique, and certainly very different from those of its fellow "competitors" in such a heterogeneous line-up.

Most Cabernet-based wines are dominated by the fruity, often blackcurrant-flavoured, intensity that can quite easily be achieved by this grape. But Haut-Brion is shaped much more obviously by its terrain, its 100 acres (40 hectares) of Guntz, once Pyreneean, gravel on a favoured, well-placed hillock in Pessac, the southerly suburb of Bordeaux that now has its own appellation, Graves-Pessac. The taste of a mature or maturing Haut-Brion is dominated not by fruit but by something that seems of a more mineral origin, a very particular flavour described by some as tobacco, others as dusty, others, less oppressed by literalists, as the broad, lazy aroma of bricks warmed in the sun.

Haut-Brion is more subtle than intense, a fact that may owe something to Monsieur Delmas's belief in late bottling. Whereas others rush to preserve youthful vigour in the bottle, Jean Delmas chooses, for vintages as formidable as 1985 and 1986, to bottle as late as the January of the wine's third winter. Even such light vintages as the 1980 and 1987 were bottled in July, a conventional bottling time for big vintages elsewhere.

His theory put simply is that tannins, especially in powerful vintages, need to be softened or tamed a little before being cooped up in a bottle for the rest of their lives. This policy can certainly result in wines that age fast relative to the first growths of the Médoc, wines that tend to whisper seductively rather than shout which, however subtle and appealing, is rarely an advantage in a big taste-off.

One aspect in which Haut-Brion is exceptional is in the fact that its owners the Duc and Duchesse de Mouchy now control the next-door La Mission-Haut-Brion estate, Haut-Brion's old rival, too. The estate is also marked out by Jean Delmas' unusually inspired and painstaking research project. He is striving to develop a colony of complementary clones designed to maximise the quality and quantity at Château Haut-Brion.

With typical thoroughness Delmas has been monitoring the results of microvinifications from his plant nursery of 360 different clones using advanced computer analysis, and by the year 2000 he reckons he will have cracked the problem. He clearly takes the educational and technological side of wine-making very seriously indeed and the results of his experiments are awaited with great interest. He also plans to add an acre (half a hectare) each of Petit Verdot and the ancient Carmenère to the current 55:20:25 Cabernet Sauvignon:Cabernet Franc:Merlot profile of this, one of the world's most distinctive vineyards.

Earlier vintages

Jean Delmas's own comments are: "The 1970, a good but definitely not great vintage for us, still very young. The 1971 was charming but is fading. The 1966 is gorgeous and almost at its peak. The 1964 is à boire. The 1961 is not yet ready while the 1959 is my favourite for current drinking. The 1955 and 1945 are very, very good but I'm no great fan of very old wines." The 1924 and 1929 tasted good to me in 1986.

1978 Quite high in Haut-Brion characteristics such as the dusty "warm bricks" smell. Good colour but tawny at the rim. A less powerful bouquet than the 1979 with a distinctly herbaceous, less-than-fully-ripe note. Good balance. Dry, mineral-laden wine: already approachable.

Weather and timing

Very good vintage, small crop.

Wet winter. Wet, cool spring. Fine summer. Fair, dry autumn. Harvest Oct 5-14.

Quantity produced

10,000 cases released at Fr f880 a case. Graves production: 1,140,000 cases.

1979 Glowing with health and youth. Brilliant ruby colour out to rim. Opulent and flattering with a slightly burnt top note on the full, luscious and slightly dusty fruit. Neat with gorgeous nuances of *terroirisme*. Very soft tannins, great fan of flavours on the finish. Ready to drink.

Weather and timing

Very good vintage, large crop. Late, dry season. Wet spring. Hot July, cool Aug. Harvest Oct 1-11.

Quantity produced

14,000 cases released at Fr f880 a case. Graves: 1,800,000 cases.

1980 Light and rather dilute. Definite shading towards the rim and quite evolved with a distinct if

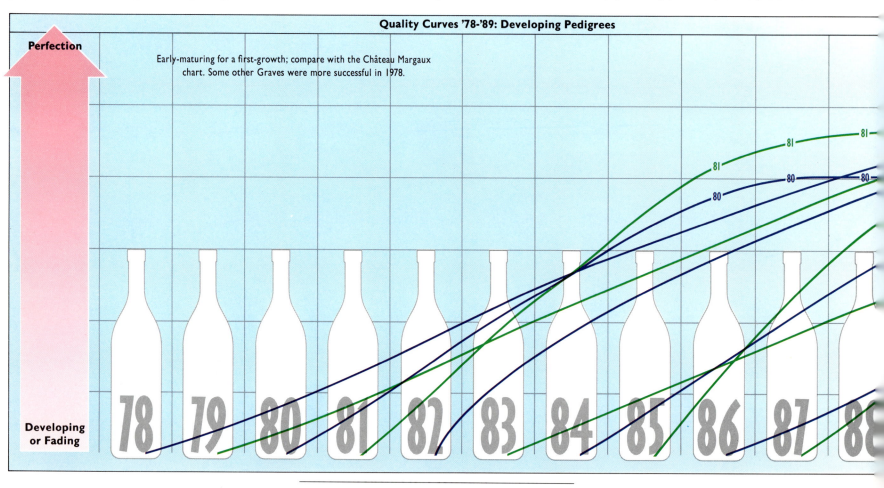

Quality Curves '78-'89: Developing Pedigrees

Perfection

Early-maturing for a first-growth; compare with the Château Margaux chart. Some other Graves were more successful in 1978.

Developing or Fading

78 79 80 81 82 83 84 85 86 87 88

low-key bouquet of secondary flavours. Some meatiness and tannin but needs more extract and even acidity.

Weather and timing
Average vintage, small crop. Cold, wet spring. Cold, wet, windy weather badly affected flowering. Harvest Oct 6-18.

Quantity produced
10,000 cases released at Fr f960 a case. Graves: 1,200,000 cases.

1981 A forward, exceptionally plump Haut-Brion with an extremely deep, rich, ruby colour. Verges on being heavy and unappetising. Merlot perceptible through a cooked prunes flavour. Some charred wood and blackcurrant notes. An uneven wine that developed early but has enough tannin for the medium term.

Weather and timing
Very good vintage, small crop. Poor spring: incomplete flowering. Hot, dry autumn. Sept fair, then wet. Excellent for harvest Sept 24 to Oct 4.

Quantity produced
12,000 cases released at Fr f1,500 a case. Graves: 1,120,000 cases.

1982 Jean Delmas likens this to the 1959 and the 1985 to 1961. It is impressive, but less charming than the 1985. Deep crimson. The rich mix of extract, tannins and acidity leave the palate tingling almost with pain: a chunky wine that for years will express the vintage rather than the property. The structure is dominated by the tannins and the flavour by stewed blackberries.

Weather and timing
Great vintage, very large crop. Almost perfect season. Hot, dry Apr. Thundery June. Hot summer and harvest which began Sept 15.

Quantity produced
19,000 cases released at Fr f2,040 a case. Graves: 2,050,000 cases.

1983 A powerful wine for this vintage with a rich, gamey bouquet. The almost excessive tannin level is disguised until the very dry finish. Full-bodied, seductive, long, with an almost chocolaty richness. This is a 1986 with body, which will provide superb drinking while the 1986 ripens.

Weather and timing
Excellent vintage, large crop. Wet spring. Dry June. Hailstorm July 3-4. Tropical Aug. Perfect for harvest Sept 26 to Oct 7.

Quantity produced
17,000 cases released at Fr f2,040 a case. Graves: 1,800,000 cases.

1984 A tell-tale pale rim: this is not up to Haut-Brion's very best. On the nose there is some chocolaty richness but some herbaceousness too, indicating Cabernets that had to struggle to ripen. Both acid and tannin are noticeable. Balance and structure but no concentration or charm.

Weather and timing
Good vintage, below average crop. Cold, wet spring. Hot, dry July. Harvest Sept 27 to Oct 12.

Quantity produced
11,000 cases released at Fr f2,040 a case. Graves: 1,400,000 cases.

1985 The indisputable star. All the ingredients of the miraculous 1985. Already complex, with all the elements that make a great wine and those that make Haut-Brion. There is enormous weight and ripeness, together with dust, tobacco and hot bricks. Layer after layer of fascinating flavour elements and nuances. Dry with lovely acid and soft tannins.

Weather and timing
Outstanding vintage, normal crop. One of the hottest years on record. Mist early Sept prevented excess drying. Harvest Sept 23 to Oct 8.

Quantity produced
17,000 cases released at Fr f2,640 a case. Graves: 1,500,000 cases.

1986 The longest-term of these wines. Excellent crimson and youthful fruit, good concentration and richness with notable viscosity. Classic and rigorous on the palate. Extremely correct, neat, clean, powerful and well balanced and should develop beautifully over the next two decades. A more polished version of the 1978, perhaps?

Weather and timing
Excellent vintage, large crop. Cold spring. Clear for flowering then hot and dry right through to harvest (Sept 29 to Oct 10).

Quantity produced
16,000 cases released at Fr f2,160 a case. Graves: 1,900,000 cases.

1987 (Cask sample) Another agreeably forward wine from this bad-mouthed vintage. Healthy crimson but without great concentration at the rim. Aromatic Cabernet aromas: low-key rather than opulent. Well balanced, well structured wine with good impact and smooth texture. Tannin for the medium term.

Weather and timing
Good vintage, normal crop. Variable weather throughout spring and summer. Unripe grapes removed at end Aug. 10 hot days in Sept. Poor for harvest Sept 28 to Oct 13.

Quantity produced
10,000 cases released at Fr f1,512 a case. Graves: 1,500,000 cases.

1988 (Not tasted) Reported as being very typical of the terroir. Strong tannins and high acidity. One to keep.

Weather and timing
Excellent vintage, above average crop. Wet early spring. Average summer. Uneven ripening: unripe grapes removed. Warm, dry Sept. Harvest began Sept 28.

Quantity produced
18,000 cases.

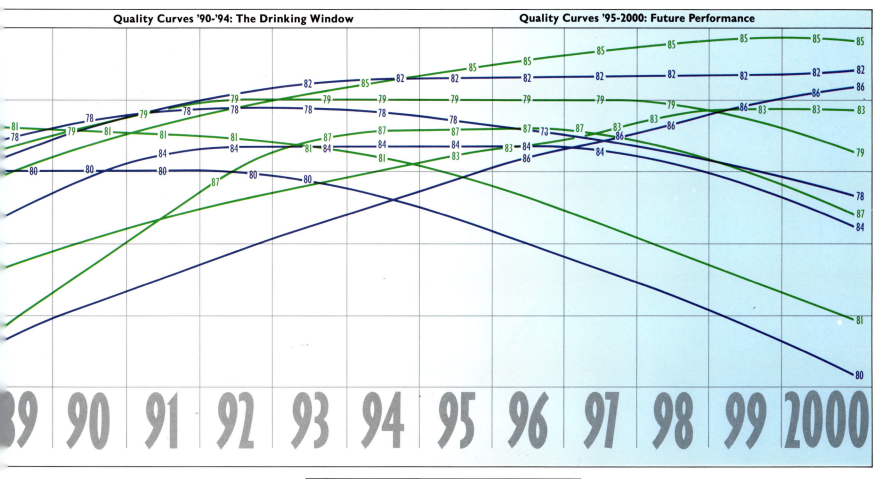

Quality Curves '90-'94: The Drinking Window   Quality Curves '95-2000: Future Performance

RIGHT BANK

Château Petrus (page 44) – where care and francs are lavished on the unique vineyard rather than the surprisingly simple, uninhabited, château building.

Three Timecharts have been assembled to illuminate the patterns of evolution of collectable wines made on the right bank of the Gironde: one from tiny but democratic Pomerol and two from diverse St-Emilion with its delicately nuanced classification system.

Pomerol presents its thirsty fans (notably Belgians) with a unique concentration of ageworthy wines. Almost every drop of wine produced in the commune goes into a bottle that is worth keeping for a few years – with the possible exception of that rarity, generic Pomerol. Château Petrus is the commune's indisputable superstar, selling at prices which sometimes make the wine hard to swallow. It is made by the team responsible for a high proportion of Pomerol's other top properties, led by the Libourne wine merchant Jean-Pierre Moueix.

Pomerol is small enough to be a climatologically homogeneous area, although in 1987 Château Petrus was treated to a localised remedy for badly timed rain, its very own grape-drying helicopter. It thereby produced one of the best wines of the vintage (although miniscule Château Le Pin did well too). Most Pomerol properties should follow the relative maturity patterns of Petrus (although not too many of them managed to produce a 1984 at all –

let alone one of such quality – and 1980 was also particularly successful for Petrus). Few Pomerols last as long as Petrus, however, although Châteaux Lafleur and Trotanoy, and in vintages such as 1986 L'Evangile, Certan de May and the rather harder, renovated Vieux Château Certan, can do so. For most Pomerols, accelerate the Petrus chart by two years, three if you have managed the near impossible and found an inexpensive one.

St-Emilion is represented by one of its most seriously managed *Premiers Grands Crus Classés*, Château Canon; and one of the most popular of the myriad lesser properties which export approachable emissaries for Bordeaux all over the world, Château Monbousquet.

In terms of weather and vintage variation, however, one of St-Emilion's most illustrious clusters of châteaux – Cheval Blanc and all of those with Figeac in their name on the *graves* plateau – are much closer to Château Petrus than to the main concentration of St-Emilion's châteaux around the medieval town itself. Château Cheval Blanc and Château Figeac mature quite similarly to Château Petrus, and can last every bit as long. For the other St-Emilion châteaux on the *graves* plateau, accelerate the Petrus chart by two years.

The plateau of St-Emilion is among the densest areas of vine cultivation in the world. Little wonder that this is also a hotbed of wine politics, with one of the few wine classification systems which is actually open to change.

To establish a maturity pattern for any other St-Emilion property (generics on the market should be ready for drinking) first look on the label for its classification. A simple *Grand Cru*, or no mention of rank at all, means that the wine is likely to be of Monbousquet status (although it may have had more success with the 1983 vintage). Accelerate the Monbousquet chart by two years for a St-Emilion *petit château*, the status of which will probably be signalled by its price. If, on the other hand, the words *Grand Cru Classé* appear on the label, signalling that this wine stands somewhere between a *Grand Cru* (no "*Classé*") and a *Premier Grand Cru Classé* in rank, advance the Canon chart by a year, with the proviso

that Canon's 1979, along with Château Pavie's, is a particularly successful one.

Most *Premier Grands Crus Classés* should follow a very similar pattern to that of Canon. *Grands Crus Classés* which are now making wines to equal many a *Premier Grand Cru Classé* include Châteaux L'Arrosée, La Dominique and Soutard.

For wines from the so-called satellite appellations of St-Emilion, those whose appellations include a prefix to St-Emilion such as Lussac, Montagne and Puisseguin, accelerate the Monbousquet chart by two years. For Pomerol's "satellite", Lalande de Pomerol, accelerate the Petrus chart by three years, four in backward vintages.

Château Petrus

Those who can afford the rare and great wine Petrus tend to know the story of this small château. To those who cannot, the tale only adds to the wine's mystique. Briefly, Petrus is a wine raised from pre-war obscurity to international star status by the old owner Madame Loubat and the merchant Jean-Pierre Moueix, who has held exclusive selling rights since 1961.

The vital statistics are these. Just 28 acres (11 hectares), are planted almost exclusively with Merlot, Pomerol's vine. Grapes from these vines owe their unique (an overworked word that in this case is accurate) concentration to a unique (ditto) deposit of iron-rich clay in the gently elevated vineyard. An average of only 3,000 cases of Petrus are produced each year.

Petrus now commands such a price that the cellar and particularly vineyards are treated to every luxury. Pruning and January selection of the vats for the *grand vin* (the offcuts are tantalisingly "lost" in M Moueix's cellars in Libourne) is passionately stringent. The vines are cossetted into ripe old age. There was no piecemeal replanting, for example, to replace the eight per cent of vines lost in the 1985 frosts and 12 per cent frozen to death in 1987. There will simply be a forlorn and costly gap in the row until it is the turn of that particular hectare to be replanted, and that might not be for decades since a different single-hectare parcel is replanted every nine years.

If there is danger of dilution through wet weather at vintage time, the grapes are carefully fanned dry by the rotating blades of a helicopter, no less, as happened in 1987 and in 1970 when helicopters were also drafted to administer a vital blow-dry. On the second occasion, continuous rain had made the vineyard too muddy for tractors so more sophisticated (if slightly less than traditional) equipment had to be summoned to protect the potential of this valuable crop. Picking is concentrated into three consecutive afternoons so that ripeness is uniform and no dew dilutes the result.

If the vineyard is the domain of Jean-Pierre Moueix's talented son Christian (who is democratic enough to have his own vineyard in California), the freshly scrubbed cellar is that of Jean-Claude Berrouet, Moueix's unusually cerebral oenologist. Although on a financial basis Petrus easily merits 100 per cent new oak every year, he carefully judges the mix of casks suitable for each vintage year. He selected only 20 per cent new oak for the 1980, and exclusively one-year-old barrels (already used for maturing the 1982 vintage) for the light 1984 crop, for example.

In really ripe years Petrus is dangerously easy to drink young, but this is crazy. Better by far to drink lesser Pomerols young or to go for an off vintage, when Petrus can so often provide an exceptional order of pleasure at even six or seven years old (they say eight), just like the earthly Pomerols it so proudly sweeps along in its train.

Earlier vintages

The 1921 was glorious in 1986, the 1934 a bit too muscular. In 1980 the 1926 was over the top; the plummy 1945 outshone the meaner 1947. 1948 and 1949 were respectable and lively: the 1952 successful. The 1953 was lighter than expected and ready; the 1955 too light and acid to be fun. The 1959 beautifully perfumed and balanced; the 1960 past it. The 1961 has a port-like status. The 1962, 1964 and 1966 should be in their prime but the 1967 is fading and the 1969 softening. Among 1970s, 1971s, 1975s and 1976s, Petrus is youthful and outstanding, 1970 and 1975 have years to go. The 1973 is years ahead of the now ready 1972.

1978 A hint of tobacco and the herbaceous notes of undergrowth and mushrooms. Acidity and tannin are unintegrated. A medium-weight, chunky, over-valued wine.

Weather and timing
Good vintage, normal crop. Cold winter. Dull to mid-Aug then hot and dry. Late, irregular flowering. Harvest began Oct 14.

Quantity produced
3,500 cases released at Fr f864 a case. Pomerol production: 620,000 cases.

1979 Deep crimson right out to rim; so much extract and concentration that the youthful bouquet takes time to emerge. Slow-developing, full of ripe fruit, almost munchable texture. Still too big, in a 1982 way, in 1989.

Weather and timing
Good vintage, large crop. Mild winter. Cold, wet Apr and May. Fine for flowering. Excellent July-Oct. Harvest began Oct 12.

Quantity produced
4,200 cases released at Fr f900 a case. Pomerol: 910,000 cases.

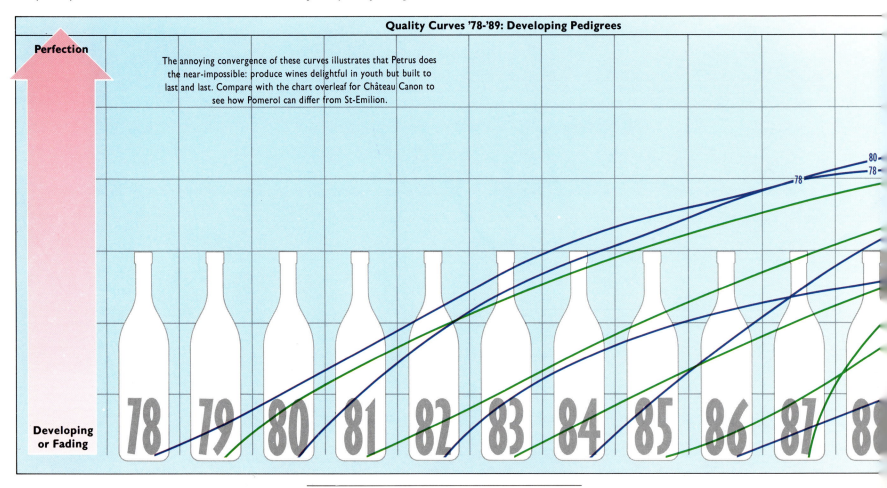

Quality Curves '78-'89: Developing Pedigrees

Perfection

The annoying convergence of these curves illustrates that Petrus does the near-impossible: produce wines delightful in youth but built to last and last. Compare with the chart overleaf for Château Canon to see how Pomerol can differ from St-Emilion.

Developing or Fading

78 79 80 81 82 83 84 85 86 87 88

1980 A particularly good vintage at Petrus. Exciting, with supple ripe fruits complemented by nervy acidity and even tannin. A lighter-weight Petrus, but unctuously mouthfilling.

Weather and timing
Average vintage, small crop. Late, incomplete flowering. Cold July then warm, sunny Aug and dry Sept. Grapes reached 13% alcohol. Ideal for harvest Oct 20-22.

Quantity produced
2,000 cases released at Fr f996 a case. Pomerol: 530,000 cases.

Other details
No chaptalization. Favourable exchange rate increased American demand 1980-1986.

1981 Less concentrated than usual for a Petrus: paler than the 1980. Lots of easy, ripe fruit flavours with some woodsmoke: just starting to form a bouquet in 1989. Unadorned Merlot flavours of plump, simple blackberries.

Weather and timing
Good vintage, below average crop. Cold winter. Dry, hot Aug-Sept then rain late Sept. Early harvest began Sept 29.

Quantity produced
3,000 cases released at Fr f1,500 a case. Pomerol: 620,000 cases.

1982 Gigantic dimension. Glowing ruby and black with a seductive cocktail of exotic spices, licorice and toasted fruits. The fruit and lush opulence disguises ripe tannins. Layers of flavour. Could already be drunk but there should be glorious development as shown.

Weather and timing
Outstanding vintage, large crop. Dry, sunny spring. Even flowering. Good maturation. Hot Sept concentrated grapes. Excellent harvest began Sept 16.

Quantity produced
4,500 cases released at Fr f2,040 a case. Pomerol: 630,000 cases.

Other details
Severe thinning of harvest. 100 rating by Robert Parker!

1983 Less concentration in every way than the 1982 with relatively open aromas, notable acidity, harsh tannins and a dry finish. An angular wine. Needs time.

Weather and timing
Fine vintage, large crop. Humid winter. Cold spring. Dry for flowering. Scorching July. Warm, wet Aug encouraged rot. Dry Sept. Harvest began Sept 28.

Quantity produced
4,500 cases released at Fr f2,040 a case. Pomerol: 730,000 cases.

Other details
Some thinning of harvest, but not the strictest selection.

1984 Light and soft, slightly diluted but welcoming. As dark as the 1983 with seductively ripe, evolved bouquet. Slightly short but very respectable.

Weather and timing
Poor vintage, very small crop. Coldest May for 25 years. Incomplete flowering. Dry, warm to mid-Aug; deteriorated in Sept. Harvest began Oct 3; interrupted by hurricane Hortense on Oct 4.

Quantity produced
1,000 cases released only for US at Fr f2,040 a case. Pomerol: 390,000.

1985 A wonder. The evolution of this (and the 1982) will be fascinating. A slow start, but by 1989 was opening out into a rich cocktail: game, roast chestnuts and *surmaturité*. Lots of acid and fruit: less tannin than usual.

Weather and timing
Excellent vintage, above average crop. Arctic Jan and Feb damaged roots. Mild Mar and Apr. Good for flowering, dry summer. Harvest began Sept 30.

Quantity produced
4,200 cases released at Fr f2,700 a case. Pomerol: 720,000 cases.

1986 In the classic, slightly austere 1986 mould. Youthful, bluish crimson, lighter than 1985: high toned aromatics. Some cinnamon and definite oak still. An attractive thoroughbred, if lean. Energy and polish with marked tannin. A long future.

Weather and timing
Good vintage, large crop. Winter frosts. Late spring. Dry summer then rain in Sept. Ripened well. Harvest began Oct 6.

Quantity produced
4,000 cases released at Fr f2,160 a case. Pomerol: 1,050,000 cases.

Other details
Jean Veyssiere's son, François, succeeded him as *maître de chai*.

1987 (Cask sample) More concentration than one would expect. Alluring, youthful, ripe animal Merlot flavours. Plump, if not enormous.

Weather and timing
Average vintage, small crop. Cold

winter. Uneven ripening. Harvest began Sept 30. Wet after Oct 10; strict selection.

Quantity produced
About 2,800 cases released at Fr f1,560 a case. Pomerol: 660,000.

Other details
Helicopter used to dry grapes before picking.

1988 (Cask sample) Port-like colour: black in the middle and shocking pink at rim. Floral high notes on an opulent, unctuous mix of ripe fruit. Heady, rich, powerful with magical spice and great vigour. Starting to harden in early 1989. A dry finish. Jean-Claude Berrouet thinks this is a cousin of the '85.

Weather and timing
Very good vintage, below average crop. Wet start to year. Variable summer. Indian summer. Harvest began on Oct 3.

Quantity produced
About 3,500 cases.

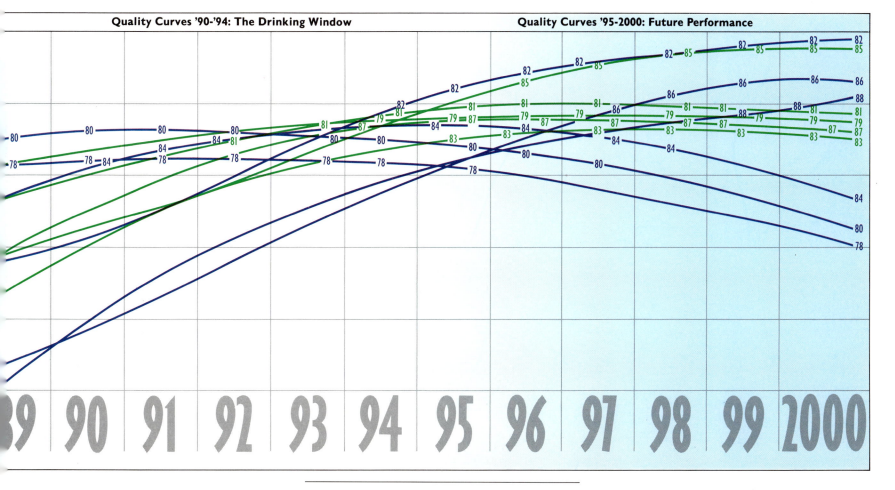

Quality Curves '90-'94: The Drinking Window

Quality Curves '95-2000: Future Performance

Château Canon

Of all the wines depicted in this book, those of Château Canon show the least qualitative variation and one of the most consistently long life-cycles. Compare the vintages charted below, for instance: only Canon 1980 is in any sense a disappointing wine, and even this exception to Canon's rule of firmness and concentration is a fine wine in the vintage context. The gentle or indeed non-existent downward slopes on the right hand side of this chart are significant, and indicate the tenacious lasting quality of these wines: one notable side of St-Emilion that is not illustrated by the Château Monbousquet Timechart overleaf.

Like Château Margaux, Château Canon is tailor-made for analysis in the period since 1978. It was with the 1978 vintage that the influence of the dynamic Eric Fournier could first be tasted in the bottle.

As the youngest of three brothers and the one least committed to a career elsewhere (one brother, an engineer, has played a considerable part in the eighties refurbishment of the Médoc châteaux), Eric gradually took over management of the family wine estates from his father and grandmother in the early seventies.

First he went to the Faculty of Oenology at the University of Bordeaux and then he began to look critically at the state of Château Canon. By 1976 he knew enough to come back the the winery and persuade the rest of the family that restitution of soil nutrients and stricter pruning were necessary in the vineyard, and that new fermentation vats and many more new barrels were needed in the winery.

By 1978 and 1979 these policies were starting to take effect, and by 1986 Château Canon had a second wine, Clos J Kanon, to soak up lesser *cuvées*. There was also an average yield of fully ripe, healthy fruit of around 38 hl/ha; full destalking; enough covered wooden fermentation vats to treat all the crop to the three-week temperature-controlled warm *cuvaison* that Fournier likes in order to leach soft tannins and colouring matter out of the must, and between 50 and 60 per cent new oak barrels each year.

He is usually described as "young Fournier" because of his boyish modesty (he describes himself as *régisseur* rather than anything grander) but is now into his fifth decade, and, confident about the success of his new policies, he remains unrepentant about the new oak flavours that mark his "strong, almost rude" traditionally built wines in their youth.

The property itself is on the outskirts of the town of St-Emilion between Château Magdelaine and Clos Fourtet. Two-thirds of the 45-acre (18-hectare) vineyard is planted with 35- to 40-year-old *coulure*-prone vines on the unyielding clay and limestone plateau, the rest is on the sandier *côtes*, the steep hillside onto which St-Emilion and such neighbours as Châteaux Belair and Ausone cling. Merlot usually constitutes between 60 and 65 per cent of the blend and the Cabernet is all Cabernet Franc.

Earlier vintages

Canons are lasters and the 1929 and 1947 are still concentrated, lively wines. The three great wines of the fifties are still in wonderful shape: the 1953 is splendidly rich and lively, the licorice-scented masculine 1955 is still developing and the flattering, complex 1959 perhaps the nearest its decline. The 1961 is less succulent, the 1962 fading fast while the 1964 shares some of the faded perfume of violets with all these wines. The 1970 is still angular and chunky, the 1971 plummy and flattering but losing substance, the 1975 is skinny and the 1976 is now on its last legs.

1978 Eclipsed by the 1979 but a serious, sturdy wine. A more open, herbaceous, loose textured bouquet suggesting a dusting of minerals on a base of classic, warm, spicy St-Emilion fruit. Less substantial and fleshy than 1979 but long and built to last.

Weather and timing

Good vintage, small crop. Cold, wet winter then cold spring. Long flowering. Lovely from Aug 6. Harvest Oct 11-19.

Quantity produced

5,400 cases released at Fr f384 a case. St-Emilion production: 3,800,000 cases.

Other details

Hard pruning after severe frost in Mar 1977 affected the vines for three harvests.

1979 A concentrated yet supple, meaty wine that still shows its high proportion of new oak. A powerful wine constructed to hide the easy warmth of Merlot for the moment. With its heady tarry scent, it seemed in 1989 the nearest St-Emilion will get to producing a Barolo.

Weather and timing

Good vintage, small crop. Hard

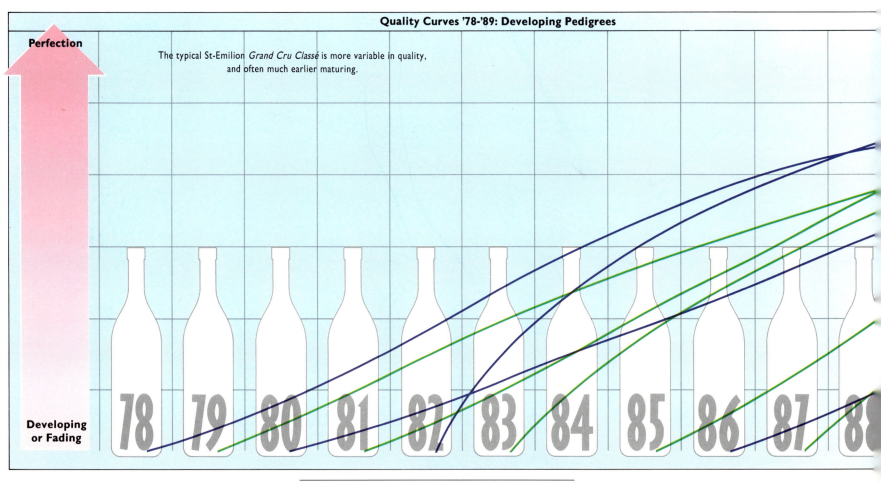

Quality Curves '78-'89: Developing Pedigrees

Perfection

The typical St-Emilion *Grand Cru Classé* is more variable in quality, and often much earlier maturing.

Developing or Fading

78 79 80 81 82 83 84 85 86 87 88

winter; cold, wet spring. Late flowering. Warm summer. Fine for harvest Oct 7-17.

Quantity produced
5,300 cases released at Fr f384 a case. St-Emilion: 5,150,000 cases.

Other details
Closed vats used for the first time enabling long *cuvaison*.

1980 A respectable "luncheon claret". Light crimson shading to a ruby rim. Lightweight with an evolved bouquet, good balance and some floral notes. Lovely fan of flavours on the finish but high acidity.

Weather and timing
Average vintage, small crop. Dry winter, wet spring. Frosts. Cold, wet June. Late ripening. Latest harvest since 1932 began Oct 17.

Quantity produced
4,000 cases released at Fr f384 a case. St-Emilion: 3,250,000 cases.

1981 A triumph. Excellent colour right out to rim. Statu-

esque build and richness with only slightly less concentration than the 1982. Rich, ripe Merlot fruit and a Cabernet backbone. An exciting fruit cocktail but with much more obvious tannins than the 1982. Powerful, long wine that tastes younger than it smells.

Weather and timing
Good vintage, below average crop. Humid spring. Fine for flowering. Overcast July, stormy Aug, dry Sept. Harvest Oct 3-9.

Quantity produced
5,700 cases released at Fr f480 a case. St-Emilion: 6,000,000 cases.

1982 Wonderful deep, rich colour. Relatively closed in 1989 but packed with exciting things. Rich scent and velvety texture thanks to the soft tannins. Plum pudding elements with some gaminess and good acid levels. Full-bodied but unformed yet.

Weather and timing
Outstanding vintage, large crop.

Mild spring. Excellent flowering began June 2. Splendid summer with rain end Aug. Ideal harvest Sept 15 to Oct 1.

Quantity produced
9,800 cases released at Fr f660 a case. St-Emilion: 5,250,000 cases.

1983 Expresses the property more than the vintage (unlike the 1982): developing fast. The wine was ruby by 1989 and fading at the rim with obvious secondary aromas melting into a medium-intensity bouquet of spiced, dried fruit compote. A well-mannered wine with good balance and strongly Merlot character, but just a note of dryness in the finish that suggests it will be good rather than great.

Weather and timing
Fine vintage, normal crop. Snow in Feb. Cold, wet Apr. Fine and hot from end May. Warm, stormy summer then fine and dry from Sept. Hot for harvest Oct 1-9.

Quantity produced
7,700 cases released at Fr f780 a case. St-Emilion: 4,800,000 cases.

1984 Failure of Merlot crop. No Château Canon.

Weather and timing
Poor vintage, very small crop. Worst May for 25 years. Fine for flowering. Hurricane Hortense Oct 4.

Quantity produced
St-Emilion: 1,850,000 cases.

1985 A broad, spicy, brawny specimen which in 1989 was just organising its ripe powerfully scented fruit backed up by good acid and unobtrusive tannin levels.

Weather and timing
Exceptional vintage, large crop. Harsh winter but vines remained virtually undamaged. Humid spring. Flowering June 7. Excellent summer with showers end Aug. Hot, dry Sept. Harvest Sept 27 to Oct 12.

Quantity produced
10,000 cases released at Fr f1,200 a case. St-Emilion: 3,250,000 cases.

Other details
Introduced second wine called Clos J Kanon.

1986 Where the 1985 is broad and floral the 1986 is piercing and fruity, with strong oak elements just starting their integration early in 1989. Deep crimson and slightly austere. Marked Cabernet rigour. To watch.

Weather and timing
Good vintage, large crop. Mild winter. Record rain in Apr. Quick flowering. Good summer. Excellent harvest Oct 1-15.

Quantity produced
9,700 cases released at Fr f1,080 a case. St-Emilion: 5,700,000 cases.

Other details
Tough selection especially of young Merlot.

1987 Deep colour: extremely healthy. A respectable meld of

fruit, oak and spice with acidity more prominent than tannin but sparkling clean. Good structure.

Weather and timing
Average vintage, small crop. Hard winter. Good spring. Cold June and beginning of July: late, slow and incomplete flowering. Harvest Oct 1-13; wet from Oct 3.

Quantity produced
5,300 cases released at Fr f816 a case. St-Emilion: 3,950,000 cases.

Other details
New fermentation room installed. Chaptalized.

1988 (Not tasted) Great concentration, tannic and with a good colour.

Weather and timing
Excellent vintage, small crop. Mild, humid winter. Wet spring. Poor flowering: incomplete set. Magnificent summer. Perfect for harvest Oct 1-11.

Quantity produced
About 5,800 cases.

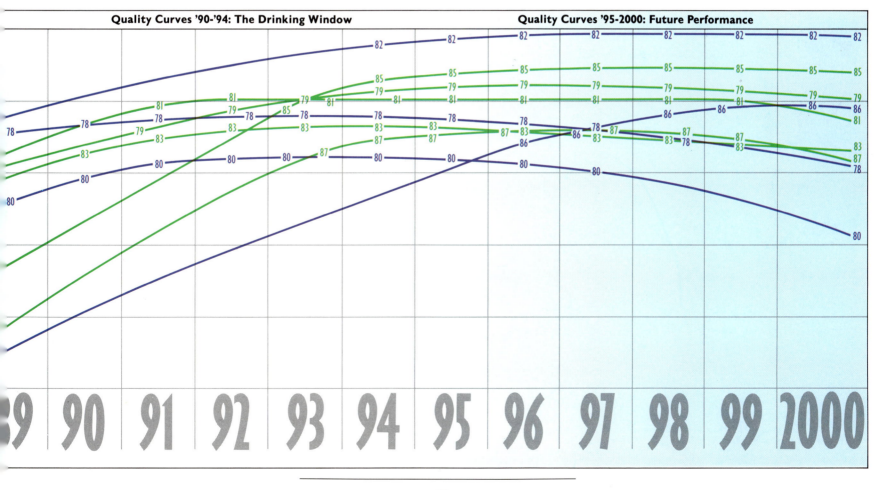

Quality Curves '90-'94: The Drinking Window

Quality Curves '95-2000: Future Performance

Château Monbousquet

If the Médoc is characterised by its noble estates, owned as likely as not by Parisian insurance companies or bankers, St-Emilion is a region of smallholdings, owned and managed by intense individualists. They are proud to produce a wine that may not be grand, but nevertheless forcefully expresses their own patch of one of France's most historic appellations.

Such an individualist is Alain Querre, who with his brothers runs a general wine business but whose passion is Château Monbousquet. This is a fairly typical, though unusually large, example of the hundreds of middle-range properties sold around the world as *Grand Cru* or *Grand Cru Classé* St-Emilion. This long roll-call of confusingly similar names is the right bank's answer to the Médoc's more tightly marshalled army of *Crus Bourgeois*, and can in good years provide an equally good source of value and potential. Monbousquet produces about 150,000 bottles a year, of which Alain Querre, in the admirably hospitable tradition of St-Emilion, gives away about 5,000.

About 100 acres (40 hectares) of exceptionally deep sandy gravel, with the odd iron oxide deposit in the subsoil, are planted at Monbousquet on the flatter land due south of the town of St-Emilion. If the property's reputation today is considerably higher than its unclassified status may suggest, it is because of the energy and cash invested in the property since it was taken over in 1945 by the Querre brothers' father Daniel. With the counsel of some of Paris's top restaurateurs,

his aim was to produce a wine tailor-made for restaurant wine lists: one that could be drunk young but would also age for 10 years or so if circumstances allowed. He accordingly set about replanting and revitalising a property even more run-down than the Bordeaux post-war norm, with an *encépagement* that supplemented an equal split between the Merlot and Cabernet Franc of St-Emilion with about 10 per cent Cabernet Sauvignon. The last Cabernet Sauvignon vine was pulled out in 1984 because of the usual right bank problems of ripening this late variety. The aim is now to maintain an equal split between the two other varieties, although the 1985 frosts cost Monbousquet many a Merlot vine.

Wine quality from a quality-conscious property at this level seems to vary enormously. In some years such as 1983 and 1985 the wine is frankly unexciting, whereas in others, especially some of the lesser vintages, Monbousquet can outshine many much higher ranking St-Emilions. Alain Querre is proud of the strictness of his selection – his wine company's generic St-Emilion can easily absorb the offcuts – but connoisseurs will query his current policy of moving away from oak ageing. By 1988 only 20 per cent of Monbousquet was being aged in wood and this proportion is declining. This seems to result in skinnier wines although "to me", says Alain Querre, "the personality of the fruit itself is more important than the oak and anyway, so much of the oak sold today is so *bad*."

Earlier vintages

Monbousquet's 1947 is legendary, an all-Merlot Querre debut wine that is still alive and kicking. The 1962 and particularly 1961 are vigorous and the 1964 is gorgeously opulent and velvety, although starting to decline. Monbousquet's 1975 is a triumph, one of the château's finest wines ever with its ripe, full, headily sensual Merlot flesh and flavours completely enveloping any residual tannins. A few years' more life in it. The 1976 is better and more vigorous than one might expect, although it will not improve.

1978 A wine for the long term, deeper but rather browner than the 1979. Good rich, full-bodied fundament on which there is a cocktail of secondary aromas considerably more intriguing than 1979's bouquet. Monbousquet's tell-tale scent of licorice is also

there, and a very slight hint of damp wood.

Weather and timing

Very good vintage, below average crop. Late start. Flowering June 12-28. Good summer. Hot, dry Aug; good maturation. Late harvest.

Quantity produced

15,110 cases released at Fr f456 a case. St-Emilion: 3,800,000 cases.

Other details

According to the year, 10-20% of the figure above is sold as the second wine.

1979 Good purple colour and elegant aromas to which some Cabernet herbaceousness adds interest. Attractive, harmonious, ripe, open but unsubtle. Confident yeoman style.

Weather and timing

Good vintage, above average crop. Cold, wet spring delayed flowering. Fine summer. Harvest began Oct 2.

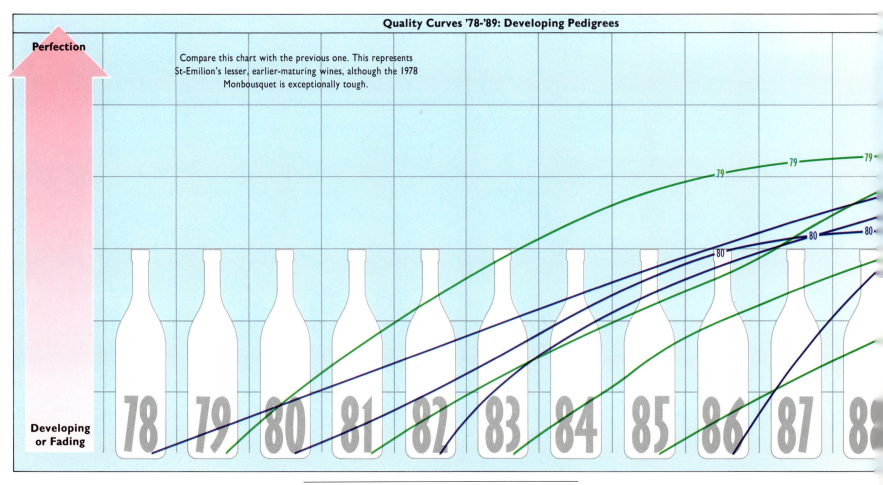

Quality Curves '78-'89: Developing Pedigrees

Perfection

Compare this chart with the previous one. This represents St-Emilion's lesser, earlier-maturing wines, although the 1978 Monbousquet is exceptionally tough.

Developing or Fading

78 79 80 81 82 83 84 85 86 87 88

Quantity produced

17,770 cases released at Fr f421 a case. St-Emilion: 5,150,000 cases. **1980** A light wine that is ready to drink. Pale ruby colour with some tawny at the rim. Slightly weedy nose with some high-toned mineral notes. Lightweight, low-key, quite pretty but with notable acidity. Medium length of flavour.

Weather and timing

Average vintage, below average crop. Mild, wet winter. Fine Apr and May. Cool, wet June; late, uneven flowering. Fine Aug and Sept. Harvest Oct 13-29 interrupted by showers.

Quantity produced

15,470 cases released at Fr f304 a case. St-Emilion: 3,250,000 cases. **1981** Dark ruby but with definite age at rim. Mature, spicy, interesting bouquet of no great intensity but real quality on the palate. Very lively dried fruit and

spice flavours reminiscent of rich fruit cake. Vibrancy and length.

Weather and timing

Good vintage, large crop. Variable start to season. Good flowering. Excellent growing season; ripened well. Good harvest Sept 28 to Oct 10.

Quantity produced

15,110 cases released at Fr f695 a case. St-Emilion: 6,050,000 cases. **1982** Enormous in every way. Deep dark concentrated colour with lively crimson right out to rim. Powerful mushroom and truffles aromas with intriguing secondary aromas. Dark, mysterious, not even obviously St-Emilion. Exciting concentration of ripe fruit flavours with surprisingly marked acidity. Darkly intense and chewy although not, compared with the 1982 norm, particularly opulent.

Weather and timing

Outstanding vintage, large crop.

Good start to year; early, even flowering May 30 to June 10. Very hot early Sept. Rain interrupted harvest Sept 14 to Oct 2.

Quantity produced

20,455 cases released at Fr f755 a case. St-Emilion: 5,250,000 cases.

Other details

Mechanical harvester used for the first time. Vats had to be cooled. Strong US$ affected the market until 1986.

1983 A lightweight wine for early consumption. Mid-ruby that is visibly ageing towards the rim. Broad, evolved, slightly vegetal nose with some perfume and licorice. Light but attractive aromas. Definite Merlot spice with tannin and acid underneath. A little ungenerous although perfectly straightforward.

Weather and timing -

Fine vintage, normal crop. Mild winter. Very cold mid-Feb. Variable Apr-May. Warm, humid July;

vines treated for rot. Good from Sept 18. *Botrytis*-free harvest Sept 23-Oct 6.

Quantity produced

15,775 cases released at Fr f832 a case. St-Emilion: 4,800,000 cases. **1984** None made.

Weather and timing

Poor vintage, very small crop. Feb and Mar cold and dry. Wet end Mar. Hail mid-May. Early June showers; flowering June 8. Fine Aug. Wet during harvest which began Oct 3.

Quantity produced

6,555 cases sold in bulk. St-Emilion: 1,850,000 cases. **1985** Unexceptional Monbousquet. Good deep dark crimson with little excitement on the nose. Marked tannins underneath the velvety spice of Merlot. A bit downbeat but there is sufficient here to meld into a good, typical lesser St-Emilion for the early nineties.

Weather and timing

Exceptional vintage, below average crop. Harsh Jan and Feb. Wet Mar-Apr. Poor for flowering. Fine Aug-Sept; good ripening. Harvest Sept 24 to Oct 10.

Quantity produced

15,554 cases released at Fr f962 a case. St-Emilion: 3,250,000 cases. **1986** An exciting, nervy wine. No great weight or concentration but plenty of vibrant red fruit flavours and piercing leafy aromas with an attractive, open spiciness. Light and fragrant.

Weather and timing

Good vintage, above average crop. Cold start: some vines killed by frost. Fine for flowering. Sunny, hot July and Aug. Fine Sept. Harvest Sept 29 to Oct 14.

Quantity produced

16,665 cases released at Fr f625 a case. St-Emilion: 5,700,000 cases. **1987** No wine to be sold as Château Monbousquet.

Weather and timing

Declassified vintage, below average crop. Snow and severe frost late Jan. Flowering began June 3. Harvest Sept 28 to Oct 10. Many Merlot vines died.

Quantity produced

8,880 cases sold in bulk. St-Emilion: 3,950,000 cases. **1988** (Cask sample) Not being a member of the *Union des Grands Crus*, Alain Querre had no qualms about showing his lastest baby before it reached its first April – and very impressive it was too. Excellent colour and concentration of fruit. Good tannin and acid levels and the gorgeous plumpness of young ripe fruit.

Weather and timing

Excellent vintage, small crop. Fine, cold Jan-Mar. Few storms Apr-May. Excellent flowering. Good harvest Sept 26 to Oct 10.

Quantity produced

11,110 cases. Release date: 1989.

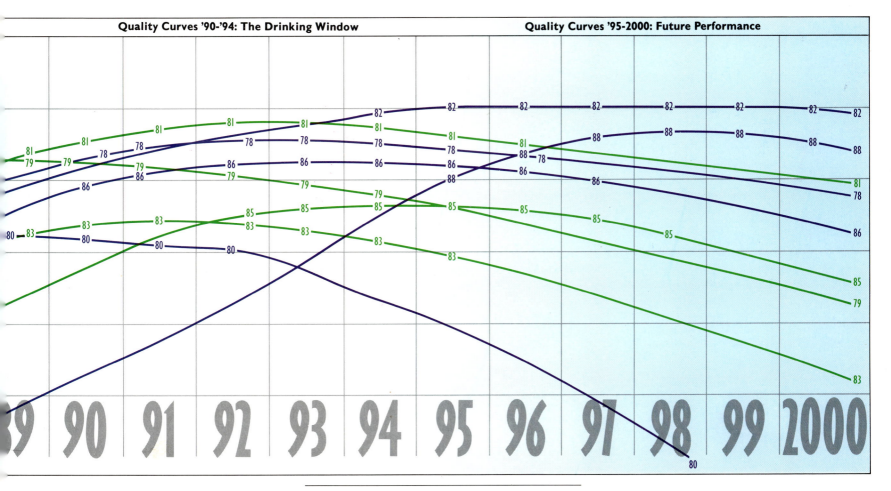

Quality Curves '90-'94: The Drinking Window

Quality Curves '95-2000: Future Performance

SAUTERNES

Colour may hint at the maturity of a red wine, but great Sauternes can be deep gold or even tawny and yet still be in its youth.

Bordeaux provides France with most of its longest-living white wines, the great sweet wines of Sauternes, and examples of some of the worst white wine-making in the country.

As Pomerol is dominated by Château Petrus, so Sauternes (including Barsac) is dominated, consistently and magnificently, by Château d'Yquem. Few other Sauternes properties have been able to afford the expensive techniques and selection processes necessary to make, from every vintage, a great sweet wine destined to last for decades. This makes generalisation about Sauternes particularly difficult.

What does apply to the entire region is the extent to which each autumn's weather encourages the single element that makes a sweet wine ageworthy and great rather than merely pleasant: the beneficial development of *Botrytis cinerea*. Regarded as "noble rot", this fungus shrinks the quantity of wine produced but dramatically boosts its quality by concentrating the apparent sugar and endowing it with a wide range of more delicious (and long-living) characteristics. It is encouraged by early morning moisture but needs warm, sunny days to dry out the bunches and stop the *Botrytis* splitting and ignobly rotting the grape, as it is wont to do to red grapes. Sauternes is in an ideal situation for good *Botrytis* development, with its nearby river and gentle hillside vineyards, and has clearly nurtured its own colonies of suitable *Botrytis* strains. But the late autumn weather is critical.

Too often the reputation of all white Bordeaux (indeed of all French wine) is made (or lost) by the performance of red Bordeaux. There is no direct correlation between the factors that make good Sauternes and those that make good red wines, even in nearby Graves, except that the summer has to have been sufficiently warm and dry. In 1982 for example the Sauternes crop suffered from heavy October rain, which the early-ripening reds escaped, while in 1985 October was so dry there was no *Botrytis* – good for reds, a poor show for sweet whites.

The vital period for Sauternes is during the weeks immediately after the red and dry white grape harvests, when proprietors pray for morning mists and long sunny days. Those who can afford to be quality conscious may send pickers through the vineyard up to a dozen times right into December, harvesting each grape at ideal maturity. But some of the best quality Sauternes are produced in vintages that are the easiest to harvest, when conditions are so good that only two or three relatively early pickings are needed. Such years included 1986, when the September rainstorm left the ground damp enough to promote morning mist, and 1976.

Other vintages in the Timechart span that produced good to excellent Sauternes were 1983, when real dedication and risk-taking were required to wait for the humidity needed; 1981 when sugar levels were at their highest since 1976 (but very few proprietors sat it out until late October when it was dry enough to pick); 1980 when only the poker players waited for the dry late autumn; and the great 1975 during which the heavily Botrytised grapes needed careful selection.

Just what is wanted at Château d'Yquem (page 52) of an autumn morning – lots of moisture at ground level to promote the spread of the magical mould, *Botrytis cinerea* or noble rot, a major life-preserver for sweet white wines wherever they are made.

The difference in quality between Yquem and the rest is particularly marked in lesser vintages since few other properties can afford the cash or commitment to pick so often or to be so selective with the results. Dedication is now much more important than official classification, and the most demonstrably quality-conscious Sauternes Châteaux are de Fargues, Raymond-Lafon (neither of them are officially classified but both are run similarly to Yquem), Rieussec, Climens, Coutet, Lafaurie-Peyraguey (especially since 1983), Guiraud (especially 1980 to 1986), Suduiraut, Nairac, Doisy-Daëne, Rayne-Vigneau (from 1986) and two real triers, Lamothe-Guignard and Bastor-Lamontagne.

To establish the maturity patterns of these properties, accelerate the Yquem chart by three years – five years for most other Sauternes properties. Château Gilette provides an interesting exception to all this by carefully maturing wine for decades in concrete and bottling only when it is ready to drink. "Current" delicious vintages include 1959 and 1962.

Most other, inevitably lesser, sweet white Bordeaux matures at two to three years and has a maturity pattern similar to that shown on Chart B (page 19). But in years that are particularly good for *Botrytis*, well-run châteaux in Loupiac and, occasionally, Ste-Croix-du-Mont, can produce wines worth keeping for five years.

Château d'Yquem

Yquem is not a wine of our times. The Yquem that was picked last autumn will not be bottled for three years, perhaps not sold for four years and, in really good vintages, may not reach its peak for four decades.

The outsider has every right to question the superlatives that cling to Yquem as surely as the noughts on the end of its price. The only property designated a *Premier Grand Cru Classé*, Yquem sells at up to five times the price of other first growth Sauternes. But no-one who has ever tasted it alongside other top Sauternes can retain their scepticism. The wine produced is simply of a different order and will evolve from a vital, *Botrytis*-scented youngster to a rich *crème brulée* quintessence of a wine.

Nowhere does this vitality show itself more than in the time demanded by this wine, illustrated at the right hand side of the chart below. Even the most forward vintages such as the 1980 and the 1976 plead to be left alone for well over 10 years. There is no such phenomenon as a hasty decline with Yquem, and every year brings a new level of subtlety and force. Colour, incidentally, is in Yquem's case no indication of maturity. It can still be vibrant in its third century, when it is the same fox red as a fine red wine of the same age.

The explanation for this lies partly in Yquem's privileged geographical position. With ideal soil and an altitude higher than any other Sauternes property its grapes (mainly Sémillon with one in five vines Sauvignon, the classic Sauternes *encépagement*) are perfectly placed for maximum attack and subsequent concentration by *Botrytis*. Yquem's pre-eminence is also self-perpetuating. Because it sells at such fabulous prices, the Lur Saluces family have been able to lavish every luxury on it, including miles of drainage pipes; an uncompromising replanting and pruning programme, an unlimited number of *tries* or passages through the vineyard, picking individual grapes at just the right moment; the most traditional wine-making methods including 15 rackings and the very finest oak in the cellar and the new and controversial cold room to dry surplus moisture off grapes.

The average yield of wine *before* this selection is only 9 hl/ha and in some years such as 1974, 1972 and 1964 none of this will end up as Yquem. The highest proportion selected was 90 per cent in 1976. In general the better the year the easier the vintage, the fewer the number of *tries* necessary and the higher the proportion of total wine allowed into Yquem. The exceptions to this are the lines representing the 1985 and 1986 vintages of Ygrec, the dry white wine produced at Château d'Yquem from an equal blend of Sémillon and Sauvignon grapes whenever conditions are right. Yquem must is ideally between 20 and 22 per cent potential alcohol and will be fermented out to 13 to 14 per cent alcohol. Ygrec, with just about a third of a degree of residual sugar, is big, heady stuff which is rarely better at ten years than at three, although 1979 still had some youthful freshness about it in 1986.

Earlier vintages

I have only once tasted an Yquem past its best. It was made in the mid-eighteenth century. At the same marathon feast at the Château itself we were served an 1811 just starting to fade, a vigorous 1847, an aggressive 1858 and the sensational 1921 and 1937. The 1921 was deep, dark, burnished gold with an exotic, spicy richness: seems perfect. The 1937 was bursting with vivacity but seemed far from ready. The 1928 and 1929 are also recognised greats and other favoured years since then include the 1945, 1947, 1949, 1953, 1955, the magnificently *brûlé* 1967, the stately 1970 and the much more open 1971 which is perfect for now.

1975 A classic vintage: slow but sure to 1976's more obvious charms. Demands intellectual attention, more even than the 1983.

Deep gold and rigorously structured for the long term with good acidity and a dynamite character on the palate.

Weather and timing

Very good vintage, large crop. Spring frosts. Good for harvest Sept 29 to Nov 7.

Quantity produced

Sauternes production: 415,000 cases.

1976 Gorgeously ripe and opulent. Already deepening in colour and extremely viscous even by Yquem standards. A leap up in quality from the 1977 with rich animal flavours and seductive unctuousness. An enormous wine without the nerve and subtlety of 1983 but so rich and gorgeous it is difficult to resist.

Weather and timing

Very good vintage, below average crop. Hot, dry summer; high sugar levels. Poor conditions during harvest Sept 21 to Oct 13.

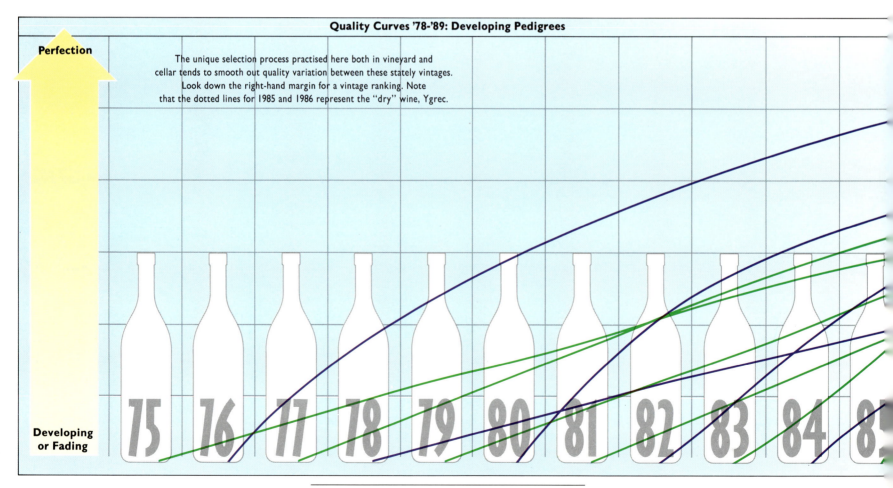

Quality Curves '78-'89: Developing Pedigrees

Perfection

The unique selection process practised here both in vineyard and cellar tends to smooth out quality variation between these stately vintages. Look down the right-hand margin for a vintage ranking. Note that the dotted lines for 1985 and 1986 represent the "dry" wine, Ygrec.

Developing or Fading

75 76 77 78 79 80 81 82 83 84 85

Quantity produced
Sauternes: 290,000 cases.

1977 Unusually pale and green for an Yquem: it should stay so because of its low oxydase level. Youthful. A light, sinewy vintage with good backbone and some charm. The Comte de Lur-Saluces suggests it is ideal for savoury dishes: it even has a whiff of smoked sausage.

Weather and timing
Poor vintage, very small crop. Severe spring frosts damaged vines. Poor summer. Late harvest Oct 20 to Nov 26.

Quantity produced
Sauternes: 95,000 cases.

1978 A notably tart, slow-developing wine whose big, open, waxy nose distracts from the textured, nervy wine underneath. Still relatively unknit and doesn't have the weight to last centuries. Skinny for an Yquem but creditable for this vintage.

Weather and timing
Average vintage, below average crop. Cold spring. Cool summer. Dry, warm Sept and Oct. Ideal for harvest Oct 25 to Dec 8.

Quantity produced
Sauternes: 285,000 cases.

1979 Comparatively dull. The nose is ripe and powerfully broad but on the palate there is a slight lack of concentration. A floral and muted 1981. Designed to be drunk with savouries.

Weather and timing
Average vintage, above average crop. Wet winter and spring. Fine June, good flowering. Dull, cold summer. Showers throughout harvest Oct 15 to Nov 29.

Quantity produced
Sauternes: 340, 000 cases.

1980 A relatively loose-textured enveloping bosomy Yquem. Richly concentrated green/gold with lush ripe pineapple flavours, floral perfumes. Marvellous soft velvety texture. Liquorous: teetering between plumpness and flab but a good structure.

Weather and timing
Excellent vintage, average crop. Poor for flowering. Hot, dry Aug. Wet before harvest which began Oct 20.

Quantity produced
Sauternes: 300,000 cases.

1981 An unusual, characterful wine. Something spicy and rather unsauternes-like on the nose – licorice perhaps? Fairly light, but with lots of sweetness and acidity. Real *brûlé* character underneath and a long finish. It should last well but needs time to knit together.

Weather and timing
Very good vintage, average crop. Hot, dry summer; high sugar levels. Autumn rains then fine for harvest Oct 5 to Nov 13.

Quantity produced
Sauternes: 315,000 cases.

1982 Hugely successful for the vintage. Wonderful orange-tinged gold, very unctuous with richness and distinctly toasted, burnt notes. An edge of nuttiness but no marked *Botrytis*. More open than the 1983. Very Semillon and very slightly loose-textured.

Weather and timing
Average vintage, above average crop. Ideal for flowering. Early Sept hot and dry; late Sept very wet. Harvest Sept 16 to Nov 7; first third of crop used in Yquem.

Quantity produced
Sauternes: 335,000 cases.

1983 Wonderful. Rich gold: not that much on the nose yet but the palate is stunned by the concentration of *Botrytis*, fruit and acid. There are burnt, textural notes and a mouthful really does last minutes after swallowing. Explosively exciting with notes of peaches and the vegetal range of *Botrytis* flavours. Magical.

Weather and timing
Excellent vintage, large crop. Wet spring, fine June. Very hot July, wet Aug. Indian summer before harvest which began Sept 29.

Quantity produced
Sauternes: 350,000 cases.

1984 Very seductive (unless tasted alongside the 1983). Alluring bouquet of figs, pineapple, toast and some *Botrytis*. Lightish for an Yquem and with a slight bitterness on the finish. It wants to be left alone for a while.

Weather and timing
Average vintage and crop. Wet, cold May. Good for flowering. Fine summer. Harvest delayed until after hurricane Hortense (Oct 4). 75% of crop used in Yquem; harvest Oct 15 to Nov 13.

Quantity produced
Sauternes: 315,000 cases.

1985 Ygrec. Rich, toasty and with sufficient power and acid to last a while.

Weather and timing
Very good vintage, above average crop. Severe winter. Fine, dry summer, excellent autumn. High sugar levels but little *Botrytis*. Ideal conditions during harvest Oct 1 to Dec 19.

Quantity produced
Sauternes: 340,000 cases.

Other details
Record number (11) of *tries* needed to select the grapes for Yquem (20% of crop).

1986 Ygrec. *Crème caramel* nose, lemony, light and clean but without great extract.

Yquem. Looks set to be an extraordinarily good vintage.

Weather and timing
Excellent vintage, large crop. Good spring. Very dry June-early Sept then wet; downpour on Sept 23. Wet soil contributed to morning mists. Good harvest.

Quantity produced
Sauternes: 365,000 cases.

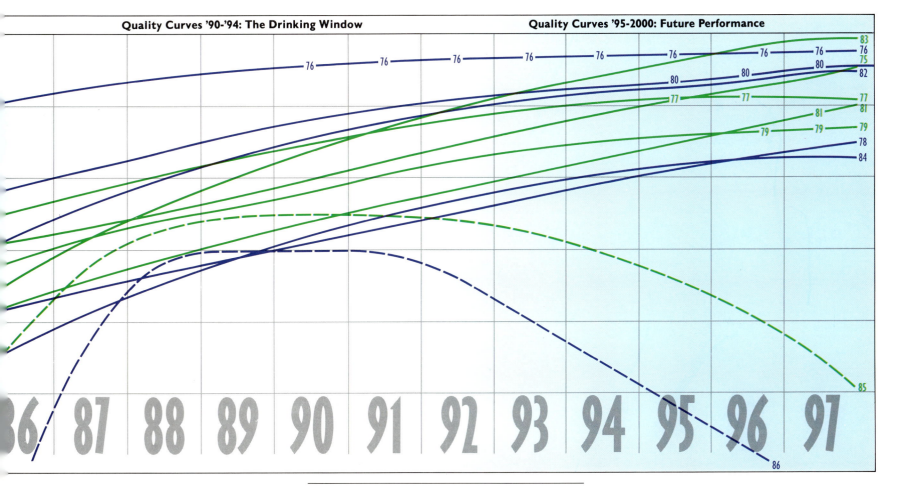

REST OF BORDEAUX

DRY WHITE WINES

Considering the quantity of white wine produced in Bordeaux – a million hectolitres of *Appellation Contrôlée* white a year, often more than a quarter of the amount of AC red produced – its quality is shocking. With few exceptions, these are wines to drink as young as possible: their Timecharts would too closely resemble Chart A on page 19. This applies to most wines whose AC is plain Bordeaux, to any other AC with the word Bordeaux in it and to Entre-Deux-Mers or Graves de Vayres – although the best of them such as Château Thieuley would qualify for Chart B (also on page 19). The superior Graves appellation should have more substantial whites to offer. Chart B, sometimes plus a year's more life, would apply to the whites produced by most *Crus Classés* and by unclassified properties as serious as Châteaux Chantegrive, La Louvière and Rahoul. De Fieuzal and Malartic-Lagravière produce white Graves that are considerably more ageworthy than the Chart B archetype – but this has only recently been the case at Fieuzal. Good recent vintages for dry white Graves include 1987 and 1984 (which illustrates the lack of correlation between red and dry white Bordeaux performance) although the 1985s and superb 1983s should last as long.

The exceptional dry white Graves, on the other hand – Châteaux Haut-Brion Blanc, Laville-Haut-Brion and Domaine de Chevalier Blanc – repay much longer keeping, although they are produced on such a minuscule scale that this can be difficult. Haut-Brion Blanc is designed to be drunk at five to six years, whereas the team producing Laville-Haut-Brion until 1983 maintained that the wine (now made by Haut-Brion) should never be drunk before 10 years and was usually at its best between 15 and 30. "*Crème de tête*" *cuvées* of Laville-Haut-Brion produced in 1948 and 1964 were still developing in 1987, as was the regular bottling of the 1970. Domaine de Chevalier Blanc is leaner but its many devotees are still savouring particularly successful vintages such as 1970, 1971, 1973 and 1976.

Château Margaux's Pavillon Blanc has been challenging these dry whites since 1978 – and seems to be best either at around three years old or, as a mature wine, around seven or eight.

RED WINES

One effect of an increasing fastidiousness in assembling the wine to be sold under the Château label is the emergence of a host of "second wines" from impeccable sources, Pavillon Rouge du Château Margaux and Les Forts de Latour are two of those with the longest history and highest reputation. Réserve de la Comtesse and Clos du Marquis are two more faultless examples from Châteaux Pichon-Lalande and Léoville-Las Cases respectively. Second wines generally mature three years ahead of their role models so Timecharts should be advanced accordingly. Nevertheless they should accurately reflect the character of each vintage – it is arguably their job to do so even more emphatically than the *grands vins*. Most of the lesser red Bordeaux on the other hand, are Chart B-type wines which are less dramatically influenced by the conditions of individual vintages. Most of those whose appellation contains the word Bordeaux should be ready two years after the vintage, although the number of more ambitious proprietors is increasing.

The sturdy, slow-developing wines of Fronsac just east of Pomerol and its superior heartland Canon-Fronsac, are also special cases. Accelerate the Petrus chart by two years for most Fronsacs, by one for such concentrated wines as Châteaux Canon, Canon de Brem, Mazeris and Moulin-Pey-Labrie.

Most of the wines of the Côtes de Bourg and Premières Côtes de Blaye are of Bordeaux Supérieur quality and are often labelled as such. Assume they will be ready to drink at two years and in very good vintages may still be lively at five.

BURGUNDY: CÔTE D'OR

Precious *Grand Cru* vineyard land (page 58) all the way up to the tree line above which the extra height would expose the vines to too much wind and, occasionally, critically low temperatures.

In every survey involving the wines of the world, the surveyor has at some point to throw up his or her hands and admit that of all the world's wine regions, the Côte d'Or refuses, charmingly, majestically, but obstinately, to submit to any form of systematization.

This privileged slope of vineyard that constitutes the heartland of Burgundy is so narrow that it produces only a fraction of the wine produced in, for example, Bordeaux's heartland the Haut-Médoc. But the Côte d'Or is the same length, about 35 miles (55km), and therefore, as in the Haut-Médoc, particular areas can be subject to localised setbacks – heavy rainstorms and, the bane of the Cote d'Or, hail. In both 1986 and 1982 for example, Volnay in the southern half of the Côte d'Or, the Côte de Beaune, was badly hit when early June hail destroyed buds, and in the world-famous vineyards of Vosne-Romanée in the Côte de Nuits, hail wiped out most of the 1978 crop. Climate is in any case a most sensitive issue in this region where the relatively thin-skinned Pinot Noir is not only easily affected by rain but also difficult to ripen fully. It is notable for instance that 1985, by far and away the best vintage in our span, was the only year in which Burgundy enjoyed more than 2,000 recorded hours of sunshine and its lowest rainfall. The wettest year by many wet millimetres produced the miserable 1981 vintage, so often tainted by hail and rot.

What makes it particularly difficult to generalise about the maturity of burgundy, with red burgundy (as usual) notably wayward, is the wide variation in philosophies and techniques employed by the many different wine-makers.

Cellars separated only by a damp stone wall under a Burgundian back-street may be occupied on one side by casks of wine that have been made to provide luscious, lively drinking within a year or two of being bottled and on the other by casks of much denser, darker, more tannic wine that, once it is eventually bottled, should be hidden away in the furthest corner of a wine collection and forgotten for a decade. And these two styles of wine could well carry exactly the same appellation.

When Pinot Noir vines are extremely old, their concentrated produce is *typically* identified as "Vieilles Vignes" on the label. The red wines of – from north to south – Marsannay, Fixin, Côtes de Nuits-Villages, Hautes Côtes de Nuits, Ladoix-Serrigny, Pernand-Vergelesses, Savigny-lès-Beaune, Côte de Beaune, St Aubin, Santenay, Côte de Beaune-Villages and Hautes Côtes de Beaune are usually raspberry coloured, non-extractive, fairly delicate and often delicious liquids that can provide charming wines to be drunk between three and six years after the vintage. They will certainly vary in overall quality and characteristics from year to year, but are very rarely wines worthy of being kept for the next generation.

There are some who would argue that it is precisely in this capacity for early maturation that Pinot Noir distinguishes itself. They feel it is wrong to expect from Pinot Noir wines the long ageing structure of a wine made from grape varieties such as Cabernet Sauvignon, which initially have a more surly nature.

Some Burgundians therefore, even in the Pinot Noir *vignoble* where it is technically possible to produce wines with sufficient extract to last 20 years and more, do not choose to do so. Some see five years hence as the proper focus for their labours and purposely take the wine off the skins fairly early in order to restrain the tannin and anthocyanin levels and make the wines approachable in youth.

Others achieve early drinkability less honourably. Maintaining the bad habits which Burgundians have acquired owing to the disproportionate worldwide demand for their output, they carelessly overproduce high-yielding Pinot vines and make lightweight, heavily filtered, eviscerated red wines bearing only a fraction of the potential character of their particular slice of the Côte d'Or.

The third possible option is that the wines are hand crafted and nurtured to express dramatically their provenance. They manage this only after seven years or more in bottle, thanks to the concentrated essences of fully ripe, low-yielding vines that can, in youth, seem almost chewable.

As one would expect of this region, it is extremely difficult to tell from a red burgundy's label whether or not it is one of these long-term "type three" burgundies designed to repay long-term cellaring. What can be said is that a red wine carrying an appellation that belongs to any of the following could, in theory, be one of them. From north to south: Gevrey-Chambertin, Morey St Denis, Chambolle-Musigny, Vougeot, Echézeaux, Vosne-Romanée, Nuits-St-Georges, Aloxe-Corton, Beaune, Pommard and Volnay.

As for which producers have their sights set on the longer term, only the broadest of guidelines can be offered. It would take a large volume indeed to detail each producer's policy for each wine he produces. Very generally speaking, wines seen outside France that specify *Mise en Bouteille au Domaine*, or "domaine bottled", tend to be made for ageing. This is partly because most of the individual growers whose wines are exported are serious individuals and, if the wine comes labelled thus from one of Burgundy's *négociants*, or mer-

chants, rather than from an individual wine farmer, it will be from the *négociant*'s own vineyards. *Négociants* who make all their wines for the very long term include Faiveley, Louis Jadot (page 60) and Maison Leroy. The wines of Joseph Drouhin are good medium-term bets, as are the Domaine du Château wines of Bouchard Père et Fils.

The two wines whose Timecharts have been chosen to represent paradigms of red burgundy evolution are both serious, third option wines, La Tâche from the world-famous Domaine de la Romanée-Conti and one of Louis Jadot's most successful Beaunes, their own monopole vineyard, Clos des Ursules. This gives us, respectively, wine from a grower and a *négociant*; one wine from the northern and southern halves of the Côte d'Or, the Côte de Nuits, the Côte de Beaune; one *Grand Cru* and one *Premier Cru*; both of them made very much for the long term but also to express the individual characteristics of each vintage.

The most important step towards deciding which Timechart a given wine relates to is working out from the clues above whether or not it is a "third option" wine designed for keeping. If it is not, the wine could be drunk at three to seven years in a poor vintage, five to nine years in a good one. If it is, determine whether it comes from the Côte de Nuits or Côte de Beaune and choose the appropriate Timechart. On the Côte de Nuits the Domaine de la Romanée-Conti's wines are famously slow developers. Accelerate the Tâche Timechart by two years for most other *Grands Crus*, three years for *Premier Crus* and four years for "village" wines coming from a larger or less grand area than a specific *Cru*. The end of the maturity span for such wines in vintages like 1981 and 1984 would be well in sight by the midnineties. On the Côte de Beaune, most Cortons and other *Premiers Crus* from long-term wine-makers should age at the same rate as the demonstrably longlived Clos des Ursules. For village wines, accelerate the chart by three years but note that Jadot was particularly severe with the amount of juice run off as *saignée* in 1982 (so the 1982s are more concentrated than most) and that other, simpler, less rigorous 1982s have peaked already.

The 1983 vintage (not unlike the 1976) poses the most questions for those of us attempting to provide a burgundian crystal ball – and this applies as much to

The village of Chassagne-Montrachet within whose boundaries a substantial part of the great Montrachet vineyards fall. This sheltered square mile of white wine country produces an extraordinarily high proportion of the world's most ageworthy dry whites.

whites as to reds. Rot left its mark on many reds, most of which have so much tannin that only those with the most concentrated fruit will live to see it fade to palatability. In white burgundies, alcohol is often at an unacceptably high level, and that will not diminish with age. As for 1983 white burgundies, Leflaive is the undisputed king of Puligny-Montrachet and he, like his nephew Olivier, is convinced that all will resolve itself in his Chevalier in the end. The Timechart reflects this confidence but I would counsel extreme caution over 1983 white burgundies. Most are too big for their boots and only those with perceptible acidity can be kept in the hope that their overpowering richness will be tamed into something more subtle.

No white burgundy will last longer than Leflaive's Chevalier – except perhaps one from 1982 when the other great domaines of Sauzet and Ramonet managed nervier wines – but note how much more rapidly white burgundy ages than red. The Chevalier Timechart should apply to other *Grand Cru* white burgundies but should be accelerated one year for *Premier Cru* white burgundies and two years for village wines.

Chart B (page 19) applies to the basic red, white and pink burgundian appellations (Chart A for some Aligotés) although Bourgogne Rouge from the most conscientious producers' top vintages, such as 1988 and 1985, can provide interesting drinking for up to 10 years.

La Tâche, Domaine de la Romanée-Conti

La Tâche is far more than a Côte de Nuits *Grand Cru*. It is fabulous. Not just because of the quality of the wine but also because, along with its even smaller sister vineyard of La Romanée-Conti, La Tâche provides the inspiration for so many of the wine world's fables.

These two *crus*, La Tâche only 15 acres (six hectares) and Romanée-Conti less than a third of that size, are the *Grand Crus* owned exclusively by the Domaine de la Romanée-Conti of Vosne-Romanée, so famous throughout the world that it is often referred to simply as "the Domaine". This does nothing to suppress the price of the Domaine's wines, which in turn does nothing to lower expectations of their quality. Yet methods at the Domaine are not geared to the requirements of a wine market that is eager for thrills straight off the bottling line. The Domaine's vineyards, every one a *Grand Cru*, are picked later than most of their neighbours, but La Tâche and Romanée-Conti are picked last of all. This, together with the vines' venerability, strict pruning, fastidious selection, extended maceration, exclusively new oak and relatively rustic cellar methods, makes for exceptional wines.

The annual production of La Tâche averages just 24,000 bottles, each label zealously guarded and numbered. About half will find their way to the United States, although there are collectors as far away as Australia who would willingly divert some of this transatlantic traffic. Domaine de la Romanée-Conti wines represent almost the sole burgundies

tradeable in the saleroom, which of course helps to stimulate demand still further. Concentration and richness tend to replace purity and delicacy in the Pinot Noir canon. The wines contrarily gain colour and depth as the dose of sulphur they were given at bottling dissipates. The ebullient Madame Lalou Bize-Leroy, co-owner with Aubert de Villaine and a somewhat fabulous creature herself, counters the inevitable criticisms with the argument that the less promising the vintage, the longer it takes to show its charms.

The owners describe La Tâche as sinewy, lean and slightly austere in youth. It has a herbal note which after 15 or so years in bottle gives way to ethereal flavours with more animal influence and an unctuous, velvety texture in which there is both rigour and something slightly rustic. In cask the wines are certainly beguiling, and can remain so until up to two years after bottling. During bottling they typically close up, although by no means all vintages in this range require the full 15 years to open out again.

After a nasty experience in California, Lalou stresses the importance of storing wine, particularly her wine, in fairly damp conditions (more difficult in the US than the UK). She would prefer to see bottles kept too warm than corks too dry. The chart applies to bottles kept at the Domaine throughout their lives. The more travelled they are or the more aridly and/or warmly they have been stored, the earlier they could be enjoyed.

Earlier vintages

Even vintages of La Tâche older than those below could still be good. **1959**: holding up well in early 1988. **1962**, the especially gorgeous **1964**, **1966**, the **1971** (slightly too voluptuous for Madame) and the more typically La Tâche **1972** are all capable of giving pleasure now. The **1976** should start to shine in the nineties.

1978 Deep crimson, even hinting at purple, right out to the rim. Luscious bouquet belying visible signs of youth. Delicate top layer of mature burgundy flavours with burnt molasses top notes. Well balanced base in which softening tannins are still evident. For hedonists, and fairly soon.

Weather and timing

Classic vintage, above average crop. A dry year. Cold June and July delayed and slowed

flowering, then hot and dry. Ideal harvest Oct 16-26.

Quantity produced

1,976 cases released in 1981. Côte de Nuits production: 480,000 cases.

1979 Even more open than the 1978. Mature colour and bouquet with well-developed aromas in which fruit (prunes?) and vanilla-scented oak are still evident. Heady and ethereal rather than blockbusting. Delightful, soft, and proof of the treasures yielded by this vintage.

Weather and timing

Excellent vintage, small crop. Good bud break. Hail during flowering drastically reduced crop. Ideal conditions for rest of season. Harvest Oct 11-20.

Quantity produced

633 cases. Côte de Nuits: 580,000 cases.

Other details

Hailstorm allowed harvesting of

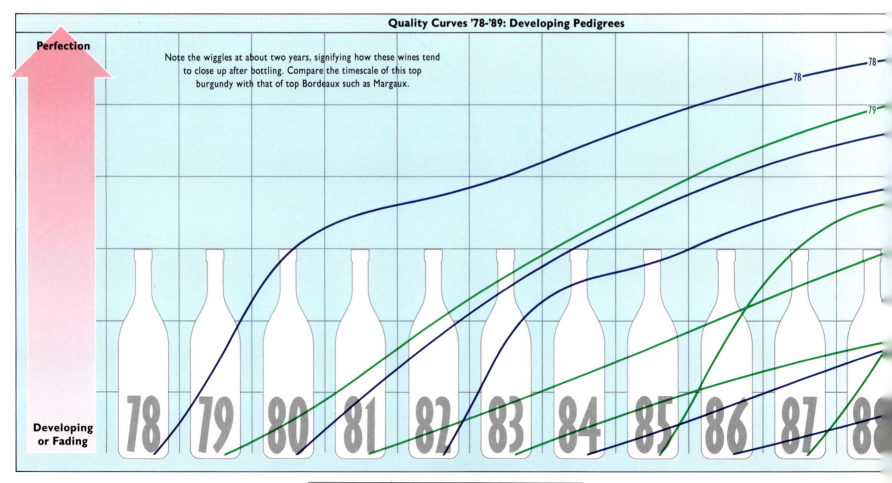

Quality Curves '78-'89: Developing Pedigrees

Perfection

Note the wiggles at about two years, signifying how these wines tend to close up after bottling. Compare the timescale of this top burgundy with that of top Bordeaux such as Margaux.

Developing or Fading

78 79 80 81 82 83 84 85 86 87 88

verjus (second generation grapes) in Nov, used to produce *Fine de Bourgogne*.

1980 Blackish ruby right out to rim. Powerful but still indistinct, smudgy aroma. Big block of almost overripe fruit. Full, round, but without complexity at eight years.

Weather and timing

Exceptional vintage, normal crop. Cold winter and spring delayed bud break and flowering. Sunny Aug. Cool, dry Sept. Late harvest Oct 18-26 allowed full maturation.

Quantity produced

1,191 cases. Côte de Nuits: 580,000 cases.

1981 Deep ruby with amber rim. Powerful, rich, truffley aroma with hints of chocolate and licorice. Fleshy with good texture and constitution.

Weather and timing

Fair vintage, small crop. Vines still affected by 1979 hailstorm. Cold

June, incomplete flowering. Hot July, cold Aug, rain in Sept. Hot from mid-Sept. Sunny harvest Oct 5-10.

Quantity produced

963 cases. Côte de Nuits: 320,000 cases.

1982 Direct, charming nose. Lurking violets. Rich, full, ripe flavours making an enticingly pretty whole. Very La Tâche, according to Lalou.

Weather and timing

Fine vintage, very large crop. Ideal conditions. Early bud break. Good growing season. Excellent harvest Sept 27 to Oct 9.

Quantity produced

2,685 cases. Côte de Nuits: 1,170,000 cases.

1983 After 1975, this was the Domaine's most controversial vintage. Deep garnet with light brick rim. Pale for La Tâche. Not quite frank on the nose: a mustiness that masks the ripe fruit

qualities evident on the palate. High tannin levels, a metallic note and a drying effect at the end.

Weather and timing

Famous vintage, below average crop. Good start to season. Excellent flowering. Dry summer. Hailstorm hit crop on July 23; damaged grapes removed in July and Aug. Rain in Sept. Good conditions for harvest Oct 3-11.

Quantity produced

1,096 cases. Côte de Nuits: 630,000 cases.

1984 Looks *much* older than the 1985 with a more developed colour than the 1983. Sweet notes of vegetation and decay on the nose suggesting truffles but clean, light fragrance. Tannins obtrude but this should turn into a very respectable and typical La Tâche vintage. Jewel-like texture.

Weather and timing

Light vintage, small crop. Effects of 1983 hailstorm still present.

Good start to the year. Rain during flowering. Hot summer. Wet Sept. Good harvest which began Oct 8.

Quantity produced

811 cases. Côte de Nuits: 520,000 cases.

Other details

André Noblet, manager, retired after 40 years. Succeeded by Gérard Marlot as vineyard manager and Bernard Noblet as cellar master.

1985 A wine produced by the vintage rather than the vineyard. Sturdy roasted aromas that are rich and sweet, redolent of prunes and redcurrants yet with gamey notes already. Explosive glory on the palate with acidity and tannins creeping in fast to try to subdue it. A revelation.

Weather and timing

Outstanding vintage, above average crop. Hard winter. Frost hit lower part of La Tâche. Late

flowering. Hot growing season. Superb Sept. Excellent harvest Oct 2-8.

Quantity produced

1,624 cases. Côte de Nuits: 640,000 cases.

1986 Vibrant, youthful scents of bitter cherry. Fragrant with acidity and tannins increasing. Savoury, dry, some evidence of oak. Not charming at two years but a promisingly powerful fan of flavours on the finish.

Weather and timing

Very fine vintage, normal crop. Cold, wet spring delayed bud break, then fine. Early, short flowering. Rain in July. Good growing season with storm mid-Aug and rain in Sept. Fine, dry harvest Oct 1-8.

Quantity produced

1,694 cases released in 1989. Côte de Nuits: 970,000 cases.

1987 (Cask sample) Attractive, relatively delicate blend of

oak and simple, open fruit. Less voluptuous than the 1986, perhaps more La Tâche.

Weather and timing

Good quality vintage, very small crop. Early bud break. Cold, wet May and June caused incomplete flowering. Hot Sept. Harvest Oct 5-10.

Quantity produced

35 *pièces* (7,980 litres). Côte de Nuits: 800,000 cases.

1988 (Not tasted) An early assessment from the Domaine found this to be chewy with very fine tannins which will assure it a good future.

Weather and timing

Superb vintage, large crop. Gentle winter. Early bud break. Wet Apr and May then fine. Quick flowering. Hot and dry from early Aug. Excellent harvest Sept 26 to Oct 7, with some rain.

Quantity produced

24 *pièces* (5,472 litres).

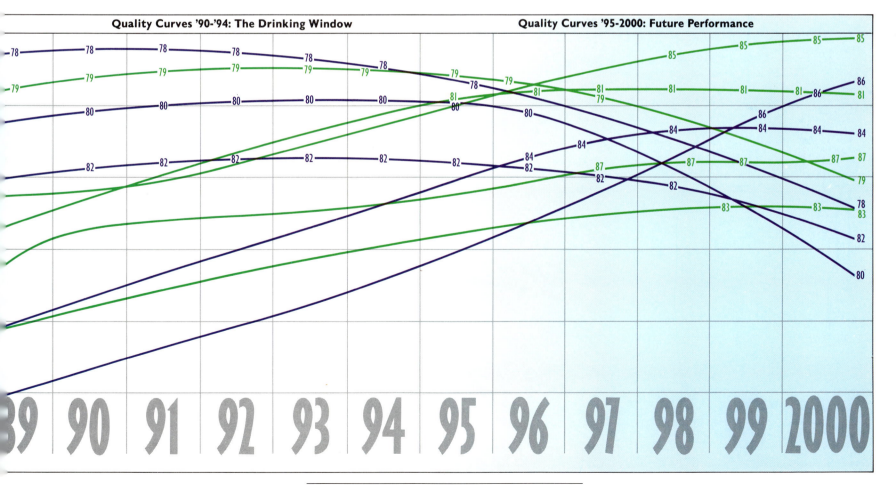

Beaune Vignes Franches, Clos des Ursules, Louis Jadot

Clos des Ursules is usefully representative of top quality Beaune (and a timely reminder that *négociants* too produce top quality wine). There are few single vineyard red burgundies more widely available than various Beaunes that aspire to be top quality. The domaine bottled wines of Volnay, Pommard and Aloxe-Corton are shipped to an enthusiast here, a knowledgeable fan there, while the *négociants* can afford to tell the world about Beaunes such as Bouchard Père's Grèves, Vigne de l'Enfant Jesus and Louis Latour's Vignes Franches.

Jadot's Clos des Ursules is just down the hill from Joseph Drouhin's equally well-loved Clos des Mouches and next door to Les Boucherottes, another of Jadot's top-ranking *Premier Cru* Beaunes. Clos des Ursules is halfway up the east-facing slope and made up of alluvial deposits on a base of clay and limestone.

The eminent, almost pre-eminent Beaune house of Louis Jadot could fairly be said to have been founded on the Clos des Ursules. The acquisition of this 5.5 acre (2.2 hectare) enclave in the Beaune Premier Cru, Vignes Franches, in 1826 marked the advent of Louis Jadot the vine grower or *viticulteur*, and led to the founding of Louis Jadot the burgundy merchant or *négociant* 33 years later. As is so often the case in Burgundy, the derivation of the name Clos des Ursules is ecclesiastical, the Ursulines being a teaching order established in Beaune since the early seventeenth century.

Today the merchant house of Louis Jadot is well entrenched in Burgundy's spectacularly vaulted, tiled, turreted and labyrinthine capital. Typically for one of the town's top *négociants* Jadot have their traditional roots sunk well below the surface of the town (in Jadot's case most spectacularly at the Clos des Jacobins). But they conduct most of their winemaking business in a specially constructed, modern warehouse way outside the medieval ramparts.

André Gagey and his son Pierre-Henri continue to steer a determined course towards wine quality and longevity, apparently little affected by the acquisition of Jadot by their American importers Kobrand in 1985. Their steward in this enterprise is Jacques Lardière, a passionate oenologist who has been following the evolution of the Jadot vintages since the 1959s and 1961s. He admits that the house philosophy of designing wines for the long term, by allotting them more than their fair share of polyphenols (including tannins) initially, can make Jadot wines difficult to taste when young. There are vintages, as demonstrated on this chart, which have sufficient fruit to triumph briefly over this initial charge of tannins. But most Jadot reds go through a long and distinctly surly stage before the phenolics are finally precipitated to show the evolved fruit flavours in all their glory. Jacques Lardière literally looks, by holding the base of a bottle up to the light and inspecting for sediment, to see whether one of his wines has reached maturity.

Earlier vintages

1947 Gorgeous intrigue and fan of flavours yet with some delicacy. André Gagey's first vintage. **1957** Rich, velvety, fascinating and still evolving. **1961** Gamey, seductive, mature wine that may be slightly too big for its boots for purists but will still be gorgeous in the mid-nineties. **1964** Lovely rich, well balanced, bitter-cherry flavoured Pinot with 10 years' life yet. **1971** Still a relatively crude mix of fullness and sweetness with a note of truffles. **1976** Extraordinary wine still developing. Powerful rather than delicate but with a seductive balance of truffles, game, concentration and soft tannins. A second tranche will be put on the market in 1990.

1978 Gamey bouquet. Pretty balance between simple fruit flavours and noticeable acidity but still in retreat at 10 years.

Weather and timing

Excellent vintage, small crop. Mild winter. High humidity during spring badly affected flowering. Sunny July. Rain in Aug and Sept. Excellent for harvest which began Oct 10.

Quantity produced

600 cases. 1988 price: Fr f 1,800. Côte de Beaune production: 1,350,000 cases.

1979 Rich, spicy nose belies the relatively lightweight palate with little evident complexity. A note of firmness at the end suggests that patience will be rewarded but this is for the intellectually curious rather than the sensualist.

Weather and timing

Good vintage, large crop. Another mild winter. Fine spring, good flowering. Sunny spells throughout growing season. Dry, hot Sept helped to ripen grapes. Healthy harvest began Oct 1.

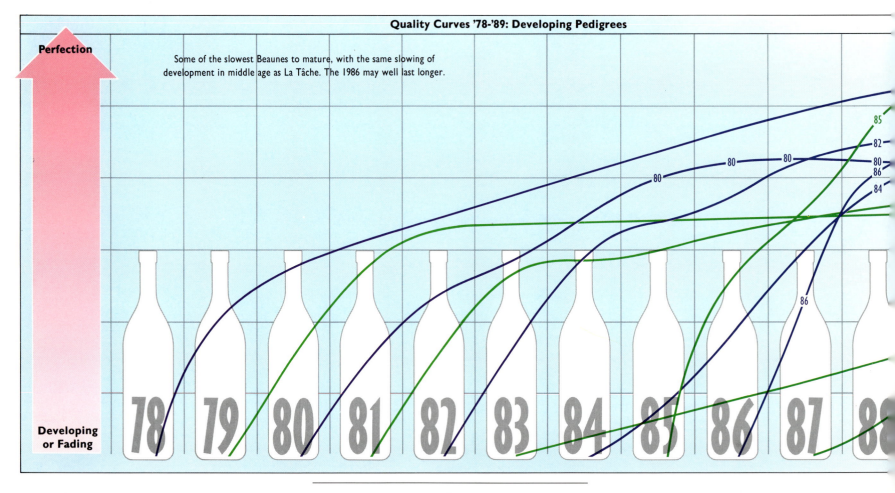

Quality Curves '78–'89: Developing Pedigrees

Perfection

Some of the slowest Beaunes to mature, with the same slowing of development in middle age as La Tâche. The 1986 may well last longer.

Developing or Fading

78 79 80 81 82 83 84 85 86 87 88

Quantity produced

950 cases. 1988 price: Fr f1,476. Côte de Beaune: 1,850,000 cases.

1980 Some orange already noticeable at the rim. Simple, slightly vegetal nose. Lack of concentration on the palate. Very muted power.

Weather and timing

Good vintage, small crop. Poor year; lowest recorded sunshine hours for years. Cold weather during bud break and flowering reduced crop. Rain during harvest which began Oct 10.

Quantity produced

750 cases. 1988 price: Fr f1,176. Côte de Beaune: 1,600,000 cases.

1981 Deep blackish tinge. Rather musty, bark-like notes on the nose, presumably due to hail damage. Palate better, opening out to flattering, foxy richness.

Weather and timing

Good vintage, small crop. Raw winter. Wet spring. Saturated soil

and cold temperatures adversely affected flowering. Wet June. Poor growing season. Cold, wet harvest which began Sept 28.

Quantity produced

550 cases. 1988 price: Fr f1,188. Côte de Beaune: 1,010,000 cases.

1982 Good mid-ruby with pale but not orange rim. Very low-key nose with slightly medicinal notes. Mouthfilling, easy, charming and *flatteur* on the palate. A touch of bitterness at the end. *Un Pinot facile.*

Weather and timing

Good vintage, very large crop. Gentle winter followed by early flowering. Sunny growing season. Hot Sept and Oct. Perfect for harvest which began Sept 20.

Quantity produced

1,070 cases. 1988 price: Fr f1,212. Côte de Beaune: 2,490,000 cases.

1983 Big and bizarre. Entrancing aromatic cocktail of young fruits – morello cherries

and plums. 1983's almost bitter tannins increase their grip on the palate but this particular wine suggests that there could just be life after their demise. There are 300 bottles in the Gagey cellar.

Weather and timing

Exceptional vintage, below average crop. Normal winter. Good flowering. Sept sun concentrated grapes. Harvest began Sept 29.

Quantity produced

670 cases. 1988 price: Fr f1,524. Côte de Beaune: 1,650,000 cases.

1984 Light cherry red with direct cherry-based fruit aromas. Clean, frank expression of light- to medium-bodied Pinot with tannins evident only at the very end. Appealing if not desperately serious.

Weather and timing

Average vintage, small crop. Unexceptional year. Poor flowering. Rain during harvest which began Oct 3.

Quantity produced

800 cases. 1988 price: Fr f1,092. Côte de Beaune: 1,465,000 cases.

Other details

About 3° chaptalization. Lightly filtered. Unfined.

1985 Frank and still simple: young healthy fruit with strawberry flavours. Round, attractive mouthfilling fruit. Explosive on the palate with some oak still evident. *Flatteur* though not big. Great delicacy and balance in its youth and already charming. Chosen for the Gagey personal cellar.

Weather and timing

Excellent vintage, below average crop. Harsh winter. Cold spring with late but quick flowering. Average summer followed by perfect Sept brought grapes to full maturity. Harvest began Sept 30.

Quantity produced

820 cases. 1988 price: Fr f1,740. Côte de Beaune: 1,625,000 cases.

Other details

Louis Jadot acquired by the American Kobrand Corporation.

1986 A deceptive wine at two years old with simple strawberry flavours but definite elegance. A gentle charmer of a wine with lovely ripe fruit, if relatively lightweight. Excellent balance. Good for early drinking.

Weather and timing

Excellent vintage, large crop. Cold winter, mild spring. Sunny June; good flowering. Excellent conditions end Sept and beginning Oct. Good weather for harvest which began Sept 29.

Quantity produced

1,030 cases. 1988 price: Fr f1,212. Côte de Beaune: 2,310,000 cases.

1987 (Cask sample) Aromatic with good if slightly lean fruit underneath. Very rigorous structure for such a lissome wine with good tannins and attractive fan of flavours at the end. A laster.

Weather and timing

Good vintage, large crop. Cold Feb. Long flowering. Average summer. Good spells in Sept. Harvest began Oct 5. Clos des Ursules picked last. Low alcohol levels.

Quantity produced

650 cases. Côte de Beaune: 2,135,000 cases.

1988 (Not tasted) According to Pierre-Henri Gagey this is probably the second best vintage of the decade after 1985. Full-bodied with good balance for long ageing. Tannins less powerful than 1985.

Weather and timing

Good vintage, normal crop. Mild winter followed by poor spring. Good, quick flowering. Excellent weather in Aug and Sept. Grapes ripened well. Harvest began Sept 26.

Quantity produced

700 cases.

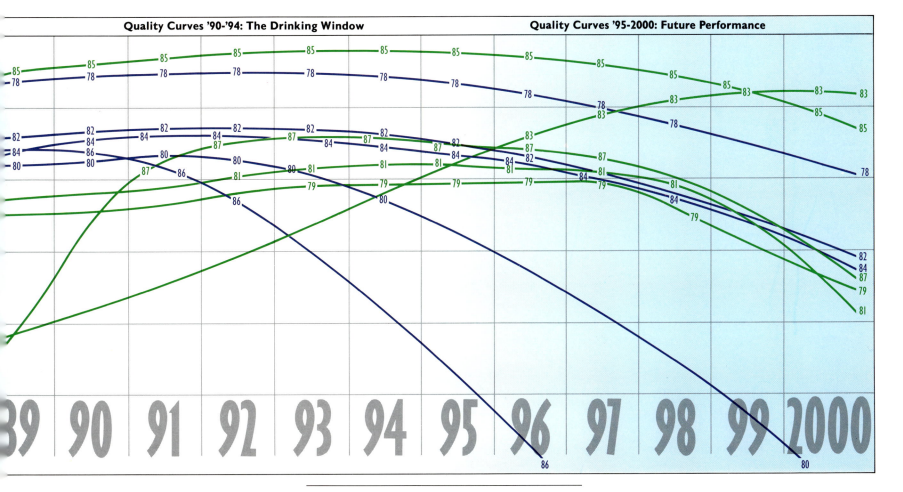

Quality Curves '90-'94: The Drinking Window

Quality Curves '95-2000: Future Performance

Chevalier-Montrachet, Domaine Leflaive

In their various corners of the wine world, those who aspire to make top quality Cabernet Sauvignon may argue whether their model is Château Lafite, Latour, or some geographically closer archetype. There is little dispute among Chardonnay producers who know Leflaive's white burgundies, however, that this domaine provides an ideal to strive for.

Leflaive's wines are not faultless. No producer of genuine burgundies, wines notoriously subject to vintage variation, can achieve perfection every year. But the Leflaive hallmarks of sublime purity of fruit and expression of *terroir* have shone so brightly and so often that they are recognised and admired throughout the world.

This 250-year-old family firm is run today by Vincent Leflaive with his nephew Olivier, now a *négociant* in his own right, as adjutant; and Pierre Morey (only a very distant relative of the Moreys of Chassagne) as wine-maker.

According to Vincent Leflaive, the characteristics of the domaine are simply: "good vines, well placed and cared for; clinical cleanliness; and the work done by nature whenever possible".

Leflaive's 55 acres (22 hectares) of vines are certainly exceptionally well placed. None is in the Montrachet vineyard itself, source of so many expensive disappointments, but sizeable chunks are in its *Grand Cru* neighbours: steely-fine Chevalier-Montrachet, plumper Bâtard-Montrachet

and often gorgeous Bienvenues-Bâtard-Montrachet as well as in equally carefully nurtured *Premiers Crus* and other sites around the village.

It takes two weeks of September and October to pick their 22 hectares (55 acres). Both fermentations and the initial *élevage* are in small oak casks, up to a third of which are new for the *Grands Crus*. Before the next harvest however the wines are transferred to Vincent Leflaive's pride and joy: small, pristine stainless steel tanks slotted neatly into the spotless cellars with a centimetre or two to spare. (So thorough is their regard for hygiene that the visitor is likely to be warned twice against the customary burgundian cellar practice of spitting on the earth floor.) Spending their second winter in tank means that the wines are clarified naturally by the burgundian chill.

Chevalier-Montrachet is Leflaive's most revered wine and the one which usually repays cellaring so handsomely. Vincent describes it as "an androgynous flirt. It comes and goes, and the bottom of the bottle is usually best. Bâtard may be a wine for banquets, but Chevalier is a *vin d'intimité*".

Visitors from as far afield as California and Australia make regular pilgrimages to this Chardonnay shrine, always trying to get Leflaive, Morey or his predecessors François Virot and his son Jean to divulge the "recipe". Details of their traditional techniques are eventually exported but the real secret, the mythical vineyard sites themselves, can never be.

Earlier vintages

These are built to last and stand a better chance of withstanding the ravages of decades on acidity and fruit levels than most White Burgundies. Look particularly for 1974, 1973, 1971 and 1969.

1978 The last bottle from Leflaive's private cellar was deep gold and powerfully, almost bizarrely, scented of smoked sausage or white truffles. Definitely the most evolved, most rich and smoky on the nose. Enormous impact, vigour and power. Too much for some but Vincent's favourite among 1978-1987.

Weather and timing

Excellent vintage, very small crop. Fine end to season; perfect maturation. Healthy harvest Oct 16.

Quantity produced

450 cases released at Fr f1,128 a case. Total Côte de Beaune production: 1,350,000 cases.

Other details

About an acre (½ ha) replanted each year to maintain the balance between old and young vines.

1979 Not razor sharp but complete and fascinating. Well-knit, fully open bouquet with lots of plump fruit on the palate: suggests sugared almonds. Medium-weight with a good, aromatic finish. Olivier's favourite. Ready.

Weather and timing

Good vintage, above average crop. Good bud break; perfect flowering. Excellent Sept; grapes matured well. Harvest Oct 13.

Quantity produced

550 cases released at Fr f1,340 a case. Côte de Beaune: 1,850,000 cases.

1980 Touch of *Botrytis* suggests Sauternes on the aristocratic nose with its hints of smoked bacon. Less weight than some – a ballet dancer rather than an opera singer – lovely elegance and life.

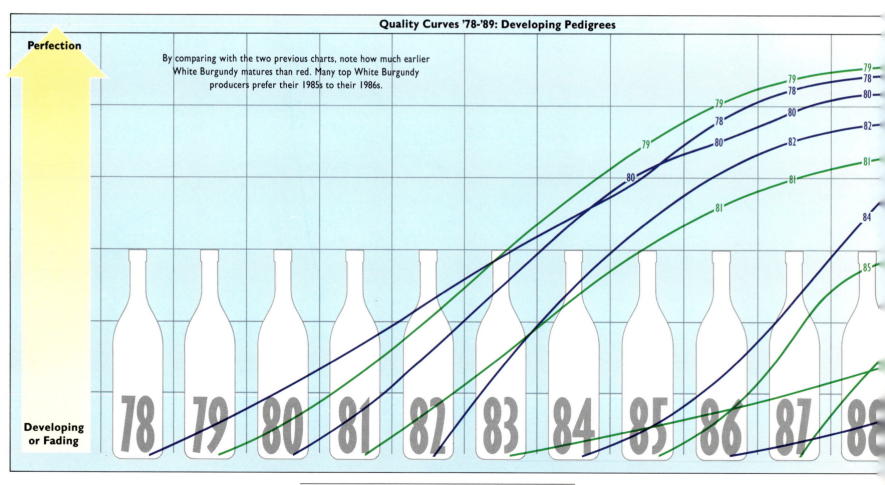

Quality Curves '78-'89: Developing Pedigrees

Perfection

By comparing with the two previous charts, note how much earlier White Burgundy matures than red. Many top White Burgundy producers prefer their 1985s to their 1986s.

Developing or Fading

78 79 80 81 82 83 84 85 86 87 88

Not a big wine but great quality and neatness. Still *nerveux* though already giving enormous pleasure.

Weather and timing
Good vintage, below average crop. Slow start to the season. Late flowering. Sunny Aug and Sept. Late harvest Oct 21.

Quantity produced
625 cases released at Fr f1,354 a case. Côte de Beaune: 1,595,000.

1981 Savoury notes as in 1984 but a little scrawny for Chevalier. Lots of acid and some toasted elements in the bouquet. Real attack. Very correct, with layers of nutty flavour, but not one of the most generous.

Weather and timing
Fine vintage, small crop. Spring frosts and localized hailstorms reduced crop. Harvest Oct 7.

Quantity produced
400 cases released at Fr f1,480 a case. Côte de Beaune: 1,010,000 cases.

Other details
First harvest of 1978 vines.

1982 One of Leflaive's less successful vintages relative to its peers. The Chevalier lacks definition although there is no shortage of mouthfilling, silky fruit on the palate. Slightly hot and already ready to drink.

Weather and timing
Good vintage, large crop. Frost-free spring. Excellent flowering in spite of hail. Good summer then especially sunny Sept; good maturation. Early harvest Sept 25. High sugar levels.

Quantity produced
1,000 cases released at Fr f1,579 a case. Côte de Beaune: 2,490,000 cases.

1983 An extraordinary deep golden wine, reaching 13.8 with no help from the sugar sacks. Tasting it at five years was like trying to lick a whale-sized popsicle. For several more years it

will be difficult to discern anything other than the extract, the sweetness of the alcohol, a bit of oak and the impressively high (for this vintage) acid level. A wine to wait for, hoping the acidity is high enough for such a heavyweight.

Weather and timing
Exceptional vintage, normal crop. Hot, dry summer. Effective control of grape moth (*Eudemis*) attack in July. Sept showers. Warm for harvest Oct 1.

Quantity produced
1,125 cases released at Fr f1,861 a case. Côte de Beaune: 1,650,000.

Other details
No chaptalization.

1984 Unusually for a Leflaive wine of this stature, ready to enjoy at four years old. Savoury, open bouquet with less steely delicacy than is usual for Chevalier. A note of more Bâtard-like earthiness, chewy texture and life from acidity rather than opulence.

Slightly honeyed but skinny.

Weather and timing
Average vintage, below average crop. Normal bud break. Difficult flowering mid-June to mid-July: uneven cluster size. Fine summer: varied Sept. Harvest Oct 12.

Quantity produced
625 cases released at Fr f1,974 a case. Côte de Beaune: 1,465,000.

1985 Extremely easy to appreciate, for me overshadowed by 1986 but Vincent, the maestro after all, thinks it will always be better than the 1986. Much more evolved than the 1986 with gorgeously ripe greengages and mossy undergrowth already apparent in the bouquet. Good balance and some spice on the finish with very slightly less obvious acidity than the 1986. Drinking divinely even at three years old.

Weather and timing
Excellent vintage, large crop. Harsh winter and strong, local-

ized spring frosts: late flowering. Very sunny, hot summer and autumn. Fine for harvest Oct 2.

Quantity produced
1,000 cases released at Fr f2,538 a case. Côte de Beaune: 1,625,000 cases.

1986 Taut, dense, extremely aristocratic and reserved. Exceptional acid/alcohol balance. Direct, neat, dry with some oak still and layers of youthful floral but somehow masculine scents. Extremely rigorous and promising although only hinting at its future glory.

Weather and timing
Excellent vintage, large crop. Late bud break. Dry, warm for quick flowering. Hot summer with some showers (Aug 15 and Sept 15). Harvest Oct 1.

Quantity produced
1,250 cases released at Fr f2,679 a case. Côte de Beaune: 2,310,000 cases.

1987 Great finesse and elegance. Much more forward than the 1986. Not a wine for keeping. Pretty, open, floral. Hints of putty and hazelnuts.

Weather and timing
Good vintage, normal crop. Average season. Incomplete flowering. Harvest Oct 5.

Quantity produced
750 cases released at Fr f2,961 a case. Côte de Beaune: 2,135,000 cases.

1988 *(Not tasted)* An abundant harvest: selection necessary for inclusion in the appellation. Good conditions throughout the year bode well for this wine.

Weather and timing
Fine vintage, large crop. Good start to year. Ideal for early flowering. Fine summer with some showers. Harvest began on Oct 4.

Quantity produced
1,290 cases. Release date 1990.

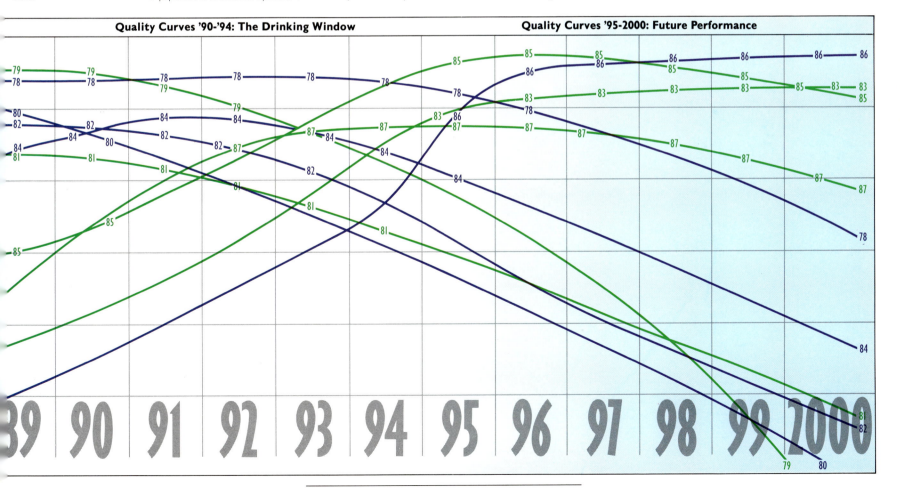

GREATER BURGUNDY

Chablis from new vineyards that increasingly encroach on the surrounding farmland are unlikely to demonstrate Chablis' ageability as eloquently as a *Grand Cru*.

Greater Burgundy is quite different from the Côte d'Or – only coincidentally, it sometimes seems, sharing major grape varieties. The most dramatic example of this is in Burgundy's isolated northern outpost, Chablis. Here the wines shed quite a different light on Chardonnay from the broader whites of the Côte d'Or. Years such as 1979 and 1981 show how Chablisien maturity patterns are quite distinct from those of the Côte d'Or, the first year maturing so much faster in Chablis, the second so much slower and more magnificently.

The example of Chablis' longest-living *Grand Cru* from one of the town's most diligent vinifiers gives an idea of the upper limits of Chablis' longevity. *Grands Crus* from Raveneau, Dauvissat, William Fèvre, Moreau and Michel should follow the Timechart overleaf; for their *Premiers Crus*, and the *Grands Crus* of many others, the chart should generally be advanced by a year. For the *Premiers Crus* of others advance the chart by two years, bearing in mind that Montée de Tonnerre can be regarded as a *Grand Cru* for its ageing ability if not for its complexity.

Basic Chablis should be ready to drink within two years of the vintage but study the Timechart for guidelines on how long it will last. Petit Chablis is a Chart B-type wine (page 19).

The rolling countryside immediately to the south of the Côte d'Or is interspersed with the up-and-coming vineyards that comprise the Côte Chalonnaise. Weather patterns and crop levels are very similar to those reported for Chevalier-Montrachet on page 63, especially for the good value Chalonnaise whites Rully and Montagny, which should be ready to drink two to three years after the vintage. The reds of Mercurey and Givry share some of the vintage characteristics of any Côte de Beaune red (see page 61) and should be mature between three and five years after the vintage – although producers such as Michel Juillot can imbue them (and his whites) with serious Côte d'Or structure.

South of the Côte Chalonnaise is the huge sprawl of Mâconnais vineyards, producing generally undistinguished Mâcon Rouge of Chart A or Chart B type. Much more promising in terms of quality is Mâcon Blanc, although only a small proportion of it is worth keeping longer than Chart B suggests. Domaine Vincent in Château Fuissé has, like Raveneau, been chosen to show the upper limits of ageing potential in this region – although the Chardonnays of the Mâconnais age notably faster overall than those of Chablis (thereby confirming the role of acidity in white wine evolution). Some St Vérans, the odd Mâcon-Viré and Thevenet's Mâcon-Clessé can be worth cellaring past their fourth birthday. Note the steepness of the initial curve for Château Fuissé which shows how rapidly the various vintages mature. Otherwise, only serious Pouilly-Fuissés are worthy of Timechart consideration. Accelerate the chart by two years for a good Pouilly-

The village of Fuissé, with its twelfth-century church, is home to the unofficial first-growth of the appellation, Château Fuissé.

Fuissé (which has a life expectancy very similar to a Côte Chalonnaise white).

At the southern end of Greater Burgundy, providing a corridor to the Rhône Valley and the Midi, are the Beaujolais vineyards about which generalisation is relatively easy. (For Beaujolais Blanc, which is to all intents and purposes St Véran, see above.) Beaujolais epitomises the charm of wines that are clearly made to be drunk young. Fruity, flirtatiously light and frisky, with a white wine's whisk of acidity, most Beaujolais is Chart B wine par excellence, designed to be drunk as soon as it is released. In the case of Nouveaux this is from a few weeks after the harvest, although a good one can still provide perfectly pleasant drinking a year later. The wine that is one grade up, Beaujolais-Villages, can be drunk well into the year after that, especially if it was made in one of the years shown as having a long peak on page 70/1's Timechart. The Beaujolais illustrated there represents the third most substantial category of Beaujolais, one of the 10 *Crus*, in this case Morgon, which produces some of the longest-living wines of the region. These are wines worth keeping, although not, as the chart quite deliberately shows, for too long.

Note how varied are the life expectancies of the different vintages of *Cru* Beaujolais. Individual domaines' Moulin-à-Vent, some Fleuries and some Juliénas should certainly last as long as this fine Morgon, although they may well not share its stunning performance in such off vintages as 1982 and 1984.

This is an area however in which a *négociant*'s blend, even of one of these most long-lived *Crus*, is likely to age as fast as any Chart B wine unless it is labelled as coming from a single property.

Chablis Grand Cru, Les Clos, Raveneau

Jean-Marie Raveneau does not sell his family's wine. He meticulously allocates it to those who have been begging for it the longest. Those lucky enough to taste what Jean-Marie and his father François make from their 17 acres (seven hectares) of Chardonnay vines can understand the widespread thirst inspired by the name Raveneau. Steely and whistle-clean, Raveneau wines exemplify the almost austere style of Chardonnay on which Chablis, a pocket of vineyards halfway between Paris and Burgundy proper, seems to have the universal monopoly.

Although the wines of Chablis share some of the qualities of fresh, tart, Sauvignon-based wines, the best of them can age as well as good Côte d'Or whites – in fact after two or three decades they can begin to taste more like a wine made in Meursault or Puligny. Raveneau's wines are some of the slowest to reveal their charms. In principle, *Premier Cru* Chablis outlasts straight Chablis by a good five to eight years while *Grand Cru* Chablis demands the most patience, evolving at the most stately pace of all.

Of all the *Grands Crus*, Les Clos enjoys the widest respect. The only restaurant of note in the tiny town of Chablis is the Hostellerie des Clos. Les Clos tends to produce those wines most worth long- to medium-term cellaring. François Raveneau has just over three-quarters of an acre (a third of a hectare) of Les Clos, or Clos as it is economically designated on Raveneau labels, and this is their most sought-after wine.

In the war that rages in Chablis over the use of oak, Raveneau steer an impeccable middle course. Their slim cellar below Rue Chichée is lined with a mixture of Burgundian *pièces* and the smaller *feuillettes*, carefully fitted in according the height of the vaulted roof. Most of their wines, and certainly all their Clos, are fermented in oak, often the newest oak they have. Great care is taken to avoid any hint of oak-derived flavour on the nose of the wine, and to keep just a hint of cask on the structure of the palate. Bottling (and sealing with thick yellow wax) usually take place either in September or March, depending on the vintage.

Steeped in Chablisien lore (Jean-Marie's elder brother is technical director of the Pic-Regnard empire and his uncle is Monsieur Dauvissat), the Raveneaus are respectful of the different characteristics of each vintage – which arguably vary more here than in any other wine region. This is reflected not only in how they make each wine, but also how they sell it and whether or not they hold stocks back for extended maturation. They held back 60 bottles (an enormous cache in Chablis terms) of the 1978s made from Les Clos and Montée de Tonnerre, for example, whereas they have to struggle to find a bottle of 1980 because it, unlike its immediate successor, was judged such an early-maturing vintage, as reflected in the chart below. Little 1987 and 1988 will be held back, on the other hand, because these were relatively ordinary years, with less than 7gm/litre of acidity.

Earlier vintages
The Raveneau family are currently enjoying wines from the 1971, 1974 and 1975 vintages (along with the 1982s and 1984s). The vintages which François chose to bottle in magnum for his own cellar are 1969, 1971, 1973 and 1974.

1978 A wonderful year for Chablis, it produced a Raveneau Clos that is still in its youth. Exceptionally high levels of acidity are married with exceptionally high levels of extract which makes this a wine to wait for. Five dozen bottles of Clos and Montée de Tonnerre were stashed away chez Raveneau.

Weather and timing
Great vintage, small crop. Wet start to the season. Average summer with dry, sunny Aug. Fine conditions for harvest which began Oct 16.

Quantity produced

Chablis regional production: 550,000 cases.

1979 Mature bouquet with hints of both mushrooms and almonds but with much more concentration and nervy acidity than the 1980. Lively, if slightly rustic and textured – the opposite of polished – but very, very long.

Weather and timing
Average vintage, above average crop. Snowy Jan and Feb. Sunny July. Wet Oct; harvest Oct 8-16.

Quantity produced
Chablis: 1,275,000 cases.

Other details
Planted one acre/⅖ ha of Chablis Premier Cru Vaillons and 1⅘ acres/¾ ha of Chablis Grand Cru Valmur.

1980 Mature, relatively full-blown and notably less excitingly austere than most.

Weather and timing
Average vintage and crop. Cold, wet spring. Dry Apr. Poor

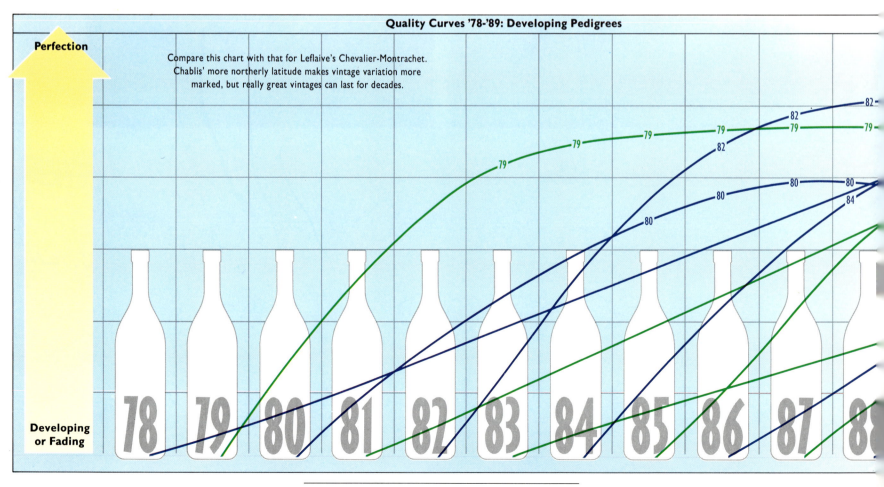

Quality Curves '78-'89: Developing Pedigrees

Perfection

Compare this chart with that for Leflaive's Chevalier-Montrachet. Chablis' more northerly latitude makes vintage variation more marked, but really great vintages can last for decades.

Developing or Fading

78 79 80 81 82 83 84 85 86 87 88

flowering; *coulure*. Wet July. Humid growing season. Late harvest Oct 16-24.

Quantity produced
Chablis: 917,000 cases.

Other details
Planted 1⅓ acres/½ ha of Chablis Premier Cru Butteaux.

1981 A majestic wine that demands respect. Great quality and concentration are apparent, yet it also displays obvious finesse. Marked acidity on the palate confirms this is a wine just coming out of its shell. Very rigorous with ripe green fruit well encased in a steely structure. Lovely waves of fruit on a long finish. This is a vintage to seek out for current drinking.

Weather and timing
Fair vintage, small crop. Dull season (sun hours 25% below average). Spring frosts. Cold and wet for flowering. Wet during harvest Oct 5-10.

Quantity produced
Released at Fr f516 a case. Chablis: 500,000 cases.

1982 Blanchots. (Blanchots is usually a faster-maturing *Grand Cru* than Les Clos.) Most attractive well-knit bouquet suggestive of wet stones. Resolved, firm palate with real charm which, according to Jean-Marie Raveneau, has always been evident on the 1982s.

Weather and timing
Very good vintage, large crop. Warm, sunny and relatively dry season. Normal bud break. Beautiful flowering. Dull June and Aug. Ripened early. Harvest Sept 23-Oct 2.

Quantity produced
Released at Fr f540 a case. Chablis: 1,300,000 cases.

1983 As further south, this was an atypically hot vintage. Rich, alcoholic, very slightly overripe nose. The development of this wine seemed blocked in the late eighties. There is some nuttiness but the fruit does not sing out and the acid is by no means obvious. Jean-Marie thinks that this wine is marked by heat, and that one must wait for it longer than most. Let us hope he is right.

Weather and timing
Great vintage, large crop. Extended flowering. Good summer. Very ripe crop; even young vines achieved 14.7% alcohol. Isolated spots of noble rot. Harvest Sept 29-Oct 7.

Quantity produced
Released at Fr f576 a case. Chablis: 1,580,000 cases.

Other details
No chaptalization.

1984 An underrated vintage producing very typical Chablis. Notably clean, lean and stylish. Masses of acid, but quite enough silky fruit to balance it provided this somewhat sinewy wine is drunk with food. (Probably about the same acid level as the 1986 but with much less flesh.) Long, steely and delicate.

Weather and timing
Good vintage, above average crop. Very humid season which encouraged rot. Rain during harvest Oct 10-19. Low alcohol. High acidity, low sugar levels.

Quantity produced
Released at Fr f600 a case. Chablis: 1,250,000 cases.

Other details
Chaptalized.

1985 A slightly low-key wine with a floral bouquet to which smoky top notes add interest. Lacking concentration (despite the low yield) and lacking a little acid. For early drinking.

Weather and timing
Great vintage, below average crop. Winter and spring frosts badly affected bud break. Wet May to mid-June. Poor flowering. Hot, sunny Sept. Slow to ripen due to dry conditions. Harvest Oct 7-13.

Quantity produced
Released at Fr f720 a case. Chablis: 1,000,000 cases.

1986 Real concentration of green fruit flavours and exciting impact. Still quite rustic and aggressive in youth but with wonderful palate impact and great acid. A powerhouse of impressions, taut as a crouching sprinter and with excellent length.

Weather and timing
Excellent vintage, large crop. Harsh winter, heralded a slow start to the season. Feb frosts. Dull Apr. Fine June and July. Very wet Sept 12-17 which encouraged *Botrytis*. Harvest Oct 1-8. Good acid/sugar balance.

Quantity produced
Released at Fr f756 a case. Chablis: 1,480,000 cases.

Other details
No chaptalization.

1987 Clean, lean, aromatic, almost Sauvignon in its piercing quality. Very slightly dilute with the acidity more marked on the palate than the fruit. Relatively lightweight.

Weather and timing
Average vintage, large crop. Wet spring. Excellent flowering. Excellent Sept. Rain during harvest Oct 8-17. Low acidity levels.

Quantity produced
Estimated release price: Fr f780 a case. Chablis: 1,475,000 cases.

1988 (Cask sample) Good medium weight with a certain sturdy meatiness and a strong impression of green apples but not a tremendously strong impact on the palate.

Weather and timing
Good vintage, large crop. Normal winter. Warm Apr; early bud break. Average summer. Cold, wet Sept delayed ripening. Harvest early Oct.

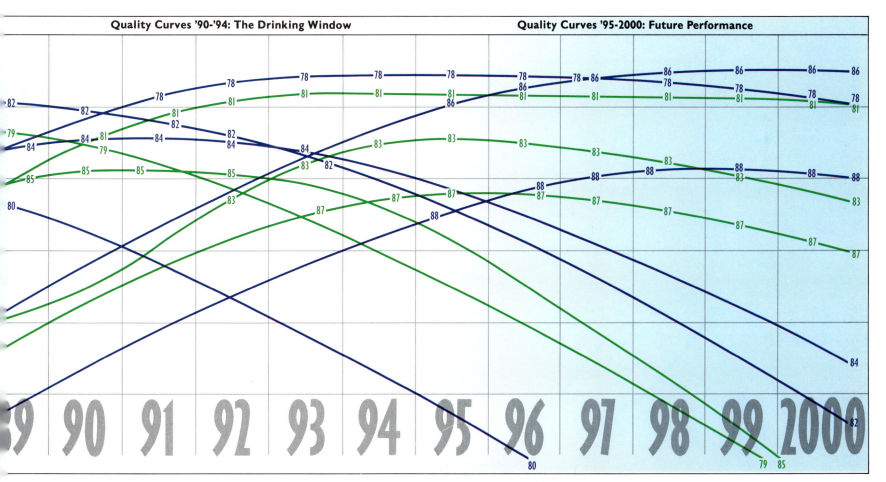

Quality Curves '90-'94: The Drinking Window

Quality Curves '95-2000: Future Performance

Château Fuissé, Vieilles Vignes, Jean-Jacques Vincent

Like its red counterpart, the superior Beaujolais charted overleaf, a Timechart for Château Fuissé only just belongs in this book. Most Mâconnais whites are relatively evanescent: their charms start to fade after about three years, four or five in really good vintages such as 1986 or 1988.

Pouilly-Fuissé is incontrovertibly the best appellation in the Mâconnais, where Chardonnay shines so much more brightly than Pinot Noir and Gamay. And Château Fuissé seems to have the monopoly on producing truly great, as opposed to good (and often highly priced), Pouilly-Fuissé.

The 44 acres (18 hectares) of Domaine du Château Pouilly-Fuissé vineyard perhaps owe their ability to concentrate a double helping of flavour and extract to their steepness and exposure to the midday sun. These admirable raw ingredients are then nurtured by one of the Mâconnais' top wine-makers. Jean-Jacques Vincent, the fifth generation of the Vincent family to make wine here, has the dedication necessary to maintain and even improve the reputation of this remarkable estate, being a trained oenologist who still teaches at the local Lycée Viticole and exhibits a distinctly unburgundian obsession with constant improvement.

While some of his basic Pouilly-Fuissé is fermented in tank like most other Mâconnais whites, Monsieur Vincent treats his Château Fuissé bottlings to 100 per cent fermentation and ageing in oak, of which a good fifth is new each year. There is no doubt that the wine needs it. Here is a classic case of ripe to over-ripe grapes which can not only take but are enhanced by the extra rigour and dimension that are invariably provided by a stint in small oak casks.

The very finest expression of Pouilly-Fuissé as a wine worthy of cellar space is the top, Vieilles Vignes *cuvée* from Château Fuissé. Although its precise provenance varies from year to year, the selection being made chiefly on the basis of taste and analysis, Vieilles Vignes tends to come from those vines within the Domaine du Château which are 35 to 40 years old.

These grapes achieve extraordinary levels of ripeness (and in some years, noble rot), always at least a full degree more even than the regular Château Fuissé, which is itself perceptibly more powerful than most other Pouilly-Fuissés. In years such as 1983 it can even nudge an extraordinary 15 degrees of natural alcohol.

Jean-Jacques Vincent keeps such wines from falling over themselves by studiously suppressing malolactic fermentation for a suitable proportion of the blend even though, as a direct result, they need even longer in bottle to soften the initial harshness of the malic acid and integrate it with the lushness of the fruit.

As a general rule the regular Château Fuissé bottling of Pouilly-Fuissé and the very best Mâconnais whites such as Pouilly-Loché and Pouilly-Vinzelles peak two to four years before the Vieilles Vignes charted here.

Earlier vintages
Tending to show their age.

1978 The deep, coppery colour of old fino but with no signs of unhealthy browning. Extremely savoury, meaty cocktail of old Chardonnay-and-oak flavours with a subtlety still not seen outside Burgundy. Full-blown: not to every palate's taste, but a miracle of integrated acid and balance with real nerve and excitement.

Weather and timing
Fine vintage, very small crop. Uneven flowering. Perfect Aug and Sept; excellent maturation. Harvest began Oct 8.

Quantity produced
About 550 cases released at Fr f691 a case. Mâconnais production: 2,180,000 cases.

Other details
Small reserve stock. Strong American demand. Experimented with oak types.

1979 A fully mature wine showing some of the asparagus vegetal notes of old Chardonnay. Some smokiness too. Evolved tertiary aromas but good balance. Not big but neat and long with extremely good acid.

Weather and timing
Very good vintage, large crop. Perfect weather during flowering. Healthy harvest began Oct 3.

Quantity produced
About 1,330 cases released at Fr f604 a case. Mâconnais: 2,900,000.

1980 The least successful of this range. Gold as deep as 1983 with little other than alcohol and a hint of incipient oxidation to show for itself. Not subtle.

Weather and timing
Good vintage, small crop. Disastrous spring. Bad flowering. Cold, humid summer. Very late harvest began Oct 14.

Quantity produced
About 780 cases released at Fr

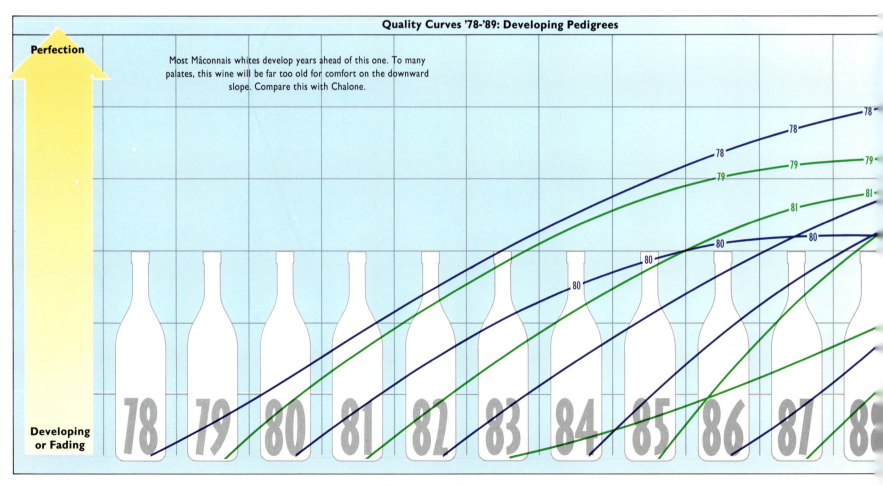

Quality Curves '78-'89: Developing Pedigrees

Perfection

Most Mâconnais whites develop years ahead of this one. To many palates, this wine will be far too old for comfort on the downward slope. Compare this with Chalone.

Developing or Fading

78 79 80 81 82 83 84 85 86 87 88

f480 a case. Mâconnais: 2,220,000 cases.

1981 Full, rustic, Michelot-type Meursault. Almost oily caramel notes on the nose. Ready to drink (the straight Château Fuissé started to dry out in 1988).

Weather and timing
Good vintage, small crop. Spring frosts cut crop by a third. Hail in June caused damage. Bad flowering. Ripened well: early harvest.

Quantity produced
About 600 cases released at Fr f720 a case. Mâconnais: 1,145,000.

1982 This delicate wine looks much younger than it smells. Still pale green/gold, it has a powerful toasted, almost gamey nose with a fascinatingly broad, charred quality. One of the few Vieilles Vignes which tastes like Pouilly Fuissé rather than something grander. Appetising and not too rich.

Weather and timing
Excellent vintage, large crop. Heavy, humid spring. Good for early flowering. Fine growing season. Harvest began Sept 19.

Quantity produced
About 1,330 cases released at Fr f814 a case. Mâconnais: 3,590,000.

Other details
Snazzy dark flask replaced bright green burgundy bottle.

1983 Deep gold with markedly high glycerol and a distinct burnish. A rich, fat wine headily scented with *Botrytis*. Enormous impact suggesting smoke on butterscotch and some tropical fruits in much denser concentrations than so much New World Chardonnay. On the palate the acidity is dominant. It will take years to tame and might not make it.

Weather and timing
Botrytised vintage, small crop. Warm, humid spring; good flowering. Late Aug very hot. Harvest began Sept 25 (20% *Botrytis*). High alcohol level.

Quantity produced
About 780 cases released at Fr f914 a case. Mâconnais: 2,620,000.

Other details
Malolactic fermentation suppressed. Favourable exchange rate stimulated American demand.

1984 Some bottle variation but the wine can be meaner and leaner than one would expect. Uncomfortably high acidity and low concentration for this wine. Some vegetal Chardonnay oxidation already.

Weather and timing
Good vintage, normal crop. Cold, humid spring. Normal flowering. Fresh, wet summer. Rain during harvest which began Oct 5.

Quantity produced
About 890 cases released at Fr f1,124 a case. Mâconnais: 2,430,000 cases.

Other details
New fermentation temperature-control system introduced.

1985 A highly successful wine showing admirably both the appellation and the individual wine style. Extremely healthy fruit with broad, open, melon, lemon and smoke flavours. Has not the intensity of the 1986 but shares its balance and exuberance. A slight impression of sweetness but not the slightest hint of flab. Lovely layers of flavour.

Weather and timing
Excellent vintage, normal crop. Perfect flowering. Dry summer, scorching Sept. Healthy harvest began Sept 27.

Quantity produced
About 1,070 cases released at Fr f1,124 a case. Mâconnais: 2,620,000 cases.

1986 Simply gorgeous: only the somewhat obvious unintegrated toasty oak elements stop this one from being gulped down at three years. Very powerful, as 1983 was, but this time in wonderful balance. Extremely stylish with the zip of lime zest. Fully ripe fruit elements underneath too. The acidity is already much better integrated and less aggressive than in the 1983. Vincent thinks this the best ever.

Weather and timing
Good vintage, above average crop. Good start to year. Fine flowering. Superb summer; dry with light rain. Great harvest began Sept 24.

Quantity produced
About 1,110 cases released at Fr f1,300 a case. Mâconnais: 3,160,000 cases.

1987 Surprisingly successful. High in acid but by no means raw, with some of the elements of a crisp green apple as well as distinctly youthful floral notes. Apricot flavour underneath recalls Viognier. Medium- to full-bodied with an explosive finish. One to watch.

Weather and timing
Partly Botrytised vintage, above average crop. Fresh, humid spring. Poor for flowering. Dull summer. Scorching Sept. Harvest began Sept 30.

Quantity produced
About 1,070 cases released at Fr f1,300 a case. Mâconnais: 3,110,000 cases.

Other details
New stainless steel equipment introduced.

1988 (*Not tasted*) Good acid/alcohol balance, according to Jean-Jacques Vincent. Fine aromas with a floral note.

Weather and timing
Very good vintage, above average crop. Warm, spring: excellent flowering. Fine growing season. Good maturation. Harvest began Sept 21.

Quantity produced
About 1,110 cases released at Fr f1,360 a case.

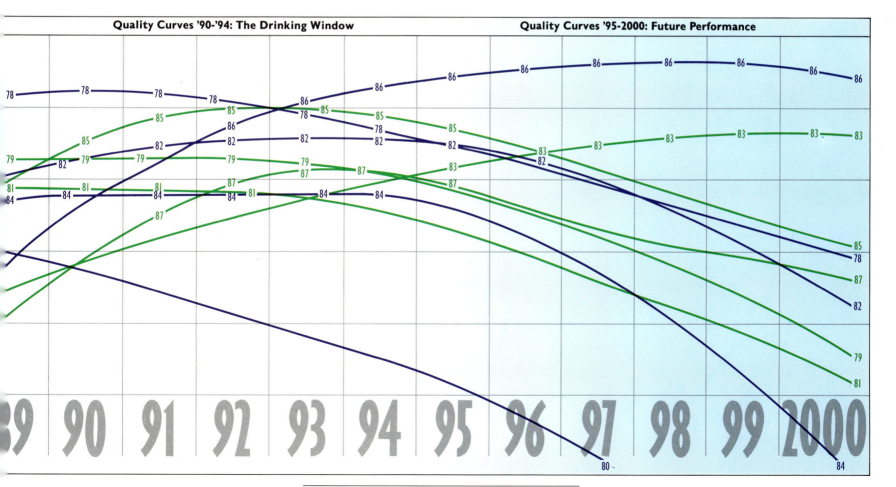

Quality Curves '90-'94: The Drinking Window   Quality Curves '95-2000: Future Performance

Morgon, Jean Descombes

The story of this ageworthy Beaujolais concerns not just Jean-Ernest Descombes, one of the village of Morgon's most conscientious wine producers, but also his impresario Georges Duboeuf. It is Duboeuf's bottling and shipping business that now threatens to engulf the sleepy village of Romanèche-Thorins a few miles down the hill from Morgon.

Over the last three decades Georges Duboeuf has earned his personal appellation as King of Beaujolais by nurturing and promulgating throughout the world the wines of a select band of the region's finest producers: *vignerons* who, in spite of the quality of their product, could not otherwise hope to promote themselves on an international scale.

Apart from what he keeps for his own robust consumption, Jean Descombes sells all the wine from his 32 acres (13 hectares) of Morgon vines to Georges Duboeuf, an agreement based on a simple handshake 20 years ago. A much earlier character than the smoothie depicted on his Duboeuf label, Jean Descombes is truly a son of the soil, dedicated to extracting the maximum quality from his vines. The vines are mainly in their third or fourth decade and in four well-placed parcels, Le Py, La Roche Pilée, Bellevire and Les Pillets. His pickers may be sent several times through each vineyard – a rare luxury for a Beaujolais.

He has travelled as far afield as America and Japan, but once a year at least there is no doubt where Jean Descombes

will be. During vintage time he is rooted to his fermenting room and cellar, monitoring the safe discharge of every truckload of Gamay grapes from the unloading bay above into his workmanlike vats. They are fermented *à la beaujolaise* in whole bunches and given a six or seven day *cuvaison* so that the resulting wine is high in extract, concentration and, for a Beaujolais, quite high in tannins.

Regular Beaujolais is quintessentially for early drinking, Beaujolais-Villages lasts perhaps a year longer and most of the wines of the Beaujolais *crus* are designed to be drunk at about two years old. Only some of the *crus* are generally capable of producing wines which can age longer than this: some St Amour, some Chénas, Morgon, Fleurie, Juliénas and, most ageworthy of all, Moulin-à-Vent. In some cases this can last for decades, developing some of the characteristics, if not always the finesse, of a mature burgundy.

A fine Morgon therefore makes a good candidate to illustrate the ageability of suitable *cru* Beaujolais, although the charts show how widely, and often unexpectedly, the performances of the different vintages vary. Beaujolais at all quality levels evolves relatively rapidly, and the state of the 1978 tasted in 1988 suggests that when the end approaches for a mature Beaujolais, it does so at some speed. It is also worth noting that Descombes' wines in particular, like many serious wines, can suffer a temporary diminution of charm, in this case in their second year.

Earlier vintages
One would not normally recommend Beaujolais more than 10 years old, but isolated examples from the **1945** and **1947** vintages have given enormous pleasure in the seventies and eighties. Descombes' **1970** Cuvée de la Reine is a delicate, jewel-bright vindication of his wine-making skills (and a toast to his daughter Nicole who was Reine de Beaujolais in 1969/70). His **1976**, which was a particular success for Descombes, now tastes almost like mature claret, it is so full-bodied and powerful. I served it in quantity at my 30th birthday party but this, the last bottle chez Duboeuf, showed me that I should have kept some back.

1978 Yellow rim and fading fast. Some strawberry sweetness and delicacy of body but the acid is encroaching on pleasure.

Weather and timing
Excellent vintage, normal crop. Late season. Wet June delayed flowering. Good growing season. Harvest began Oct 1.

Quantity produced
Duboeuf produces approx. 7,780 cases of Domaine Jean Descombes each year. This varies by only 100 cases from year to year. Total Beaujolais production: 13,122,000 cases.

1979 This wine could still charm. Aged red burgundy nose with some interest but almost faded fruit on the palate and aggressive acidity.

Weather and timing
Fair vintage, normal crop. Cold, wet winter. Excellent weather for harvest which began Sept 20. Low acidity levels.

Quantity produced
Release price: Fr f234 a case. Total Beaujolais production: 13,122,000 cases.

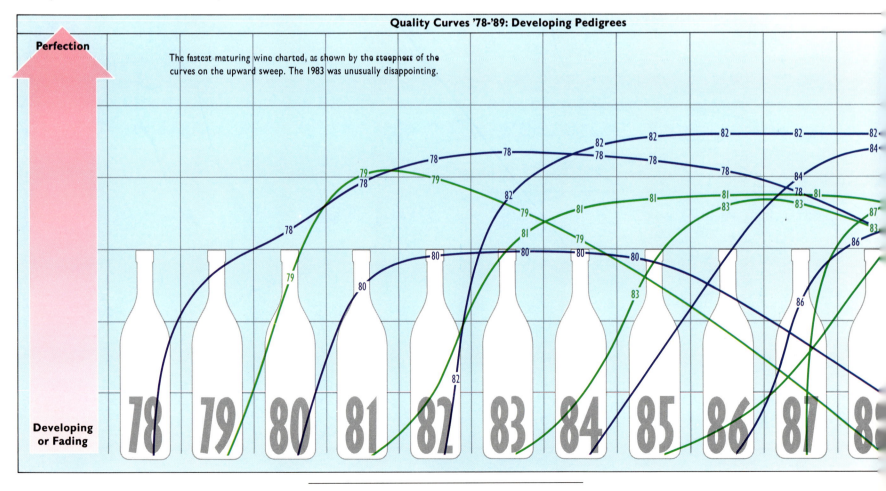

Quality Curves '78-'89: Developing Pedigrees

Perfection

The fastest maturing wine charted, as shown by the steepness of the curves on the upward sweep. The 1983 was unusually disappointing.

Developing or Fading

78 79 80 81 82 83 84 85 86 87 88

1980 Another yellowing wine with a relatively simple nose, pronounced acidity and a hot, sweet finish.

Weather and timing

Unexceptional vintage, small crop. Poor spring, month-long flowering, hot growing season. Harvest began late on Oct 9.

Quantity produced

Release price: Fr f240 a case. Total Beaujolais production: 13,077,000.

1981 Excellent deep, healthy colour. Big and muscular. Impressive rather than charming. Some tannin lingers but the fruit is fading.

Weather and timing

Good vintage, small crop. Frost on Apr 26 badly damaged crop. Normal flowering. Sun during Aug and Sept advanced harvest which began Sept 14.

Quantity produced

Release price: Fr f264 a case. Total Beaujolais production: 12,267,000.

1982 Glorious nose that is pure Morgon (as opposed to old burgundy, old claret or simply old red) and surprisingly youthful. Real Gamay lightness of touch. Well evolved but still with slight sweetness and definite zip of acidity. Lovely in late 1988 but, according to Duboeuf, has always been supple.

Weather and timing

Good vintage, very large crop. Mild spring followed by early, rapid flowering. Good growing season. Fine for harvest which began on Sept 8; high sugar and low acidity levels.

Quantity produced

Release price: Fr f270 a case. Total Beaujolais production: 14,311,000 cases.

1983 A vintage of good repute but this wine has aged in a disappointingly jammy, "cooked" fashion. Lots of glycerol and good depth of colour: typical rather than delightful aged Beaujolais.

Weather and timing

Exceptional vintage, normal crop. Long, hard winter. Wet spring, dry summer which ended with rain. Hot, sunny Aug and Sept. Harvest began on Sept 24.

Quantity produced

Release price: Fr f282 a case. Total Beaujolais production: 13,978,000 cases.

1984 The surprise of this range. This vintage, so acid at first, has produced wines that have aged superbly and now have an enticingly complex, mature bouquet. Arguably more burgundy than Beaujolais with hints of coffee and bitter chocolate, and good structure on the palate although a lack of weight hints at fast decline.

Weather and timing

Excellent vintage, normal crop. Dominated by the success of the flowering; wet, cool conditions caused a very uneven set. Good July and Aug followed by cool, humid Sept.

Quantity produced

Release price: Fr f336 a case. Total Beaujolais production: 13,422,000 cases.

1985 An excellent vintage whose reputation is vindicated in this wine. Very deep colour. Aromatic, powerful fruit with some primary Gamay aromas still evident. Unusually for Beaujolais, some mineral notes add spice to the bouquet. Still in retreat in late 1988 but expected to reveal all from 1989.

Weather and timing

Excellent vintage, normal crop. A year of extremes. Harsh winter with frost damage on the more humid slopes. Sunny July, Aug and Sept. Harvest began Sept 16.

Quantity produced

Release price: Fr f372 a case. Total Beaujolais production: 13,356,000 cases.

1986 Muted, resolved nose but without too strident a shriek of Gamay. Low-key fruit and a slight lack of power. Lightweight, easy and flattering.

Weather and timing

Fair vintage, large crop. Long, cold, wet winter delayed vines (three weeks behind in Apr). Sun in June redressed the balance. Harvest began Sept 18.

Quantity produced

Release price: Fr f372 a case. Total Beaujolais production: 15,056,000 cases.

Other details

Morgon Jean Descombes won the gold medal at the Paris wine fair.

1987 Good straight purple with floral nose and youthful vigour. Sings, even shrieks, typical exuberant Gamay. Packed with fruit although relatively lightweight. Not a long future but attractive in youth. Good balance. The 1988, with more body, should be a better cellaring candidate.

Weather and timing

Good vintage, large crop. Harsh winter then a cold, wet spring followed by a hot, humid early summer. Slow flowering. Perfect Sept; harvest began Sept 29.

Quantity produced

Release price: Fr f378 a case. Total Beaujolais production: 14,500,000 cases.

1988 This vintage has far more character and body than the 1987; also more tannin. Rich, fruity but less sweet. A Beaujolais for the cellar.

Weather and timing

Good vintage, large crop. Mild winter; no frost or snow. Hot, stormy May. Excellent July and Aug. Exceptionally sunny Sept. Harvest began Sept 15.

Quantity produced

Release price: Fr f390 a case. Total Beaujolais production: 14,146,000 cases.

Quality Curves '90-'94: The Drinking Window   Quality Curves '95-2000: Future Performance

CHAMPAGNE

The question of champagne ageing is both controversial and seriously under-reported – two good reasons for exploring it in some detail here. Consumers are left more than usually ignorant about the bottle they are buying if that bottle contains the undated non-vintage champagne which forms between 80 and 90 per cent of all wine produced in Champagne. The point about NV, we are told, is that it should be blended to smooth out all variation between different vintages so that a bottle of Brand X's should taste the same whether the consumer buys it in 1986 or 1990.

The Champenois philosophy of branding their wines stylistically with the mark of the house rather than, as elsewhere, with the mark of the year and/or the vineyard should in theory make the consumer's life easier. But the theory is severely marred by the fact that in practice champagne is one of the most fragile of wines. A typical NV is not designed to be aged in bottle and, if stored in anything less than ideal cool, dark conditions (and how many cool, dark bottle shops do you know?), it can deteriorate fast and seriously. This means that the consumer is at the mercy of the many individuals along the distribution chain. We cannot know whether a champagne bottle has been badly stored at some point in its life, which is particularly worrying since so many retailers act as though champagne bottles, like moths, are attracted to the light source. Because of this the Champenois have been investing heavily in training retailers and in research into various champagne bottles that filter out the rays close to the ultra-violet wavelength which, through sunlight and fluorescent light, can spoil the taste.

But just as serious as the question of spoilage is that of age. We have no way of telling how old a bottle of NV champagne is. The extent to which the cork has been pressed into a mushroom shape indicates how long ago it was disgorged (recorked after the second fermentation's sediment was expelled). But no clues are given on label or cork as to when the champagne was blended and bottled – except to those who happen to be privy to (or who have managed to crack) the relevant in-house bottling codes now printed discreetly on the back of champagne labels.

The pressures of modern commerce usually mean that the NV currently being wholesaled is simply the most recently released, and therefore made from a blend based on the last vintage but one in the case of most labels, the last vintage but two or even three in the case of the more quality-conscious houses. But the retail chain can easily provide exceptions to this rule so that the consumer cannot tell whether a bottle of NV champagne could (in the case of three-year-old wine) or should (in many cases of two-year-old wines) be kept. The Champenois have so far rebuffed suggestions that now is the time for *glasnost*. But since there are as many consumers who enjoy youthful champagne as enjoy its mature counterpart, it seems that the champagne producers would have a happier matching of wine styles to customers to gain, and nothing to lose – except of course for those producers who do not have enough reserve wines to compensate for the effect of poor quality vintages on their NV blends. It is during, or rather two or three years after, catastrophic vintages that the best *grandes marques*, the traditionally famous Champagne houses, come into their own.

What happens to champagne or any other sparkling wine with age is that, like other white wines it deepens in colour, its acidity seems less pronounced – presumably as other compounds form to distract from it – and it starts to lose its fizz.

The official line from Epernay and Reims is that an NV champagne is ready to drink as soon as it is released from their cellars, but several British importers admit that NV champagne is better, less raw, after six to eight months' "landed age". Some wine merchants are even thoughtful enough to give their customers the benefit of this conviction.

In the case of champagne, travel seems to broaden the taste; distance from Champagne can be directly proportional to the apparent maturity of the champagne on sale. The very same champagne drunk in France can taste aggressively "green" to a British palate whereas its counterpart in America, Australia or the Far East can have acquired during the journey itself just the maturity that the British wine merchant seeks from his six-month cellaring. This softening of the very high initial total acidity is a particularly rewarding treatment for cheap NV

The Champagne region shows its northerly latitude and continental climate most winters with at least a dusting of snow. Here at Cuis the snow seems particularly appropriate to the area, the Côte des Blancs.

champagnes bought two years after a poor vintage, even though these are not wines that will improve with more than a year or two's cellaring after the champagne has been disgorged and released.

What is clear is the unsurprising fact that the finer the initial champagne, the longer it will last. Most NV *grande marque* champagnes bearing famous names will last if well-kept in cool dark conditions for up to four years after disgorgement (Moët & Chandon officially sanction their NV champagne for two years after purchase, their vintage wines for five). Champagnes that repay ageing considerably longer than this are Bollinger, Alfred Gratien, Roederer and those from the houses that deliberatly suppress the softening malolactic fermentation such as Lanson, Piper-Heidsieck, Salon and Krug.

The safest way to enjoy really mature champagne is to buy old vintages that have only recently been disgorged. Bollinger RD (the RD being their trade-mark and standing for *récemment dégorgé* or recently disgorged) is the most famous.

Some connoisseurs actually like their champagne to be not just mature but old: deep gold, hardly fizzing, and with more than a hint of oxidation. This stage that supposedly satisfies the *goût anglais* is charted as decline on the charts overleaf. Roederer Cristal has been chosen because, with Dom Pérignon, it represents the pinnacle of champagne's ability to age, and it is made in even more vintages.

The Cristal maturity curves should represent fairly accurately the ageing pattern of Dom Pérignon as well as all of Krug and Salon's wines. For other de luxe cuvées, which are so easily identifiable by their horrifying price, advance the Cristal chart by one year and for "ordinary" vintage champagnes accelerate the chart by three years.

Roederer Cristal

While the champagne houses spend thousands of francs on PR denying the importance of vintage variation, they are all happy to sell a vintage-dated product at a premium price. Most houses release a vintage champagne only every two years or so, which would result in a somewhat incomplete chart.

The champagne that manages to combine seriousness of purpose with frequency of appearance is Louis Roederer's de luxe vintage dated *cuvée* Cristal. To prove the Champenois' point that it is possible to find top quality champagne in even the least starry vintage, some of Cristal's most successful wines in recent years have been the 1974 and 1977.

The house of Louis Roederer in Reims is one of Champagne's surprisingly small élite. It owes much of its *réclame* to the unparalleled extent to which it controls its own production: Roederer own more than 450 acres (180 hectares) of well-distributed top vineyard land which supplies an enviable 70 per cent of their needs. Most of this land is rated 100 per cent on Champagne's official vineyard scale. Roederer can therefore use for Cristal 100 per cent grapes they have grown and, more importantly, vinified themselves: a rare luxury conferring several advantages. Although they practise rigorous selection at the press-house, Roederer have found, for example, that because of superior training and attention, the grapes from their own vineyards average a good one per cent higher sugar levels than their bought-in counterparts.

Cristal is perhaps the most recognisable of all luxury *cuvées* with its clear glass bottle, burnished gold livery, gold cellophane wrapping and no punt. This fancy packaging is a historical hangover from the days when Roederer Cristal, then a sweet wine, was made to order for Tsar Alexander II under the supervision of his personal cellarmaster.

Since 1917 Cristal has evolved into a sophisticated dry wine, clearly put together in the hope that the wine will be kept for a decade or even two before being drunk.

The house style of Roederer as evinced in their Brut Vintage and, to a lesser extent, in the non vintage Brut Premier, is fairly full and clearly Pinot-dominated. It is made of up to 60 per cent Pinot Noir and the balance is Chardonnay. But Cristal displays much more elegance as well as the solid structure needed for long ageing. This doubtless owes something to the influence of Roederer's unrivalled stocks of older Reserve wines: the house has 700,000 litres which are kept, unusually, in old oak *foudres*.

Despite its quality, Cristal is not of minority interest. It can easily represent 25 per cent or more of the house's annual output, and in years such as 1985 its managing director the energetic Jean-Claude Rouzaud has wished out loud that it could represent 100 per cent.

The 1985-based Brut Premier, which was sold throughout 1988, is certainly worth seeking out; the Cristal 1985 will not be sold before 1991.

Earlier vintages

1974 Some bottles are just starting to show signs of *goût anglais* age but others are simply miracles of maturity. At the peak of its undoubted powers. Such bottles of older vintages as still exist are likely to please only the strange palates of the English. All the wines below had remarkably similar colours and, a Cristal trademark, exceptionally small, persistent bubbles.

1975 A deep flavoured wine which still seemed to have an exciting future – even in 1989. Deep gold with an evolved savoury, biscuity bouquet, enormous impact and noticeably more acid than the 1976. Hazelnuts and extraordinary fruit even at 14 years. Very long and substantial.

Weather and timing
Excellent vintage, below average crop. Mild winter followed by cold start to spring. Good summer. July and Sept storms damaged and rotten grapes removed before harvest.

Quantity produced
Exact production figures for Cristal are not released. Production for the Champagne region 14,050,000 cases.

1976 A flattering wine that is heavily perfumed, creamy, luscious and smooth. Open, slightly candied notes with a particularly lively mousse. Just an edge of decay nudging into an attractive palette of flavours.

Weather and timing
Excellent vintage, average crop. Ideal June. Hot June-Aug. Earliest harvest this century.

Quantity produced
Champagne: 16,960,000 cases.

1977 Still very pale gold. Lean, steely and somehow Chablis-like in build (as opposed to the more Meursault-like character of

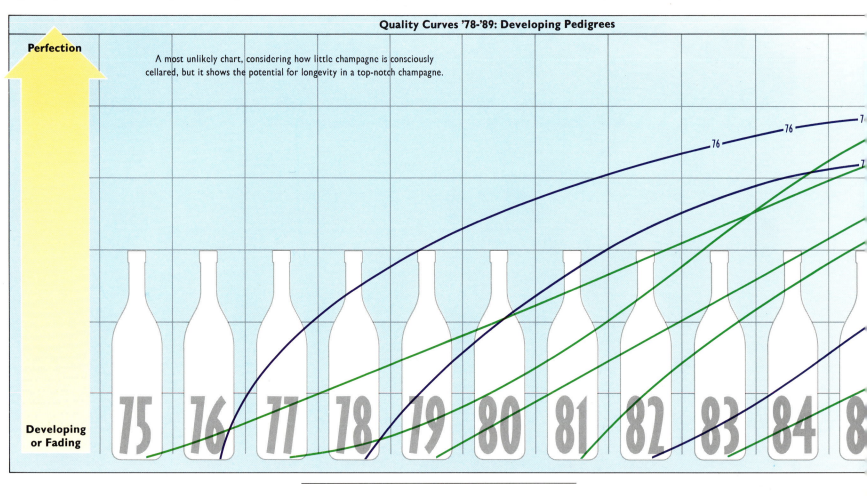

Quality Curves '78-'89: Developing Pedigrees

Perfection

A most unlikely chart, considering how little champagne is consciously cellared, but it shows the potential for longevity in a top-notch champagne.

Developing or Fading

75 76 77 78 79 80 81 82 83 84 8

the 1976) which suits this particular wine well. Hazelnuts and a range of high-toned aromas give way to exceptional balance and great constancy on the palate. Long, dancing flavours go on and on, as this wine will. Roederer see it as similar to the 1974.

Weather and timing
Average vintage, normal crop. Spring frosts. Damp summer; mildew and grey rot. Hot, dry Sept.

Quantity produced
Champagne: 15,560,000 cases.

1978 One of the least pleasurable wines to taste in 1989, and one of the fastest-maturing Cristals. Definite gold, the wine looks one of the the most mature and has some of the vegetal notes of early oxidation. Jean-Claude Rouzaud admits this wine could have been released earlier. There is now a slight syrupiness on the palate which is relatively loose textured.

Weather and timing
Good vintage, very small crop. Poor June; late, irregular flowering. Dry, warm summer.

Quantity produced
Champagne: 6,610,000 cases.

1979 A full-bodied, substantial wine for current drinking, this is a good typical Cristal with aristocratic concentration, deeper and fuller than the 1981 and somewhat masculine and steely. Just a note of biscuity maturity.

Weather and timing
Good vintage, above average crop. Good spring. Fine throughout summer. Good maturation and harvest.

Quantity produced
Champagne: 19,050,000 cases.

1980 No Cristal was made in this ill-fated vintage.

Weather and timing
Poor vintage, small crop. Cold, wet June-July; incomplete flowering. *Millerandage*. Unexceptional summer. Excellent Sept induced full maturity.

Quantity produced
Champagne: 9,430,000 cases.

1981 This wine, slightly paler than 1982, should be drunk well before the later vintage for it is much lighter and less forceful. It has some attractive nuttiness and a good full-blown, fairly evolved bouquet, but no weight on the palate to make it a long-term prospect. Very positive finish.

Weather and timing
Very good vintage, small crop. Frost end of Apr. Hail in May. Cold for flowering early July. Hot Aug. Wet Sept; derogation obtained in order to start picking before the official harvest date of Sept 28. Excellent acid/sugar balance.

Quantity produced
Champagne: 7,690,000 cases.

1982 A wonderful, if embryonic, wine packed with flavour and substance. Very powerful and already showing its full, toasty nose. Lots of refreshing acid and some aromatic bloom but it is clear that this is a very backward wine into which the elements have been packed in excellent balance . . . but for our delectation at some future date. In 1989 it still had marked acidity and an almost abrasive finish.

Weather and timing
Excellent vintage, large crop. Almost perfect season. Frost-free winter and spring. Long, warm summer. Excellent for harvest.

Quantity produced
Champagne: 24,600,000 cases.

1983 More classic, masculine and angular than the 1982. Fresh notes of apple complemented by smoke and violets followed by an almost prancingly youthful mouthful of fruit with lovely stern acidity. Finely textured with substantial build and a note of youthful astringence on the finish.

Weather and timing
Very good vintage, average crop. Excellent season. Sunny, warm summer followed by wet, cool Sept. Fine Oct.

Quantity produced
Champagne: 25,170,000 cases.

Other details
Decision to increase to 350 lb/160 kg (from 330 lb/150 kg) the amount of grapes required during pressing to produce one hectolitre (175 US gals) of must.

1984 No Cristal made in this small, mean harvest.

Weather and timing
Poor vintage, small crop. Late flowering followed by indifferent summer. Cold, wet Sept which encouraged some rot. Late harvest began Oct 8.

Quantity produced
Champagne: 16,580,000 cases.

1985 Not tasted but said to be exceptional. No malolactic fermentation.

Weather and timing
Very good vintage, small crop. Harsh winter. Severe spring frosts killed many vines. Wet, dull early summer. Perfect Sept and Oct; grapes ripened well. Healthy harvest.

Quantity produced
Champagne: 12,650,000 cases.

1986 No Cristal made.

Weather and timing
Very good vintage, large crop. Poor spring. From June 10 hot and sunny; good flowering late June. Good summer. Heavy rain late Aug and early Sept. Fine for harvest.

Quantity produced
Champagne: 21,660,000 cases.

Prospects
1987 Unlikely to be a vintage. Large crop. Good flowering. Very rainy season saved by Indian summer. **1988** First indications are of a good quality harvest. Above average crop. Early flowering.

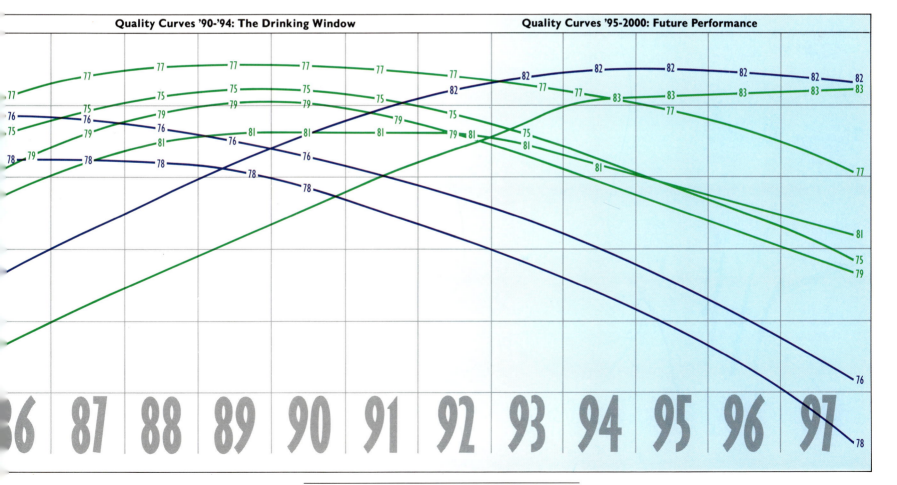

Quality Curves '90-'94: The Drinking Window **Quality Curves '95-2000: Future Performance**

ALSACE, LOIRE & RHÔNE

The Rosacker *Grand Cru* vineyard above Hunawihr in Alsace
– provenance of Trimbach's Clos Ste-Hune (page 80), a white wine
so concentrated it demands many years in bottle.

ALSACE

Few Alsace wines last longer than Trimbach's Clos Ste-Hune, but a wide variety of them last almost as long. Most producers' top-of-the-range Rieslings, such as those from *Grand Cru* vineyards or equivalent and those labelled (often irritatingly discreetly) *Cuvée Particulière* or *Réserve Personnelle*, will follow similar curves of evolution to the Clos Ste-Hune. But the majority slope upwards towards drinkability rather faster than this particularly steely, reserved bottling from Trimbach, whose wines tend to be anachronistic slowcoaches. Trimbach's own Riesling Cuvée Frédéric Emile, made from several different vineyards' produce, is perhaps more like the average top quality Alsace Riesling. For this wine and most top Reislings, accelerate the Close Ste-Hune Timechart by a year.

Gewürztraminers and Tokays tend to mature respectively two and one years faster than equivalent quality Rieslings, so project forward accordingly on the Clos Ste-Hune chart. The vintages of single vineyard, Reserve and *Réserve Personnelle* Gewürztraminer to broach in 1990, for example, will be those specified for Clos Ste-Hune in 1993, and of top quality dry Tokay, those vintages of Clos Ste-Hune suggested for consumption in 1992. But note the exceptions of the 1985 vintage, in which the Riesling was markedly less successful than the other two

noble *cépages* of Alsace, and 1982, and 1984 and 1986 when the reverse was generally the case.

The rich, rare, late-picked wonders which achieve *Vendange Tardive* and *Séléction de Grains Nobles* ripeness levels on the other hand are exceptions which usually have the ballast of considerable residual sugar and can take even longer to develop than Clos Ste-Hune. Most of the 1976s reached their prime in the second half of the eighties. The 1983s should provide gloriously indulgent drinking between 1993 and the end of the century. Few of the 1985s quite matched their 1983 equivalents, but some may well have more staying power.

For other more basic Alsace wines, combine Chart B on page 19 with the Clos Ste-Hune Timechart on page 80/1.

LOIRE

The Vouvray chart on page 82/3 provides a good, if representatively varied, picture of the fortunes of serious Chenin-based wines made in the favoured middle stretch of the Loire Valley since 1977.

Names such as, working east across the Anjou-Touraine from the mouth of the river, Quarts de Chaume, Savennières, Coteaux du Layon, Bonnezeaux, Touraine Azay-le-Rideau, Vouvray and Montlouis are hardly internationally famous but they are a largely untapped source of top quality

The Vosges mountains to the west of the cosseted vineyards of Alsace help concentrate the wines. They shelter the vineyards immediately in their lee from the moisture in clouds like these. Long, dry summers result in powerful yet ageable wines.

white wine, many of the best labelled as sweet (*Moelleux*) or medium dry (*Demi Sec*) but with quite enough acidity to make them appetizing aperitifs and partners for a wide range of savoury foods. The appellations listed above are all consistently worthy of space in the serious collector's cellar, though lesser quality Coteaux du Layon and Vouvray can be found. Price is a good, if not infallible, indicator of quality and potential here.

In general terms, most *sérieux* white wines made from the Chenin Blanc or Pineau de la Loire will follow the curves outlined on the Vouvray chart, but 1986 was a notably better year for *Botrytis* in the Anjou-Saumur sweet white appellations of Quarts de Chaumes, Coteaux de Layon and Bonnezeaux than in the Touraine appellations of Azay-le-Rideau, Vouvray and Moutlouis.

The wines of Savennières, flowery but dry and piercingly, uncompromisingly, tart in youth, need a decade or two to start to unfurl and can continue to soften for three or four decades, thanks to the acidity inherent in the Loire's best Chenin. The quality indications given above for Anjou-Saumur apply to Savennières, and to those pockets of top quality whites with Anjou or Saumur appellations. For Jasnières, take Vouvray as a guide. For other (non-Chenin) Loire wines, see pages 88–90.

NORTH RHONE

In the northern Rhône Valley, where so much of the wine produced is of good to great quality, there can be perceptible differences in vintage performance between appellations. The charts for Guigal's Côte Rôtie and Jaboulet's Hermitage La Chapelle on pages 84–87 perhaps justify themselves on the basis of the differing performances in 1985 alone, a vintage so much more successful for the Côte Rôtie vineyards on the west bank than for those of Hermitage to the south and east.

Jaboulet dominates the hill of Hermitage above Tain in the northern half of what the wine collector knows and treasures as the Rhône Valley.

To gauge the maturity of most Côte Rôtie, the chart can be taken as a fairly accurate guide, with the proviso that no other producer's wines take longer to mature than Guigal's, and the Côte Rôties of the likes of de Vallouit, Delas and less successful vintages of Jaboulet mature two to three years earlier.

Hermitage La Chapelle charted on page 86/7 also shows how the longest-lasting Hermitages such as those from Chave and the top *Cuvées* of Chapoutier and Delas develop. Run-of-the-mill generic Hermitage matures three to five years ahead and most Crozes-Hermitage is ready for drinking within three years of the vintage. The major exception is Paul Jaboulet Aîné's superior *cuvée* of Crozes-Hermitage, Domaine de Thalabert, which reaches its peak only about four years before the great Hermitage La Chapelle (although the peak is rather lower).

The super-concentrated wines of Cornas demand time, are well priced and could prove to be any cellar's best investments, reaching drinkability only a year or two ahead of Hermitage La Chapelle. Qualitatively they follow the Hermitage pattern but with 1985 being more successful in Cornas.

The most difficult appellation to prescribe is St Joseph which stretches all the way down the west bank from Côte Rôtie to Cornas. In general terms, this one follows the quality and maturity patterns of a superior Crozes-Hermitage.

Finally, a note on the white wines. In all but a handful of cases, these should be drunk young, and the cheaper the wine the younger it should be drunk. The best Condrieus provide relatively rare examples of wines that are both serious and early-maturing. There are very few white wines from St Joseph, Crozes-Hermitage or even Hermitage – with the exception of those produced by Chave and Chapoutier – which can afford the loss of freshness that is inevitable after three or four years in bottle. A bottle of middle-aged Château Grillet may well be a collector's treasure, but no wine drinker should feel any qualms about drinking North Rhône whites, particularly the often overweight St Péray, as young as possible.

SOUTH RHONE

The southern Rhône vineyards are rather more homogeneous in terms of their vintage variation, such is the calming influence of the Mediterranean. The chart of any Châteauneuf-du-Pape would look similar to that of Château de Beaucastel except that it would be compressed into a much shorter timescale and achieve less ambitious peaks of quality. Only Château Rayas consistently makes such slow-maturing wines as Beaucastel (and this applies to the Côtes-du-Rhône produced at the two estates Château de

While the soil of Hermitage is forever slipping down the steep hillside, it would take more than the local *mistral* to shift the rocks of Châteauneuf-du-Pape. These reflectors put the southern Rhône sunshine in the grapes and, subsequently, in bottle.

Fonsalette and Cru de Coudoulet respectively). Most of the rest mature between three and five years ahead, price being a good indicator of potential longevity. Generic Châteauneuf-du-Pape bottled by a merchant rather than at the domaine can be drunk three years after the vintage, like most red Lirac.

Most Côtes-du-Rhône matures even more rapidly and it is significant that much of it today is made *à la beaujolaise* to be drunk at two years, the average Côtes-du-Rhône-Villages being at its peak at three. Individual village wines such as Vacqueyras, Cairanne and, especially, Rasteau, can be made of

much sterner stuff. They can improve for up to four years, while most Gigondas is as concentrated as all but the finest Châteauneuf and is only about three years ahead of Château de Beaucastel, although its lower tannins will make it more approachable in youth. The 1984 vintage was discernibly more successful in Châteauneuf than in any surrounding appellations.

The plentiful whites and dry rosés of the southern Rhône are definitely for early drinking. Only the white Château de Beaucastel, outlined in some detail on page 88/9, is worthy of cellar space.

Riesling Clos Ste-Hune, Trimbach

If Gewürztraminer is the most popular and easily appreciated face of Alsace, the top Rieslings are the wines of which the producers themselves are most proud. They show sublimely, and extremely slowly, the savoury, steely purity of this grape variety rather than its more perfumed, honeyed, floral aspects. And few would argue with the proposition that Trimbach's Clos Ste-Hune represents what can be achieved with the Riesling grape in the world's most under-appreciated wine region.

Every few years, such as in 1988, 1985, 1983 and 1976, nature gives the quality-minded producers a chance to show what they can do with ultra-ripe grapes in the way of the special late harvest wines sold as *Vendange Tardive* or, even sweeter, *Séléction de Grains Nobles*. These wines can be wonderful, but would have provided a sparse and rather simple chart. Trimbach's strength is at the other end of the sweetness scale, in producing year in and year out steely, stately, dry wines in the traditional Alsace style even from humble grape varieties such as Sylvaner, but most gloriously from their top Riesling vines. These minimally treated wines are difficult to appreciate when young, so harsh can the malic acidity seem. And the fact that Trimbach is the most prominent Alsace house in the US has done nothing to enhance their top wine's reputation there.

Trimbach's second most respected Riesling is their Cuvée Frédéric Emile, named after a prominent nineteenth century forefather (the Trimbachs have reached their twelfth wine-making generation in Bernard's sons Pierre and Jean). Cuvée Frédéric Emile comes from a vineyard by the winery in Ribeauvillé and takes perhaps 10 years to reach the stage at which it can be drunk with confidence.

The Riesling from Trimbach's three-acre (1.25-hectare) Clos Ste-Hune plot in the Alsace *Grand Cru* vineyard of Rosacker is an even greater wine than Cuvée Frédéric Emile, however. The vines, now well into their thirties, face south-southeast above the village of Hunawihr. The soil is heavier, deeper and less stony than that of the Frédéric Emile vineyard and can boast an even more varied mineral base. This gives the wines even more intensity and finesse, even if it can take 12 to 15 years for this to become apparent. (The pH levels in Riesling musts such as Trimbach's help to explain how these wines retain their youthful hue and acidity well into their third decade: 2.8 to 3.2, while the pH of Alsace Gewürztraminer is more likely to be around 3.5 or 3.6.)

Yields in Alsace have traditionally been high relative to those in the rest of France but Clos Ste-Hune's meagre area has been stretched to yield 8,000 bottles in an average year. And this average is likely to drop as Trimbach consolidate their policy of summer pruning, begun in 1984. They claim that by trimming off about a third of the potential Riesling crop in late July or early August, the eventual alcohol level can be increased by a whole degree.

Earlier vintages

Like the equally austere Riesling Kabinetts of Dr Prüm across the German border, these are extremely long-lived wines which show a remarkable consistency. There is no hurry to drink any wines from the seventies. The 1971, a classic vintage, seemed to have achieved a lean, creamy, powerful state of perfection, if slightly ascetic, by 1988. The 1967 Clos Ste-Hune Vendange Tardive is at the peak of its powerful form.

1975 A near-perfect example of Riesling qualities: intensity of aroma, delicacy, structure and elegance. A particularly smoky, pungent specimen with strong vegetal notes and a well-developed bouquet. Evolved.

Weather and timing

Classic vintage, average crop. Fine, humid spring. Heavy and warm for flowering and good summer. Normal Sept: good maturation. Harvest Oct 23.

Quantity produced

800 cases. Alsace production: 8,800,000 cases.

1976 Majestic. Deep green/gold at first sniff; very meatily evolved, but an almost painfully high level of underlying acidity suggests this wine will go on and on. There is enormous richness and extract even though it is a dry wine. Like an essence, with a wonderfully long finish.

Weather and timing

Outstanding vintage, small crop. Snow in Jan. Hot, dry for flowering June 6-15. Showers in July and early Oct. Fine, warm harvest Oct 7.

Quantity produced

700 cases. Alsace: 9,800,000 cases.

1977 Austere, but it recalls the 1977 Wehlenuhr Sonnenuhr Kabinett in its admirable structure. Powerful evolved mature nose with kerosene elements.

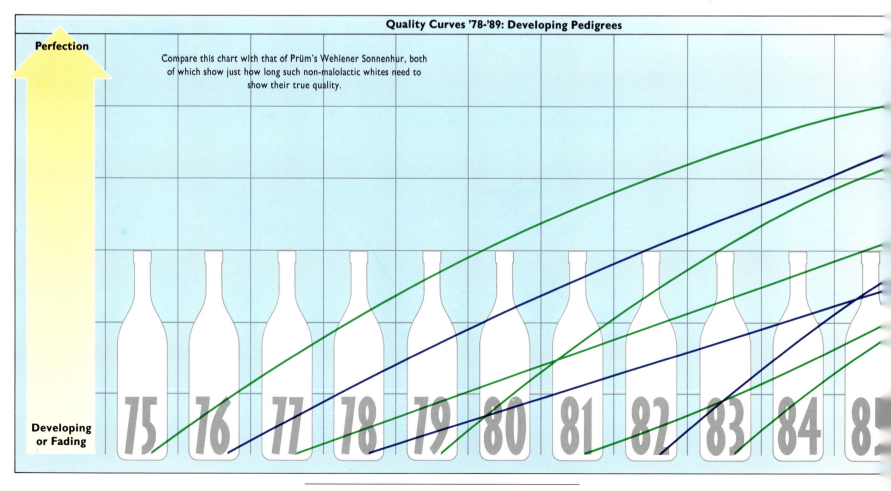

Quality Curves '78-'89: Developing Pedigrees

Perfection

Compare this chart with that of Prüm's Wehlener Sonnenhur, both of which show just how long such non-malolactic whites need to show their true quality.

Developing or Fading

75 76 77 78 79 80 81 82 83 84 85

Savoury and steely. Lean and perhaps more admirable than pleasurable.

Weather and timing
Poor vintage, large crop. Mediocre spring; late bud break. Harvest late Oct.

Quantity produced
800 cases. Alsace: 10,600,000.

1978 The wine with the highest acid (5.3 gm/lit) and the driest apart from the 1977. The dryness seems to dim Riesling's customary perfume. The wine shows meticulous wine making but is still hard work, demanding food to mitigate its rigorous structure. Time should soften it.

Weather and timing
Fair vintage, below average crop. Normal spring. Cold June lengthened flowering: incomplete set. Fine summer. Main harvest late Oct, completed Nov 20-22.

Quantity produced
750 cases. Alsace: 7,690,000 cases.

1979 Remarkably advanced for Trimbach Riesling (like the 1979 Prüm wine). Green/gold with a high level of glycerol. Smoky nose but unpleasantly reminiscent of slightly rotting cabbage. Very dry and lean with lots of texture, but quite approachable already.

Weather and timing
Very good vintage, large crop. Cold spring then warm for flowering. Early July cool. Warm, stormy Aug. Harvest Oct 30 and Nov 27.

Quantity produced
900 cases. Alsace: 11,900,000.

1980 None made.

Weather and timing
Average vintage, small crop. Poor flowering. Good Sept and fine for harvest.

Quantity produced
Alsace: 6,660,000 cases.

Other details
Planted 24 acres/10 ha of vines.

1981 A particularly interesting, elegant wine. Deep straw colour with a penetrating bouquet: aromas of kerosene, mature Riesling, grapefruit and spice. A certain oiliness of texture but the wine is in no way fat. Piercingly high acidity and still very young.

Weather and timing
Very good vintage, above average crop. Humid May. Good for flowering. Dry summer. Humid for harvest Oct 2-22.

Quantity produced
800 cases. Alsace: 10,040,000 cases.

Other details
New fermenting room: temperature-controlled, stainless steel vats.

1982 One of the more flowery, Germanic versions of this Alsace Riesling. Relatively forward with some honeyed characteristics but a slightly narrower, duller flavour profile.

Weather and timing
Very good vintage, enormous crop. Foggy, cold Jan then mainly fine. Warm Sept. Harvest Oct 7 to Nov 4; selective picking to maximise quality.

Quantity produced
1,000 cases. Alsace: 15,450,000 cases.

1983 The most alcoholic at 13.1%. Exuberantly powerful on the nose with a lovely range of floral perfumes and luscious notes of ripe fruit. It would be easy to drink this rich dry wine as soon as it is launched in 1989 although it is clearly a heavyweight that will provide intellectual sustenance as it develops over the next two decades.

Weather and timing
Exceptional vintage, large crop. Mild, wet winter. Rained all May. Late June warm and dry for flowering. Dry July-Aug. Harvest Oct 6-27 and Nov 21-24.

Quantity produced
850 cases. Alsace: 10,970,000 cases.

1984 None made.

Weather and timing
Good vintage, average crop. Warm, early spring. Cold for flowering: incomplete set. Dull summer and autumn. Selective picking to avoid rot.

Quantity produced
Alsace: 8,970,000 cases.

1985 The residual sweetness of this wine, nearly 5 gm/lit, is perceptible and would make the wine approachable earlier were it not for its extraordinarily high acidity. Very pungent, smoky and high-toned. Full and neat but tightly packed with flavour. Great extract and balance and rigorously fermented fruit that was clearly gloriously healthy. More straightforward than the 1983.

Weather and timing
Excellent vintage, above average

crop. Severe frosts. Late Apr cold and wet. Good flowering then fine and dry to Oct. Harvest Oct 7-24 (end of Nov cold with snow) and Nov 28 and Dec 2-5.

Quantity produced
900 cases. Alsace: 9,950,000 cases.

Other details
New bottle cellar.

1986 Piercing young steely Riesling aroma. The most floral, with the scent of elderflowers. Extremely high acid and the steeliness of a wine that knows not the softening process of "le malo". Very positive with a real beginning, middle and end already.

Weather and timing
Very good vintage, large crop. Cold, snowy Feb. Excellent for flowering. Hailstorm July 23 damaged crop. Harvest Oct 20-31, Nov 3-6.

Quantity produced
Not yet determined. Alsace: 13,280,000 cases.

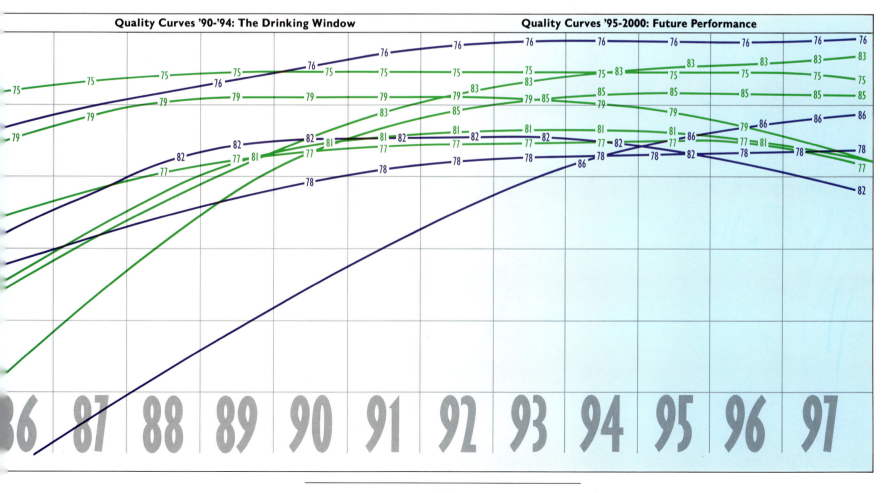

Quality Curves '90-'94: The Drinking Window   **Quality Curves '95-2000: Future Performance**

86 87 88 89 90 91 92 93 94 95 96 97

Vouvray, Prince Poniatowski

The inclusion of this wine may surprise many well-versed wine enthusiasts. The existence of top quality, ageworthy white wines made from Chenin Blanc vines grown in the middle Anjou-Touraine stretch of the Loire Valley is a secret appreciated by only a small fraction of the world's wine collectors.

Yet, arguably more than any other white wine, these bottles should be destined for the least accessible corner of wine cellar. This is particularly true of the coolest, most easterly twin appellations of Vouvray and Montlouis (the Sancerre and Pouilly-Fumé of the Touraine). Here wines are often so high in acidity in youth that they demand at least a decade in bottle before they even begin to be broachable. But when at last they are ready to be opened, there should be no great hurry as the acidity continues to preserve many vintages for a long plateau of perfection, as illustrated on the chart.

The Chenin Blanc grape from which they are exclusively produced is naturally high in acidity, particularly when grown here at the northwestern limit of vine cultivation. Even grapes picked late into November have acidity levels that some Californians would kill for.

In most other wine regions whites from even the tartest vintage are softened by the second, malolactic fermentation, and the wine is matured before bottling by many months in cask. But in the Loire both malolactic fermentation and extended barrel maturation are avoided.

As with vintage port, the moment of bottling (in March or April following the vintage in this case) is the start of the wines' long maturation process. They are *meant* to develop slowly, taking on extra nuances of honey, quince and hazelnuts as the acidity almost imperceptibly softens. In particularly cool years such as 1972, 1974, 1979 and 1984, the wines manage very little residual sugar. They are in effect dry or *Sec* – but they need even longer than the sweeter *Demi Sec* and *Moelleux* (literally "full of marrow") wines before they give pleasure, like their German counterparts.

Vouvray's handful of quality-conscious producers include Gaston Huet, Foreau, Marc Brédif, Daniel Allias and Prince Poniatowski, who bottles the wine produced on the 12-acre (five-hectare) vineyard, Clos Baudoin, separately whenever the vintage warrants it. The rest of his still wine, from his additional 42 acres (17 hectares) of vines, is bottled as Aigle Blanc, although the produce of grapes which fail to reach sufficient ripeness for a still *Sec* is made into the Aigle d'Or *méthode champenoise* sparkling Vouvray, another wine with unexpected longevity. In 1977 for instance, he produced nothing but Aigle d'Or whereas in 1976 not a single bottle of it was produced. Unusually, Poniatowski chooses not to label his wines *Sec*, *Demi Sec* or *Moelleux* on the basis that these labels are subjective and the impression made by wines changes with each year in bottle. Prince Poniatowski practises minimal chemical treatments in both vineyard and cellar.

Earlier vintages

This century's great vintage for sweet Loire whites was **1947**, followed by **1976** for which *Moelleux* wines, with strong *Botrytis* influence, are just starting to come into their own but will continue to develop for many decades. Other great sweet wine vintages were **1959**, **1929**, **1921**, **1964** and **1970** for slightly less ripe grapes. **1945**, **1955** and **1969** produced particularly good drier wines but any older vintage of *sérieux* mid-Loire white is worth trying: it should be underpriced.

1978 Aigle d'Or (disgorged 1980). Deep green/gold with fine, lively mousse. Meaty nose reminiscent of gingerbread. Full-bodied, much more vinous than champagne and certainly more youthful than most 1978 champagnes would be, with a suggestion of almonds in the aftertaste.

Weather and timing

Average vintage, small crop. Good start to the season. Rain disrupted flowering. Harvest Oct 10 to Nov 10.

Quantity produced

4,900 cases. AOC Vouvray production: 627,860 cases.

1979 Clos Baudoin. An exceptional, experimental wine bottled as late as September to prove why Vouvray should be bottled in spring. Deep orange gold (almost the same colour as a 1955 tasted alongside). Much broader, more evolved bouquet than normal with the customary acidity but without fruit concentration to hold it together. Slightly bitter.

Weather and timing

Good vintage, normal crop. Good season with rain in spring and during harvest. High acidity.

Quantity produced

5,340 cases. Vouvray: 987,789 cases.

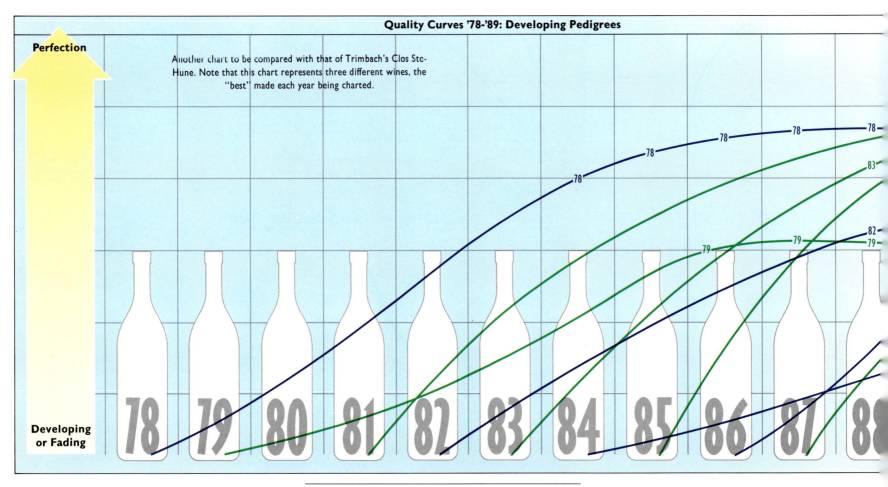

Quality Curves '78-'89: Developing Pedigrees

Perfection

Another chart to be compared with that of Trimbach's Clos Ste-Hune. Note that this chart represents three different wines, the "best" made each year being charted.

Developing or Fading

78 79 80 81 82 83 84 85 86 87 88

Other details

Good year for the *méthode champenoise*.

1980 Stocks non-existent.

Weather and timing

Unexceptional vintage, below average crop. Snow during harvest Oct 10 to Nov 11.

Quantity produced

5,155 cases. Vouvray: 769,178 cases.

1981 Aigle Blanc (*Sec*).

Undeveloped nose with still youthful floral notes together with a slight suggestion of cordite. Great palate impact because of the concentrated fruit flavours. Only just entering its honeyed phase. Very, very youthful.

Weather and timing

Good vintage, very small crop. Frost on Apr 4 burnt the buds. Dry during harvest.

Quantity produced

3,200 cases. Vouvray: 467,045 cases.

1982 Aigle Blanc (*Sec*).

Deep gold. Light floral scent. Taut, not to say tight, and skinny. To be attempted only with food. Relatively light-bodied. The opposite of flattering.

Weather and timing

Good vintage, large crop. Could have been an outstanding year if it hadn't been for bad weather during harvest.

Quantity produced

9,340 cases. Vouvray: 1,243,578 cases.

Other details

First crop from the 45 acres/18 ha planted in 1970. Began to establish a reserve.

1983 Clos Baudoin (*Demi Sec*). Deep green/gold. Jewel bright aroma with hints of minerals somewhat like the 1986. More apparent acidity than the 1985 but very powerful, rich and long. Has the potential to develop beautifully and should be given time.

Weather and timing

Good vintage, large crop. Very wet year. Poor first half of season. Excellent Sept and Oct. Dry harvest. Higher acidity levels than 1982.

Quantity produced

10,050 cases. Vouvray: 1,301,678 cases.

Other details

Increasing proportion of the wine exported, mainly to USA, England and Germany.

1984 Clos Baudoin (*Sec*).

Green/gold. Pretty, low-key nose with perceptible Chenin fruit. Very dry with pronounced acid. Quite coarse textured and for very long ageing.

Weather and timing

Poor vintage, below average crop. Wet start to season then dry until Sept. Rain during harvest. High acidity levels.

Quantity produced

9,300 cases. Vouvray: 898,223.

Other details

Large reserves due to high acidity levels; needs long ageing.

1985 Clos Baudoin (*Sec*). A greenish gold as intense as the aroma. More quince than honey and flowers but definitely fruity with mineral overtones. Very noticeable acidity at this stage, relatively lean, loping and powerful. "More typically Vouvray than 1986 or 1987" says the Prince. "Lots of people like it now but they shouldn't."

Weather and timing

Great vintage, large crop. Rain in early spring. Dry from June until after harvest. Good acid/sugar balance: too rich for sparkling wine.

Quantity produced

10,150 cases. Vouvray: 1,196,645 cases.

1986 Clos Baudoin (*Sec*). Gold with green highlights. Very rich, mineral-flavoured nose with notably honeyed undertow. Real substance. Medium weight with a touch of almonds. Still very youthful. Slight astringence on the finish.

Weather and timing

Good vintage, average crop. Wet start to season. Rain at end of harvest.

Quantity produced

9,100 cases. Vouvray: 1,026,489 cases.

Other details

New pneumatic press installed, replacing two old mechanical ones. Introduced Cuvée Abbé Baudoin as top selection of Aigle Blanc.

1987 Aigle Blanc (*Sec*). Lovely green/gold colour and extraordinarily clean and pure fruit flavours for a young Vouvray. Seductively pure and simple and, unusually, this one could easily be enjoyed in its youth. Delicate and slightly muted.

Weather and timing

Good vintage, above average crop. Difficult season. Wet early spring and during harvest.

Quantity produced

8,860 cases. Vouvray: 1,063,723 cases.

Other details

47% exported, mainly to USA, Europe and Japan.

1988 Clos Baudoin (*Sec*). "A good Sec year", according to Prince Poniatowski, with "great finesse and aroma". Probably better than 1985 and with very high alcohol level.

Weather and timing

Excellent vintage. Wet spring. Good for rest of season. Fine during harvest.

Quantity produced

7,400 cases. More than 50% exported.

Other details

New fermentation temperature-control system introduced.

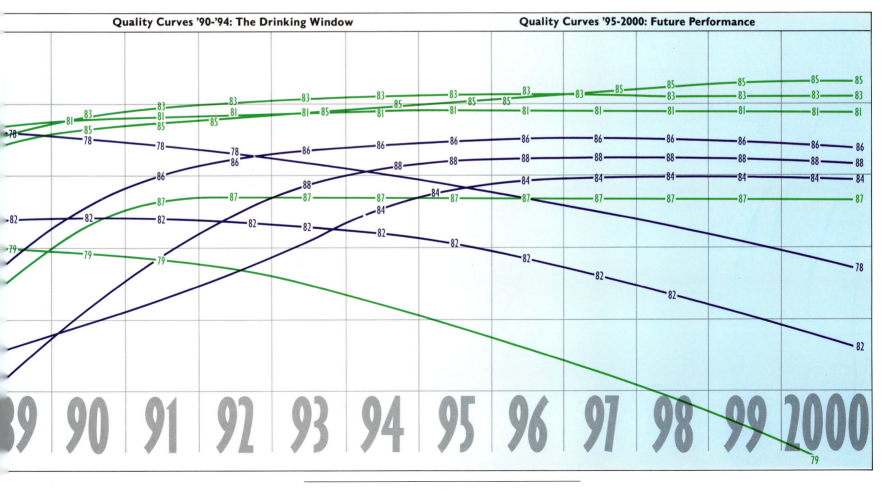

Côte Rôtie, Côtes Brune et Blonde, Guigal

Guigal's 1985 and 1983 single vineyard vintages may have attracted the rare distinction of perfect scores from Robert Parker, but any wine enthusiast whose interest in this north Rhône house was sparked by such an accolade would surely be disappointed by the face that Guigal presents to the passing tourist.

Top quality Côte Rôtie may for the moment have joined first growth Bordeaux and *grand cru* burgundy as one of the most sought-after red wines in the world, but its commercial capital, Ampuis, is an undistinguished village spurned by the Guide Michelin and all but ignored by the passing local traffic on the right bank of the Rhône. Guigal's headquarters, with its stocks of arguably the scarcest wines in France – unreleased vintages of La Mouline, La Landonne and La Turque – are signalled by an unprepossessing warehouse-like structure on a bend in the road.

Guigal's strong suit is quality in bottle rather than show business, history or aesthetics. The house was founded only in 1946 by Etienne Guigal. He had been in charge of the cellars and vineyards at the most ancient house in Ampuis, Vidal-Fleury, which dates back to 1781. Indeed Guigal still buys in wine from about 40 other *vignerons*. But before Etienne died in late 1988, handing over to his formidably astute son Marcel, he had the satisfaction of seeing his new enterprise take over his former employers' business. Over the next three years he oversaw the rationalisation of the two houses, a

process which was carefully designed to maximise their respective qualities rather than simply to effect the most expedient union.

Guigal's basic (although in this context the word seems inappropriately downbeat) Côte Rôtie is labelled Côtes Brune et Blonde, signify that it is made, like many of the finest Côte Rôties, from a blend of wines produced in the two major areas that go to make up the appellation. These are the long-living, firm wines of the clay-based Côte Brune and the lighter, more aromatically precocious wines of the Côte Blonde where limestone predominates.

Like their most famous single vineyard wines, named after La Mouline from the Côte Blonde and La Landonne and La Turque from the Côte Brune, Guigal's regular Côte Rotie is, unusually for this appellation, graced with time in new oak casks from Burgundian coopers. This is after whole bunches of grapes have been fermented in a closed vat for up to three weeks. Both fining and filtration are avoided if possible, the object being to produce extremely long-lived wines. The length of time they stay in *pièces*, or in the larger oval *foudres*, is controversial. It may be up to three years, but gives them an extra richness and concentration which means that even at this level Guigal's Côte Rôtie is worth waiting for longer than anyone else's.

Happily for the consumers, Guigal will not be hurried. His 1985s were just being shipped in late 1988.

Earlier vintages

Guigal's chief fan Robert Parker recommends in *The Wines of the Rhône Valley and Provence* La Mouline from 1976 and 1969 and regular Côte Rôtie from 1964 and 1961. Unfortunately for most of us, such recommendations are likely to be academic.

1978 Looks much older than the 1979 with some pale brick. On the nose this is a lighter, more evolved, open wine than the 1977. Notes of spearmint and cinnamon give way to easy current drinking with a spicy finish.

La Mouline. Luscious colour. Treacley rich nose, still youthfully concentrated with slightly floral top notes but essentially smoky roasted almost burnt flavours. Long, rich aftertaste too. Could be enjoyed in the nineties.

La Landonne. The debut year for this wine, the result of 10

years' careful piecemeal acquisition. Even more intensely tinted than La Mouline, this wine is a good decade behind it. The aromas are even more concentrated and piercing, closed rather than broad and supple. There is so much tannin that tasting is almost painful but the power of the fruit suggests that Marcel is probably right in recommending half a century for this wine.

Weather and timing

Great vintage, average crop. Very good year. Dry, hot summer. Early harvest.

Quantity produced

9,000 cases. Côte Rôtie production: 34,000 cases.

1979 Excellent depth of colour. Well-integrated bouquet of prunes and sandalwood. Great concentration and guts although still unyielding. Perhaps slightly too dry, but with lots of flavour for the future.

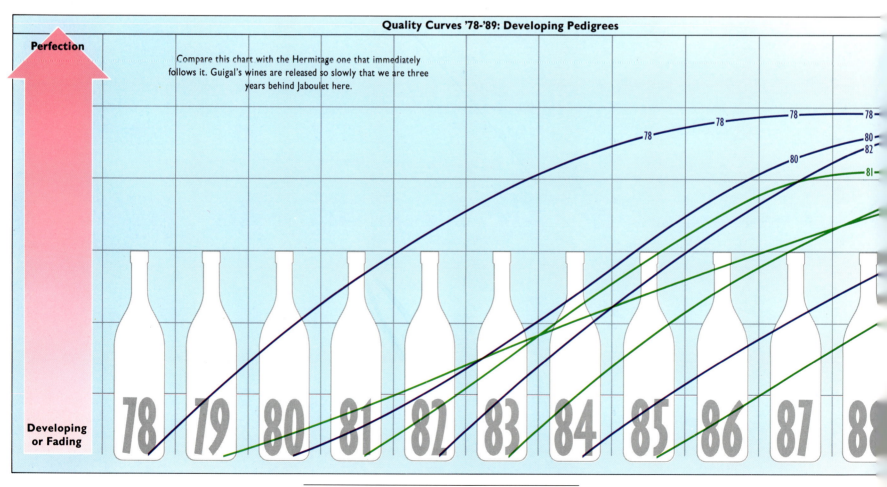

Quality Curves '78-'89: Developing Pedigrees

Perfection

Compare this chart with the Hermitage one that immediately follows it. Guigal's wines are released so slowly that we are three years behind Jaboulet here.

Developing or Fading

78 79 80 81 82 83 84 85 86 87 88

Weather and timing

Good vintage, large crop. Mild spring. Good, quick flowering. Cool until July then hot and dry through to harvest; good maturation. Fine during harvest which began late Sept.

Quantity produced

12,000 cases. Côte Rôtie: 46,000 cases.

1980 Deep colour with autumnal tints at the rim. Prunes, spice, ripe fruits and some herbiness on the nose. Flattering in its mouthfilling, voluptuous fruit flavours; tannins noticeable only at the end. Approachable.

Weather and timing

Very good vintage, small crop. Cold, wet spring delayed flowering. Incomplete set. Fine from mid-July through to harvest. Harvest affected by *le Mistral*.

Quantity produced

10,000 cases. Côte Rôtie: 38,000 cases.

1981 Very deep with some blue shades still evident at seven years. Relatively light, evolved bouquet of autumn leaves and herbs. One of the less opulently structured wines with a dry finish and some tannin still in evidence.

La Mouline. Gorgeous layer of extra riches, spices, perfumes, and smoke. Full-bodied throat-warmer. Powerfully spicy. Rich.

Weather and timing

Fair vintage, large crop. Warm spring but then cool and wet. Late harvest disrupted by rain.

Quantity produced

9,000 cases. Côte Rôtie: 47,000.

Other details

Increasing international demand for long-lasting Rhône wines. Favourable export market due to weak French franc.

1982 Crimson with lots of youthful blue. Very warm, well-integrated bouquet but without the concentration of the 1985.

Nuts, oak and a hint of tawny port. Ripe, flattering, not a blockbuster but an early developer.

Weather and timing

Excellent vintage, large crop. Dry season. Very hot June to Aug. Storms early Sept. Early harvest. Low acidity.

Quantity produced

12,000 cases. Côte Rôtie: 52,000 cases.

1983 Very deep shading to a crimson rim. Solid and sturdy with lots of tarry concentration suggestive of dry wood. Highly spiced fruit just starting to take over from the heavy oak influence. Tannins intrude only at the end. One to wait for.

Weather and timing

Excellent vintage, large crop. Early spring. Good flowering. Hot summer. Excellent weather during harvest.

Quantity produced

11,000 cases. Côte Rôtie: 53,000.

1984 Almost as deep in colour as the amazing 1985 but more acid and aromatic. Dry, almost dusty but without great fruit concentration. Relatively lightweight.

Weather and timing

Average vintage, small crop. Fair spring and summer. Late flowering. Rain in Aug and Sept. Cold during late harvest; fermentation vats needed heating.

Quantity produced

12,000 cases. Côte Rôtie: 39,000 cases. Average increase of 10% in Rhône wine prices.

1985 Black in the middle of the glass, thick prune colour at rim. Overpowering scent of young Syrah plus spice and texture. Full of black pepper; voluptuous, but on the palate the gorgeous satiny ripe fruit overlays a very high level of dry tannins. Very long and fruity.

Weather and timing

Excellent vintage, average crop.

Normal flowering. Dry, hot growing season. Heat continued into late harvest; fermentation vats had to be cooled.

Quantity produced

13,000 cases. 30% increase in Rhône wine prices.

Other details

Bought back Vidal-Fleury vineyard. First Côte Rôtie "La Turque" released.

1986 (Not tasted) Not the most luscious vintage: rains spoiled a promising harvest before it was picked but Guigal managed to make a well-structured, if for the moment uncharming, wine destined for the long term.

Weather and timing

Very good vintage, average crop. Average season but then rains at beginning of harvest meant that careful grape selection was necessary.

Quantity produced

14,000 cases. Côte Rôtie: 42,000.

Other details

Temperature-controlled fermentation introduced.

1987 (Not tasted) For Guigal, soft and forward, so like most other Côte Rôties in a good year.

Weather and timing

Excellent vintage, enormous crop. Good flowering. Dull growing season. Harvest early Oct.

Quantity produced

16,000 cases. Côte Rôtie: 94,000 cases.

1988 (Not tasted) Very promising indeed. Could this bring the 22nd century within Marcel Guigal's sights for his single vineyard wines?

Weather and timing

Outstanding vintage, average crop. Rain during flowering; incomplete set. July-Sept sunny and hot; grapes matured well. Harvest late Nov/early Oct.

Quantity produced

11,000 cases. Release date 1991.

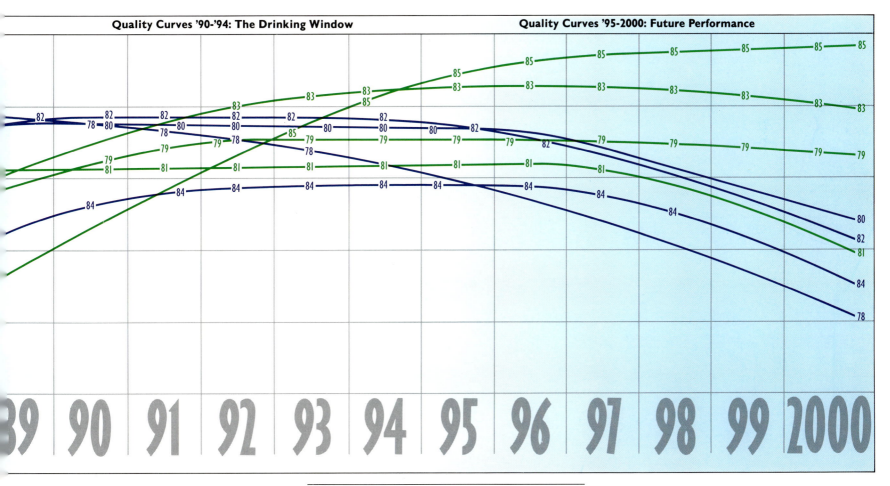

Quality Curves '90-'94: The Drinking Window   Quality Curves '95-2000: Future Performance

89 90 91 92 93 94 95 96 97 98 99 2000

Hermitage La Chapelle, Paul Jaboulet Aîné

La Chapelle is a wine designed for inclusion and analysis in this book, being one of the world's great reds, fashioned for an intense and exceptionally long life, yet with relatively wide vintage variation.

The Jaboulet family of Tain have been making top quality wine for well over 150 years, as long as their vines have clung to the steep, dusty hill of Hermitage just behind the town. The family are major vineyard owners on this unique hillside, a point made quite clearly on their vineyard terrace walls to anyone thundering along the left bank of the Rhône just south of Lyon by road or rail.

La Chapelle takes its name from a small stone chapel on the hillside which was bought by the Jaboulets for Fr f500 in 1929. About two-thirds of the grapes come from Le Méal, revered for its elegance, and one third from Les Bessards, better known for tannic, characterful wines. Just as important as these vines' position and the thinly-covered granite to which they cling, however, is their age. They boast an average age of about 35 years and are replanted terrace by terrace, but the produce of no vine less than 12 to 15 years old is allowed into La Chapelle. The grape is the noble Syrah, which has evolved in this spot over the decades. It is now superbly adapted to the precise requirements of this steep, often baked, site. Cuttings from these vines have been taken by – among others – many of those now trying to replicate the greats of the Rhône in California and by Penfolds for Grange (see p 150).

Wine-making follows a traditional pattern that has demonstrated over the decades what it can produce. The wines can have extraordinary concentration in youth yet in their second and third decade can develop wonders of subtle power with layers of autumnal scents and rich briary spice. They share the structure for longevity *and* complexity with top quality classed growth claret.

But there are no fancy modern tricks here: the grapes are the thing. Up to 70 per cent of stalks are retained and the must spends its first four days reaching 30°C in the unromantic cement fermentation vats. Here, the special qualities of the Jaboulet Hermitage fruit is extracted over three weeks, the results of one light press being included. New oak is kept below a third of all the burgundian barrels used and, despite the suspicions of some connoisseurs who claim to have tasted different bottlings, the Jaboulets insist that La Chapelle has been bottled from a single vat as far back as 1961.

Certainly the wines from good years are very tannic in youth but they rarely suffer a completely dumb period in the same way as some similarly structured Italian or Bordeaux wines do. And once these wines from favoured years reach their peak, they tend to stay there for year after year, as demonstrated on the chart.

There are lighter years aplenty however, and several of these add their shape to the chart below. They can be the result of not enough sunshine, as in 1987, or too much, as in 1975.

Earlier vintages

1961 This La Chapelle, for which the yield was hardly a third of the usual, is legendary. Connoisseurs have confused it with Château Latour 1961 when tasting it blind. It continues to astound. **1964**, **1971**, **1972** and **1973** are all vintages to drink now with great pleasure. By 1991 the **1966** and **1969** will be ready.

1978 Spectacular. The colour is still as deep as the 1985 and only slightly browner at the rim. An extraordinarily dense wine developing secondary aromas but with a long and exciting way to go. Gorgeous scent of prunes, game and spice. Lovely concentration, integration and length. Already good, but should be even more splendid in the late nineties.

Weather and timing
Great vintage, small crop. Cold, wet winter and spring. Incom-plete set. Excellent Sept and Oct. Good harvest Oct 5-23.

Quantity produced
4,650 cases released at Fr f392 a case. Hermitage AOC production: 35,000 cases.

Other details
Helicopter spraying of vines for the first time.

1979 Not a typical La Chapelle. Overheating on the nose but with hints of green leaf aromas too. Bigger than the 1980, and not subtle. Dry, without real fruit concentration.

Weather and timing
Good vintage, large crop. Long winter. Cold Feb. Sun and thunderstorms in May. Dry June-Aug. Showers during harvest Sept 25 to Oct 22.

Quantity produced
9,150 cases released at Fr f378 a case. Hermitage: 54,000 cases.

1980 Mild, low-key wine. Already a lightweight pleasure.

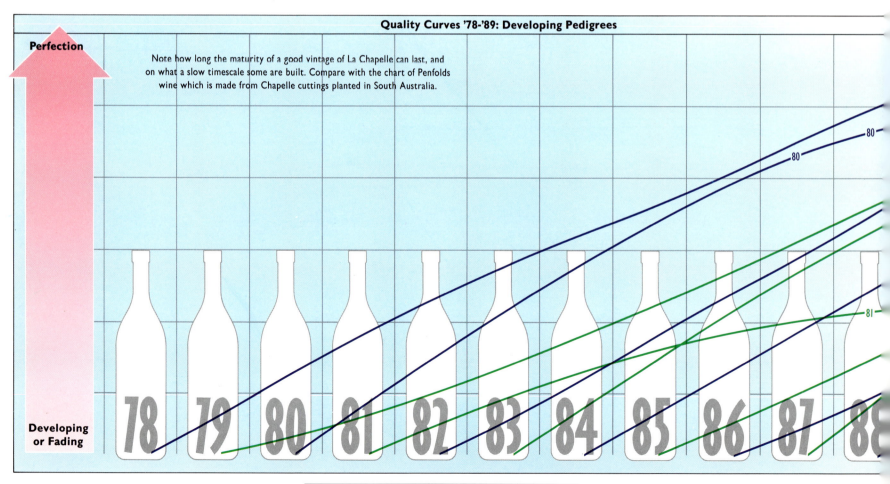

Quality Curves '78-'89: Developing Pedigrees

Perfection

Note how long the maturity of a good vintage of La Chapelle can last, and on what a slow timescale some are built. Compare with the chart of Penfolds wine which is made from Chapelle cuttings planted in South Australia.

Developing or Fading

78 79 80 81 82 83 84 85 86 87 88

Aromatic with the simpler burnt rubber elements of Syrah. Harmonious and ready to drink. Typical Hermitage, if simple.

Weather and timing
Fair vintage, average crop. Mild winter then cold, wet spring. Poor weather until July 23; late flowering, incomplete set. Fine Aug-Sept 20 then rain. Late harvest Oct 8-30.

Quantity produced
6,700 cases released at Fr f408 a case. Hermitage: 51,000 cases.
1981 Unbalanced: too acid, no tannin.

Weather and timing
Declassified vintage. Long, hard winter. Good July to Sept. Rain during harvest Sept 22 to Oct 8.

Quantity produced
7,000 cases sold as plain Hermitage. 1,000 La Chapelle sold in US. Hermitage: 49,000 cases.
1982 A Hermitage for hedonists. Perfectly balanced and in

double-quick time too. Less concentration than 1983 and a shorter-term proposition than 1985 but secondary dense autumnal flavours already quite evolved. Solid on the palate: tannins noticeable at the end. Warm, comforting, easy and early maturing.

Weather and timing
Good vintage, normal crop. Mild winter. Dry spring. Showers before flowering June 10-20. Dry July, wet Aug. Hot during harvest Sept 13-30: had to cool grapes.

Quantity produced
7,500 cases released at Fr f582 a case. Hermitage: 60,000 cases.
1983 A wonder of concentration. Nearly a 1961? A dense, truffly mulch of rich compost and ripe fruit flavours. Enormous potential. Chewy and substantial with layers of fruit and spicy Christmas flavours. A less developed 1978. Relatively hard tannins decree a longish wait.

Weather and timing
Outstanding vintage, below average crop. Wet autumn. Cold winter. Poor, late spring. Warm for flowering. Fine throughout growing season and harvest Sept 16 to Oct 6.

Quantity produced
6,000 cases released at Fr f1,140 a case. Hermitage: 52,000 cases.

Other details
Rhône wines began to gain international recognition.
1984 Pale for La Chapelle but some discernible purple. Aromatic, leafy but with an undertow of pruney fruit. Well balanced, open, relatively light-bodied. Low-key and slightly too green but should provide useful drinking in the early nineties.

Weather and timing
Acceptable vintage, normal crop. Very dry, mild winter then cold spring. Temperature dropped to freezing due to *le Mistral* on Apr 3.

Late Apr hot. Rain early May. Changeable during growing season and through harvest: Sept 27 to Oct 15.

Quantity produced
7,850 cases released at Fr f816 a case. Hermitage: 44,000 cases.
1985 Unusually for Jaboulet, they had more success with their Côte Rôtie Les Jumelles than with La Chapelle. Powerful meaty/gamey aromas with lots of concentration but, young, it is full-blooded rather than fascinating. Not as typically Syrah as the 1986.

Weather and timing
Very good vintage, large crop. Long, hard winter; very cold Jan. Late spring. Cold, wet May. Good flowering and growing season. Harvest Sept 23 to Oct 8.

Quantity produced
10,000 cases released at Fr f1,200 a case. Hermitage: 60,000 cases.
1986 Deep purple right out to rim. Exceptionally peppery nose

with some herbaceousness. High acid level and very high tannin (not bottled until Aug 1988 because of its toughness) but a good balance of fruit. Very dry finish. For the long term.

Weather and timing
Good quality vintage, normal crop. Nov-Apr cold. First warm weather mid-May. Good flowering. Mixed weather during growing season. Good harvest Sept 22 to Oct 11.

Quantity produced
6,700 cases released at Fr f1,140 a case. Also 2,080 cases of plain Hermitage. Hermitage: 48,000.
1987 Light crimson, well-shaded at the rim. Aromatic floral notes with more than a hint of bergamot or Earl Grey tea. Lightweight and low in tannin but relatively fruity. For early consumption.

Weather and timing
Modest vintage, normal crop.

Spring-like autumn then hard winter. Sunny, wet spring. Rain during flowering; incomplete set in older vines. Storms in Aug. Harvest began Sept 22; bad weather disrupted harvest – completed Oct 16.

Quantity produced
6,000 cases released at Fr f726 a case. Hermitage: 69,000 cases.
1988 The grapes were some of the healthiest ever. Extra-long maceration gave enormous colour, finesse, complexity and concentration. Juicy but destined for a 25 year life.

Weather and timing
Very good vintage, large crop. Wet autumn caused soil erosion. Warm, humid spring caused some mildew; disease checked by warm July. Hot Aug with rain. Harvest Sept 19 to Oct 8.

Quantity produced
About 9,150 cases. Release date: 1990.

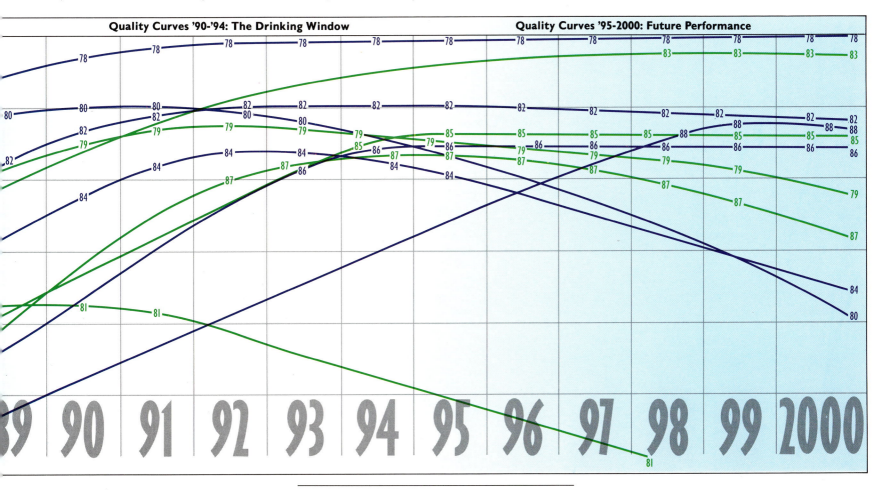

Château de Beaucastel, Châteauneuf-du-Pape

The wine world today is dotted with individuals driven for a wide variety of reasons to achieve a level of quality far in excess of the minimum required. The Perrins are the leading exponents of this philosophy in southern Rhône. They can prove it with their Vieille Ferme business, concentrating on top quality Côtes du Ventoux and Côtes du Rhône, their outstanding Cru de Coudoulet Côtes du Rhône, their planned "Californian-style" *négociant* house and most notably with their extremely solid base in Châteauneuf-du-Pape, Château de Beaucastel.

Jacques Perrin was one of the few Châteauneuf growers to persist with each of the 13 (often obscure) vine varieties allowed. His sons, François who is now in charge of the 325-acre (131-hectare) Château de Beaucastel domain and Jean-Pierre who is installed at La Vieille Ferme, have reaped the benefits of these rich building blocks in flavour and structure and are certainly taking advantage of them.

With even more prescience, Jacques also laid the foundations for Beaucastel's policy of minimal chemical intervention in the cellar and, especially, the vineyard. There is also Jacques Perrin's special vinification method, which starts with careful selection of individual grapes, includes warming the must before fermentation instead of adding sulphur dioxide, and often a good 18 months in large casks.

This makes the wines perceptibly more concentrated and textured than most Châteauneufs, possibly more prey to the ravages of poor storage, but certainly more interesting and more worthy of cellar space.

This applies as much to the whites, to which the Perrins address themselves with noble and unique perseverance, as the reds. Regular whites are made from about 80 per cent Roussanne with its alcohol level boosted by 20 per cent Grenache Blanc. This is to meet the arguably impractically high legal minimum of 12.5 per cent, but in years as good for whites as 1986, François is experimenting with barrel fermented wines made entirely of their top Roussanne vines, labelled Vieilles Vignes.

They reckon most of their Châteauneufs, red or white, need seven to 10 years to reach their peak but this can sometimes be an underestimate.

It is another important element in their unusual philosophy that, as they say, "all our wines are designed to be drunk with food". It is certainly difficult to imagine tackling any Château de Beaucastel wine, red or white, without the mitigating effect on the digestive system of some solid matter. These are strong wines, although the flavour elements that add such interest to the sheer alcohol are tangibly, almost chewably, present.

As one might expect, this attribute entails unusual ageability in the wines, inevitably in the reds at least, even though the whites in lesser years are wines designed for the converted.

Earlier vintages
The red 1972 was still gorgeous in 1988, as was 1970, 1967, 1966 and 1962.

1978 (Red) Exceptional vintage. Amazing depth of colour. Nose still closed but with silky texture. Flavours of tobacco and leather with smoked bacon and a red fruit *brûlée*. Mouthfilling. Nowhere near its peak.

(White) Deep gold with many layers of mature bouquet. Good acid with power, honey and impact. Drink up to 1996.
Weather and timing
Excellent vintage, below average crop. Wet Apr then dry. Hot summer. Harvest Sept 22 to Oct 9.
Quantity produced
16,000 cases released in 1980 at Fr f420 a case. Châteauneuf-du-Pape production: 1,000,000 cases.
Other details
Jacques Perrin died.

1979 (Red) Concentrated colour. An integrated whole with candied plums. Full and charming with length. Very Beaucastel.

(White) Not as successful and lively as 1978: dull and astringent on the palate.
Weather and timing
Good vintage, normal crop. Dull season with heavy rain late Oct. Harvest Sept 4-27.
Quantity produced
20,000 cases released at Fr f456 a case. Châteauneuf-du-Pape: 1,099,000 cases.
1980 (Red) Looks deeper and more youthful than the 1982. Smoky bouquet of ripe, roasted, red fruits and cinnamon. Slight on the palate. Marked acidity.

(White) Extraordinarily pale green/gold. Honeysuckle nose and good acid. Drink up to 1995.
Weather and timing
Good vintage, large crop. Late flowering. Little sun May-July.

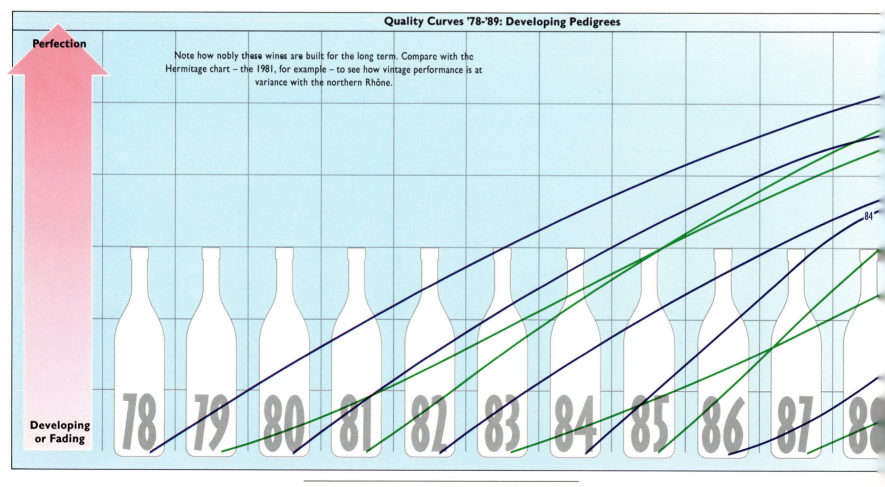

Quality Curves '78-'89: Developing Pedigrees

Perfection

Note how nobly these wines are built for the long term. Compare with the Hermitage chart – the 1981, for example – to see how vintage performance is at variance with the northern Rhône.

Developing or Fading

78　79　80　81　82　83　84　85　86　87　88

Warm with light rain during harvest Sept 25 to Oct 24.

Quantity produced
22,000 cases released at Fr f498 a case. Châteauneuf-du-Pape: 1,115,000 cases.

Other details
New 500,000 bottle cellar.

1981 (Red) A stunner. Suggestion of glowing embers in its blackish ruby with tawny rim. Glorious rich cocktail of gamey flavours. Powerful nose and the savoury, ripe berry and tar elements are starting to make an exciting whole.

(White) Deep gold with an odd suggestion of coffee. Big: needs more acidity. Drink 1986-1991.

Weather and timing
Fair vintage, small crop. Dull season. Cold weather during flowering caused incomplete set. Harvest Sept 14 to Oct 6.

Quantity produced
15,000 cases released at Fr f540

a case. Châteauneuf-du-Pape: 953,000 cases.

Other details
Installed new crusher/destemmer .

1982 (Red) Light for Beaucastel, the rim browning. Open, evolved almost burnt nose with some jamminess. A hint of tannin at the back of the palate.

(White) Honeyed nose: sweetness on the palate. Good greengage acidity. A lovely, well-knit, powerful-long wine. Drink 1987-1995.

Weather and timing
Good vintage, large crop. Dry year. Flowering June 3. Rain during harvest Sept 7 to Oct 9.

Quantity produced
11,000 cases released at Fr f540 a case. Châteauneuf-du-Pape: 1,144,000 cases.

1983 (Red) More floral than the 1985 with a lovely blackberry mulch of autumn flavours. More classically built, less opulent and

generous than the 1985 but showing a gamey middle-age. Still reserved.

(White) Deep lemon colour with a powerful aroma of dried lemon peel and greengage. Full, exciting and layered but not fully developed. Drink up to 1997.

Weather and timing
Good vintage, small crop. Bud break early Apr. Cold, wet May. Flowering June 8. Warm, wet July-Sept. Harvest Sept 12 to Oct 6.

Quantity produced
13,000 cases released at Fr f840 a case. Châteauneuf-du-Pape: 881,000 cases.

1984 (Red) Dark red: warm, open, resolved bouquet suggesting charred wood. High acidity and fairly lightweight impact. Simple but good balance.

(White) Was not at its best in late 1988: apparently oxidised and fairly dull. Perhaps merely in repose? Wait until 1991.

Weather and timing
Average vintage, small crop. Cold May. Cold Aug and Sept. Late harvest Sept 19 to Oct 12.

Quantity produced
11,000 cases released at Fr f600 a case. Châteauneuf-du-Pape: 900,000 cases.

1985 (Red) Deep crimson; ruby at the rim. Rich and textured. Lots of smokiness with mulberries underneath. Youthful, rich, sweet, almost overripe. Already drinkable though still unresolved.

(White) Fresh if subdued. Perceptible oak on full-bodied if fairly neutral fruit. Drink from about 1989.

Weather and timing
Good vintage, very large crop. Cold and wet in May. Flowering June 7. Hot, sunny Sept. Harvest Sept 16 to Oct 11.

Quantity produced
22,000 cases released at Fr f840

a case. Châteauneuf-du-Pape: 1,256,000 cases.

1986 (Red) Deep crimson. Aroma of wood-smoke and bacon; marked acidity. Should last.

(White) Particularly deep green/gold. Rich, concentrated nose with a whiff of ginger and lots of acid. Drink up to 1995. 1986 Roussanne Vieilles Vignes, has oak-suppressed nose and some youthful astringence. Should be exciting drinking from 1993.

Weather and timing
Very good vintage, large crop. Very dry, hot May; flowering May 29. Hot with storms June-Sept. Harvest Sept 11 to Oct 8.

Quantity produced
22,000 cases released at Fr f864 a case. Châteauneuf-du-Pape: 1,163,000 cases.

1987 (Red) Dark purple. Young, still unevolved smoky nose suggesting prunes in armagnac. Acidity balanced by ripe

fruit. Lots of extract and spice.

(White) Lovely smell of ripe pears. Good fruit, acid and real substance. Young and simple but elegant. Drink 1990-1996.

Weather and timing
Average vintage, normal crop. Wet May and June. Humid Aug-Sept. Harvest Sept 18 to Oct 17.

Quantity produced
About 10,000 cases released at Fr f780 a case. Châteauneuf-du-Pape: 1,034,000 cases.

Other details
Two pneumatic presses installed.

1988 (Not tasted) The Domaine believes this to be a great vintage. Fruity nose and strong tannin, but not aggressive.

Weather and timing
Excellent vintage, normal crop. Wet, humid spring. Excellent flowering. Hot, sunny growing season. Harvest Sept 8 to Oct 7.

Quantity produced
About 20,000 cases.

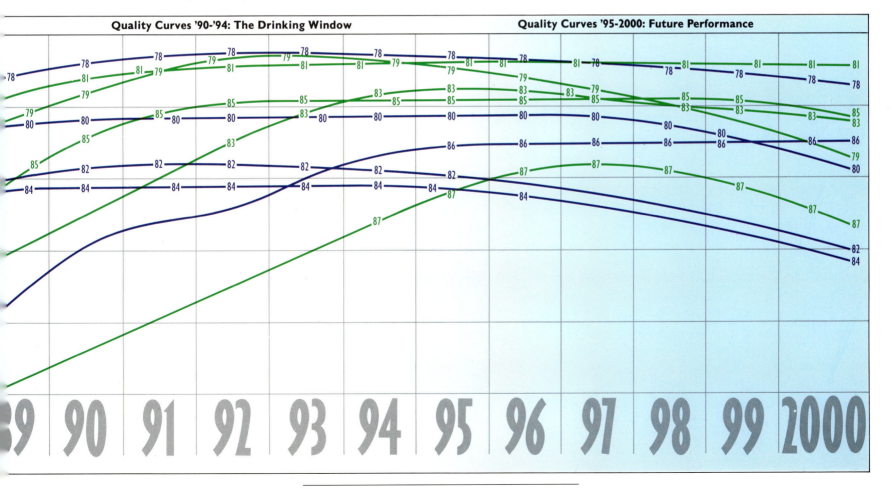

REST OF FRANCE

This section applies to all wines produced in France other than those already addressed. To all these, certain general rules on wine maturity apply:
– *Vin de Table* or Table Wine matures typically as shown on Chart A (page 19) and should be drunk as young as possible whatever colour it is;
– a typical white *Vin de Pays* also matures as shown on Chart A;
– any wine labelled *Nouveau* or *Primeur* may mature even earlier than shown on Chart A and should also be drunk as young as possible – although its process of decline is no more sudden or critical than that of any other wine.

It is more difficult to be dogmatic about red *Vin de Pays*. Most of them are made in the Midi, and the cheapest can mature as fast as shown on Chart A. Others, particularly those whose labels specify a *cépage* such as Cabernet Sauvignon, Syrah or Merlot and those which boast of oak ageing (*Vieilli* or *Elevé en Fût de Chêne* or *Chêne Neuf*) mature as shown on Chart B, (also page 19).

The exception to this is the celebrated Mas de Daumas Gassac which is an extraordinary *Vin de Pays* whose red should be kept for a decade at least before drinking.

In general the non-champagne sparkling wines of France are ready to drink when they are released. Unfortunately for the producers of sparkling Saumur, Vouvray, Blanquette de Limoux, Crémant d'Alsace and Crémant de Bourgogne, demand for their produce is not so rapacious as demand for "the real thing" and market forces, or the lack of them, tend to complete the maturation process. Sparkling wines reflect the quality of the still wine from which they are made; sparkling Vouvray is one of the longer-lived *vins mousseux*. Storage, as with champagne, is important (see page 72/3).

The still wines of Champagne, Coteaux Champenois, are in my experience Chart B-style wines, although the red grapes are so seldom ripe enough for an attractive still red wine that the likes of Bouzy Rouge 1976, for example, are pressed into service long after their notional "Sell By" date. The red wines of Irancy and other Yonne wines such as Sauvignon de St Bris are definitely designed for early consumption, as in Chart B. Sauvignon is not a grape designed to give long-term pleasure.

Some Sauvignon de Touraine matures as fast as Chart A suggests although the more expensive bottlings nudge onto Chart B. Like Reuilly, Quincy and Ménétou-Salon, most bottlings of Sancerre and Pouilly-Fumé, the prototype Loire Sauvignons, age along Chart B lines, with the amount of fruit and acid varying slightly with the year. Muscadet and, particularly, Gros Plant Nantais should also be drunk as young as possible although exceptional bottlings of Sancerre, Pouilly-Fumé and Muscadet can last.

Most Loire reds are also designed for early consumption, within three years of vintage, although in really fine years such as 1976, 1983 and 1985 the best Chinon, Bourgeuil and especially St Nicolas de Bourgeuil can last a decade.

In general, and with the noble exception of the superior Chenin-based wines already examined, this northwestern quarter of France cannot ripen grapes enough to produce seriously ageable wines. But the wines can boast a refreshingly high level of natural acidity in every single vintage. South of the Loire, for instance, the wines of Haut Poitou and St Pourçain-sur-Sioule benefit from a year in bottle to soften the initial acid attack.

In the far east of France the Jura produces a small quantity of fascinating wines that demand ageing and repay study, such as the curiously sherry-like but entirely natural local specialty Vin Jaune, of which Château-Chalon is the most respected. It is made only in the most suitable vintages and should be aged in bottle until it is at least 15 years old, although it will last for decades. The red wines of the Jura and Savoie are at their best between three and six years depending on the ripeness of the vintage. Study of the notes for Burgundy give clues as to the style of the Jura vintage. Drink the whites young.

On the eastern fringes of the Rhône Valley the whites and rosés should be drunk the minute they are bottled, but the medium- to full-bodied reds can be drunk within two to five years of the vintage. They are, in order of increasing longevity, Côtes du Vivarais, Côtes du Ventoux, Côtes du Luberon and

Coteaux du Tricastin, although the intentions of individual producers are all-important here. Provençal whites and pinks can be relatively full-bodied too. Most are at their best in the fruity bloom of youth within a couple of years of bottling, with the exceptions of Château Simone's extraordinary wines, Domaine Ott's best Côtes de Provence bottlings and the best white Bellet.

A high proportion of the red wines produced in Provence deserve cellaring. Bandol is the most famous and, were it easier to find outside the region, would deserve a Timechart to itself. The best wines can still be evolving at 10 to 12 years old, while none have reached their peak by four. Best recent vintages have been 1987, 1985, 1982 and 1979. Bellet reds share Bandol's vintage successes and are also worth ageing, although only usually for three to six years. Palette reds, which effectively means Château Simone's, demand at least one decade and sometimes two in bottle. Most other Provençal reds such as Coteaux d'Aix-en-Provence and Côtes de Provence are at their best three to four years after the vintage but those of Domaine de Trévallon, and to a lesser extent Château Vignelaure, require up to five years longer and can last for a further decade in years such as 1983.

Few Corsican wines escape the island but some of the reds do need at least two years' taming in bottle. The more Nielluccio in the wine the more ageworthy it is; Ajaccio should therefore be drunk before Patrimonio. 1985 and 1987 produced wines for keeping up to five years.

Most of the vast quantity of wine produced in the Languedoc-Roussillon is of *Vin de Table* and *Vin de Pays* status and should be drunk as young as possible. But quality overall has been rising admirably and the Languedoc-Roussillon now manages to produce nearly 15 per cent of all *Appellation Contrôlée* wines. Pockets of fairly serious red wine worth ageing for two or three years join the traditionally made sweet fortified wines of all colours, *Vins Doux Naturels*, as the most prized wines of the Midi. Any undated VDN should be ready to drink as soon as it is bottled, but the best producers of Banyuls, Maury and Rivesaltes sell wines of the finest vintages that, not unlike vintage port, can continue to develop in bottle for decades. For less alcoholic wines, the most recent vintage can often be the best in this region. In general terms however the reds most suitable for ageing, in ascending order of longevity, are Minervois, Corbières, Fitou, St Chinian, Côtes de la Malepère, Faugères, Côtes du Roussillon-Villages and Collioure (which is to Banyuls what Douro table wine is to port). Most Minervois are Chart B wines but the best Collioures, made from old vines with a substantial proportion of Mourvèdre, can continue to develop in bottle for up to eight years.

One important way in which the wines of the southwest differ from those of the south, the Languedoc-Roussillon, is in their life expectancy. The wines of the southwest almost invariably last longer, although there is no shortage of dry whites that conform to Chart B or even Chart A. The whites worth ageing are generally, as usual, the sweet wines of Côtes de Bergerac, Gaillac, Côtes de Montravel or Haut Montravel, Pacherenc du Vic-Bilh, Rosette, Saussignac or Monbazillac, the Dordogne's unabashedly rustic answer to Sauternes. They are listed again in ascending order of likely longevity and while most Côtes de Bergerac needs only a year or so in bottle there are some which can last for 12 years.

Much of the Monbazillac made in 1976 continued to evolve throughout the eighties. The Yquem pages (52/3) give general indications about which years were particularly good for sweet white wine (and *Botrytis*) in the southwest. Perhaps the most ageworthy southwestern white is Jurançon, a curious and noble sweet wine that is as troublesome to make well as Sauternes but as rewarding to keep when successful. The sweet version is one of the few inexpensive whites that can last for decades – particularly good years were 1987, 1983, 1981, 1975, 1971 and 1970. Jurançon Sec evolves along Chart B lines.

Reds with greater life expectancy than that outlined on Chart B are, in roughly ascending order of longevity, Côtes du Frontonnais, Irouleguy, Buzet, Bergerac, Côtes de Bergerac, Pécharmant, Cahors and Madiran. Those appellations most varied in quality are asterisked. The best Côtes du Frontonnais reds peak at three or four years while the best Madiran can enjoy a stately maturation up to 15 years. The best years for these southwestern reds have been those that were most successful for red Bordeaux: 1985 particularly.

GERMANY

The glorious, spiritually uplifting old age of fine German wines is one of the wine world's best-kept secrets. To age well the wine has to be made meticulously from carefully ripened examples of the great grape Riesling whose intense concentration of pure fruit flavour and exceptionally high natural acidity packs a young wine with all that it needs for years, decades and sometimes centuries of slow but dramatic evolution. As the colour deepens from pale straw to deep greenish gold, the Riesling scent changes from a single light floral strand to a much more intense, finely woven tapestry of different flavours. The flavours vary from flowers, blossom and leaves through fruits as varied as apples and figs to a wide range of high-toned mineral scents. Eventually the wines turn the same dark tawny as an old Sauternes – and indeed the sweeter wines become increasingly difficult to distinguish from great Sauternes of the same age, although their more delicate structure and higher acid should mark them out.

The world's oldest wine by far that is still alive and evolving is a 1653 Rüdesheimer kept in cask in the cellars under Bremen's town hall. Such venerable Rüdesheimer is one of the vindications of the Rheingau, which, along with the Mosel-Saar-Ruwer, produces most of the ageworthy bottles.

The rationale for choosing von Simmern is given on page 96. The Rheingau is arguably Germany's most homogenous wine region of which as much as 80 per cent of the intensively planted wine country is planted with Riesling. The wines charted for von Simmern are for the most part, as for J J Prüm, the ripest produced that year, except for 1980 and 1981 when a few bottles of Kabinett were made. Almost all the mainstream Rheingau vineyard slopes gently south towards the wide, fast-flowing Rhine, so the von Simmern Timechart should represent fairly accurately the maturity patterns of equivalent Rheingau wines.

The Mosel river on the other hand, with its tributaries the Saar and Ruwer, provides a jigsaw of aspects and altitudes for its slate-based vineyards. Much of its wine is thin, early-maturing stuff made from new, lesser vineyards in the hinterland or overproduced from more traditional sites. Only committed wine-makers at the great estates continue to demonstrate the unique ageability of Mosel Riesling.

Happily, these estates – though small – continue much as they have for decades. There was therefore no shortage of suitable candidates for the Mosel paradigm in this book, except that a number of the obvious ones – Egon Müller, von Hövel, Dr Fischer, Zilliken and von Schubert at Maximin Grünhaus – are in their own delicious backwaters, the Saar and Ruwer. J J Prüm is, like so many others, in the mainstream middle stretch of the Mittel Mosel and satisfies the criteria of consistency and extreme longevity. These Prüm wines last probably longer than any other Mittel Mosel representatives and as long as the even more acid (although more delicate) wines produced up-river around Trier or in the Saar and Ruwer. For most other Mittel Mosel wines of the same quality level, accelerate the Prüm chart by two years.

It should be easy to draw up a set of rules governing the maturity of German wines. No other country has such an apparently orderly and objectively quantified quality ranking system. The ripeness of the grapes, measured as must weight in the all-important German unit of *Oechsle*, determines a wine's rank, upwards from the tiny *Tafelwein* category, through *Landwein* (Germany's answer to *Vin de Pays*) and ordinary *Qualitätswein* or QbA to the QmP wines of the *Prädikat* Kabinett, Spätlese, Auslese, Beerenauslese, Eiswein or Trockenbeerenauslese.

In theory the higher ranking the wine, the longer it can, and usually should, be kept. In practice however the less residual sugar there is in a serious German wine, the more it benefits from some bottle age – certainly two years and often many more. Thus, while an Auslese can be drunk with pleasure as soon as it is bottled (although it should continue to improve for a good 15 years) a QbA or Kabinett in a lean year from a serious producer using traditional methods will not soften to its optimum drinkability until about five years after the vintage. This is certainly true of the drier *Trocken* and *Halbtrocken* wine styles now so popular in Germany: the best 1985s are just starting to show their mettle.

Bremm, just down-river of the Middle Mosel, shows a typically disorienting twist of this famous wine river. Aspect, and elevation, are all – with the finest vineyards such as the Wehlener Sonnenuhr (page 94) facing southeast, and enjoying river reflection.

These drier wines tend to have a shorter plateau of maturity than the sweet dessert wines. Beerenauslese and Trockenbeerenauslese continue to evolve deeper textures and flavours for at least two decades in bottle. Individual vintage guidance for these wines is hardly necessary since they are made only in exceptional years. They are expensive rarities, so it seems a waste not to give them this chance.

Eiswein is a very different animal, made from ultra-healthy grapes frozen once, rather than ultra-ripe ones that have been ravaged by *Botrytis* over many days. Eiswein is less substantial, less complex than a "TBA" with excellent acid and high sugar but not the nuances brought about by noble rot (called *Edelfäule* in Germany). Of the three categories of sweet wine, Beerenauslese is at current prices by far the best buy and Eiswein the worst.

Vintages conventionally regarded as great in Germany are those which manage the highest must weights and therefore the highest proportion of QmP wine such as 1988 (48 per cent) and 1976 (83 per cent). To achieve this the flowering usually has to be early to allow for a sufficiently long growing season, the summer warm and the autumn not too cold and rainy. But this underestimates the quality of the more easily attainable. Good producers can provide QbA and Kabinett Riesling in the "poor quality" years such as 1986 and 1984 that show the pure, unadorned fruitiness for which German wine deserves more recognition.

Most non-Riesling wines from the Mosel and Rheingau should be drunk within two to three years and some of the cheapest Mosel blends within one. Mosel QbA Riesling should be drunk within anything from one year (for a commercial bottling) to 10 (for a Dr Prüm QbA, for example). The "poorer" the vintage (that is, the higher the initial acidity), the longer the QbA could and should be kept.

Wehlener Sonnenuhr, J J Prüm

The house of J J Prüm has been producing quintessential Mittel Mosel Rieslings for well over a century, a history that seems quite in keeping with the extraordinary longevity that characterises these apparently delicate, almost frail, lightweight whites.

The enthusiastic Dr Manfred Prüm and his wife Amei are in the enviable position of being the largest single owners in the Wehlener Sonnenuhr vineyard, arguably the most dependable source of top quality wines in the famous middle stretch of the Mosel.

Having more than 10 acres (four hectares) means that in some particularly ripe vintages he can afford the rare but distinctly advantageous luxury of making more than one grade of Auslese. His Auslese Goldkapsel is the modern equivalent of the pre-1971 Feine Auslese and those wines with an extra-long gold capsule, "lange Goldkapsel", have replaced the old Feinste Auslese.

The chart below illustrates the likely evolution of the ripest Wehlener Sonnenuhr produced by J J Prüm in each year since 1975.

Wine-making techniques at Prüm are just as slow as the wines' evolution. Particularly ripe musts are allowed to ferment at their own pace, over many months if necessary. Particularly acid wines are allowed to soften in cask until the second spring after the vintage, miraculously retaining all their freshness and delicacy, before bottling.

This has been one of the most difficult charts to draw up, chiefly because the charms of a Kabinett are so different from those of a Spätlese, while each Auslese presents quite distinct virtues and pleasures again.

The Kabinett wines have been evaluated as a Kabinett, the Auslese wines as an Auslese and so on, which is why the surprise star of the Kabinetts, the 1977, reaches as high a pinnacle as some of the Auslesen, even though the grapes themselves did not score nearly so highly on the Germans' own measure of success, the *Oechsle* scale.

There are marked and perhaps unexpected differences in maturity times between the various quality categories too. The drier, more acidic Kabinett wines take far longer to soften to drinkability than their riper counterparts (as in the Loire). In a Spätlese and an Auslese the youthful acidity is often mitigated by a good dollop of residual sugar and a distracting panoply of ripe fruit flavours. That said, anyone who knows German wines knows that however gulpable a three year-old Auslese may seem, it would be a crime to drink it at this stage when it has a good 10 years' more slow, complex evolution ahead.

When interpreting this chart therefore it is worth remembering that the sweeter the wine, the earlier it *can* be drunk with pleasure, especially by those who are able to ignore the extra dimensions it will achieve when it reaches its true peak, conservatively indicated below.

Earlier vintages

The consistency and youthfulness of the wines below suggests that any older Prüm wine of quality (except for the QbA wines sold under the Dr M Prüm label) would still be in good shape. Prüm's British importer treasures memories of a **1904** Graacher Himmelreich Auslese tasted in 1964. The magic preservative is the high level of natural acidity. Approaching its third decade the Wehlener Sonnenuhr Auslese **1971** was a model of vibrant fruit with no signs of drying out. There was maturity on the nose, yet on the palate it was still fresh with light, fruity ripeness.

1975 Auslese lange Goldkapsel. Miraculously young and elegant, a taut contrast to the 1976. Still pale green/gold with blossom notes on the nose. The truest Riesling in this range, dec-

ades behind the 1976 in development. High acidity but great balance. Sheer class and extreme longevity shone through.

Weather and timing

Good vintage, large crop. Average summer. Good autumn. Harvest Nov 13-18.

Quantity produced

60 cases released at Dm720 a case. Total Mosel production: 18,000,000 cases.

1976 Auslese lange Goldkapsel. The richest and deepest-coloured of these wines by far with a coppery tinge and a gloriously powerful *Botrytis*-packed bouquet. An unctuous, complex mix of minerals and a touch of smoky char. A very sweet wine.

Weather and timing

Great vintage, below average crop. Early flowering. No rain June to mid-July: crop reduced due to loss of small grapes. Hot with showers Aug-Sept. Tropical

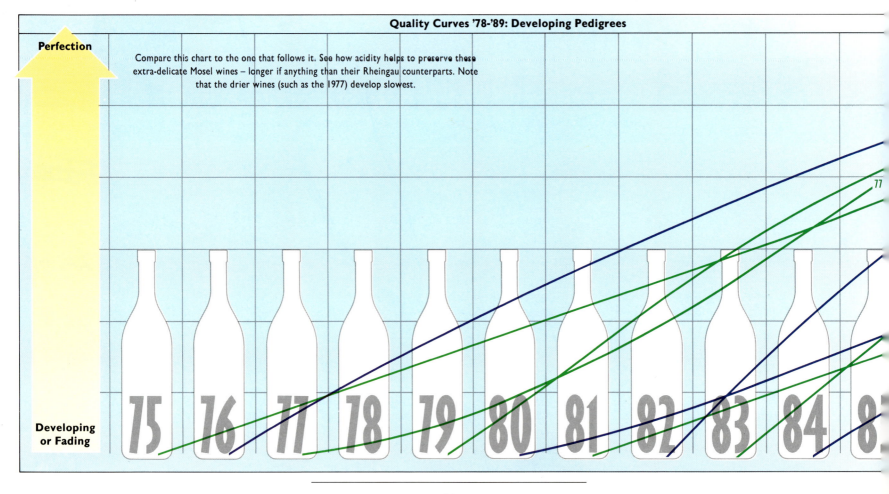

Quality Curves '78-'89: Developing Pedigrees

Perfection

Compare this chart to the one that follows it. See how acidity helps to preserve these extra-delicate Mosel wines – longer if anything than their Rheingau counterparts. Note that the drier wines (such as the 1977) develop slowest.

Developing or Fading

75 76 77 78 79 80 81 82 83 84 8[5]

early Oct then rain Oct 18-19: *Botrytis*. Hot and dry for harvest Oct 20-28.

Quantity produced
225 cases released at Dm900 a case. Mosel: 11,550,000 cases.

1977 Kabinett. A revelation from a poorly rated vintage which was entering its prime in 1989. Light-bodied with delicate vivacity: no hint of age. Balanced steely Riesling characteristics.

Weather and timing
Average vintage, above average crop. Cool summer and autumn. Harvest Nov 3-18.

Quantity produced
1,167 cases released at Dm120 a case. Mosel: 16,080,000 cases.

1978 Not one of Prüm's most successful vintages.

Weather and timing
Fair vintage, below average crop. Late flowering. Cold, wet summer followed by dry, warm autumn. Harvest mid-Nov.

Quantity produced
1,165 cases released at Dm120. Mosel: 10,062,000 cases.

1979 Auslese Goldkapsel. The relatively evolved nose of this highly successful wine belies its extremely youthful, pale spritzy gold. Already more mature than the 1975. A bouquet of blackcurrant leaves but a hint of the mature Riesling kerosene notes. Not an ultra-rich Auslese but sweet.

Weather and timing
Good vintage, below average crop. Average spring followed by moderate summer. Better autumn. Harvest Nov 8-15.

Quantity produced
330 cases released at Dm360. Mosel: 11,820,000 cases.

1980 Kabinett. Still young compared to the 1977, this mid-gold wine has natural fizz (and tartaric acid crystals that look like glass). At nine years old it was still tart, light-bodied and highly aromatic. Suggests wet stones, and should keep much longer than any vintage chart would suggest.

Weather and timing
Good vintage, small crop. Poor conditions throughout year. Cold summer and autumn. Frost in Nov killed leaves. Harvest Nov 6-15.

Quantity produced
1,160 cases released at Dm120. Mosel: 5,763,000 cases.

1981 Spätlese. Extremely delicate. Muted. Pale green/gold with some spritz. Has layers of flavour but is still steely and relatively hard.

Weather and timing
Good vintage, below average crop. Harvest Nov 4-12.

Quantity produced
2,000 cases released at Dm216 a case. Mosel: 12,903,000 cases.

1982 Auslese lange Goldkapsel. Slight mousey whiff but much to be enjoyed. There is considerable richness and extract balanced, as always, by lovely acidity. Not one of the longest-living but not clumsy.

Weather and timing
Very good vintage, enormous crop. Fine until end Sept. Rained for first half of Oct then fine again: *Botrytis* spread well. Excellent harvest Nov 4-10.

Quantity produced
30 cases released at Dm768 a case. Mosel: 25,874,000 cases.

1983 Auslese Goldkapsel. Gloriously, and deceptively, enjoyable. Darker gold than all except the 1976. Pure, rich, honeyed flavours suggesting, like the 1979, blackcurrant leaves. Much richer than the 1985 and balanced between the ultra-ripe panoply of spicy floral flavour and the acidity. Resonant finish but still young.

Weather and timing
Excellent vintage, large crop. Very wet in May. Fine weather from June through to harvest. Normal flowering. Excellent harvest Nov 8-15.

Quantity produced
67 cases released at Dm936 a case. Mosel: 19,910,000 cases.

1984 Kabinett. Still shy, this straightforward wine is fizzing pale green/gold with great acid and characteristic young Mosel smell of wet stones. Neat and unadorned but the acidity suggests a long plateau of drinkability.

Weather and timing
Fair vintage, below average crop. Dull season. Cool, wet summer. Fine autumn. Harvest Nov 8-17.

Quantity produced
1,666 cases released at Dm156 a case. Mosel: 12,211,000 cases.

1985 Auslese. A combination of richness with delicacy. Pale straw with spritz. Youthful with a ragbag of jaggedly mixed raw ingredients. A perfumed gloss on some lovely Riesling flavour elements that are pure but hard for the moment.

Weather and timing
Excellent vintage, below average crop. Poor conditions until the end Aug. Unusually warm, wet Sept allowed vines to catch up. Harvest Nov 7-19.

Quantity produced
2,000 cases released at Dm300 a case. Mosel: 12,172,000 cases.

1986 Spätlese. The free sulphur is evident as the bottle is opened, but it is not meant for consumption until the sulphur has nursed it through its infancy. Healthy, vibrant, confident fruit.

Weather and timing
Very good vintage, above average crop. Excellent until mid-Aug then wet and cold for three weeks. Rain again mid-Oct. Harvest Nov 3-18.

Quantity produced
2,000 cases released at Dm240 a case. Mosel: 16,112,000 cases.

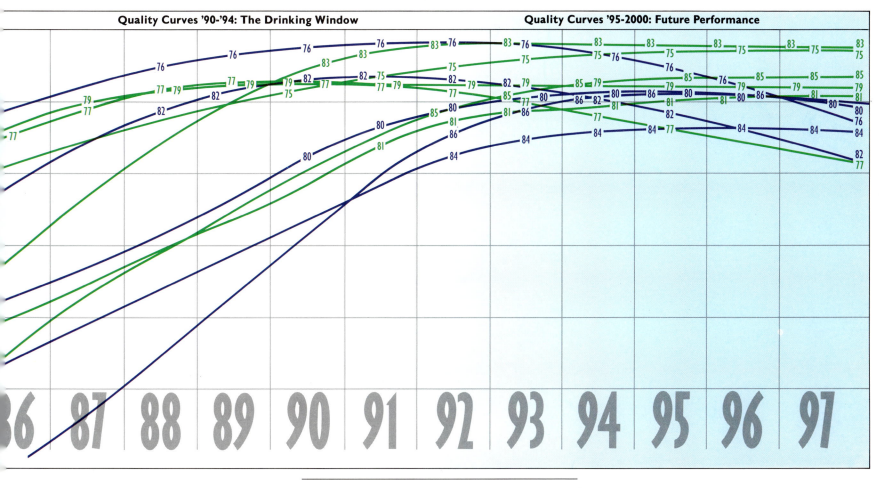

Hattenheimer Mannberg, Langwerth von Simmern

The wine world is agreed that the Rheingau represents Germany's greatest concentration of top quality Riesling. It is difficult to name a single property that has produced an unbroken run of successes with no major change of direction, particularly since the German wine trade has been buffeted in recent years by a series of difficulties, including that most demanding variable: consumer taste.

A number of properties, for example, have tailored their output to match the German market's current love affair with dry or *Trocken* wines. Others have changed hands or their reputation has suffered as a result of temporary setbacks in cellar or vineyard.

At the Baron Langwerth von Simmern estate, Freiherrlich Langwerth von Simmern'sches Rentamt, there has been reassuring continuity. The cellarmaster Josef Schell, for example, has worked to the same brief since 1958, aiming to produce long-living wines of unimpeachable purity which reliably express the individual nuances of each of von Simmern's top ranking vineyards.

The estate's holdings include some of the finest sites in the important central slice of vineyards just above the banks of the Rhine between Hattenheim and Eltville. The 125 acres (50 hectares) are shared between such famous sites as Hattenheimer Nussbrunnen, Erbacher Marcobrunn, Rauenthaler Baiken and Eltviller Sonnenberg so that they include a range of the Rheingau's diverse soil types.

Erbacher Marcobrunn is perhaps von Simmern's most famous single wine, partly because it impressed America's first serious wine collector, Thomas Jefferson, 200 years ago. The estate's director Helmut Kranisch points out however that his Hattenheimer Mannberg was originally considered part of "Marcobrunn". Herr Kranisch controls 4 acres (1.7 hectares) of Erbacher Marcobrunn and 15 acres (6.3 hectares) of Hattenheimer Mannberg, which gives von Simmern almost a monopoly on this second, exceptionally well favoured site.

All von Simmern's wines are meticulously well made. Even if the Marcobrunn wines are just a little fuller than the Mannberg examples, both are ideal vehicles for the unique combination of honeyed Riesling fruit and mineral-scented earthiness that characterises the Rheingau.

Like its counterpart from the Mosel, the chart below traces the development of the ripest wine produced in any quantity in each of the vintages since 1978. (So sought after are von Simmern wines that Herr Kranisch had to recall for this tasting some of the older ones from private cellars.) The chart demonstrates the vicissitudes of growing vines here. The Rheingau's acid levels, lower than these of the Mosel, are apparent in the slightly earlier ageing patterns of these wines, although the level of ripeness achieved in this range is notably lower than those Dr Prüm managed in his exceptionally favoured site in Wehlen.

Earlier vintages
Some of von Simmern's output from the 1971, 1975 and 1976 vintages would still be superb – if traceable.

1978 QbA. Only a handful of wines above this mediocre quality level were produced in the entire Rheingau and this humble example is a miracle of survival. The colour is still pale straw. There are signs that the wine is slowly losing fruit and excitement but the vibrancy and completeness of the Riesling fruit is a vindication of both the grape and the estate.

Weather and timing
Average vintage, below average crop. Dry winter then harsh, wet spring. Flowering July 1. Cool, dry summer. Harvest Nov 3.

Quantity produced
3,600 cases (100% of the estate's Hattenheimer Mannberg produc-

tion) released at Dm86 a case. Total Rheingau production: 1,108,000 cases.

1979 Spätlese. Extraordinarily youthful. Mid-gold with an intense bouquet of hazelnuts that manages to be both pure and complex. Wonderful honeyed fruit underneath, good weight and much more zip than the 1982 Spätlese. Lovely acid and slight astringence on the finish still.

Weather and timing
High quality vintage, small crop. Fine, dry spring; early flowering June 26. Harvest Nov 8.

Quantity produced
2,376 cases (72%) released at Dm144 a case. Rheingau: 1,652,000 cases.

1980 QbA. This mid-gold wine is the youngest to be showing any signs of age. The bouquet is broad, open and has lost its freshness without gaining any complexity. Things are more ex-

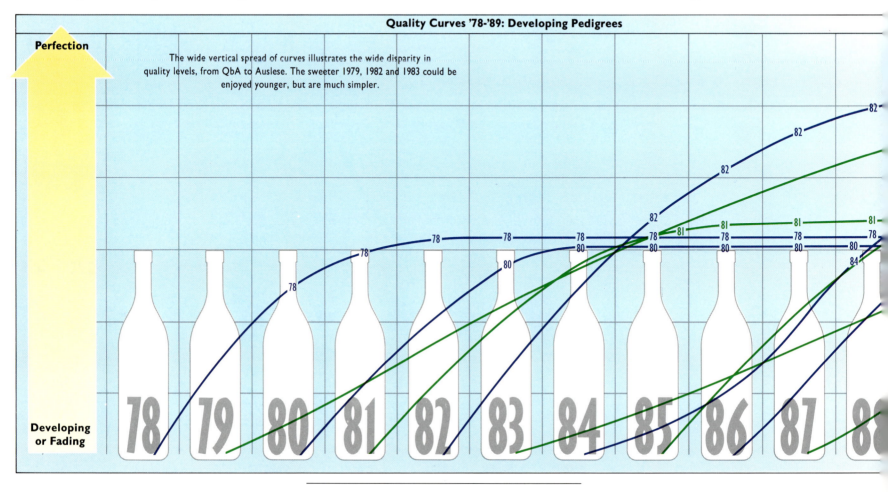

Quality Curves '78-'89: Developing Pedigrees

Perfection

The wide vertical spread of curves illustrates the wide disparity in quality levels, from QbA to Auslese. The sweeter 1979, 1982 and 1983 could be enjoyed younger, but are much simpler.

Developing or Fading

78 79 80 81 82 83 84 85 86 87 88

citing on the palate where there is much respectable spice and evidence of *terroir*. An attractive mouthful of fruit that is fading: could do with a bit more acid.

Weather and timing
Good vintage, small crop. Cold, wet year. Cold, dry autumn. Harvest Nov 3. High acidity.

Quantity produced
1,986 cases (77%) released at Dm90 a case. Rheingau: 509,000 cases.

1981 QbA. A respectable Rheingau Riesling showing its wet stone and blackcurrant leaf aromas but still holding its own thanks to a higher acid level than the 1980. Still some fruit perceptible and marvellous flavours on the finish.

Weather and timing
Good vintage, very small crop. Mild, wet winter. Cool spring and summer. Normal flowering. Dry autumn. Harvest Oct 21.

Quantity produced
1,332 cases (74%) released at Dm93 a case. Rheingau: 1,055,000.

1982 Spätlese. A great year for von Simmern although the size of the crop and the late rains show in the lack of extract and acidity respectively. Admirable ripeness and some chalky notes on top of ripe honeyed fruit in the bouquet, the only one showing any sign of kerosene. An excellent bottle packed with spicy Riesling flavours and good initial impact, if a slightly dilute finish.

Weather and timing
Very good vintage, double normal crop. Wet, cold winter. Beautiful spring. Flowering June 16. Hot summer. Wet autumn. Harvest Nov 5.

Quantity produced
616 cases (11%) released at Dm144 a case. Rheingau: 2,500,000 cases.

Other details
Size of vintage led to national storage problems causing a slump in the wine market.

1983 Auslese. A raw, unformed marvel. Viscous straw gold. Luscious yet low-key aromas in a distinctly primary state. Smoky, mineral, earthy Riesling scents underneath and then, after sweet fruit flavours, almost painful acidity. Beautiful balance and intensity with earthy acidity.

Weather and timing
Outstanding vintage, very large crop. Mild winter, wet spring. Flowering June 25. Good summer and autumn. Harvest Oct 21.

Quantity produced
66 cases (1½%) released at Dm420 a case. Rheingau: 1,654,000 cases.

Other details
Strong dollar stimulated American market.

1984 QbA. A real lightweight but very attractive. Deep straw with the piercing aroma of wet stones and high acidity. Pure Rheingau Riesling fruit flavours with spicy overtones. Good honest stuff with excellent balance.

Weather and timing
Average vintage, below average crop. Mild, dry winter followed by cold, wet spring. Flowering July 11. Harvest Nov 7.

Quantity produced
268 cases (81%) released at Dm96 a case. Rheingau: 959,000 cases.

Other details
Difficult to sell after 1983.

1985 Kabinett. Not a success, marked by the Orthene stink that marred so many German wines in the early eighties. Good, splashy, broadly painted fruit flavours, hints of lemon but not quite enough acid for the long term.

Weather and timing
Excellent vintage, very large crop. Cold, wet first half of the year. Flowering June 26. Hot summer and fine autumn. *Botrytis*-free harvest Nov 4. High acidity.

Quantity produced
3,033 cases (68%) released at Dm124.80 cases. Rheingau: 1,106,000 cases.

1986 Kabinett. Real zip, class and concentration on this powerful wine with smoky mineral scents. So racy it seems to vibrate on the palate. You could enjoy this wine at three years but probably shouldn't.

Weather and timing
Beautiful vintage, average crop. Harsh winter. Mild spring. Flowering June 21. Great summer. Stormy autumn. Harvest Oct 25.

Quantity produced
1,052 cases (54%) released at Dm124 a case. Rheingau: 1,476,000 cases.

1987 Kabinett. Less intense and nervy than the 1986 but very clean, delicate and pure. Honest, earthy flavours with overtly unadorned fruity acid. Neat and well balanced but not showy.

Weather and timing
Excellent vintage, average crop. Wet winter then fine spring. Flowering July 6. Poor summer. Wet autumn. Harvest Nov 3.

Quantity produced
2,698 cases (71%) released at Dm126 a case. Rheingau: 1,197,000 cases.

Other details
Difficult export market due to currency rates.

1988 (Not tasted) The average quality Spätlese was reported as full-bodied, with a high alcohol level. Mature acidity.

Weather and timing
Excellent vintage, below average crop. Mild, wet winter followed by even wetter spring. Flowering June 14. Fine summer but then dull, foggy autumn. Harvest Oct 14 to Nov 4.

Quantity produced
1,720 cases released at Dm 228 a case.

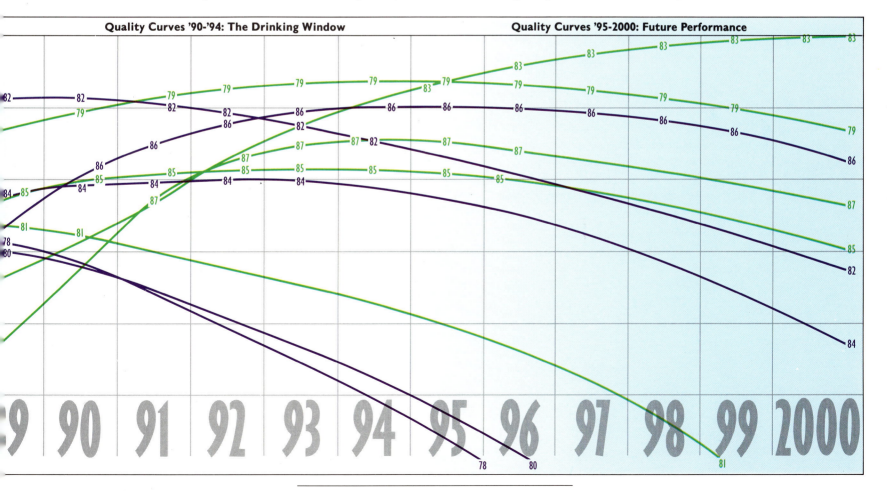

Quality Curves '90-'94: The Drinking Window

Quality Curves '95-2000: Future Performance

REST OF GERMANY

All Tafelwein, Landwein, all Liebfraumilch and most other QbA wines from outside the Mosel and Rheingau should be drunk as young as possible. Most Müller-Thurgau also comes off the bottling line and starts to go downhill, and Silvaners should generally be drunk within a year or two of bottling (but note the Franken exceptions below).

Other widely planted German grape varieties whose wines age notably rapidly are Bacchus, Morio-Muskat, Ortega, Optima and Reichensteiner. Kerner and Scheurebe are the only two new(ish) crossings whose wines are worth ageing, although they tend to decline at least five years before Riesling.

The total quantity produced in a given year does have an effect on quality, although the brake of Nature is unfortunately the only one most German vine-growers will heed for the moment. The bumper crop of 1982 for instance must be counted as one of Germany's least successful vintages ever. Other generalisations include the fact that, as in Burgundy, 1984 turned out some slightly austere but distinguised whites; 1982 was marked by September rot almost everywhere, and 1980 and 1978 were generally seen as poor, rather hard and definitely unripe vintages. Guidance on maturity given below refers to the wines of conscientious producers (membership of the VDP estates group distinguishes some of them).

In the Rheinpfalz, where wines tend to be characterised by a certain earthy richness, the 1975s seem delightfully stuck at a stage of perfect but still refreshing maturity, while a few 1976s are over the hill. Most of the wines made from 1977 to 1980 should have been drunk but 1979 and, particularly, 1981 were successful and there are still some good, higher grade QmP wines to be found. In general, these have lasted much better than the overpowering and generally flabby Pfalz 1983s. Lessons were learnt and put into practice with the 1985s, a great success resulting in powerful, fruity Pfalz wines that can already be drunk with pleasure but will last into the mid-nineties. 1986 was almost as ripe as 1985 and more closed in infancy while the 1987s were high in extract and the 1988s, as everywhere, much trumpeted after a perfect flowering. However, in the Rheinhessen the 1983 vintage was more successful than the 1985 which was hit by poor flowering conditions and turned out rather leaner wines. The very sweet 1975 and 1976 Rheinhessen can now be tackled, and the very best of 1978's bad bunch are, thanks to high acid, still improving in bottle. 1979 is regarded as the finest recent vintage after 1983 and is ready to drink at higher levels, although it is fading in the lower reaches. The 1983s are the wines to be opening now and should last into the early nineties, while the less luscious 1985s will definitely outlast them. The 1986s, on many of which September rain left its mark, are better than the thin 1987s but they are nowhere near as successful as the 1988s.

Baden is the only other sizeable German wine region. Few of its wines are built to last although some of the Black Forest Spätburgunders and Rieslings can improve with a couple of years in bottle. The only part of Baden whose wines have consistent ageability is Badisches Frankenland, the very northern spur that is viticulturally, even if not politically, part of Franken or Franconia.

Franken wines, quite distinct from those made in the rest of Germany, are difficult to find outside Franken, but are fine whites worthy of cellar space. Franken's winters are harsher and its summers much warmer than the rest of Germany so that yields vary enormously. The wines are less acid so the best vineyards face north and most of the wines are vinified dry.

The most long-lived recent vintages in Franken have been 1975 rather than the fatter 1976; 1979 and 1985 rather than the much less stable 1983. Silvaner, the local Rieslaner and even Müller-Thurgau are better bets over two, sometimes three, decades in bottle, than Riesling which has difficulty in ripening fully before the cool autumn sets in.

In the Nahe 1983 was the ripest year but 1985 was more concentrated while 1979 Spätlese wines are just coming into their own.

The jury is out on the cellar potential of the new *barrique*-aged Rieslings, although Weissburgunders should age quite gracefully for about five years.

PIEDMONT & TUSCANY

Piedmont's most famous grape, Nebbiolo, is actually named after the local mist, or *nebbia*, that swathes the hillsides and is so important to ripeness in Barolo and Barbaresco.

Italy provides lovers of fiercely distinctive reds with some of their longest-lasting bottles, even if, as elsewhere, the great majority of their wine is straightforward stuff designed to keep the thirsty Italians going until the next vintage. But Italian basic reds generally have more lasting qualities than their French counterparts, thanks to a warmer climate and less puny grape varieties. Further up the quality scale, the country the Greeks called "the land of wine" produces an extraordinary quantity and variety of wines worth ageing (see page 110) but that very variety makes them poor Timechart candidates.

PIEDMONT

Piedmont and Tuscany however are the two regions which regularly produce a substantial quantity of similarly-styled wines that demand attention and cellar space from the world's connoisseurs. And while the need to age Tuscan reds may be exaggerated in some cases, it is difficult to overestimate the time needed by some of Piedmont's examples.

In fact Piedmont (or Piemonte) is probably the region with the most serious designs on the world's cellars, specifically with its nearly black wines made from the intense, thick-skinned Nebbiolo grape. Barolo and Barbaresco are the two famous names. In youth, these are powerful, brooding hulks with enormous extract, alcohol and an almost painful grip

on the palate, but they eventually unfurl to a majestically harmonious whole emitting an extraordinary range of perfumes – violets, tar, truffles and *sottobosco*, or forest undergrowth.

This process takes longest for the wines made most traditionally. Some involve up to five weeks' leaching of phenols from the grape skins, often by keeping them submerged in the fermenting vat; no softening malolactic fermentation; and as much as eight years in large chestnut barrels or *botte* before bottling. Some of the most reliable traditionalists are Borgogno, Cavalloto, Clerico, both Aldo and Giacomo Conterno, Giacosa, Guiseppe Mascarello, Prunotto, Rinaldi and, to a certain extent, Vietti.

Although there is wide disparity in philosophy, the new wave of modernists may now ferment in stainless steel, encourage malolactic, and wood-age the wine for not much more than the legal minima of one year for Barbaresco and two for the generally more intense and long-lived Barolo. Good producers who embrace some aspects of modernism include Castello di Nieve, Ceretto, Cordero, Fontanafredda, Franco-Fiorina, Gaja, Marchesi de Gresy, Pio Cesare (in recent vintages) and the late pioneer of modernism, Renato Ratti. Angelo Gaja is a modernist whose Barbaresco lasts as long as many modernists' Barolo, it is so carefully invested with phenols and flavour elements. So the Gaja Timechart should be a fairly accurate guide to the ageing patterns of modernists'

Montalcino's altitude, above 1,600 feet (500 metres) gives the vines a long,
slow ripening period – like Brunello di Montalcino's in bottle.

Barolo: accelerate the chart by a year for other modernists' Barbaresco – and adjust as indicated overleaf for Gaja's single vineyard Barbarescos. Retard, rather than accelerate, the Gaja Timechart by two years for traditionalist Barolo.

Vintages matter enormously in this region, which is so high and therefore cool that it can be difficult to ripen the late Nebbiolo after a poor summer. The grape has to be planted on south-facing slopes to stand any chance at all of regular ripening. As in Burgundy, a region with which it shares an intricate latticework of individual vine-yards, hail is a persistent spring and summer threat. La Morra, a village which usually produces the most fragrant Barolos, for instance, was badly hit by hail which severely reduced the crop in May 1986.

There can however be subtle distinctions of overall performance between Barolo and Barbaresco within the same vintage. When inter-preting the Timechart, note that Barbaresco made in 1983 tends to have considerably more fruit than Barolo from the same year. And in 1984 some producers, particularly in Barolo which was more successful than Barbaresco, bottled a 1984, unlike Gaja. But most '84s are light and ready to drink. The recent star vintages are the 1985, 1982 and 1978, but the 1979s are worthy of serious consideration too. They all enjoy a period of maturity considerably longer than that of most other wines. It tends to be more of a plateau, too, because mature fine Barolo and Barbaresco is remarkably stable, in terms of its microbiology and its evolution.

The comments above refer to Barolo and Barbaresco from conscientious producers: many lesser examples hardly improve after they are put on the market. *Novello* bottlings such as Gaja's Vinot should be drunk as young as possible.

Most other local Nebbiolo wines, such as Roero and wines with Nebbiolo in their name, are only medium-bodied, quickly vinified wines which are designed to be drunk young. Like the other attract-ive reds made from the Dolcetto, Barbera, Freisa, Brachetto and Grignolino grapes grown in the region, these are wines with the sort of lifespans shown on Chart B on page 19. Nebbiolo-based wines which deserve cellaring, and for which the Gaja Timechart should be accelerated by two years (three for a particularly cheap bottle) include Boca, Bramaterra, Bricco del Drago, Bricco Manzoni, Caramino, Carema, Fara, Gattinara, Ghemme, Lessona, Sizzano, Spanna, and Nebbiolo d'Alba from the best producers. Even the region's most expensive non-Chardonnay whites rarely improve in bottle, and Piedmont's Asti and Moscati should be drunk straight from the corking machine.

TUSCANY

The Tuscan reds worth ageing tend to be made either from the local Sangiovese, from Cabernet Sauvignon imported from France, or from a blend of the two. But the Sangiovese vine has been allowed, even encouraged, to degenerate shamefully in central Italy and only carefully nurtured clones, selected for their suitability to individual sites and for the uncompromising quality of the fruit, are capable of producing ageworthy wines.

The most obvious example of this is the Brunello clone of Sangiovese selected by Biondi-Santi for Montalcino more than a century ago. In Biondi-Santi's wines Brunello shows the limit of durability that can be achieved by a Sangiovese: to trace their maturity patterns retard the Poggione Timechart by a generation – or a decade at least. The Poggione scale of evolution should be about right for most other quality-conscious Brunello producers such as Altesino, Fattoria dei Barbi-Colombini, Caparzo, Case Basse, Castelgiocondo, Col d'Orcia, Costanti, Lisini, Talenti and Val di Suga.

For the lighter and much more approachable Rosso di Montalcino, accelerate the Timechart by three years (except for the 1984 which was as disastrous in Montalcino as 1976 and 1972 and is not worthy of the name Brunello). Brusco dei Barbi has a similar timescale.

Vino Nobile di Montepulciano is subject to the same sort of vintage variation as wines from the Brunello area next door. But the wine produced is less concentrated and long-lived because the impact of Montepulciano's Sangiovese clone is diluted by other grapes and, perhaps, because wine-making there is less conscientious. Vino Nobile is in essence a Chianti Classico *Riserva* made south of the Chianti region near Montalcino. Accelerate the Poggione Timechart by two years, noting that Montalcino was particularly badly hit by hail in July 1981.

Most Tuscan reds are made to be drunk young but Chianti, which is effectively Tuscan for red, is maddeningly variable. Certainly almost all regular Chianti is at its best within three years of the vintage (four for one of the vintages signalled as especially good on the Tignanello chart). If however the Chianti is a *Riserva*, it should have been made of superior fruit, aged in oak for three years, and be built for the longer term. Although I have experienced respected Chianti *Riservas* well into their third decade, I have yet to taste one, even from the best Chianti Classico, Chianti Rufina and Chianti Montalbano zones, that tasted better at 12 years than eight. Those who appreciate fruit in their wines should accelerate the Tignanello Timechart by two years for most Chianti *Riservas*, noting that 1982 was

much more successful for Chianti Classico than Tignanello. The longest-living wines usually come from Chianti Rufina and Chianti Classico, but 1985 was a great year throughout the region.

Chianti may contain 10 per cent Cabernet Sauvignon, since 1984 when this highly satisfactory union was officially sanctioned. Tignanello represents the army of *barrique*-aged Tuscan reds made with more than usual care from various proportions of Cabernet and Sangiovese (often called Sangioveto when allied with aspirations to quality). Such wines can be recognised by their high prices, their Vino da Tavola designation and their fanciful and utterly impenetrable names. Coltassala, for example, is Castello di Volpaia's Tignanello counterpart, while Antinori's Solaia, Villa Banfi's Tavernelle and Frescobaldi's Mormoreto are made principally from Cabernet. *Barrique*-aged wines such as Monte Vertine's Le Pergole Torte contain only Sangiovese, on the other hand. The chart for the relatively forward Tignanello should be retarded by two years for most of these serious examples, although there are subtle distinctions between each.

The forerunner of these Sangiovese/Cabernet blends, embraced by the often untrustworthy DOC system, is Carmignano which is made in the Chianti Montalbano area. Accelerate the Tignanello chart by one year, two years for the local Barco Reale, but note that 1980 was particularly successful for Carmignano (as was 1978, 1975 and 1973).

Sassicaia is Tuscany's prototype all-Cabernet wine and, being made on the coast, well outside the Chianti zone, obeys its own rules. It shares disastrous vintages with Tignanello, is ready to broach at seven to eight years, and is at its peak at 10 to 12.

Novellos of all sorts should of course be drunk as young as possible. Most other Tuscan reds exported in any quantity are ready to drink at two to four years, Morellino di Scansano perhaps at three to five. In recent years almost all Tuscan whites need to be drunk as young as possible to preserve what little freshness they have. But good Vernaccia di San Gimignano and some of the few whites carefully made from Malvasia, the other indigenous variety, can repay two to three years in bottle. Oak-aged Chardonnays such as Frescobaldi's Il Benefizio are clearly being sculpted for a four- to five-year span. White wines were particularly successful in 1986.

Barbaresco, Gaja

At the conferences, symposia and celebrations that punctuate the international wine calendar it is often Angelo Gaja, graduate of wine schools in Alba, the Midi, Burgundy and Germany, who is the lone representative of the world's biggest wine producing country. His presence is particularly striking. With his deep-set eyes, almost translucent pallor and unnaturally angular features, he can look more like an image of Futurism than a man; though it is impossible to think of him without thinking of his very real dynamism.

Before Angelo took over as fourth generation head of the firm, Gaja was simply one of Barbaresco's more respectable and dependable *cantine*. In Angelo's hands Gaja has become famous for flaunting every local convention. Some updating was perhaps inevitable in the hidebound cellars of Piedmont, but Angelo Gaja has imported his own whirlwind of almost frenetic change.

Using the family's 137 acres (55 hectares) of prime vineyard land as a canvas Angelo has painted a new landscape with childlike energy and enthusiasm. In 1978 he began to plant rows downhill and vines much closer together, closely pruned so that, to mitigate his philosophy of reducing time in oak, each one produces less but better fruit. He erected three weather stations in the vineyard to provide him with better pre-spraying intelligence and pulled up Nebbiolo vines, the area's lifeblood. In their place he planted Cabernet Sauvignon and Chardonnay, releasing them to considerable applause in the early eighties. In the winery he introduced *barriques* experimentally as far back as 1969, played with carbonic maceration and, for more conventional wines, altered the maceration time to between 20 and 25 days. In 1981 he introduced an even more tauntingly modern element, computerised stainless steel fermentation tanks in which temperatures can be maintained at around 80°F (26°C). There must be times when the villagers of Barbaresco wonder what they talked about in pre-Angelo days.

But these are just some of the means towards some incontrovertibly delicious ends, notably the Gaja range of Barbarescos. The regular bottling, on whose label the name Barbaresco is dwarfed by the name Gaja, has been joined by Gaja's trio of individual vineyard or *cru* bottlings: the luscious, extravagantly perfumed Costa Russi, the fought-over long-distance runner Sori'Tildin, and the extraordinarily concentrated Sori'San Lorenzo which seems to combine the attributes of the other two.

These *cru* wines sell at considerably higher prices than Bordeaux first growths (they are admittedly produced in much smaller quantity) but seem to be establishing themselves, along with Biondi Santi wines, as Italy's only surefire wine investments. Costa Russi usually takes two years longer to mature than the regular Barbaresco while the other two *crus* may need an additional five and will continue to evolve for perhaps 15 years rather than 10.

Earlier vintages
Angelo's father also made extremely good, if slower-maturing wines. The (fading) 1961 and rather longer-lived 1964 still repay serious attention. The powerful 1971 is also a great vintage and showed more colour than the 1982 when they were tasted alongside each other in 1986. The 1974 was another successful vintage, with more concentration than the 1973.

1978 A very great, stately vintage that displays more traditional, oxidative techniques than any others since. Extraordinarily deep crimson with more concentration than any other wine in this range. Wood-smoke and tar on the still quite unresolved nose. Savoury and many-layered. Not entirely unlike a great young Landonne with almost aggressive briariness warning the taster off for many a year. Long.

Weather and timing
Great vintage, small crop. Normal winter. Cool, wet spring. Hot from mid-June. Dry Sept. Fine for harvest. High tannin and alcohol levels.

Quantity produced
7,150 cases released at L78,000 a case. Barbaresco DOCG production: 293,620 cases.

Other details
New vineyards, closely planted.

1979 A very successful, voluptuous wine from an accessible vintage overshadowed by the 1978. Gorgeous layers of Barbaresco's characteristic violets and tar flavours already emerging from this relatively soft, heady specimen.

Weather and timing
Very good vintage, above average crop. Cold Jan. Mild spring. Good for flowering. Average summer. Wet early Oct then fine.

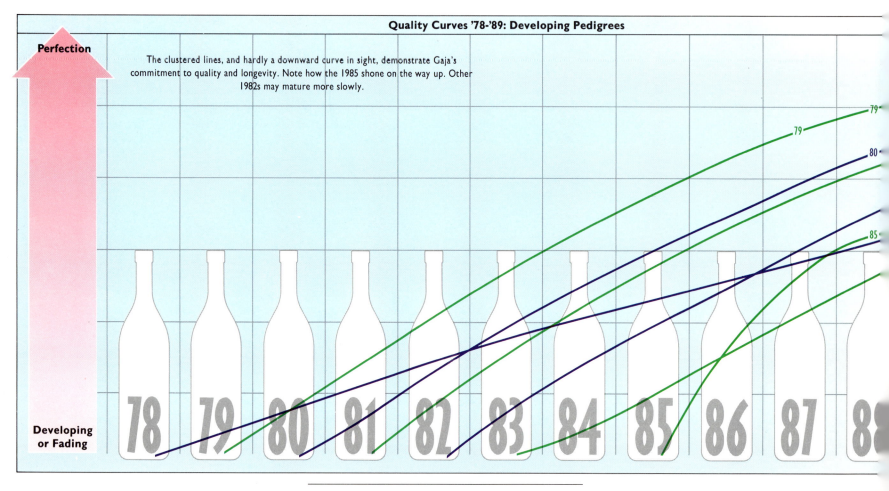

Quality Curves '78–'89: Developing Pedigrees

Perfection

The clustered lines, and hardly a downward curve in sight, demonstrate Gaja's commitment to quality and longevity. Note how the 1985 shone on the way up. Other 1982s may mature more slowly.

Developing or Fading

78 79 80 81 82 83 84 85 86 87 88

Quantity produced

10,130 cases released at L108,000 a case. Barbaresco: 293,544 cases.

1980 The first of a pair of rather unexciting vintages in which it may be necessary to head *cru*-wards for real spark. Light crimson with a low-key, relatively undistinguished nose and a hint of compost. Lightweight for a Barbaresco with aggressive tannin and acid more in evidence than fruit in 1988.

Weather and timing

Average vintage, normal crop. Mild winter, little snow. Wet spring. Cool June and July then hot and dry. Rain end Sept and early Oct: harvest delayed.

Quantity produced

6,550 cases released at L120,000 a case. Barbaresco: 293,678 cases.

1981 A less concentrated rehearsal for 1982. Smoky, autumnal, *sottobosco* flavours with good acid and tannin but in late 1988 it

seemed to need a little more ripe fruit concentration.

Weather and timing

Good vintage, normal crop. Cold winter. Hot, humid June and July. Early Aug hot and dry then some rain. Dry and cloudy for harvest: careful selection needed.

Quantity produced

6,830 cases released at L168,000 a case. Barbaresco: 308,022 cases.

Other details

New temperature-controlled fermentation tanks. Improved disease control system.

1982 A much vaunted vintage showing its paces in terms of size, solidity and richness. Deep crimson with real evolution at the rim. Enormous fruit convinces the palate it will eventually ride out the tannin (which is lower than in many more typical Barbarescos). Scents of charcoal and chestnut flatter the nose but the palate is more flattered by the 1985.

Weather and timing

Great vintage, normal crop. Very dry spring. Snow storm Apr 24. Dry summer. Rain early Oct. Fine for harvest.

Quantity produced

9,250 cases released at L336,000 a case. Barbaresco: 306,467 cases.

1983 A relatively floral, aromatic wine hinting at violets, luscious prunes and toast. Relatively taut, dry and restrained. Serious stuff.

Weather and timing

Very good vintage, normal crop. Dry winter, no major snow storms. Rain during flowering. Hot, humid July; careful disease control. Variable Aug and Sept. Good for harvest.

Quantity produced

8,790 cases released at L336,000 a case. Barbaresco: 323,689 cases.

1984 Rotten vintage entirely declassified. It is in years such as this that Gaja's carbonic macer-

ation Nebbiolo Vinot presumably comes into its own.

Weather and timing

Poor vintage, small crop. Cold, wet May; late flowering. Variable season, often cool. Incomplete maturation before harvest.

Quantity produced

Barbaresco: 318,422 cases.

1985 Simply extraordinary. Angelo Gaja regards this as his best vintage ever. This regular Barbaresco should confound those who maintain that the *cru* bottlings have prejudiced the quality of the basic blend. Exceptional depth of colour and still perceptible oak flavours on the wine just after its release late in 1988. Charred autumnal fruit flavours. Quite youthful aromatic nose in which it is easy to perceive the scent of violets. Like a punch in the mouth at this young stage but with a dry finish already showing layers of fruits and flowers.

Weather and timing

Great vintage, below average crop. Two large snow storms in winter. Hot, dry July and Aug (rain Aug 25). Grapes matured well. Perfect for harvest.

Quantity produced

8,270 cases released at L480,000 a case. Barbaresco: 313,944 cases.

Other details

Increasing interest, especially in Germany, USA, Switzerland and Austria, continued to push up the price.

1986 *(Not tasted)* Reported as having good concentration and backbone with brilliant colour.

Weather and timing

Very good vintage, normal crop. Cold winter. Higher than average humidity throughout the year. Aug very hot and humid. Dry, cool Sept. Fine for harvest.

Quantity produced

Unknown. Release date 1989. Barbaresco: 316,200 cases.

1987 *(Not tasted)* More forward than the 1986, according to Gaja. Elegant with ripe tannins.

Weather and timing

Good vintage, normal crop. Long winter; snow in Mar. Cool spring. Very hot July with storms. Harvest completed before rain began on Oct 10.

Quantity produced

Unknown. Release date 1990. Barbaresco: 309,244 cases.

1988 *(Not tasted)* Gaja reported that this wine had great concentration of colour and extract with impressive fruit and firm tannin.

Weather and timing

Outstanding vintage, below average crop. Dry, mild winter. May 8-15 wet. Wet June. July hot and dry then hot and humid. Light rain end Aug. Perfect Sept. Oct 10-16 wet otherwise warm and dry.

Quantity produced

Unknown. Release date 1991.

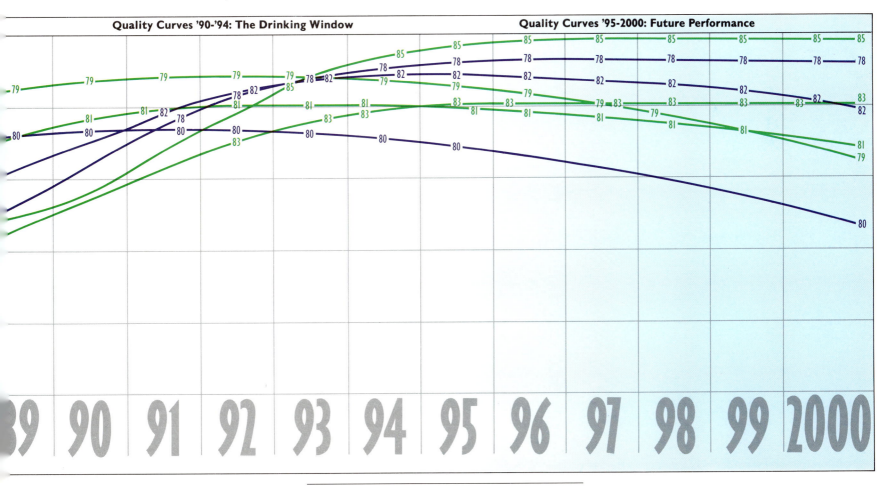

Quality Curves '90-'94: The Drinking Window   **Quality Curves '95-2000: Future Performance**

Tignanello, Antinori

For Marchese Piero Antinori, who is so determinedly situated at Italy's interface with the rest of the world, Tignanello is "the top, the number one, not just for what it represents for Antinori but, not to seem immodest, for what it represents in the evolution of Italian oenology".

In Tignanello we have the past, present and future of the Chianti Classico region. Like so many of the wines it has spawned, Tignanello is sold (in some quantity) as a mere *vino da tavola*. Yet this wine, conceived in the late sixties and eventually released only with the 1971 vintage, demonstrated a way forward for a region then beset with the problems of over-productive vines and oenological torpor.

Antinori, one of the most ancient yet dynamic Tuscan wine houses, showed how Sangiovese grapes grown in the heart of the Chianti Classico region could be sculpted into a red of world class quality and depth, albeit slightly rustic. Techniques were introduced such as pumping over the must for maximum colour extraction; malolactic fermentation to strengthen character and soften acidity, and significant maturation in small oak barrels rather than in the traditional large old wooden *botte*.

Four years later the second vintage of Tignanello, the 1975, then showed how a seasoning of Cabernet Sauvignon (first planted by Piero's father back in the thirties) could complement a wine produced solely from a Sangiovese clone. The clone was specially selected by Antinori for the 110-acre

(45-hectare) Tignanello vineyard in their Santa Cristina estate which is about 1,300 feet (400 metres) above the warmth of the Mediterranean, and on Tuscany's distinctive calcareous *galestro* soil.

The ideal proportion of Cabernet Sauvignon in the blend has finally been settled at 20 per cent. The Cabernet is drawn from a 25-acre (10-hectare) vineyard adjacent to Tignanello which also produces the raw material for Antinori's rather tougher, grander (and considerably more expensive) all-Cabernet wine, Solaia.

Despite its Cabernet element, Tignanello is still essentially a Tuscan wine, unlike Solaia or Sassicaia which has been produced by Antinori from vineyards on the Tuscan coast. It serves to illustrate how a top quality Chianti such as Chianti Classico, or indeed a well-made example of the new Tuscan breed of Sangiovese/Cabernet blend, can age, and how much each vintage depends on its climatological history.

As reflected in most bottles of Chianti, these are wines whose life expectancy is short relative to many of the other red wines in this book, notably those of the Rhône, Bordeaux and Piedmont. Part of the reason for this fairly rapid evolution is that the wines hold only a short plateau of perfection, continuing to change quite perceptibly even during their ideal period for drinking. But this is just one of several respects in which Tignanello is so typical of the Chianti region's wines.

Earlier vintages

1971 Already old, particularly in terms of its volatility. Drying out but obviously initially well-balanced and voluptuous. **1975** A famous but rare vintage of which only 2,500 cases were produced. Starting to fade. **1977** Lovely, complete, luscious yet savoury wine at its peak with real grip and vigour.

1978 A controversial wine which has its devotees but Piero and I are not among them. A little more Slavonian oak than most which perhaps explains the dryness and slight mustiness on the nose. Lacks fruit to hold it together.

Weather and timing
Good vintage, small crop. Poor start to the year. Wet during flowering June 12. Fine growing season. Separate harvests began Sept 20 (Cabernet) and Oct 1 (Sangiovese).

Quantity produced
16,330 cases released at L63,600 a case.

Other details
Continued ageing system introduced in 1977, in which one third of the wine was kept in new oak, one third in barrels that had previously completed one ageing cycle (18-24 months) and one third in barrels that had completed two cycles.

1979 Hint of chocolate on the nose but overall a hollow, ungenerous sort of wine without much staying power.

Weather and timing
Excellent vintage, large crop. Good conditions throughout the season. Perfect flowering June 10. Early maturation. Harvest began Sept 18 (Cabernet) and Sept 28 (Sangiovese).

Quantity produced
21,000 cases released at L75,600 a case.

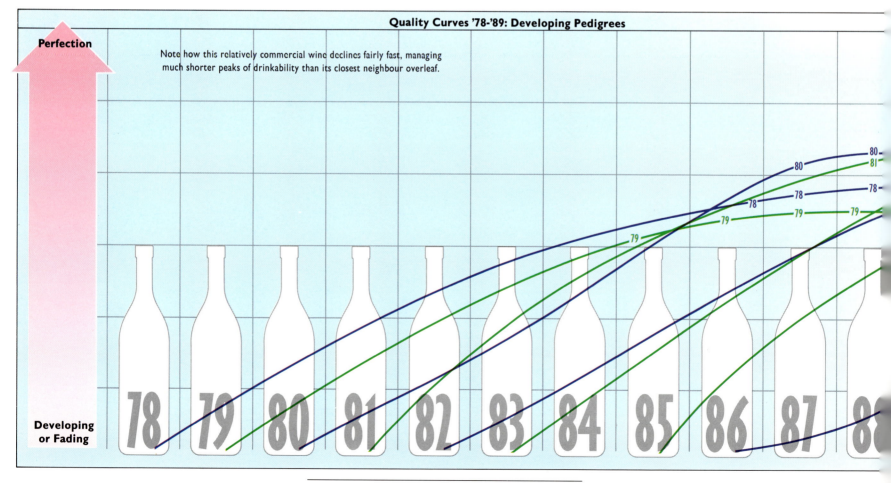

Quality Curves '78-'89: Developing Pedigrees

Perfection

Note how this relatively commercial wine declines fairly fast, managing much shorter peaks of drinkability than its closest neighbour overleaf.

Developing or Fading

78 79 80 81 82 83 84 85 86 87 88

Other details
Wine aged in 30% semi-new and 70% new oak.

1980 Looks younger than 1981. The Cabernet is a particularly obvious ingredient in the bouquet. Strong cassis: warm blackcurrant fruit gums. Young, with an undertow of warmth.

Weather and timing
Good vintage, below average crop. Flowering mid-June. Late harvest began Sept 25 (Cabernet) and Oct 5 (Sangiovese); interrupted by rain.

Quantity produced
20,556 cases released at L94,800 a case.

Other details
Wine aged in 30% *Tronçais* oak, 70% Yugoslavian oak. Tall, dark bottle introduced for extended bottle ageing.

1981 Already orange at the rim. A brawny character with no marked Cabernet. Could be mis-

taken for a particularly good Chianti Classico. Confident and ready to drink with mouthfilling flavours of undergrowth.

Weather and timing
Outstanding vintage, above average crop. Good start to year then mixed weather with frost and hail. Wet during harvest which began Sept 20 (Cabernet) and Sept 26 (Sangiovese).

Quantity produced
21,667 cases released at L114,000 a case.

Other details
70% Slavonian oak, 30% *Tronçais*.

1982 Already quite evolved on the nose with some suggestion of chestnuts and very slight cheesiness. Big, solid, still quite tannic very Sangiovese. Very slighty coarse.

Weather and timing
Excellent vintage, above average crop. Flowering early June. Hail early Sept. Harvest began Sept 20

(Cabernet) and Sept 28 (Sangiovese).

Quantity produced
27,778 cases released at L150,000 a case. Total Tuscan production: 50,600,000 cases.

Other details
50% Slavonian oak, 50% *Tronçais*.

1983 One of Piero's favourites. Relatively herbaceous and youthful even though deceptively full and flattering with tannins well hidden by attractive fruit. Some oakiness. Should develop into something exciting.

Weather and timing
Outstanding vintage, average crop. Average rainfall. Flowering early June. Harvest began Sept 22 (Cabernet) and Sept 30 (Sangiovese).

Quantity produced
27,778 cases released at L168,000 a case. Tuscany: 52,100,000 cases.

Other details
40% Slavonian oak, 60% *Tronçais*.

1984 Year of the introduction of DOCG for Chianti, and an unmitigated disaster in terms of weather and therefore wines.

Weather and timing
Poor vintage, below average crop. Wet Apr-June; flowering early June. Dull, cool summer. Late harvest.

Quantity produced
None made. Tuscany: 39,200,000 cases.

1985 Deep purple concentration. Warm, integrated, full-flavoured slightly rustic nose which was going into retreat in late 1988, not least because of the sublime concentration of ripe fruit. Should become something absolutely splendid and very serious. A great year.

Weather and timing
Outstanding vintage, small crop. Flowering June 1. Hot, dry summer followed by hot autumn. Good harvest began Sept 15

(Cabernet) and Sept 24 (Sangiovese).

Quantity produced
30,000 cases. Release date 1989. Tuscany: 36,600,000 cases.

Other details
35% *Tronçais* oak, 25% Yugoslavian and 25% Slavonian.

1986 Deep purple and attractively aromatic with notes of tobacco and chocolate. Excellent ripe fruit and excitingly classic structure. Not unlike 1986 Bordeaux in build. A thoroughbred.

Weather and timing
Average vintage, above average crop. A hot year with irregular rainfall. Flowering June 9. Rain during July. Fine Sept; harvest began Sept 22 (Cabernet) and Sept 29 (Sangiovese).

Quantity produced
30,000 cases. Tuscany: 42,600,000.

Other details
40% *Tronçais* and *Allier* oak, 30% Slavonian, 30% *Tronçais*.

1987 (*Not tasted*) A promising start.

Weather and timing
Good vintage, above average crop. Excellent during flowering. Beautiful summer. Fine for harvest which began on Sept 23 (Cabernet) and on Oct 3 (Sangiovese); rigorous selection.

Quantity produced
Not yet determined. Tuscany: 44,000,000 cases.

1988 (*Not tasted*) Will be one of the best vintages in the Chianti Classico region for the last 20-30 years with great concentration, power and harmony.

Weather and timing
Very good vintage, small crop. Cold and wet during flowering, which disrupted set. Hot, dry summer; good maturation. Harvest began Sept 22 (Cabernet) and Oct 1 (Sangiovese).

Quantity produced
Not yet determined.

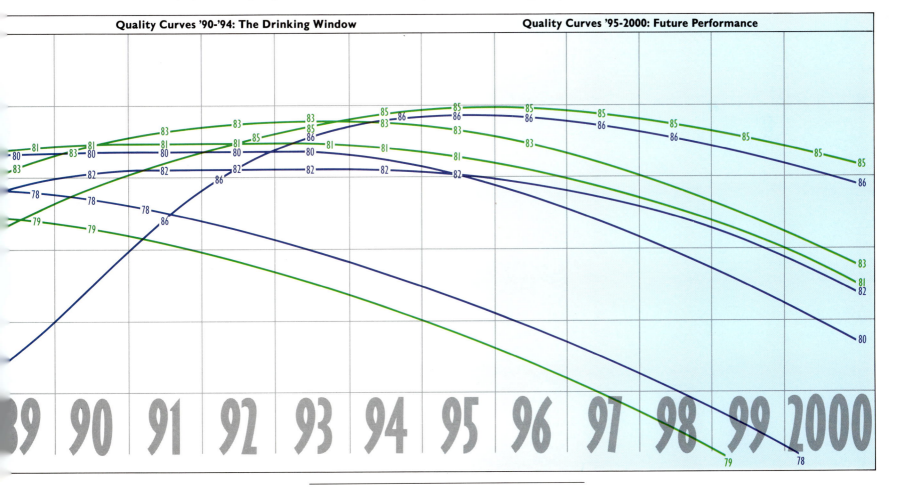

Quality Curves '90-'94: The Drinking Window

Quality Curves '95-2000: Future Performance

Brunello di Montalcino, Il Poggione

Unlike the Vino Nobile produced at nearby Montepulciano, Brunello di Montalcino fully deserved its elevation to DOGG status in 1980. There are other wine-makers in and around this bustling hill-top town south of Siena who have consistently produced vintages impressive in their concentration of local fruit and their staying power. The most famous of them all of course is the house of Biondi Santi, which can justifiably claim to have etched Brunello di Montalcino's name on the world vinicultural map. To prove it they can boast no fewer than three bottles of hundred-year-old wine in their little cellar of antiquities. The Biondi Santi style however would be difficult to accommodate on a chart such as this. Indeed it is difficult enough to accommodate in a society dedicated to projects that can be realised in a lifetime. The Brunello of Biondi Santi tastes as though it will still be around to be admired two generations hence. Brunello is of course the name of the local Sangiovese clone which was isolated at Montalcino by the Bondi-Santis of the last century.

Fine wines are also made by the likes of Altesino, Caparzo and Case Basse but the wines of the Tenuta Il Poggione seem ideally suited to the timescale of this book, offering sufficient fruit in youth to be broachable within 10 years of fermentation and with a good following abroad, where 80 per cent of all bottles are eventually enjoyed.

Wine-maker Piero Talenti manages the estate, for Clemente and Roberto Franceschi. (He has his own small

Talenti wine farm producing fine, ageworthy wines nearby on the outskirts of San Angelo in Colle, the village dominated by the Franceschis' castle.) His policy is to maintain quality by a strict selection, selling off substantial quantities of wine in bulk and bottling generous proportions as the lesser, earlier-maturing DOC Rosso di Montalcino, which is a particularly good buy from Il Poggione.

Although the estate comprises 200 varied acres (80 hectares) of clay and limestone vineyards, typically punctuated by rows of olive trees, Signor Talenti has so far resisted the temptation to adopt the fashionable "cru" notion of single-vineyard bottlings.

Instead in particularly good years there may be a Riserva, but Poggione Brunello's hallmark is a rich fruitiness that belies its mere nine-day fermentation and ageing for as long as four years, admittedly in large traditional wood rather than modish new *barriques*.

In the younger wines, the strongest hints at future form are not on the nose but in the aftertaste. Signor Talenti counsels an average age of eight years before the wines reach their plateau of drinkability, but these are wines that last much longer than most Chianti and Tuscan blends such as Tignanello.

Signor Talenti's practice is to open bottles just before the meal at which they are to be drunk, decanting them into wide jugs from which they are poured from a considerable height.

Earlier vintages
It is worth looking out for the Riservas of 1970, 1971, 1975 and 1977 but *la crème de la crème* for current drinking is the 1969 Riserva which somehow combines the ethereal scents of a fully mature red wine, strong on wood-smoke and prunes, with the friskiness of a wine so concentrated and well balanced that it has a good five years of delicious drinking ahead of it.

1978 Riserva. Big, brooding, immature wine. Looks and smells if anything younger than the 1979. At 10 years old it was still very slightly dull and clodhopping, thick and full-blooded, bigger than the 1979: apparently biding its time before resolving itself into anything more complex.
Weather and timing
Good vintage, very small crop. Normal season with average rain-

fall. Bud break Apr 10. Flowering mid-May. Harvest Oct 1-25.
Quantity produced
7,000 cases. Total production for Montalcino: 222,000 cases.

1979 Riserva. An exceptional wine, definitely ready to drink. Good deep crimson with rich tawny (and a very slight fizz) at the rim. Seductive, fully mature truffley, *sottobosco* bouquet. Masses of opulent dried fruit and nut flavours with lovely violet top notes.
Weather and timing
Good vintage, normal crop. Wet spring. Late bud break and flowering. Very hot summer, with rain, allowed vines to catch up. Harvest began early Oct.
Quantity produced
8,500 cases. Montalcino: 311,000 cases.

1980 Riserva. Fully mature colour with a brick rim. Fully integrated bouquet somehow sug-

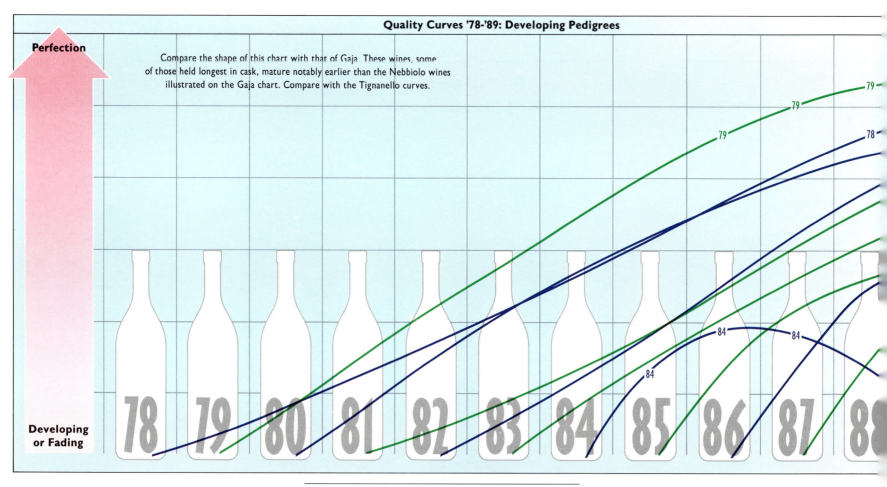

Quality Curves '78-'89: Developing Pedigrees

Perfection

Compare the shape of this chart with that of Gaja. These wines, some of those held longest in cask, mature notably earlier than the Nebbiolo wines illustrated on the Gaja chart. Compare with the Tignanello curves.

Developing or Fading

78 79 80 81 82 83 84 85 86 87 88

gests bonfires, with ripe fruit much in evidence. Slightly more interesting than the 1981. Well balanced and savoury with something prune-like on the finish.

Weather and timing
Good vintage, above average crop. Delayed start to the season; late flowering. Hot summer and fine autumn. Harvest early Oct.

Quantity produced
8,000 cases. Montalcino: 333,000.

Other details
Leopoldo Franceschi died: his sons, Roberto and Clemente, became the new owners. Established wine-making techniques continued by Pierluigi Talenti, technical director.

1981 Fairly undistinguished. Relatively pale and with a low-key bouquet. Chewy and slightly dull with some smoke and minerals in the finish. Not exciting.

Weather and timing
Good vintage, normal crop. Good

flowering. Dry summer delayed ripening. Very careful selection at harvest.

Quantity produced
6,000 cases. Montalcino: 311,000.

1982 Respectable specimen that looks more than a year older than the 1983. Something vegetal on the nose as well as strong cherry fruit. Medium weight and intensity with tannins in retreat. Good spice – nutmeg – on the finish.

Weather and timing
Excellent vintage, above average crop. Good start to the year; early bud break and flowering. Normal summer. Excellent for harvest.

Quantity produced
10,500 cases. Montalcino: 356,000 cases.

1983 Good ripe but tough wine with dark crimson hue, lots of acidity and definite life and nerve. Well balanced, well-knit bouquet of ripe red fruits, figs and

wood-smoke. Quite powerful with considerable tannin still very much in evidence. Much less charming than the 1985 because there is so much less extract, but clearly a very serious wine.

Weather and timing
Good vintage, large crop. Good spring and summer but poor autumn. Careful selection during harvest in order to maintain quality.

Quantity produced
7,300 cases. Montalcino: 389,000 cases.

Other details
Most of this wine came from vineyards planted in 1980.

1984 (Cask sample) A wine that should have been bottled at one or two years and sold as something considerably lowlier than Brunello. After four years in cask it had lost whatever fruit it had and developed merely a cheesy nose to distract from the

high acidity and attenuated character that is all this vintage could manage.

Weather and timing
Poor vintage, normal crop. Once again the first half of the year was fine then conditions deteriorated. Rain from mid-Sept through harvest.

Quantity produced
4,400 cases. Montalcino: 300,000.

1985 (Cask sample) The star of this range – although the 1987 rivals it. Exceptionally deep crimson with markedly high glycerol. Intense bouquet of roasted chestnuts. Dense, chewy, dark, very young but extremely exciting. Massive, exciting and extremely promising with a finish suggesting bitter chocolate.

Weather and timing
Excellent vintage, normal crop. Very cold winter; vines undamaged. Normal bud break. Rain during flowering; incomplete set.

Excellent summer and autumn; perfect maturation. Good harvest.

Quantity produced
10,400 cases. Montalcino: 311,000.

1986 (Cask sample) An early maturer. Relatively pale with a colourless rim showing lack of concentration. Open, smoky full-blown aromas that make a relatively low-key mouthful with a hint of bacon and a dry finish.

Weather and timing
Fair vintage, above average crop. Normal conditions throughout the year. Poor autumn.

Quantity produced
9,000 cases. Montalcino: 330,000.

1987 (Cask sample) Exceptionally attractive ripe mellow cocktail of warm, ripe aromas. Very attractive in youth with its ripe fruit and soft tannins but an impressively long, rich finish suggests that this wine will last too.

Weather and timing
Good vintage, above average

crop. Normal spring. Excellent summer; hot with rain. Ripened early. Good harvest.

Quantity produced
10,000 cases. Montalcino: 330,000.

1988 (Cask sample) Lighter than the 1987 although a good purple colour. Young, straight-forward fruit flavours showing great health and skilful wine-making. Quite openly aromatic with the scents of ripe red fruits. Medium weight with marked acidity and good structure. This one will almost certainly put on flesh to rival the 1987 during barrel ageing.

Weather and timing
Excellent vintage, above average crop. Cold Apr then warm; normal flowering. Dry summer. Early harvest.

Quantity produced
11,000 cases. Montalcino: 330,000 cases.

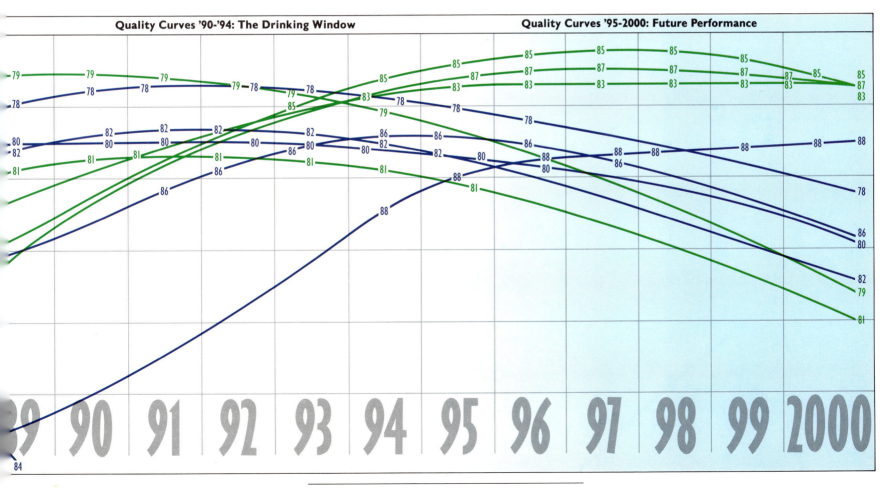

Quality Curves '90-'94: The Drinking Window

Quality Curves '95-2000: Future Performance

REST OF ITALY

As a very general observation, any Italian wine labelled *Classico* or *Superiore* must be worthy of an extra year of bottle age on a regular bottling, and a *Riserva* is worth an extra two. Most of the wines produced in the Veneto, whatever their colour, are made for early consumption. The cheapest examples of that traduced trio Soave, Bardolino and Valpolicella follow the ageing pattern outlined in Chart A (page 19).

Medium-range examples of most Veneto wines follow Chart B, (also page 19) remembering that especially good recent years in the Veneto were 1988, 1986 and 1985. Whites that could benefit from of up to three years in bottle include the most seriously made Soaves such as Anselmi's Capitel Foscarino and Masi's Col Baraca; Maculan's dry whites and Tedeschi's Capitel San Rocco.

Veneto reds, even those based on Cabernet Sauvignon, are at their fruity best well before five years. Most Veneto "Cabernet" is Cabernet Franc, which is worth ageing for two or three years. Most ageworthy of all are Venegazzù, Riserva della Casa and Maculan's Cabernet-based reds, which need a good five years in bottle.

Apart from the exceptionally tough red made from Raboso, some of the seriously ageworthy wines produced in the Veneto are those labelled Recioto. Of these, Amarone in particular requires not only a summer in which conditions up to the harvest ripen the grapes well and extremely healthily, but also an autumn and early winter which is dry and settled enough to concentrate the grapes' sugars while warding off rot. Good years for Amarone are therefore much rarer than those for straight Valpolicella, for example. 1984 was good for Recioto but mediocre for other wines, while 1982 was poor for Amarone and fine for the rest.

These wines are so rich that their evolution is fairly slow, as shown for Masi's top Amarone (which was perhaps less successful than its peers in 1977, and more so in 1975). The Mazzano Timechart gives a good idea of the ageing of other serious bottlings of Amarone such as those of Allegrini, Quintarelli and Tedeschi. For more commercial bottlings, accelerate the chart by three years.

For straight Recioto della Valpolicella without the Amarone qualification, a rich red with about 14 per cent alcohol, accelerate the Mazzano chart by two years; four years for very commercial bottlings (of which there are few). For a Vino da Tavola made by the *ripasso* method of refermenting Valpolicella on Recioto lees, such as Masi's Campo Fiorin and Tedeschi's Capitel San Rocco, accelerate the Mazzano chart by about two years.

The sweet, tangy white Recioto di Soave matures one to two years ahead of Recioto della Valpolicella, so accelerate the Mazzano chart by three years. Tedeschi's glorious sweet Vin de la Fabrisia matures at about the same rate as a Recioto di Soave, as does Maculan's equally noble (and equally astringent in youth) sweet golden Torcolato.

Further northeast most wines are even more clearly made for early consumption. Most of the wine, red and white, of Trentino-Alto Adige and Friuli-Venezia-Giulia – typically a varietal made from one of the various Pinots, Cabernets, Merlots, Rieslings, Traminers, Sauvignons, Tocais, Ribollas, Teroldegos, Schiavas or Lagreins – is made to be drunk on a Chart B timescale. The exceptions are the odd Cabernet and Lagrein that have serious intentions. 1985 and 1983 were particularly concentrated recent years for Alto Adige reds.

Whites that can take longer ageing – up to five years in bottle – are the best sweet wines made from Picolit, the finest Verduzzo from the Colli Orientali del Friuli, some particularly fine examples of Ribolla and the startlingly dense, characterful wines made by Jermann, most notably Vintage Tunina. Only a handful of Chardonnays are also worth ageing past three years. The vintages 1986 and 1985 were both especially good for Friuli whites.

Among ageworthy reds are Carso, Tazzelenghe and the best examples of Refosco and Schioppettino, although to many palates they are at their best when their natural bite is balanced by youthful fruitiness.

Lombardy reds are, typically, bumptious fruity things which are at their best about four years after the vintage. They include Franciacorta, Ca' del Bosco's Zanelli Bordeaux blend, most Oltrepo-Pavese reds and Valtellina Superiore such as Sassella,

Grumello, Inferno and Valgella. 1985 and 1983 were exceptional recent vintages.

To the south, Emilia-Romagna is a wine region of quantity rather than quality with its most famous wine Lambrusco being the archetypal advertisement for the virtues of youth. Bottle age is no friend of even the finest Lambrusco. Sangiovese di Romagna is made from a particularly undistinguished clone and is usually local dialect for basic red. Fattoria Paradiso's Barbarossa, Baldi's Ronco and Terre Rosse's reds and Chardonnay are exceptional wines which can improve with up to five years' bottle age.

Some of the reds of the Marches on the other hand can show real interest and ageability, particularly the finest bottlings of Rosso Conero which were particularly promising in 1985 and 1982.

Umbria, right in the centre of Italy, can boast one or two wines which have for years been Italy's most worthy cellar candidates. The foremost producer is Lungarotti at Torgiano whose consistent Rubesco resembles a sun-baked, comforting Umbrian answer to the more angular charms of Tuscany's reds, and which has similar ageing potential. For straight Rubesco Torgiano, accelerate the Poggione chart by three years, while the single vineyard Rubesco Torgiano Riserva Vigna Monticchio, and in fact its Cabernet-influenced stablemate San Giorgio, should mature to a pattern very similar to that of Poggione. Torgiano has enjoyed a run of good vintages – particularly 1986, 1985, 1982, 1980 and 1975, of which the Vigna Monticchio is still a credit to Dr Lungarotti.

Although most Orvieto is best drunk on a Chart B timescale, Umbria produces some ageworthy whites. Antinori's Castello della Sala and Cervaro stand out, as do Lungarotti whites such as Chardonnay di Miralduolo which can still be improving at five years (three for Castello della Sala).

South of this, drought and consequent vine shutdown is the major problem. A good vintage is one in which the sun does not shine too mercilessly, there are at least some drops of rain and acidity levels can be kept from slipping. Whites tend either to be full and lack the acidity necessary for ageing, or to have the acidity but only because they have been picked so early or treated so harshly that they have little else. They are Chart A wines. The reds can often be satisfyingly high in character, and colour, but lack the intensity and constitution for a life longer than that indicated on Chart B.

Any Montepulciano d'Abruzzo, that underpriced, well-built red, repays two years in bottle. Some of the more firmly constituted ones can continue to develop for up to a decade. 1983 was an exceptional year.

Wines which positively demand ageing are: Taurasi (especially 1985 and 1983), impenetrably tannic when young but opening out to surprising lushness and complexity after a decade or two; the extraordinarily full, scented whites Fiano di Avellino (1985, 1983) and Valentini's Trebbiano d'Abruzzo (1985, 1983); the positively volcanic Aglianico del Vulture (1985, 1981); Apulia's Castel del Monte (1985, 1984); and the red version of Ciro from Calabria (1986). Such wines are made from well ripened grapes vinified to extract maximum phenolics. They can be barbarically aggressive in youth but reward patience just as richly as their more famous northern counterparts.

The islands are still putting their vineyards and wineries in order and can field few serious candidates for cellar space other than their sometimes magnificent fortified wines. These include superior Marsala, Moscato di Pantelleria and Vernaccia di Oristano (1985, 1982) from Sardinia which tend to earn cellar space for their rarity rather than for their need for bottle age. Sicily's reds can be too coarse to age and too alcoholic in raw youth, but Regeleali's Rosso del Conte, made only in particularly successful years, can be a heady marvel after a decade.

Amarone Mazzano, Masi

This chart is different from others in this book because Amarone, or Recioto della Valpolicella Amarone to give it its full name, is such an extraordinary wine. This is true even of the more commercial Amarones but particularly of what might be termed the "first growth" Amarones. They are made by the likes of Guiseppe Quintarelli, Allegrini, Tedeschi and, the house that has perhaps done most to revive local wine-making pride, Masi.

Under the direction of Masi's president Sandro Boscaini, the Masi team headed by wine-maker Nino Franceschetti have been taking a fresh look at the production methods of the ancient Recioto wines. From the 1983 vintage (released only in 1988), they have revitalised the wine's previously rather curious style, trying to forge for it a modern model.

Recioto wines are the most obvious candidates for long ageing among the broad range of wines produced in Italy's historic northeast. Particularly ripe Valpolicella grapes Corvina, Rondinella Molinara and perhaps Rossignola, Negrar and Raboso are picked and sorted in late September or early October. The next and most important stage in the production process is their transfer to special windowless but well-ventilated drying chambers, where the grapes are spread to dry until January, losing about a third of their weight in the process. A long, slow fermentation of these raisins follows and lasts for well over a month producing a Recioto wine that is still sweet.

Wines destined to remain sweet (Amabile) complete their ageing in wood at temperatures low enough to keep any yeasts in check. A second fermentation is encouraged in Amarone wines on the other hand by letting them spend the spring in larger barrels kept warm enough to encourage the Bayanus Superyeast strain. This nudges the alcohol level up to 16 per cent and more. The wines are then left to age for many a year in large barrels before being bottled as the world's most naturally alcoholic wine.

Franceschetti's modernisation programme, initiated in the late sixties, began with selecting sites which would be particularly suitable for Amarone wines. Compolongo di Torbe is renowned for the ultra-almondy Mandorlato wines. Vajo Armaron is being developed, but Mazzano is perhaps the truest, and certainly the highest, vineyard for Valpolicella's oddity called Amarone.

Since then work has been concentrated on reducing yields; selecting clones for simultaneous ripening; picking earlier to increase acidity; decreasing the drying period to minimise *Botrytis*; trying to control even the second fermentation through temperature supervision, and shortening the barrel-ageing time to about four years. The result in 1983 at any rate is a cleaner, more aromatic and perhaps even longer-lived wine. It will be intriguing to see in what other ways the wines evolve as the new vines, which were planted mainly in the mid-seventies, mature.

Earlier vintages

The Recioto wines of 1967, 1969 and 1971 were all above average for Masi. This producer did better than most other wine-makers with the produce of the 1971 vintage. 1974 was an outstanding vintage that fully vindicates the proposition that good Amarones are long-lived wines. Amazingly deep crimson with a tawny rim. It is headily scented and has an almost floral bouquet. Unmistakably alcoholic and rustic yet at the same time tongue-tingling and exciting. Although it is obviously older than the 1975 it still has real concentration and allure. The palate is assaulted by a fruit cocktail of damsons and raspberries. There is no doubt that this is a wine that has many years ahead of it.

1975 A surprisingly succulent wine from a vintage which doesn't have a grand reputation. Sparkling deep ruby. Mellow, mature blend of fresh and dried fruits – *panettone* dried fruits of the sweet Milanese cake, and strawberries on the palate. Definitely evolved and well-knit but with great power, confidence and length. This wine certainly demands attention.

Weather and timing

Good vintage, small crop. Average growing season and drying period.

Quantity produced

492 cases released at L91,200 a case. Amarone: 98,400 cases.

Other details

16.2% alcohol.

1976 Masi rate this wine higher than their 1975. It has an intense ruby colour with a powerful bouquet of macerated chestnuts and bitter cherries. Heady yet definitely dry. An extremely solid mouthful of rich, dry red texture.

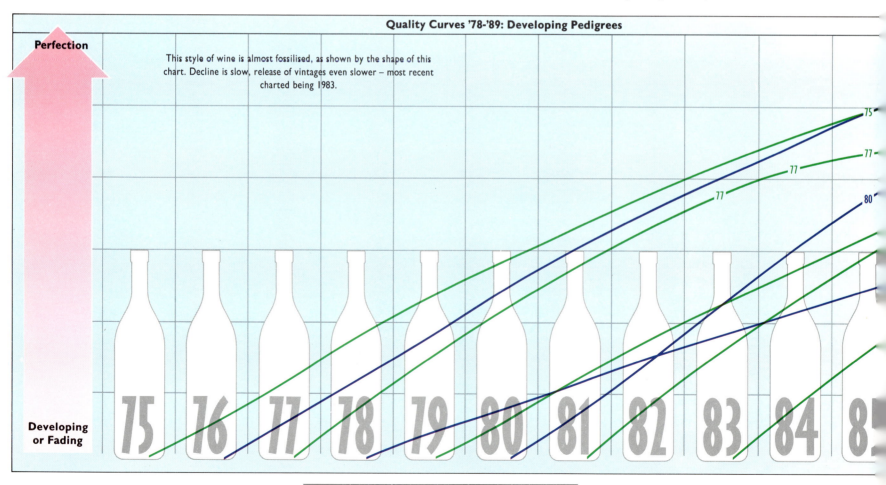

Quality Curves '78-'89: Developing Pedigrees

Perfection

This style of wine is almost fossilised, as shown by the shape of this chart. Decline is slow, release of vintages even slower – most recent charted being 1983.

Developing or Fading

75 76 77 78 79 80 81 82 83 84 85

Weather and timing

Very good vintage, small crop. Fair growing season and drying period.

Quantity produced

496 cases released at L91,200 a case. Amarone: 101,300 cases.

Other details

16.3% alcohol.

1977 Mazzano was not as successful as most Amarones in this vintage. The wine was already looking old in 1988: it tasted distinctly frail with a note of bitter almonds on the nose. The tannin level and acidity are painfully high.

Weather and timing

Good vintage, normal crop. Excellent growing season. Wet during harvest. Fine for the drying period.

Quantity produced

575 cases released at L102,000 a case. Amarone: 151,200 cases.

Other details

16.5% alcohol.

1978 Reasonably, but not exceptionally, good year. Deep ruby with a tawny rim and a strong scent of bitter almonds with dried figs underneath. A very big wine in which the alcohol and, particularly, acid are quite markedly distinct. With some tannin still in evidence, this wine desperately needs food with it.

Weather and timing

Good vintage, small crop. Average growing season and drying period.

Quantity produced

517 cases released at L132,000 a case. Amarone: 100,100 cases.

Other details

16.2% alcohol.

1979 Very lively wine. Deep ruby with smudgy meld of flavours on the nose. Overriding flavours reminiscent of dried fruits in *panettone*. Powerful note of ripe fruit on entry to the palate followed by marked acidity. Just

starting to come together but should eventually make an exciting wine.

Weather and timing

Very good vintage, large crop. Excellent growing season. Good drying season.

Quantity produced

600 cases released at L158,000 a case. Amarone: 202,000 cases.

Other details

16% alcohol.

1980 An early developer that looks older than the 1974. Concentrated, piercing aroma of high-toned, smoky, aldehyde- and fino-like essence of almonds with some bitter cherries for good measure. This powerful nose is followed by a relatively lightweight palate that it is difficult to imagine will improve.

Weather and timing

Good vintage, above average crop. Cool, damp spring. Hot, dry July-Sept. Good drying period.

Quantity produced

625 cases released at L163,000 a case. Amarone: 177,200 cases.

Other details

Some replanting. 16.5% alcohol.

1981 Very deep ruby with an even higher level of glycerol than is normal for these wines. Definitely more oxidised and rustic than most other vintages. Concentrated autumnal flavours in quite a loose textured blend which is attractive, sturdy and well balanced already. Good layered, attractively textured, dry finish.

Weather and timing

Good vintage, below average crop. Severe winter. Mid-Apr frost. Hail storms throughout summer. Fair drying period.

Quantity produced

717 cases released at L174,000 a case. Amarone: 141,200 cases.

Other details

16% alcohol.

1982 The particularly bad conditions prevailing when the grapes were supposed to have been dried meant that no Mazzano was produced.

Weather and timing

Declassified vintage, large crop. Late spring and dry summer. Sunny conditions ensured a disease-free crop and good maturation. Bad drying period.

Quantity produced

None. Amarone: 220,200 cases.

1983 Mid-ruby with a tawny edge. Strong bittersweet morello cherry scents together with almonds and even a hint of curry spices (these are curious wines, remember). Relatively youthful, straightforward aromas. Powerfully acid but with lots of clean morello fruit, if still a lot simpler than any other of these wines.

Weather and timing

Outstanding vintage, large crop. Good spring. Summer drought.

Dry sunny autumn. Good harvest. Excellent drying period.

Quantity produced

800 cases released at L216,000 a case. Amarone: 213,800 cases.

Other details

16% alcohol. A seminal vintage. The first year in which Masi's new Amarone techniques were applied.

Prospects

In 1984 and 1987 poor drying conditions prejudiced production of Amarone. 1985, to be released in 1990, was a memorable vintage according to Masi. Frost in Jan followed by a summer drought reduced the crop but the harvest was excellent. There were ideal conditions during the drying period. The 1986 harvest produced healthy grapes with high sugar content. Rapid drying occurred in the first 30 days of the drying period which bodes well for the quality of this wine.

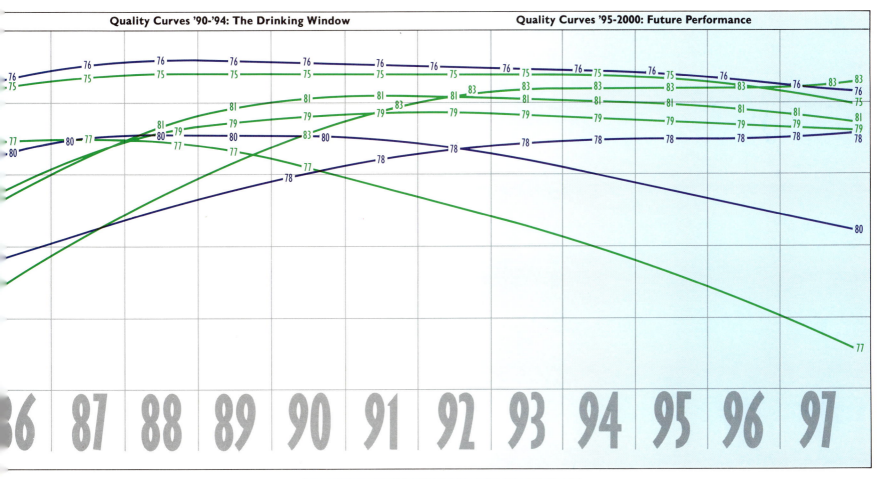

Quality Curves '90-'94: The Drinking Window

Quality Curves '95-2000: Future Performance

SPAIN

Spain occupies a special position in any survey of wine maturity. It is a most agreeable feature of Spanish wine tradition that a wine should be released only when it is ready to drink. Happily, the naturally generous Spaniards eschew the Bordelais practice of passing the cost of wine production as far down the line (towards the consumer) as early as possible.

Spanish wines in any case, particularly reds, are traditionally matured in cask for an exceptionally long time. They rely on the cask rather than the grapes to shape the wine's character to such an extent that it is difficult to see how the average wine-maker could drum up business in wine futures on the basis of one-year-old tasting samples.

The smell of a traditionally-made Spanish wine is the very obviously vanilla-scented warm, sweet flavour of the 50-gallon (225-litre) Bordeaux-sized American oak casks used so extensively in Spain's *bodegas*. This is certainly true of the red wines on which the reputation of Spain's premier wine region Rioja is built, although there has been an increase in recognition of the importance of bottle ageing over the last decade or so.

The official rules of Rioja's *Consejo Regulador* demanded in 1989 that a simple *Crianza* rioja must spend at least a year in barrel and a year in bottle or vat; a *Reserva* must have at least three years' maturation, of which at least one must be in cask; and a *Gran Reserva* should have five years' maturation in cask and bottle of which at least two were in oak. Every bottle of rioja clearly signals its official status as *Crianza Reserva* or *Gran Reserva* on the seal on the back of the bottle, although individual *bodegas* may age *Reservas* and *Gran Reservas* much longer than the official minimum.

The net result of all this tradition and regulation is that almost all red riojas are ready to drink when they are released, and this is true even of wines such as Marqués de Cáceres which are made along much more "modern", less oaked, lines. This is not to say however that none of these broachable riojas improve in bottle: the fact that they do, and the degree to which they are worth waiting for, is illustrated in some dramatic examples overleaf.

CVNE's Imperial *Reservas* and *Gran Reservas* are among the region's longest-living wines, made traditionally but from the most carefully selected fruit, and only in superior years. (Note that 1984 was a poor year throughout Rioja but the 1979 and, particularly, 1983 were good enough to produce some perfectly respectable wines that will mature long before this grand old man of Haro, CVNE Imperial, is designed to).

Other traditionally made riojas with as great an ageing potential as CVNE Imperial are: La Rioja Alta Reserva 904 and 890, Marqués de Murrieta Castillo Ygay, Muga Prado Enea Gran Reserva, Monte Real Gran Reserva from Bodegas Riojanas and Viña Tondonia from López de Heredia. For CVNE's Viña Real and most other *Gran Reservas* or *Reservas* from any of the above *bodegas*, accelerate the Imperial Timechart by two years; for any other *bodega*'s *Reserva* by three.

Basic red *Crianza* rioja has little ageing potential and should be ready to drink as soon as it is released. In general terms, Rioja Alta fruit ages more slowly than Rioja Alavesa which, in turn, ages much more slowly than Rioja Baja fruit. Most riojas, however, are a blend from two, and probably all three, of these regions.

Most white and *rosado* riojas nowadays epitomise modern, somewhat characterless white wine vinification and should accordingly be drunk as young as possible. Great, lush, lemony, unashamedly full and oak-aged whites such as those made by Marqués de Murrieta can last for up to 20 years and more, admirably vindicating the wholly traditional methods by which they are made. The white Viña Tondonia from López de Heredia can also still be lively at 10.

Although Ribera del Duero (see page 118) is Spain's hottest wine region (in terms of fashion if not climate) the amount of wine it exports is small compared with that from Penedès, where Miguel Torres produces wines that doubtless represent Spain's vinous future and are being much copied throughout the country.

His Mas de la Plana Cabernet Sauvignon, also released only when it has reached drinkability, is

Drama in the Rioja landscape. Hardly the most intensively farmed vineyard region in the world, the countryside harbours *bodegas* stacked six barrels high with wines expected to do much of their ageing in oak rather than glass.

longer-lived than any Penedès red other than the Cabernet of Jean Léon, for which the Torres Timechart indicates years of maturity, but which is notably more obdurate in youth. The 1980 is in good shape now.

For Torres Gran Coronas, the blend without the black label, accelerate the Mas de la Plana Timechart by two years and for the other Torres reds, which are even more dependent on the juicier local red grapes, accelerate it by three years. Most other Penedès reds are much lighter and unlikely to improve much in bottle after release. Most whites, *rosados* and the enormous quantities of sometimes excellent *Cava* sparkling wines should be drunk as soon as they are released, although the Chardonnays of Torres and Jean Léon are ambitiously scaled for three to five years on. Good years for Penedès have been 1988, 1987, 1985 (especially for whites), 1984 and 1982.

For the rest of Spain's exciting range of wine possibilities, see page 118.

Imperial Reserva, CVNE

CVNE or "Coonay" is the more usual name for the Compania Vinicola del Norte de España which, for over 100 years, has been one of Rioja's most quality-oriented family firms.

It is controlled by the Vallejo family of Bilbao, but the day-to-day running of this substantial *bodega* in Haro, the capital of Rioja Alta, is in the hands of viticulturist José Madrazo and Bordeaux-trained wine-maker Basilio Izquierdo.

CVNE is unusual not only in the consistent quality of its wines, particularly its red Reservas and Gran Reservas, but also in the hold it exercises over the fruit used. The *bodega* owns 1,310 acres (530 hectares) of vineyard which supply more than 65 per cent of its annual needs from relatively mature vines. Nearly 1,000 acres (400 hectares) are planted with Tempranillo, Rioja's backbone grape variety.

The vineyard project of which they are perhaps proudest is the Contino estate at Laserna just over the river Ebro into the Rioja Alavesa. Owned jointly with local farmers, it is designed to do the almost unthinkable in Rioja: to produce wine exclusively from the fruit of a single property – wine moreover that has been matured not only in American barrels but also in some French oak.

CVNE's top red wines have for decades gone to make their two famous Reservas, Imperial and Viña Real. While the latter is a riper, softer wine sold in a burgundy bottle and composed primarily of Rioja Alavesa fruit, Imperial is the top of CVNE's range, particularly in view of its longevity.

The name dates from the *annus mirabilus* of 1928 – indeed an Imperial 1928 was still in good shape in the early 1980s. Imperial is made up of top quality wine from the Rioja Alta, whose best sites are sufficiently high and calcareous to produce wines with the acid and phenolics required for a long life. Grapes come from about 250 acres (100 hectares) of vines, substantially CVNE's own Briones and Villalba vineyards. The varietal make-up of an Imperial Reserva is about 80 per cent Tempranillo supplemented by Mazuela, or Carignane, Garnacha (Grenache) and up to 10 per cent white Viura and Garnacha Blanca.

An Imperial is not made every vintage, as can be seen from the chart. While some years are reckoned worthy of Reserva status, others are thought more suitable for the even longer-matured Gran Reserva. CVNE practice is to extend the wood ageing period from two to about three-and-a-half years for Gran Reservas.

Such extended cask maturation runs counter to many tenets of modern oenology, but though some Riojas are undoubtedly faded and wan from too long in cask, most of these Imperial Reservas and Gran Reservas have the fruit quality and concentration needed to transform themselves into mature wines of a rare, yet easy-to-appreciate, style combining delicacy with richness.

Earlier vintages

1952 Gran Reserva. Great depth of colour with orange rim. Wonderfully seductive mature bouquet. Somehow manages to be both sweet and delicate. No more than medium weight, perhaps less refined and complex than the best 1952 clarets but more pleasurable than most of them. **1954** Gran Reserva. Sweet, chunky flavours reminiscent of cough pastilles. Preserved rather than evolved. Still quite chewy. **1968** Gran Reserva. Looks mature: yellow at the rim but there is still delicacy and really exciting complexity on the nose with its burgundian notes of violets and almost putrid game. Will not last long into the nineties. **1970** Gran Reserva. A classic now just starting its decline. **1976** Reserva. Sweet and gamey with the flavour of ripe berries but less sophisticated than the 1978.

1978 Reserva. Good, subtly shaded fox red. Fairly sweet, rustic burgundian perfume. Floral and vanillin notes. Well balanced blend of already integrated elements. A wine with a real beginning, middle and end.
Weather and timing
Very good vintage, very small crop. Above average winter rainfall; rains continued into spring. Poor flowering due to rain. Dry and sunny for harvest Oct 20-30.
Quantity produced
16,000 cases (4% of CVNE's total production) released in 1987 at 8,628ptas a case. Total Rioja production: 8,667,000 cases.
1979 None made.
Weather and timing
Average vintage, above average crop. Mild start to the season then fine. Heavy rain affected maturation.
Quantity produced
Rioja: 15,556,000 cases.

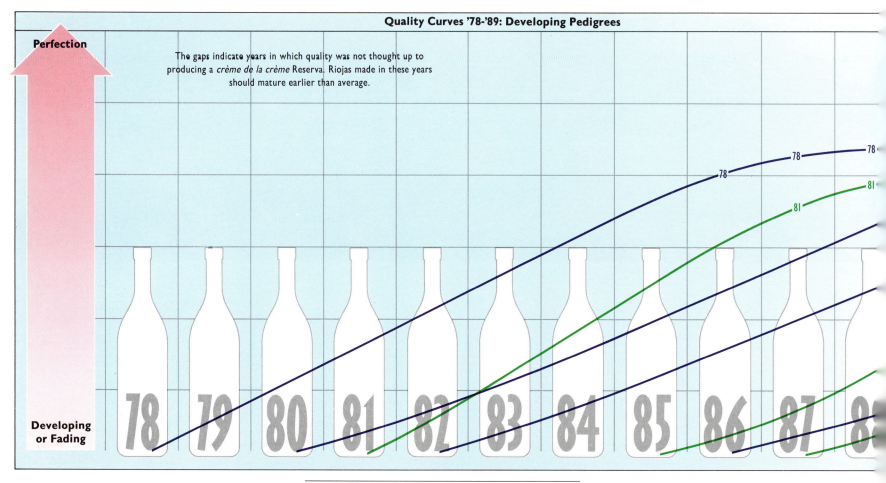

Quality Curves '78-'89: Developing Pedigrees

Perfection

The gaps indicate years in which quality was not thought up to producing a *crème de la crème* Reserva. Riojas made in these years should mature earlier than average.

Developing or Fading

78 79 80 81 82 83 84 85 86 87 88

1980 Gran Reserva. Well graded ruby out to brick rim. Aromatic and well integrated secondary flavour elements. Well balanced, harmonious whole without enormous impact but positive and confident with some acidity and tannin still perceptible. A little light but more concentrated than either 1982 or 1981.

Weather and timing

Good vintage, above average crop. Good start to the season. Cool, humid summer. Harvest Oct 5 to Nov 12.

Quantity produced

About 6,000 cases. Released in Scandinavia. Rioja: 15,667,000.

1981 Reserva. Light ruby out to brick rim. Low-key, meaty, evolved bouquet that is relatively simple but with some suggestion of smoked meat. Not very subtle; just a simple red wine but with better acidity than its immediate successor.

Weather and timing

Excellent vintage, above average crop. Cold, dry winter with frost; uneven bud break. Wet, warm spring. Early flowering. Unsteady start to the growing season which continued dry and hot through to the harvest of Oct 22-31.

Quantity produced

21,000 cases (5% of total production) released at 14,357ptas a case. Rioja: 15,000,000.

Other details

High price in response to large demand. Sold out in 1988.

1982 Reserva. Surprisingly little difference between the colour of this wine and that of the 1952. Savoury fruit with light American oak influence. By no means overwhelming. Still quite crude and rustic. (A much more impressive Gran Reserva will be released in the mid-nineties.)

Weather and timing

Excellent vintage, normal crop. Third dry year in a row. Warm winter. Dry spring and very hot growing season; vines affected by lack of water. Dry and hot for harvest Oct 22 to Nov 3.

Quantity produced

23,000 cases (5.5% of total production). Release date 1989. Rioja: 11,889,000 cases.

1983 None made.

Weather and timing

Average vintage, small crop. Cold winter. Very wet Aug. Hot for harvest.

Quantity produced

Rioja: 12,000,000 cases.

1984 None made.

Weather and timing

Average vintage, small crop. Mild, humid winter. Frost in May. Hurricane Hortense damaged crop early Oct: harvest delayed.

Quantity produced

Rioja: 11,889,000 cases.

1985 (Cask sample) Gran Reserva. Extremely promising. Exceptionally deep crimson. Rich vanillin and tobacco aromas. Austere and gentlemanly rather than the more usual feminine charms of Rioja with even a hint of bitter chocolate. Blackberry concentration. Still unresolved but with reserves and lower depths of warmth and ripe fruit.

Weather and timing

Good vintage, very large crop. Rainy autumn followed by a cold, dry winter. Good bud break. Dry, hot growing season, especially July and Aug. Very hot during harvest Oct 20-31.

Quantity produced

26,000 cases (4.8% of total production). Rioja: 18,889,000 cases. Not yet released.

1986 (Cask sample) Gran Reserva. Light crimson. Oak just starting to cast its layers over the fruit. Simple berry flavours. Less concentrated than the 1987. Dry, savoury and still simple.

Weather and timing

Good vintage, below average crop. Dry, cold winter. Spring began cold and ended hot. Late bud break. Good flowering. Rain in April. Hot, dry growing season. Rain in early Oct: dry during harvest Oct 20-28.

Quantity produced

22,000 cases (4.9% of total production). Rioja: 12,778,000 cases.

1987 (Cask sample) Gran Reserva. Very deep crimson for a Rioja (though lighter than a young Bordeaux or Rhône red) still with some blue in evidence. Very young, simple, mulberry fruit flavours. Still not much character. Quite soft with good ripe fruit in the middle palate. Young and unformed but concentrated.

Weather and timing

Good vintage, normal crop. Moderate winter. Dry, hot spring, early flowering. Growing season began cool and wet and finished hot and dry, with some autumn rains. Fine for harvest Oct 14-23.

Quantity produced

23,000 cases (4.7% of total production). Rioja: 13,889,000 cases.

Other details

37% of Imperial sales exported.

1988 (Not tasted) In spite of difficulties at harvest time this wine has great promise. Early indications suggest that this will be one of CVNE's Imperials.

Weather and timing

Good vintage, normal crop. Mild, wet winter. Spring began hot then wet right into July. Early bud break, late flowering. Set damaged by rain and cold. Aug and Sept hot. Dry, sunny days during harvest Oct 24 to Nov 2.

Quantity produced

Unknown. Bottling date 1992. Rioja: about 14,000,000 cases.

Other details

48% of Imperial sales exported. Low stocks.

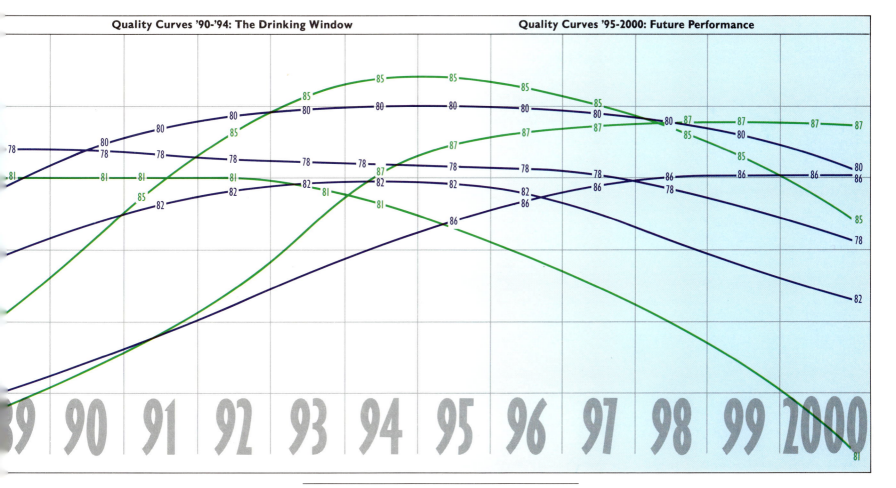

Quality Curves '90-'94: The Drinking Window

Quality Curves '95-2000: Future Performance

Gran Coronas, Mas La Plana, Torres

The wine known originally as Torres Gran Coronas "Black Label" cannot claim to be Spain's most Spanish wine. Nor is it Spain's most fashionable: that crown has been handed from Vega Sicila to its neighbour Pesquera in recent years. A blend of Cabernets Sauvignon and Franc, Black Label is, however, indubitably Spain's most famous ambassador in bottle, just as its maker is Spanish wine's most famous ambassador in person.

Miguel Torres Jr made a name for himself and this mould-breaking Cabernet Sauvignon from Penedès with its first vintage. He entered Gran Coronas "Black Label" 1970 in the top Cabernet class of the famous Gault-Millau "wine olympics" in 1979 and it came top, tactlessly "beating" the likes of Châteaux Latour 1970 and La Mission-Haut-Brion 1961.

Since then the viticultural and oenological background of this wine has evolved as Miguel has refined the original formula. The wine originally represented two dramatic departures from Spanish vinous tradition: it was made mainly from vines imported from France, and was given a mere 18 months in cask.

Curiously, the wine is unmistakably Spanish, yet it has not contained any Spanish grape varieties since the third vintage, the 1975. Since Miguel abandoned Cabernet Franc in 1977 it has been entirely Cabernet Sauvignon: unfashionably monotone on paper but, according to the composer, the song sounds better that way, exhibiting a range of flavour elements

quite different from Cabernet Sauvignon grown further north. But perhaps what hints most strongly at this wine's Spanish origins is the American oak, the oak traditionally used for wine maturation throughout Spain, from Jerez to Rioja. Miguel has not finally settled on the ideal proportion of French oak – it has been about 40 per cent in the eighties. He reports that every blind tasting analysis argues against abandoning the spice of American oak – even in favour of the most satisfactory Nevers oak they have found.

As part of a fashion-conscious move towards vineyard identification for all top Torres wines, Gran Coronas is to be known as Mas La Plana after Miguel Jr's own house. It overlooks the 48-acre (19-hectare) vineyard that exclusively supplies the raw materials for his most famous wine.

Although they export all over the world, always in bottle and notably to some of France's finest restaurants (a pet ambition), Torres retain one of the Spanish wine business's more appealing traditions. Wines, even including this superior Gran Coronas (there is a much earthier, earlier-maturing bottling of straight Gran Coronas), are sold only when they are ready to drink. This means that, with exceptional generosity, the Torres family subsidise the maturation of a wine to which few collectors would mind giving cellar space themselves. In 1988 Gran Coronas Black Label 1982 was selling for about the same price as a good bourgeois bordeaux of the same vintage.

Earlier vintages

The famous **1970** is now starting to fade but the slightly simple if still juicy **1973** will decline much more gently in the early nineties. The **1975** is the most stunning early vintage, meaty and voluptuous with tannin and oak still perceptible and every sign that this vigour will continue through much of the nineties. The **1976** is starting to dry out while the **1977** is still an exciting wine that is unusually lean and silky.

1978 Exceptionally rustic nose rather than overtly Cabernet Sauvignon. Concentrated, juicy almost damson-like fruit but definitely oaky in a slightly peasant-like fashion. Tannins already very soft. Probably at it peak in 1988.

Weather and timing

Very good vintage, below average crop. Rainy spring. Dry and mild from mid-July. Showers in early

Sept. Dry for harvest during fourth week of Sept.

Quantity produced

14,500 cases released in 1985 at 1,350ptas a case.

Other details

100% Cabernet Sauvignon. Aged for 18 months in new American white oak. Bottled in Nov 1980.

1979 Very little made and sold only in Spain.

Weather and timing

Good vintage, average crop. Mild winter followed by wet, warm spring. Good flowering. Summer drought. Mild Sept then wet for harvest.

Other details

Decided to change style of wine. Initial changes were in the vineyard, in pollenisation resulting in lower yields. Nitrogen fertilizer abandoned and only small amounts of potassium used. Lower vine vigour encouraged, resulting in greater maturity of fruit.

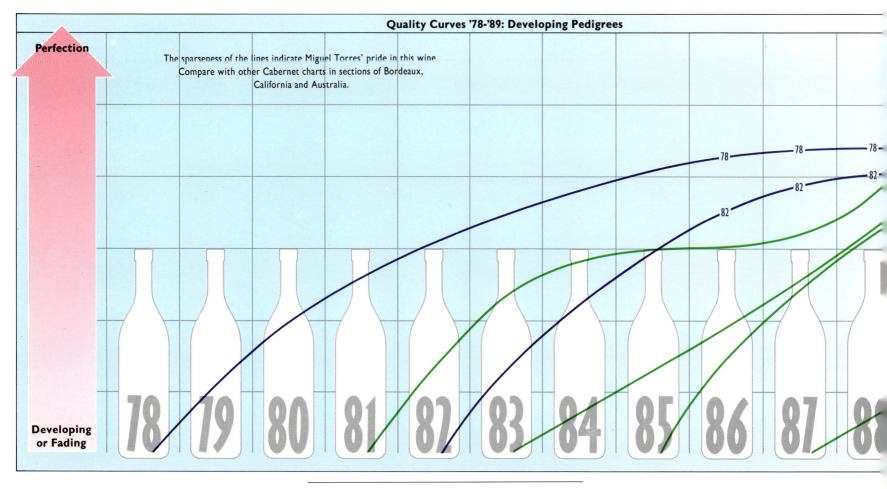

Quality Curves '78-'89: Developing Pedigrees

Perfection

The sparseness of the lines indicate Miguel Torres' pride in this wine. Compare with other Cabernet charts in sections of Bordeaux, California and Australia.

Developing or Fading

78 79 80 81 82 83 84 85 86 87 88

1980 No Black Label made.

Weather and timing
Good vintage, below average crop. Dry season. Cool, long spring. Late flowering. Short, hot summer. Dry July-Aug. Mild autumn. Fine for late harvest.

1981 Absolutely stunning. Gloriously shaded very dark crimson. Sweet, heady, explosive bouquet with lots of body and richness. Hint of minerals on a rich, spicy Châteauneuf-like base. Sweet and mouthfilling but not yet ready. Great power and length, but marked tannins.

Weather and timing
Very good vintage, small crop. Severe winter. Cold, showery spring delayed flowering. Hot, dry summer with rain mid-June and late July. Harvest third and fourth weeks of Sept.

Quantity produced
11,250 cases released in 1986 at 1,450ptas a case.

Other details
100% Cabernet Sauvignon. Aged in French oak as well as American; first six months in new wood, then in two- or three-year-old casks. Changes introduced in the vinification including longer maceration and increased emphasis on wood tannins rather than grape tannins.

1982 Gamey with rich animal scents on the nose but surprisingly and disappointingly simple on the palate. Not one of the most exciting vintages.

Weather and timing
Good vintage, above average crop. Wet spring. Saharan winds contributed to hottest July of the century. Wet Aug. Harvest first week in Oct.

Quantity produced
12,840 cases released in 1988 at 1,900ptas a case.

Other details
100% Cabernet Sauvignon. 24 months in new American white oak.

1983 Good healthy mid-ruby. Sweet, lush, warm flavours lap over the initial impression of gentlemanly rigour. An exciting wine with lots packed away for the future. Very good structure with some coffee notes at the start and a lovely warm, spicy finish.

Weather and timing
Very good vintage, average crop. Cold, snowy winter. Hot spring. Worst summer drought for 150 years. Some rain in Aug and Sept. Sunny, mild autumn: perfect ripening. Harvest first week Oct.

Quantity produced
12,700 cases released in 1989 at 1,900ptas a case.

Other details
100% Cabernet Sauvignon. Aged in American and French oak.

1984 None made.

Weather and timing
Good vintage, average crop. Much wetter, milder season compared to 1983. Fine spring. Good flowering. Mild summer slowed grape development. Late harvest.

1985 Already quite evolved bouquet with marked spicy American oak and richness. But on the palate a deceptively straightforward juicy impression gives way to notable acidity and tannins. These suggest that this wine has a distinctly promising future. Note of bitter cherries and not at all obviously Cabernet.

Weather and timing
Very good vintage, below average crop. Second drought in three years which resulted in low yields. Warm days and cool nights during ripening. High alcohol content. Harvest first week in Oct.

Quantity produced
13,800 cases. Bottled 1987. Yet to be released.

Other details
100% Cabernet Sauvignon. First six months in new oak; 60% in French oak and 40% in American oak.

1986 Whether or not a Mas La Plana will be made will be decided in 1989, but it is unlikely.

Weather and timing
Good vintage, below average crop. Another dry year. Drought which began in May was followed by the driest June for 20 years. Grapes ripened early. First rains on Aug 29. Rain throughout Sept. Rapid spread of *Botrytis* forced early harvest and selective picking.

Quantity produced
12,900 cases.

1987 Exceptional. Wonderful deep purple obscures the bottom of even a tasting glass. Great concentration of silky mulberry fruit and definite grainy oak. Not obviously sweet, but some spicy American oak. Excellent balance and very promising.

Weather and timing
Excellent vintage, below average crop. Mild winter apart from snow in Jan and Feb. Perfect for flowering. Rain early July. Hot Aug. Excellent harvest.

Quantity produced
Not yet determined.

Other details
100% Cabernet Sauvignon.

1988 *(Not tasted)* According to Torres, the Cabernet Sauvignon had an intense flavour with good tannins. Energetic and elegant, typical of the variety.

Weather and timing
Very good vintage, below average crop. Frost-free spring. Torrential rain May-June; many treatments required to combat mildew. Dry, sunny summer. Moist soil helped ripen crop. *Botrytis*-free harvest.

Quantity produced
Not yet determined. Average production for the Penedès region is about 16,700,000 cases.

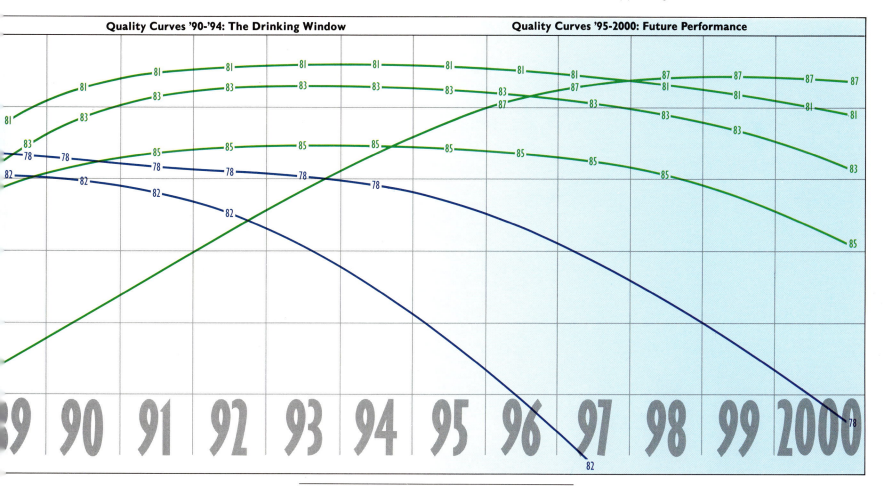

Quality Curves '90-'94: The Drinking Window   Quality Curves '95-2000: Future Performance

REST OF SPAIN

Some of Spain's most concentrated, age-worthy and intensely Spanish reds are made in the northwest in Ribero del Duero, up-river of port country and only about 60 miles (96 km) southwest across the mountains from Rioja.

For many years Vega Sicilia was the only wine widely known outside the region. Alejandro Fernández was the next Ribera wine producer to produce an internationally famous wine: Pesquera. The two wines are products of the same harsh climate but, whereas Vega Sicilia is kept in cask for up to 10 years, Pesquera looks to Bordeaux for its two-year cask maturation and, like Bordeaux, is snapped up by eager collectors many years before it sheds its youthfully tannic straight-jacket.

Vega Sicilia, whether as the vintage-dated Unico, the three- or five-year-old earlier-maturing Valbuena, or, the crowning glory, the Reserva Especial blend of different vintages, is released when it is well into its drinkable period. Only the Valbuenas may actually improve – and quite dramatically – after about three years in bottle.

As for Pesquera, it makes no concessions to "international taste" and was made unashamedly for the long term, using foot-treading for maximum extraction in shallow open vats until 1981. Particularly successful wines such as the Reserva Especial 1978 should continue to develop until the mid-nineties. The post-1981 vintages, notably the 1982 and the particularly successful 1985, are already broachable but are designed for the mid- to late nineties.

There are a host of other wines now emerging from the region, such as Protos and Peñafiel from the local co-operative and those carrying the names Victor Balbas, Peñalba López, Yllera, Viña Pedrosa and Mauro. These tend to be robust reds more in the Pesquera mould than that of Vega Sicilia, but distinctly looser-textured. Most are ready to drink between five and 10 years, their *Reservas* between seven and 15. Particularly successful years for Ribera del Duero have been the very good 1986, 1985, 1983, 1982, 1981 (which is excellent), 1976 and 1973.

Navarra is another of the few Spanish wine regions to have earned itself an international reputation, notably for light reds and *rosados* made largely from Garnacha, the Spanish forefather of Châteauneuf-du-Pape's Grenache. The *rosados* mature as shown on Chart B (page 19), while the reds are mainly at their best four to five years after the vintage (up to eight for the Cabernet blend Viña Magaña). 1984 and 1983 were much better than 1985 and 1986 for most Navarra producers.

Most other wines made in the north of Spain evolve on a timescale no longer than that outlined on Chart B. Some of the reds, especially the relatively refined ones of Cariñena, Léon and the considerably gutsier examples from nearby Toro can improve with a couple of years in bottle, as can the sweet white version of Alella.

Rueda southwest of Ribera del Duero clearly has an exciting future for characterful whites, as Marqués de Grignon and Marqués de Riscal (based in Rioja) have shown. These oak-aged Verdejos can evolve for up to four or five years.

The challenge in Galicia in northwest Spain is to find the youngest wines, especially whites, since they will be the least stale and most appetising.

In the south, the reds can sometimes benefit from two or three years' bottle age. All over Spain quality-conscious wine producers are beginning to make their presence felt. The better reds of Yecla (1985 and 1983 were especially good vintages), Valdepeñas (1986 and 1983), Utiel-Requena (1981 to 1983), Jumilla (1985) and the great plain of La Mancha (1984, 1982) show wine potential that must make the French, and Italians, quake at the knees. The whites and *rosados* should be drunk as young as possible.

In the dry fortified wine class on the other hand, Spain already leads the world – especially with the unique, tangy sherries of Jerez in the far south. They are sold when they are ready to drink and the Finos and Manzanillas are the finest wines in the "drink immediately" category.

The stronger and sweeter the wine, the longer it will keep without much apparent deterioration, but even a cream sherry loses its appeal after a few weeks in an open bottle. For this reason, the dark, sticky Malaga is a much more robust decanter wine than the delicate, lower-strength Montilla, which should be opened, and finished, as soon as possible.

PORTUGAL

Bottles of vintage port should be put in the furthest corner of the cellar
and left there for as long as curiosity will allow.

To the wine-lover and wine collector, Portugal means port, specifically vintage port. Of all wines this is the one which is – almost defiantly – designed to mature in glass rather than oak. It is packed into bottle as a fiery, awkward and unformed two-year-old, all anthocyanins and alcohol. At this stage the wine cannot be too tannic, too aggressive or too unpleasant to taste. But over the decades (at least one, preferably two and sometimes many more) it should develop, if the port shippers have got their selection right, into a mellow jewel of a wine, with lusciousness and subtlety fused into a gorgeously hedonistic, yet at the same time intellectually intriguing, whole.

The intellectual intrigue comes from the fact that vintage port, like classed growth Bordeaux, exists only as a top quality wine that is delightfully easy to codify and compare. It is produced only in superior years, three or four times each decade, and is otherwise identified only with the name of the shipper. Graham 1985 for example is the ultimate expression of the year 1985 in port, as the port shippers Graham see it. The almost black bottle itself is modestly labelled – no clever marketing concepts needed here – but the really important identification is the branding of the name of the shipper and the vintage on the cork, the assumption being that the bottle may be opened long after time has worn the label away. The reality of course is that many a restaurateur, or thirsty wine enthusiast, simply cannot afford the timescale of a vintage port, in which case the vintage port connoisseur would smartly point them in the direction of crusted and single *quinta* ports (see below).

Vintage ports from Taylor for the years 1985, 1983, 1980, 1977, 1975, 1970, 1966 and 1963 are charted overleaf. Part of being such a respected port shipper is that Taylor's performance in each year closely mirrors, and often trumps, that of the other shippers. The most notable exception is the 1966 which may never shed the Taylor backbone to become as voluptuous as so many other 1966s. The wines are certainly among the slowest-maturing every vintage year and can taste deceptively hard and ungenerous in youth.

It is worth remembering that the vintages in which there has been most variation in quality and style between the different shippers are the hugely exciting 1985 and the definitely disappointing 1975. The distinctive and perfumed 1963 however, (even

Shimmering heat on the traditionally sculpted vine terraces at Quinta de Vargellas, baking concentration into Taylor's vintage port (page 122) for which these vines provide the backbone.

though it worried some by a rather dumb patch in the early eighties), is very consistent between shippers. 1963 is the finest vintage for current drinking that still lurks in any quantity in the cellars of wise collectors around the world. 1980 and 1970, promising future pleasure, are probably the most underrated vintages. Indeed 1980, a good vintage for many second rank shippers, my well turn out better than the 1983 for some producers.

The house closest to Taylor in style is perhaps Dow, for whose ports the Timechart overleaf should be an accurate guide to maturity for current vintages – although the Dow 1970 may take even longer to open out while the 1966 developed perhaps four years ahead of Taylor's obdurate offering.

Graham has almost as good a current reputation as Taylor but the wines are considerably more lush and sweet in youth which means that for them the Taylor Timechart can be accelerated by two years. Graham was also probably more successful than Taylor in 1983.

Fonseca, under the same ownership as Taylor but much more disappointing in 1980, turns out wines that, as in 1970, can sometimes combine Taylor longevity with Graham richness. Like Graham, Fonseca usually matures about two years ahead of Taylor, as do the big, spicy, almost edible Warre vintage ports, which were so particularly gorgeous in 1963.

Quinta do Noval's vintage ports tend to be prettily scented but went through a sticky patch after declaring one of the finest 1975s with a distinctly poor 1978 and an unexciting 1982. Quinta do Noval Naçional on the other hand is a miraculously exotic, gamey port that needs at least five years longer in bottle than straight Noval. For the years when both Noval and Taylor declared a vintage port, accelerate the Timechart by three years for straight Noval and retard it by two for a Naçional. For the delicate ports of Cockburn (whose balance should then keep them going almost as long as Taylor's) and the relatively open ports of Croft accelerate the Taylor's Timechart by three years too.

Accelerate the chart by four years for the vintage ports of Delaforce and Sandeman (whose 1985 was notably less successful than the shipper's average, the 1966 more so). For the lesser known but often good value vintage ports from such shippers as Martinez, Smith Woodhouse, Quarles Harris (an excellent 1980), Gould Campbell and Rebello Valente, accelerate the Timechart by four years.

Oporto custom has it that the Portuguese-owned houses (comparatively rarely seen in the US and UK) produce much earlier-maturing vintage ports than those declared by the stiff-upper-lipped Brits. This may have been true in the past, and is certainly true of most vintage ports declared with cheerful frequency by the likes of Royal Oporto, but today shippers such as Ferreira and, from 1980, Ramos Pinto and Calem, are giving the traditionally exported ports some serious competition. Accelerate the Taylor's chart by four years for them too.

For 1984, 1982, 1978 and 1976 another sort of port is charted overleaf, Quinta de Vargellas,

Taylor's single *quinta* ("estate") port which is made from the produce of one wine farm only. Like its big, blended brother, the signs are that it too will outlast most other single *quinta* wines. Single *quinta* ports tend to follow the style of that shipper's vintage port since they each choose to bottle the *quinta* that provides the backbone for their own vintage: Quinta do Bomfim for Dow, Quinta da Rôeda for Croft and so on.

Some shippers made proper vintage ports in 1982 and 1978 when Taylors made only Quinta de Vargellas. As it happens, the Vargellas curves for these two years should fairly accurately reflect the development of a vintage port made in that year. It is interesting that Quinta de Vargellas 1978 is a noticeably better wine than the Taylor vintage port of 1975. Nature was perhaps too bountiful in the two years that followed the disaster of 1976.

The only other style of port which demands bottle age is British bottled crusting port, a blend of two or three years of superior wines which are then bottled at between three and four years old and need a further three to 10 years in bottle after the year of bottling specified on the label.

Madeira is another of the world's finest wines, made in Portuguese territory on the island of the same name. It performs the miraculous trick of being ready to drink when it is bottled, but lasting almost indefinitely in bottle, whether the bottle has been opened or not.

Moscatel de Setúbal is no rival in terms of fortified longevity, but can provide a good value earthy, grape-flavoured dessert wine made rather like a tawny port. Sold often simply as Setúbal, the wine is ready for drinking if its age is specified on the label. Otherwise, the years 1986 and, to a lesser extent, 1984, 1982, 1981 and 1974 were particularly good for this, Portugal's third fortified speciality.

The country's table wine industry is in such a state of flux that it is difficult to generalise about maturity patterns and vintages. The far north, Vinho Verde country, is subject to the same damp influences as the far northwest of Spain. Drink these wines, red and white, as young as possible, although Palacio de Brejoeira can make Vinho Verde of sufficient substance to merit two or three years in bottle.

Further south, in very general terms, whites should be drunk as young as possible. Oxidation is still widespread, but reds are still made so traditionally that they appear to keep almost indefinitely. This is certainly true of Portugal's best known Dão and Bairrada reds, most of which reach a peak at around seven years and seem to maintain it with only a slight fading of the fruit for at least another five years and sometimes more. 1985, 1983, 1980, 1975 and 1970 were specially good years for Dão and Barraida. Such wines are never luscious, but they are rarely lifeless.

Some fascinating Douro table wines are now being made in port country and demand at least four, and up to eight, years in bottle. Because of the intensely hot summers and the indigenous wine-making experience, these can have much more fruit, often markedly mulberry, than most Portuguese reds. Ferreira's Barca Velha is the most sought-after but Quinta do Côtto (also a source of excellent ports) is fast establishing a reputation. 1980 was particularly good for Douro table wines.

The wine region that most forcefully demonstrates the longevity of Portuguese reds is Colares, whose wines are almost undrinkably astringent until a good dozen years after their very traditional vinification. They can eventually reward the patient with a bouquet of some complexity but they never lose the nerve of a seaside wine. Some of Colares' finest vintages have been 1984, 1983, 1975 and 1966.

Portugal harbours many excellent value and fully mature reds which are normally sold with fairly inscrutable geographical identification but sometimes carry the word Garrafeira, "reserve", or the name of a particular *Quinta*. Those that are exported are usually mature – indeed are miracles of preservation. Most other ageable Portuguese wines are simply too difficult to find outside Portugal.

Notable exceptions are the wines of the innovative Jose Maria da Fonseca Successores and João Pires, both of whom are based just south of Lisbon on the Setúbal peninsula but buy in grapes from a wide range of different sources. The wines are made from a mixture of Portuguese and "international" grape varieties, but to California and Australian recipes. Of the whites, only the oaky Caterina is worth waiting for – about three years – but all the reds, with the exception of the soft, light, Beaujolais-like Santa Amaro, are designed to be drunk at between four and nine years old.

Taylor's Vintage and Quinta de Vargellas Port

Few could argue with the choice of Taylor Fladgate and Yeatman as our representative port shipper. Taylor's vintage ports are in the enviable position of commanding not just affection and respect from right around the world, but also that most objective measure of quality, a premium price in the saleroom.

Other shippers may excel from time to time. Graham, Dow and Cockburn are just three of the houses that have managed particularly triumphant vintages in the last two decades. But Taylor proceeds at the head of the pack year in, year out. This consistency is achieved through an extra level of density, concentration and sheer class.

Certainly Taylor's vintage ports take longer to mature than those of any other shipper, which has earned them the appellation "the Château Latour of the Douro", but because of their balance the wines are, surprisingly, not unapproachable in youth. Even the 1977, monumental in stature, can already be drunk with great pleasure by those who have a few dozen more bottles stashed away for the next millennium.

There is another parallel with Château Latour, in the form of Taylor's Quinta de Vargellas, a sort of second wine like Les Forts de Latour.

Vintage port is the ultimate expression of any serious port shipper's art but made only in particularly successful years and in tiny quantities. Shippers as quality-conscious as Taylor's

have a traditional (and very British) antipathy to having too much of a good thing and, accordingly, would never dream of declaring a vintage in two consecutive years.

Nature has no such qualms of course and it is easy to think of pairs of almost equally successful years in the Douro: 1982 and 1983, 1978 and 1977, 1967 and 1966 and 1934 and 1935, for example. Taylor's declared the second year of these pairs a vintage but this does not mean we are deprived of the very good wine that could have been produced in the other year. Since 1957 they have been laying down stocks of wine bottled, like vintage port, at 18 months. The wine is made entirely from the best fruit yielded at Quinta de Vargellas, their vineyard high in the Upper Douro, and the produce of single years that are almost as successful as those in which a Taylor's vintage port is declared.

Quinta de Vargellas is a remote farm, run by Alistair and Gillyane Robertson of Taylor's as one of the world's most hospitable and relaxed country house hotels. Along with Terra Feita, it provides the backbone of Taylor's vintage. This chart shows how these "single quinta" wines compare with their big and more famous brothers, Taylor's vintage. Like Les Forts de Latour, they are released only when Taylor's consider them broachable, which is usually at between 10 and 12 years. Unlike Les Forts de Latour, however, they are not the also-rans but the best that this famous quinta can produce in a given year.

Earlier vintages

These are the longest-lived wines in this book (with the possible exception of some Vouvray vintages). Bottles of Taylor vintages such as 1908 and 1912 could still give enormous pleasure along with the even more lively antiques from 1924, 1927, 1935 and 1945. The 1948 was magnificently mellow in the late eighties, while the 1955 is probably the youngest of the vintages which Alistair Robertson of Taylor would call "a serious old wine". The 1960 is chunky but lacks some of the class of the 1963 which has a subtle bouquet and exquisite balance. Both should see us through the nineties. The 1966 is still relatively hard. It shows some licorice and pepper but seems unformed relative to the intriguingly bitter, chocolate-scented 1970 which can already be drunk with great pleasure. There are pleasant surprises

too in older vintages of Quinta de Vargellas. The 1964 is just starting to show its age, and a slightly burnt character. The 1965 shows off the Quinta de Vargellas violet-scented hallmark to an almost embarrassing degree, taking the wine somewhere between port and rich table wine. The star is the 1967 Quinta de Vargellas, overshadowed by the 1966 vintage port in reputation but not when tasted alongside. The 1969 is respectable. Alistair Robertson advises on this, his wife's favourite, that there is no hurry to drink it. These single *quinta* wines mature relatively fast but enjoy a long peak. The 1972 is still quite dry and hard. The 1974 should be drunk immediately.

1975 Vintage. Next to other 1975s this is an incredible hulk, but next to other Taylor vintages it is a bit of wimp. Relatively ligh

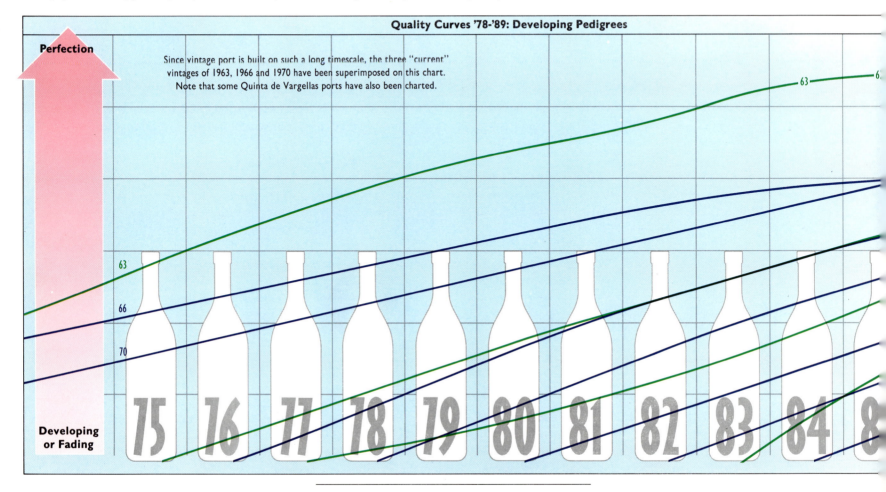

ruby with slight jamminess on the nose. Definitely ready with a little spirit showing through although much more backbone than any other port of this vintage.

Weather and timing
Excellent vintage, small crop. Wet winter. Long, dry summer. Slow maturation. Heavy rain end Sept then warm and dry. Harvest began Oct 6.

Quantity produced
Authorised port production: 6,000,000 cases.

1976 Quinta de Vargellas. A pretty wine for current drinking. Similar colour to the 1977 vintage. Sweet bouquet of licorice and violets. Delicate in structure.

Weather and timing
Average vintage, small crop. Dry winter. Hot summer. Drought: some old vines died. Rain in late Aug and Sept. Harvest began Sept 23. Continual rain from Sept 29 caused some rot.

Quantity produced
Port: 6,600,000 cases.

1977 Vintage. A marvel. The colour dropped in the late eighties so the wine was the youngest vintage in this line-up to look mature, but on the nose and palate there is no doubt that this is still a brooding giant. Aromatic with unevolved layers of hay and tea leaves. Great fruit and richness, an extremely big wine, yet with harmony, the tannin obtruding only on the end of the palate. Keep if you possibly can.

Weather and timing
Outstanding vintage, above average crop. Wettest winter on record. Bad frost May 12. Cool spring and summer. Very hot Sept. Harvest began Oct 1.

Quantity produced
Port: 7,550,000 cases.

1978 Quinta de Vargellas. Looks much younger and simpler than the 1977 with a slightly burnt, pruney nose suggesting mulled wine. Still quite tight with a hard finish.

Weather and timing
Good vintage, small crop. Second wet winter. Good flowering. Long, hot summer. Light rain in Sept. Harvest began Sept 28.

Quantity produced
Port: 6,400,000 cases.

1979 No Vintage or Quinta de Vargellas bottled.

Weather and timing
Average vintage and crop. Wet winter. Fine spring. Hot summer. Harvest began Sept 24.

Quantity produced
Port: 7,000,000 cases.

1980 An underrated year. Very good colour with better depth than the 1983. Looks extremely promising with spicy, intriguing scents already evolving into a relatively complex bouquet. Not enormous but well structured: will repay attention.

Weather and timing
Excellent vintage, above average crop. Dry winter. Cool spring; late flowering. Warm, dry summer. Hot Sept. Harvest began Sept 29.

Quantity produced
Port: 7,550,000 cases.

1981 The only poor year in the eighties. Neither Vintage nor Quinta de Vargellas bottled.

Weather and timing
Poor vintage, very small crop. Hot summer. Drought. Wet during harvest which began Sept 21.

Quantity produced
Port: 5,850,000 cases.

1982 Quinta de Vargellas. A big year for Vargellas, declared as a Vintage by some houses. Of all the Quinta de Vargellas wines of the eighties this is likely to take the longest to mature.

Weather and timing
Good vintage, small crop. Drought continued. Light rain at flowering and set. Hot summer; early maturation. Harvest began Sept 13. Very high sugar content.

Quantity produced
Port: 6,400,000 cases.

1983 Vintage. In retreat in early 1989. Deep colour and subdued nose. Good ripe fruit but not enormously tannic or concentrated, it will probably come round sooner than the 1985.

Weather and timing
Excellent vintage, small crop. Harsh Feb: snow for first time in 20 years. Wet May; poor set. Hot, dry July. Wet Aug. Fine Sept. Perfect harvest began Oct 3.

Quantity produced
Port: 6,000,000 cases.

1984 Quinta de Vargellas. A respectable but not exceptional year which will not be released until the mid-nineties.

Weather and timing
Average vintage, small crop. Dry, cold winter. Wet spring. Cool summer but very hot July. Warm and dry until Sept 28, then wet. Harvest began Sept 24.

Quantity produced
Port: 6,400,000 cases.

1985 A variable year. Excellent deep crimson suggests a wait of 20 to 25 years. Stern, rigorous structure with taut, concentrated fruit on the palate. A brooding monster for 2005 onwards.

Weather and timing
Outstanding vintage, average crop. Wet, cold winter. Late flowering. Storm in May damaged vines. Hot July and Aug. Fine for harvest which began Sept 23.

Quantity produced
Port: 7,170,000 cases.

Prospects
A Quinta de Vargellas 1986 will eventually be released and the quality of the 1987 crop is definitely up to Quinta de Vargellas quality. The **1988** crop was tiny but extremely good.

REST OF EUROPE & MEDITERRANEAN

European wines made outside France, Germany, Italy, Spain and Portugal are rarely worth serious ageing. They are either made from grape varieties designed for early consumption or, more commonly, the wine-making skills and technology are not up to crafting long-term wines.

In Switzerland, for example, wine-making skills are top-notch, but since the most planted grape variety is the somewhat dreary Chasselas – known here as Fendant, Dorin, Perlan and Terravin – Swiss wines are, typically, for early consumption. The most ageworthy wines are the finest Blauburgunders made in the northern vineyards which can develop for up to four or five years from the vintage, and the rare wines made from the old Swiss grape varieties Humagne, Armigne and, especially, Arvine.

Austria's answer to Chasselas, Grüner Veltliner, is made of slightly sterner stuff but is still best drunk young – in fact the Viennese have nurtured the concept of *nouveau* for longer than anyone else with their Heurigen. Most Austrian wines mature at a Chart B rate (page 19) but Gumpoldskirchner and many Rieslings can develop real bottle age at about four years. Most of the wines described as Auslese, Beerenauslese, Trockenbeerenauslese and the local speciality Ausbruch can take up to 10 years in bottle. Austrian wine's lower acidity level means that it is shorter-lived than its German counterparts.

Hungary can boast even more indigenous grape varieties than Austria, some of which could doubtless be turned into great wines worth ageing were the wine-making technology more advanced. For the moment Hungary can offer only the Furmint-based Tokaji as a suitable cellar candidate.

The richest Tokajis, Aszu Essencia, are aged in special casks for 10 years and can last apparently indefinitely in bottle. They lose the characteristic whiff of oxidation at about 30 years and develop a miraculous floral bouquet. Tokaji Szamorodni, made without adding the crucial Aszu paste of Botrytised berries, can be a simple rustic alternative to a fino sherry that should be drunk as young as possible. Any Tokaji Aszu of more than four *puttonyos* (literally, hods of Aszu paste) should be worth ageing in bottle for as long as you can possibly resist it.

Wine-making technology again lets us down through much of the rest of Eastern Europe, although the ageability of Bulgaria's creditable varietals is increasing every year. Some of the Reserve Cabernets may not reach their peak before six years while Mavrud and, especially, Melnik are the eastern bloc's answer to Châteauneuf-du-Pape and demand to be aged for at least six years.

There is potential for exciting reds in Yugoslavia too, especially the concentrated curios made all down the Dalmatian coast from Plavac Mali, which can easily develop for 10 years, to Vranac which needs slightly less. Romania's Feteasca Alba (called Leanyka in Hungary) makes perfumed whites which can retain their acidity for a good five years. The Soviet Union could undoubtedly produce wines worth ageing were demand not so rapacious.

One of these days Greece will surprise the world with a range of ageworthy wines made combining modern technology with its ancient grape varieties, but for the moment we must make do with one or the other. Modern technology plus classic French varieties gives us Château Carras whose ageing pattern (though not vintage variation) resembles Château Lynch-Bages. Indigenous grape varieties give us Chart A wines for immediate drinking.

The Lebanon's red Château Musar is undoubtedly the most ageworthy Mediterranean wine and ages like a second growth Bordeaux. Great vintages for current drinking are 1979, 1972, 1970, 1964 and 1961; the 1978 and 1980 should be in their prime in the early nineties. Tradition du Château Musar is designed to be drunk at between three and five years.

North Africa can produce reds for medium-term ageing, as evinced in many older bottles carrying burgundy labels. At the other extreme, the light, tart, dry wines of Luxembourg and England can benefit enormously from two to four years' softening in bottle.

CALIFORNIA

The Robert Mondavi winery is one of the best-known symbols of "sunny" West Coast wine. But the California climate is in fact variable enough to produce significantly different vintages.

California provides the most dramatic illustration of this book's central thesis: that our knowledge of what happens to wine in bottle is laughably, somehow shockingly, scant compared with what is known about every nuance of wine-making up to the moment of bottling.

Here is a multi-million dollar industry producing some wonderful wines in which, more than anywhere else in the wine world, no technological investment is too great if it helps man overcome the inconveniences of nature. And these inconveniences can be great.

Yet hardly any of those who are investing literally fortunes in California's rash of new wineries to overcome these local difficulties know for certain that they are making wines worth serious ageing. This is partly because the history of California wine is so short. Many of the wineries most highly regarded today crushed their first grapes only in the mid-eighties. The sixties represent pre-history. Few bottles survive to offer any tangible evidence of California wine's longevity.

And much of this evidence is of dubious relevance since wine-making in California has taken several different philosophical turns even in the last 20 years. A Napa Cabernet made in the early seventies and tasted in the early eighties would not be a fair representative of how its counterpart, made in the early eighties, might taste in the early nineties. There has been a switchback of wine-making styles and, increasingly, vine growing techniques since then. The trouble with making expense no object is that it leaves unlimited options, which puts no logical order on the evolution of wine styles – nor on wine evolution in general.

A French peasant may decide to invest in new oak, and will be able to afford a certain number of new casks each year. This will have a gradual effect on the resulting wines. In many California wineries on the other hand, once the word goes out that new oak's the thing, the cask hall will be piled high with virgin barrels just as soon as Séguin-Moreau or François Frères can be persuaded to deliver.

It is hardly surprising therefore that vintage charts are almost redundant in California: man is forever tinkering with the formula.

Of course there is nothing wrong with making wines which give great pleasure when young, and many West Coast wines give enormous pleasure, but it is clear that many California wine-makers are more ambitious than this. And to develop any sort of subtlety in wine, rather than sheer exuberance, takes time in bottle.

On the basis of evidence to date, only about 10 per cent of California wine is worth cellaring. Most jug wines age as shown on Chart A (page 19) while the most basic varietals are Chart B examples. Most bottlings of Gewürztraminer and Sauvignon

Blanc/Fumé Blanc won't benefit from cellaring much past their third birthday; Chardonnay their fourth birthday, Pinot Noir their fifth, Zinfandel their sixth and Cabernet Sauvignon their seventh. In the old days reds demanded cellaring in the (sometimes forlorn) hope that the overwhelming tannins would one day reveal the gorgeous fruit behind them. Nowadays however greater understanding of canopy management in the vineyard, the concept of grape maturity, the role of acid and pH in ageing and how to master oak means that an increasing proportion of California wine is being made to develop genuine interest and complexity from bottle ageing.

The seven wines whose Timecharts follow have been chosen to illustrate California cellar potential to date. They each belong indisputably to the 10 per cent of wines that do have some track record of ageworthiness, and are among the best of their type. They appear, as elsewhere in this book, in geographical order north to south of the vineyard or vineyards that supplied the grapes.

Thus Ridge's Zinfandel from Geyserville, the closest source to the Dry Creek area which produces so much fine Zin, leads as representative of those examples of the state's own grape that are worth ageing. It is there in the hope that it may encourage the growing band of those prepared to take Zin seriously. The 1973 and 1974 were only gently declining in 1988. Only Ridge can offer such a long track record but producers such as Karly, Kendall-Jackson, Nalle (a lighter style), Sausal, Storybook and, particularly, Ravenswood can show what Zinfandel can do over a similar timespan to Ridge. 1984 was a year for ageable Napa Zinfandels.

But it was with Cabernet Sauvignon-based reds that California first attracted the world's attention. The warmer climate and no shortage of investment in top quality *élevage* mean that the state can produce some of the world's sleekest Cabernet models. In the late seventies the thesis that if tannin was a sign of quality in a young wine, then a lot of tannin must be a sign of high quality was fortunately abandoned, but in favour of a flirtation with a lighter, sometimes eviscerated, more "European" style of wine. By the mid-eighties however, and certainly with the excellent 1985 vintage, Cabernet makers seemed to be getting into their stride, producing marvels of healthy flesh and balance. They have been rewarded

with a run of excellent Cabernet vintages up to 1988. This is a generalisation of course. Some producers have managed to remain unaffected by the prevailing fashions, but the Napa Valley king-pin Robert Mondavi must take responsibility for many of these changes in direction. His Cabernet Sauvignon Reserve certainly reflects them clearly. It also provides an interesting contrast to the Martha's Vineyard wine made from a nearby single vineyard, supposedly to a uniquely California recipe, by one of the business's great individuals. Tasting notes for Opus One, the most famous Franco-American wine project, have been included to animate those wondering whether it is worth paying a premium over a Mondavi Reserve.

All these Cabernets are from the Napa Cabernet heartland. For Reserve bottlings of Napa Cabernet from other producers, take the Mondavi Timechart as indicative of likely maturity, bearing in mind vintage factors outlined above. For regular bottlings of valley floor fruit accelerate the Mondavi Timechart by two years, although mountain Cabernets such as those produced by Burgess, Diamond Creek, Dunn on Howell Mountain, The Hess Collection, William Hill, La Jota, Mayacamas, Mount Veeder, Newton and Pine Ridge will probably need the timescale of the Mondavi Reserve. So will the newer mountain Cabernet labels which are doubtless being designed and printed as I write.

To calculate the likely maturity of a Sonoma Cabernet, accelerate the Mondavi Timechart by two years, one year for a reserve bottling such as a Simi Reserve or Clos du Bois' Marlstone, remembering that Sonoma Cabernets were in general less good than Napa's in 1981 and 1987, but were slightly better in 1983 and 1984.

Most Central Coast wines mature rather faster than the grandaddies of Rutherford. Accelerate the Mondavi Timechart by two years, remembering that Cabernets from the Central Coast wine regions to the south have been good in recent vintages but many were simply overripe in 1984 and too light for keeping in 1983.

Ridge Monte Bello is geographically between north and south California wine land. Its Timechart gives a good indication of the performance of mountain Cabernets made in the Santa Cruz mountains.

Like several of the other particularly impressive California wineries, Chalone is well off the beaten track.

The two Chardonnays chosen represent wines at different ends of the wine-making spectrum. The more established Chalone, using classic burgundian techniques, is producing a range of Chardonnays with a typically burgundian and distinctly un-American set of idiosyncrasies. For many tasters, the Sonoma-Cutrer line-up of more subdued wines which display consistent technical perfection will be infinitely preferable.

In fact Sonoma-Cutrer's Les Pierres has been considered a role model for California's troupe of ambitious Chardonnay starlets. This famous bottling probably has keeping qualities far in excess of most California Chardonnays, although the winery is too young to have proved it beyond doubt. Most well-intentioned Chardonnay is designed to be drunk at two to four years from the vintage. Bottlings for which the Sonoma-Cutrer may have direct relevance include Acacia, Château Montelena, single vineyard bottlings of Château St Jean, Clos du Bois Calcaire, Cuvaison, Flora Springs Reserve, Folie à Deux, Hanzell, Kalin, Kistler, Matanzas Creek, Mondavi Reserve Chardonnay, Joseph Phelps Sangiacomo, Simi Reserve, Sterling Winery Lake – and Stony Hill and Trefethen whose Chardonnays have always been built for the long term. Both 1987 and 1986 produced fine

Chardonnays for the long term, in an era when so many more wine-makers seemed interested in that variety. But when interpreting the Sonoma-Cutrer Timechart, remember that Les Pierres was more successful in 1985 than many of its peers.

The Saintsbury chart shows how surprisingly well "light" Pinots, such as most of those produced in Carneros, can age. The Saintsbury Timechart should indicate quite faithfully the longevity of all Carneros Pinot except for Acacia's most extractive bottlings. For Pinot Noir from the likes of Au Bon Climat, Calera, Chalone and Hanzell, retard the Saintsbury chart by two years, remembering that these heftier Pinot Noirs will remain drinkable for probably two years longer than the Saintsbury of the same year. 1985 was particularly good for Central Coast Pinot but, as usual with generalisations about Pinot Noir, particular caution is needed.

Uncharted, and all too often undervalued, are California's Late Harvest Johannisberg Rieslings. They last only a fraction of the time that the German prototypes do, and tend to brown after only five years in bottle, but can provide enormous pleasure at between four and eight years old. Good years for *Botrytis* have been 1986 in both Napa and Sonoma, 1985 in Napa and some Central Coast districts and 1981 in Santa Barbara and San Luis Obispo.

Ridge Geyserville Zinfandel

For many serious connoisseurs, especially those who view their cellars as long-term storehouses, Ridge Vineyards' most admirable wine is the Monte Bello Cabernet Sauvignon, which is examined in more detail on page 138.

There is a growing band of enthusiasts for full-blooded red versions of California's own vine variety, however, and Ridge's range of Zinfandels from around the state is unparalleled. This homespun winery is perched on the Monte Bello ridge above the haze of Silicon Valley. It draws grapes from carefully selected, and usually relatively antique, vineyards as far south as Paso Robles in San Luis Obispo County and as far north as Alexander Valley in Sonoma County. The final four mile zigzag up the side of a mountain must seem the ultimate insult for the truck drivers at vintage time.

The Alexander Valley wine is labelled Geyserville after the location of Leo Trentadue's vineyard just north of Healdsburg which has supplied grapes for this Ridge speciality since 1966. The Trentadue vines are on the western edge of the valley up against the foothills, so the soils are more like those of the benchland between Alexander Valley and Dry Creek Valley than those of Alexander Valley proper. Few winemakers other than Ridge's Paul Draper can claim to have worked with the same vines for even 10 years. This longstanding relationship has resulted in an admirably discernible style for Geyserville Zinfandel. Like all five Ridge Zinfandel bottlings it is serious stuff, made to last thanks to Bordeaux-style vinification and *élevage* (although the oak is American, an important Draperism). Everything is geared for a longer and more complex life than has been considered usual for a Zinfandel. The fermentation using natural yeasts, exceptional for California, is prolonged into a 12 to 14 day maceration with regular pumping over. Press wine is sometimes added for extra guts, and there is full malolactic fermentation, minimal filtration and up to 20 per cent new oak – much less than with Cabernet because of Zinfandel's intensely fruity character. For the same reason, bottling is also earlier, in the spring of the wine's second year.

The Geyserville vineyard, close to the Dry Creek area thought by many to be most suitable for Zinfandel, is on a gravel base, on the upper edges of the prehistoric Russian River Valley. A third of the vines are well over 100 years old, another third between 60 and 70 and the final third was planted in the early seventies. All these wines are spiced with a little Petite Sirah (the French Durif, about which Draper is a great enthusiast) and, from 1985, the fruit of some ancient Carignan vines.

The quality and subtlety of the oldest vintages specified here make a powerful case for according Zinfandel the respect due to any grape variety that can produce wines that age gracefully. No-one could argue that all Zinfandel currently produced is cellar fodder, but Ridge prove that much more of it could be.

Earlier vintages
1973 and 1974 fading, if pleasurably. 1975, 1976 and especially 1977 worth trying.

1978 Mature, ripe red wine rather than Zinfandel – easy to mistake for a burgundy. Scent of violets, but starting its decline.
Weather and timing
Very good vintage, normal crop. Early set followed by warm growing season. Hot Sept. Early harvest Sept 22. High sugar content.
Quantity produced
Bottled Jan 1980: 781 cases released at $90 a case. 1988 price: $240. Total California production: 159,000,000 cases.
Other details
For the first time yeast was added after pressing. 5% Petite Sirah from York Creek vineyard was included.
1979 Relatively pale and starting to brown. Strong vanillin perfume of American oak rather than fruit aromas. Old but flattering.
Weather and timing
Very good vintage, above average crop. Early but uneven set. Early harvest Sept 22. Much lower sugar levels than 1978.
Quantity produced
703 cases released at $90 a case. 1988 price: $240. California: 167,000,000 cases.

1980 Brick rim. Rather too big for its own good. Stewed blackberries on the nose, then the unintegrated impact of richness, acid and alcohol. Almost port-like.
Weather and timing
Good vintage, large crop. Cool spring followed by late set. Late harvest Oct 8 and 10.
Quantity produced
1,767 cases released at $108 a case. 1988 price: $216. California: 199,000,000 cases.

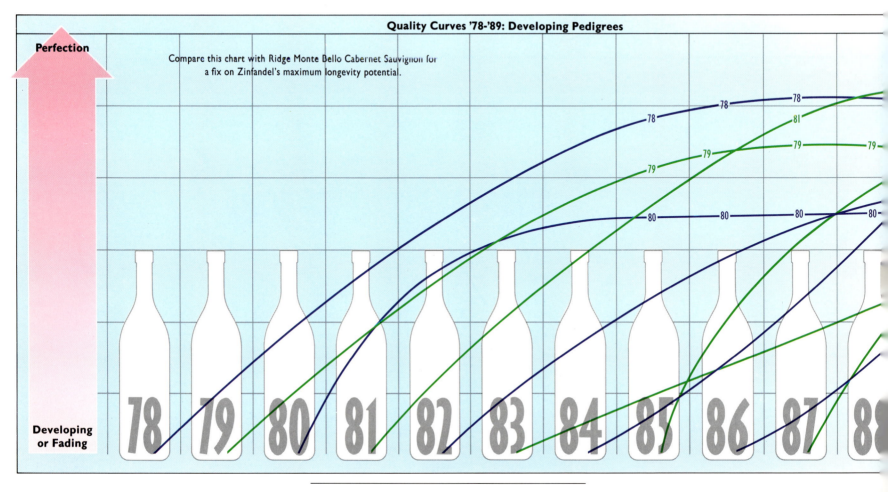

Quality Curves '78-'89: Developing Pedigrees

Perfection

Compare this chart with Ridge Monte Bello Cabernet Sauvignon for a fix on Zinfandel's maximum longevity potential.

Developing or Fading

78 79 80 81 82 83 84 85 86 87 88

Other details

Petite Sirah from the Geyserville vineyard included for the first time.

1981 One of the most massive wines of the range but in gorgeous balance. Silky-soft opulent bouquet of top quality oak-aged red rather than distinctive Zinfandel characteristics. Peak richness and complexity with some fruit.

Weather and timing

Very fine vintage, below average crop. Early set. Cool growing season then warm in early Sept. Early harvest began Sept 10.

Quantity produced

1,991 cases released at $108 a case. 1988 price: $216. California: 177,000,000 cases.

Other details

Grapes from Geyserville Township and Angeli vineyards were included to compensate for low yield. Kept in barrel for longer than usual due to high tannin.

1982 Still a way to go on this healthily crimson, gutsy wine smelling of apples and cinnamon. A higher acid level than most.

Weather and timing

Fair vintage, record crop. Damp spring led to late bud break and set. Cool growing season with rain in early Sept. Harvest began Oct 5: selective picking to avoid rot.

Quantity produced

2,045 cases released at $114 a case. 1988 price: $168. California: 216,000,000 cases.

Other details

5% of juice was drained off before fermentation to intensify wine.

1983 Deep colour, hot fruit. Relatively simple yet appealing ripe fruit flavours followed by levels of acid and, particularly, tannin that shock the palate (not unlike some 1983 red burgundies).

Weather and timing

Fair vintage, small crop. Early, wet spring followed by a cool growing season. Damp, cool Sept meant that careful harvesting was needed to avoid rot. Harvest Sept 22-28. Good sugar levels.

Quantity produced

2,533 cases released at $120 a case. 1988 price: $144. California: 162,000,000 cases.

Other details

5% of juice drained off before fermentation.

1984 Colour shows no signs of age. Vigorous, penetrating aromas of fruit and oak. Lots of ripe fruit flavours and the savoury element of pepper on the palate. Still some tannin. Confident, lively, youthful wine.

Weather and timing

Good vintage, average crop. Early flowering followed by warm growing season. Hot Sept. Earliest completed harvest on record Sept 7-12. Good sugar levels.

Quantity produced

2,322 cases released at $126 a case.

1988 price: $180. California: 168,000,000 cases.

Other details

Fined in second year. 10% Geyserville Petite Sirah was included.

1985 Concentrated crimson. Excellent, vibrant, powerful, well-knit secondary aromas. Savoury, meaty, masculine, powerful and very, very dry. A million miles from the "hot berry" stereotype Zinfandel. Definitely a Bordeaux-style Zinfandel but with a bit of extra power.

Weather and timing

Excellent vintage, below average crop. Warm spring: good flowering. Warm days and cool nights throughout growing season. Main harvest Sept 22-24 followed by the Petite Sirah Oct 1.

Quantity produced

3,881 cases released at $126 a case. 1988 price: $168. California: 174,000,000 cases.

1986 Unusually herbaceous nose. Aromatic, less ripe and lush than some, but with a rich initial impression on the palate giving way to tannin and acid.

Weather and timing

Excellent vintage, normal crop. Early flowering. Cool, spring-like growing season. Very early harvest began Sept 3.

Quantity produced

4,322 cases released at $144 a case. California: 185,000,000 cases.

Other details

Fined in second year.

1987 (Cask sample) Sweet, rich nose of ripe young berries with a touch of oaky coconut. Notable acid and stewed plums on the palate. Lively.

Weather and timing

Very fine vintage, below average crop. Warm conditions advanced the flowering: balanced by cool growing season. Oldest Zinfandel vines harvested Sept 2, 3 and 7.

Picking stopped during cool spell; Indian summer permitted continuation Sept 22, 23 and Oct 1, 5.

Quantity produced

Bottled in 1989: 5,323 cases. Estimated release price: $144 a case. California: 164,000,000 cases.

1988 (Not tasted) Comparable in style to 1985 and 1987 according to Paul Draper. Big, well-balanced with a long finish. Ripe fruit flavours with rougher tannins than 1987.

Weather and timing

Excellent vintage, average crop. Very early set. Cool growing season but with warm June and Aug. Very early start to harvest: old Zinfandel vines Aug 29, 30; young vines Sept 19-21.

Quantity produced

About 5,000 cases. California: 170,000,000 cases.

Other details

No Petite Sirah from Geyserville vineyard.

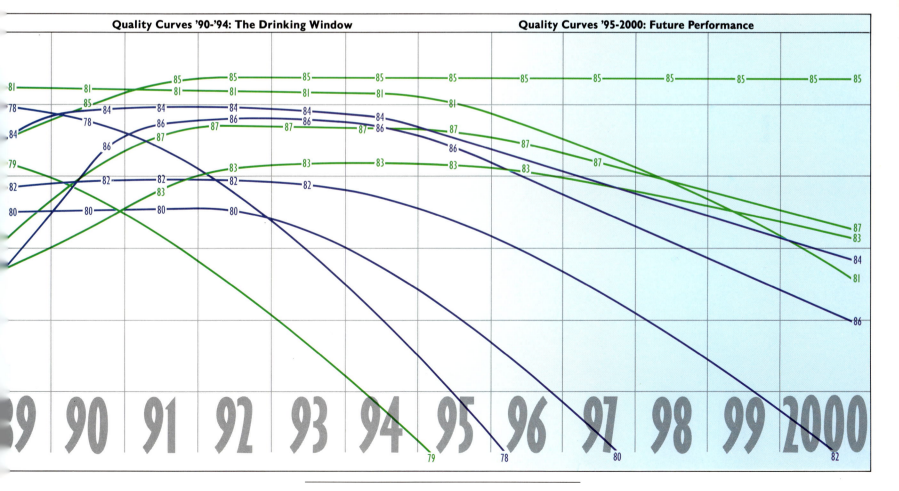

Quality Curves '90-'94: The Drinking Window   **Quality Curves '95-2000: Future Performance**

Heitz Martha's Vineyard Cabernet Sauvignon

Martha's Vineyard has long produced one of California's most distinctive and most widely admired wines. The vineyard, lined by eucalyptus trees and pressed up against the wooded hills of the western Napa Valley just south of Rutherford, was planted by Belle and Barney Rhodes. The Rhodes subsequently sold the vineyard to Tom May and his wife Martha who is, thanks to their friend Joe Heitz's success with his first vineyard-designated Cabernet Sauvignon, the most talked-about woman in California wine.

The Rhodes now own the Bella Oaks vineyard next door to Martha's, the source of Heitz's other sublime vineyard-designated Cabernet. The two wines follow similar curves of maturation, although Bella Oaks is a more supple style of wine which outdid Martha's in its debut, drought years of 1976 and 1977.

The first vintage, 1966, was a revelation to many doubters of the sheer, soaring quality that could be coaxed out of California's vineyards. No other modern classic can boast such a track record of uncompromising dedication to this peculiarly California style of wine. It is 100 per cent Cabernet Sauvignon – no namby pamby Frenchifying with Merlot or Cabernet Franc for Heitz – and has a good three years in cask, not just small French cooperage by any means, before bottling. Heitz uses a varying cocktail of old and new French and American oak, almost daring the wine not to turn out as spicily statuesque as previous, quite differently treated vin-

tages. Martha's seems to have a will and style of its own. The wine stands out like a beacon in any comparative line-up. Its smell is distinctively warm yet highly aromatic, described by many as "eucalyptus". This description elicits growls from Joe Heitz, California wine's most famous grizzly bear, who describes it as "minty".

Heitz is one of the many protegés of André Tchelistcheff, who oversaw Joe Heitz's training as a young wine-maker at Beaulieu Vineyards. It is not difficult to detect a relationship between Martha's and Beaulieu Vineyard's top Cabernet the de Latour Private Reserve.

The progress of consecutive Martha's Vineyard vintages as charted here demonstrates how well California Cabernets can age: they certainly perform as well as most red Bordeaux. Yet, with the extra fillip of ripeness due to the California sunshine, these serious red wines are approachable earlier than many of their Bordeaux counterparts (compare this chart with that on page 38/9 for Château Margaux) with the exception of such tannin storehouses as Mayacamas and Mount Veeder.

Collectors of wine trivia may be interested to hear that when Angelo Gaja (see page 102/3) visited Joe Heitz, he was so impressed by the quality of the red and rosé made from the Piedmontese grape Grignolino that he had quantities shipped back to its native region, saying "If only the Piedmontese could make wines like this!"

Earlier vintages

1968 Extraordinary reputation. Michael Broadbent's "cross between Pétrus and Mouton with years of life ahead" in 1979. Joe Heitz's "soft, sweet, cuddly little blonde" in 1988. By now mostly drunk. **1969** Copybook stuff. Quite exceptional balance with characteristic minty nose and lovely mature blackcurrant fruit. Perfectly mature, and perfectly Napa. Tannins almost imperceptible. Joe Heitz's favourite. **1970** One of Martha's most Bordeaux-like manifestations. Mature 1984-1990. **1974** Extraordinarily deep colour but with browner rim than 1969. Rich toasty bouquet with roasted red-fruit flavours and some mineral notes. Ripe, round and slightly obvious with some quite aggressive tannins on the finish. Mature 1986-2000. **1975** Overshadowed by the 1974 but one of the slowest developers.

Chosen by two out of three Heitz children for their wedding receptions.

1978 Substantial, vigorous wine with luscious cassis and hints of coffee. More suggestive of Bordeaux than Martha's. Difficult to see how it could develop further; acid and tannin levels still good.

Weather and timing

Very good vintage, normal crop. Wet winter (45"/680mm rain). Warm growing season. Harvest Sept 29 to Oct 3.

Quantity produced

4,889 cases released in 1983 at $290 a case. Sold well.

1979 Relatively light though healthy colour. Well-developed bouquet of well-mannered Cabernet fruit with a floral note. Good proportions but flavours should become yet more complex.

Weather and timing

Fair vintage. Average winter.

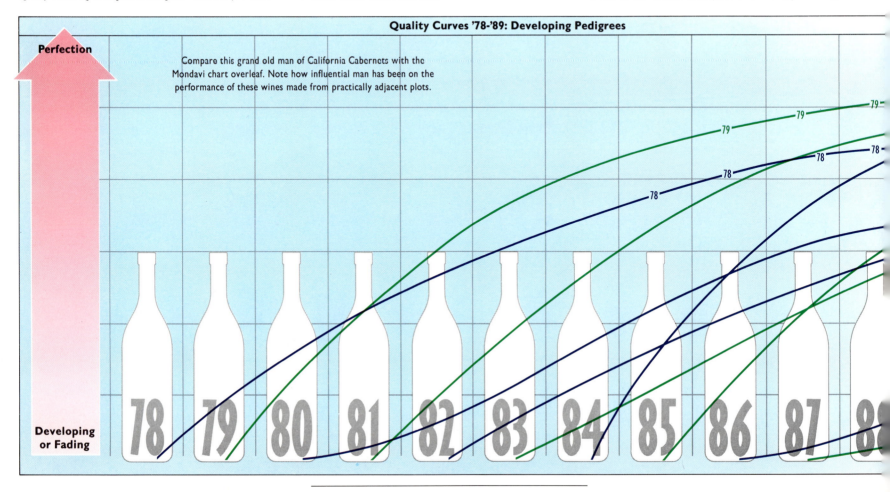

Quality Curves '78-'89: Developing Pedigrees

Perfection

Compare this grand old man of California Cabernets with the Mondavi chart overleaf. Note how influential man has been on the performance of these wines made from practically adjacent plots.

Developing or Fading

78 79 80 81 82 83 84 85 86 87 88

Frost-free bud break. Cool growing season. Harvest Oct 12-17.

Quantity produced
5,446 cases released at $270 a case. 1988 price: $540.

1980 Good attempt at a cover-up of ultimately obtrusive tannins. Powerful bouquet of gingerbread and cold tea is its most engaging characteristic. Otherwise, a tough old thing even, one suspects, in youth. Needs careful food matching.

Weather and timing
Good vintage. Wet winter then cool spring and summer. Hot Sept. Harvest Oct 6-9.

Quantity produced
2,948 cases released at $324 a case. 1988 price: $540.

1981 An underestimated star. Excellent colour. Complex mulch of tobacco and fruit flavours make an unctuously mouthfilling wine which is big, yet in perfect balance.

Weather and timing
Good vintage, below average crop. Moderate winter then warm spring. Early bud break. June heatwave shortened growing season. Fog in Sept slowed ripening. Harvest Sept 16 to Oct 1.

Quantity produced
3,172 cases released at $324 a case. 1988 price: $432.

1982 A broodingly big, spicy hulk. Not subtle but impressive and long. A somewhat jagged wine, perhaps destined for the nineties.

Weather and timing
Average vintage, below average crop. Early bud break. Windy, wet spring. Heat during flowering caused some shatter. Good growing season. Harvest Oct 13-19.

Quantity produced
5,085 cases released at $324 a case. 1988 price: $432.

1983 Martha's mint aroma. Much more forward than the 1982

with less concentration but good balance and attractively ripe Cabernet Sauvignon aromas. Might perhaps have been more interesting with a little Merlot or Cabernet Franc seasoning, but an attractively, juicy, if slightly simple early developer.

Weather and timing
Good vintage, below average crop. Very wet winter. Normal bud break. Cool summer with heatwave mid-July followed by rain in Aug. Warm early Sept. Dry harvest Oct 18-20.

Quantity produced
4,320 cases released in 1988 at $351 a case.

1984 Surprisingly approachable. Lively, rich, enticing, opulent blackberry aroma. Velvety without being spineless. Attractively soft tannins. Deft balancing act.

Weather and timing
Very good vintage, crop down by

20%. Hot season compressed the vintage. Warm, dry spring. No frost. Heatwave during May caused shatter. Second heatwave early Sept. Very early harvest Sept 10-20.

Quantity produced
4,462 cases bottled in 1988. Release date: 1989.

1985 (Cask sample) Youthfully concentrated, almost raw nose, with a hint of mint. Real mulch of dark red fruit aromas and although no secondary aromas yet, an exceptionally alluring mouthful. Sweet on entry to the palate. Very youthful and rather Rhône-like in its ripeness and spice.

Weather and timing
Excellent vintage, below average crop. Dry winter followed by Feb storms. Balmy Apr followed by cool, foggy May. Extensive shatter due to poor weather during flowering. Hot July. Rain early

Sept. Harvest Sept 24 to Oct 6.

Quantity produced
Unknown. Release date: 1990.

1986 (Cask sample) A note of bergamot on the nose of this elegant classic. Lacks the opulence of 1985, but with great balance and tannins that should see it through to Pauillac-like maturity. Dry and flavoury.

Weather and timing
Excellent vintage, large crop. Cold winter. Wet Feb. Early, long flowering. Cool, foggy summer. Aug and Sept hot. Rain late Sept. Harvest Oct 6-9.

Quantity produced
Unknown. Release date: 1991.

1987 (Cask sample) Intense, concentrated, almost herbaceous, aromatic wine with more tannin than the 1986. Very chewy. Not a heavyweight but promises a long life. Joe Heitz believes all the building blocks for greatness are present in this one.

Weather and timing
Good vintage, below average crop. Low winter rainfall. Hot late Apr. Hot during flowering. Good growing season. Harvest Sept 25 to Oct 2.

Quantity produced
Unknown. Release date: 1992.

1988 (Not tasted) According to Kathleen Heitz this vintage looks very promising. It has a deep purple colour right out to the rim with intense varietal characteristics.

Weather and timing
Good vintage, small crop. Dry winter (20"/510mm rain instead of the usual 30"/760mm). Feb heatwave. Cool, rainy Apr and May. Wet during flowering caused extensive shatter. Long growing season. Harvest Sept 21-22 and Oct 3-4.

Quantity produced
About 50% normal production. Release date: 1992.

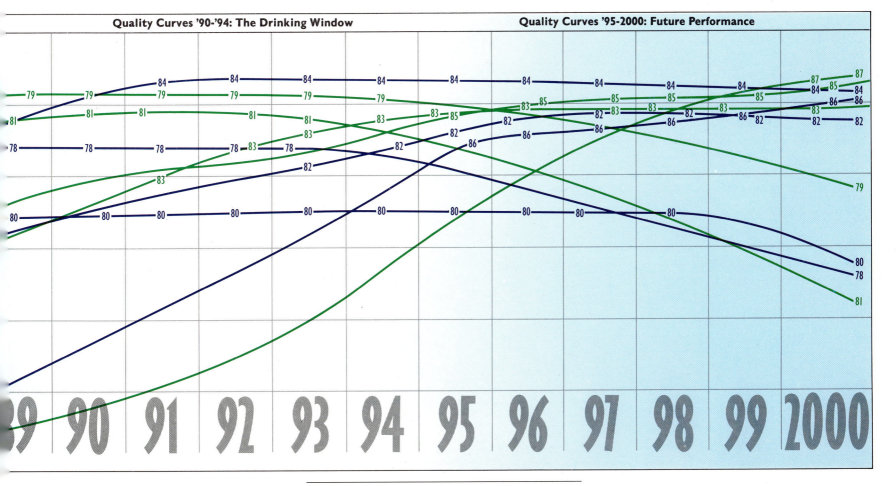

Quality Curves '90-'94: The Drinking Window

Quality Curves '95-2000: Future Performance

Robert Mondavi Cabernet Sauvignon Reserve/Opus One

This is the tale of two different but related wines. They are made from the same Cabernet-dominated cocktail of grape varieties grown near the Robert Mondavi winery just north of Oakville on the controversial "Bench".

In the late seventies, the most astute wine men of California and France got together. The Californian was Robert Mondavi, *the* California wine man, whose winery has combined quality and aesthetics with quantity since its foundation in 1966. His best lots have always been sold as his "Reserves" and the best of all is his Cabernet Sauvignon Reserve. The Frenchman was Baron Philippe de Rothschild, whose many exploits ranged across the worlds of sport, art and commerce. His precious Château Mouton-Rothschild had already been elevated to first growth status in 1973: the first change to the official classification of Médoc Châteaux since 1855.

Together the two men decided to produce a Cabernet-based wine using Napa Valley grapes and Bordeaux expertise. The name, Opus One, the terms and the packaging were agreed much later, after many a legal man-hour.

The first, 1979, vintage is by no means typical for these two wines. The Opus One 1979 was a surprisingly simple wine. It was only in 1981 that Opus One got into its stride and only perhaps since 1984 that a discernible style for each wine emerged. Opus One has a much more traditionally Bordelais structure with less aromatic herbiness than the Reserve,

harder tannins and a rigorous structure designed for a long life. The style of the Reserve wines on the other hand has varied considerably, either as a result of individual vintage characteristics or, post 1979, as a result of dramatic new directions in the winery and, recently, the vineyard. The vintages 1981 to 1983 demonstrate the desire for a lighter, more "European", or at least less obviously California style. After stumbling in 1984, subsequent vintages show the beginnings of an opulent yet concentrated style of soft-tannin wine – a sort of California Château Margaux. This is partly thanks to longer skin contact and less and later sulphur, but is also due to better control of the vigorous vines on Napa's valley floor and a lower yield forcing more flavour into each grape.

Grapes for the Reserve Cabernet now come almost exclusively from the Mondavi vineyards behind the winery, with their "J block" one of the most consistent ingredients. "P block" shares the eucalyptus element of its neighbour Martha's Vineyard (see page 130) and Tim Mondavi decided to avoid this obviously California style of fruit for Opus One, much to the relief of Lucien Sionneau, his mentor from Mouton. A block to the east of the winery has been close-planted *à la bordelaise* expressly for Opus One. Since 1982 there have been vintages of Opus One which are (almost) worth their price tag. But there are also years such as 1979 and 1985 in which the Mondavi Reserve looks a real bargain.

Earlier vintages

1968 Unfined. Ageing fast, baked overtones. Drink up now. **1969** Unfined. Warm bouquet of toasted, spicy flavours but past its peak. Drink 1980-1989. **1970** Unfined. Brick rim. Rich, well balanced whole with many secondary, mineral-laden aromas. Drink 1985-1995. **1971** 40% from the Valley's oldest Cabernet Franc vineyard. Soft, ripe and lush but the tannins just too hard for perfection ever to be reached. Drink with tannin-reducing food. **1974** Roasted blackcurrant aroma. Simple but big. Drink 1980-1992. **1975** Sweet, alluring mix of complex fruit flavours yet masses more to give. Tannins perhaps too intrusive but drink 1990-1998. **1976** Simple, sweet, relatively low acid, flattering. Drink 1985-1995.

Quantity produced

Mondavi's Reserve represents

about 10% of his total Cabernet Sauvignon production. Exact figures are not released.

1978 Raw, jagged succession of fairly simple fruit and oak flavours in a broad, direct style.

Weather and timing

Good vintage, small crop. Wet winter. Some early *Botrytis*. Good flowering. Heat-wave early June. Rain early Sept then dry. Harvest Sept 18-23.

Other details

Released in 1982 at $480 a case.

1979 Supple, hint of mint, definitely California. Deep purple with complex bouquet suggesting heady tropical flowers. Big but polished. Could drink now but the acid and well-disguised tannins promise long future.

Weather and timing

Good vintage, small crop. Average winter. Heat-wave in early May caused some shatter. Almost

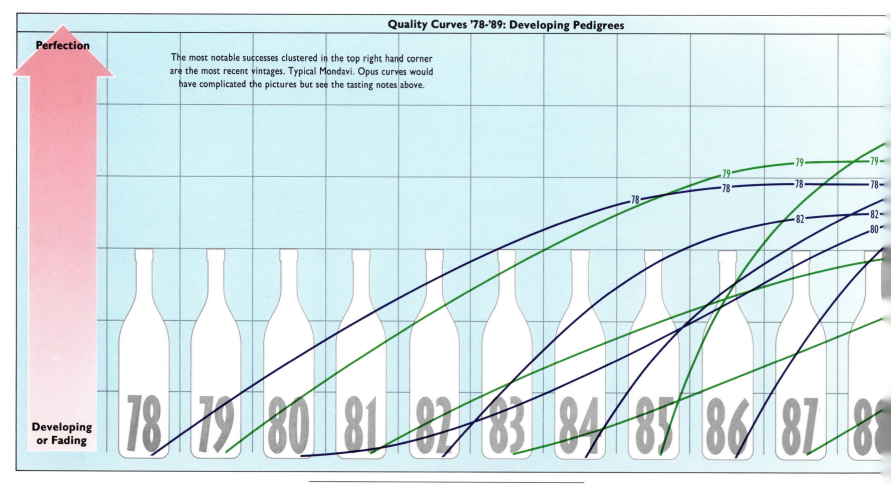

Quality Curves '78-'89: Developing Pedigrees

Perfection

The most notable successes clustered in the top right hand corner are the most recent vintages. Typical Mondavi. Opus curves would have complicated the pictures but see the tasting notes above.

Developing or Fading

78 79 80 81 82 83 84 85 86 87 88

perfect growing season. Harvest began Sept 10.

Other details
Released in 1983 at $300 a case.

1980 Brawny, slightly coarse, wine with heavy tannins. Attractive well-integrated nose: long finish. Needs careful food matching.

Weather and timing
Very good vintage, large crop. Wet winter with rain into Apr. Cool growing season. Hot in late Sept. Late harvest began Sept 21. Excellent acid/sugar balance.

Other details
Released in 1984 at $360 a case.

1981 Looks quite evolved. Simple, slightly vegetal notes on the nose. Some jamminess on the palate and an acid finish.

Weather and timing
Good vintage, average crop. Warm spring and early flowering. Excellent set. Earliest harvest on record began Aug 24. Good sugar/acid levels.

Other details
Released at $360 a case.

1982 Not a blockbuster but a well-mannered harmonious whole with cassis and light herbaceousness.

Weather and timing
Very good vintage, large crop. Perfect spring; good flowering and set. Long, cool growing season. Harvest early Oct, hampered by rains.

Other details
Released in 1986 at $276 a case.

1983 Aromatic and intriguing. Medium weight but well structured for long keeping in chewy, Bordeaux style.

Weather and timing
Good vintage, small crop. Record winter rains. Cool summer. Heatwave mid-July. Warm early Sept, then cloudy and cool. Harvest Sept 12 to Oct 15.

Other details
Released in 1987 at $330 a case.

1984 Big, warm, gamey. Less subtle than 1983 and slightly muscle-bound. Tannins slightly too obtrusive for its fruit.

Weather and timing
Very good vintage, large crop. Dry winter. Early bud break. Some shatter reduced crop. Short, hot growing season. Harvest Aug 19 to Sept 20.

Other details
1988 price, $420 a case. Less than 22 months in barrel.

1985 Exciting. More evolved and open than 1984 but promises more eventual subtlety. Mouthfilling fruit suggests ripe harvest, yet still dry and intriguing. Already approachable, but its fascination should increase.

Weather and timing
Excellent vintage, large crop. Early bud break; long season. Harvest late Aug to end Sept.

Other details
Release price: about $480 a case.

1986 Extraordinary depth of colour with purple right out to rim. Vigorous, rich brambly young fruit with a hint of oak. More resolved than 1985 with spice and better hidden tannins. Should develop well.

Weather and timing
Excellent vintage, normal crop. Heavy rains in Feb. Long, cool growing season. Rain during Sept harvest.

Other details
Release price: About $420 a case.

1987 (Cask sample) Looked like port. Young, aromatic fresh and silky. Graceful but not enormous. Classic.

Weather and timing
Outstanding vintage, small crop. Near drought year. Dry, short winter. Warm start to season. Early bud break, some shatter. Cool growing season. Main harvest Sept 1-27. Excellent acid/sugar balance.

Other details
Release date 1991. Price not determined.

1988 (Not tasted) Tim Mondavi reported that the small berry size gave concentrated flavour. Good colour. Doesn't match the 1987.

Weather and timing
Good vintage, below average crop. Dry winter. Early bud break. Long, uneven flowering. Warm growing season. Excellent harvest Aug 22 to Oct 24.

Other details
Release date 1992.

OPUS ONE

1979 Evolved but not enough fruit. Awkward. Drink 1984-1992. **1980** Rich roasted aromas. Tough and chunky but worthy meld of California fruit flavours. Drink 1990-2000. **1981** Rich fruit and tobacco character, sturdy backbone. Tannin at end. Great definition. Drink 1990-2003. **1982** Luscious, rich nose with coconut but masses of tannin at the end. Drink 1991-2002. **1983** Aromatic and well-knit. More savoury and leaner than 1982 with a dry finish. Graves-like texture. Drink 1993-2005. **1984** Rich, exotic powerful aroma of heady tropical scents and mulberry. Impressive, full-bodied. Could do with more acid. Well masked but considerable tannins. Drink 1991-2001. **1985** Rich, ripely fruity with hints of sweet coconut and the perfume of fresh green leaves. High acid and extract: excellent concentration. Drink 1992-2005. **1986** Extraordinary colour with rich red fruits and powerful oak still on the nose. Well-knit already with a little fruit lacking. Drink from 1998. According to Tim Mondavi the **1987** is vibrant and tightly knit while the **1988** is rich, broad and powerful.

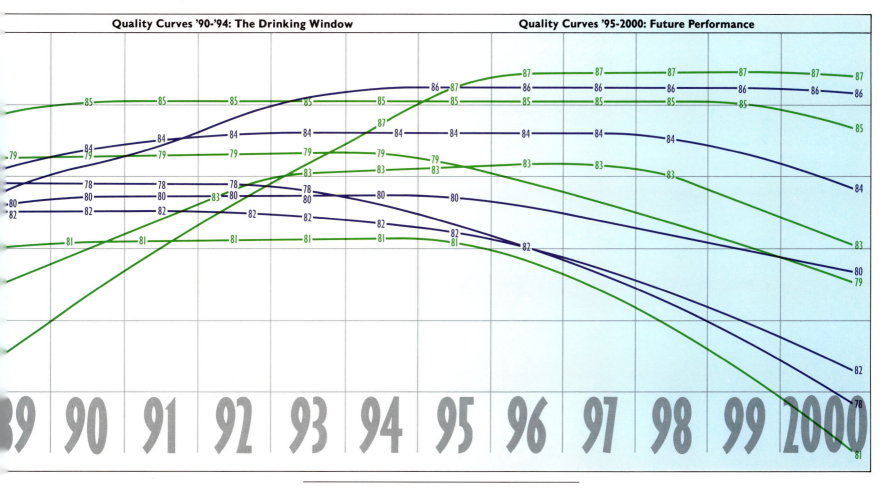

Quality Curves '90-'94: The Drinking Window

Quality Curves '95-2000: Future Performance

Sonoma-Cutrer Chardonnay Les Pierres

Sonoma-Cutrer is a dream winery – not perhaps for the tourist, nor for an investor simply after a fast return, but it would be difficult to imagine a wine operation more desirable to any wine-maker, or indeed to any croquet player. Symbolising one of president Brice Cutrer Jones' two major passions are twin international tournament croquet courts in front of the winery entrance. What lies behind that entrance demonstrates the other, his single-minded commitment to producing top quality Chardonnay no matter what the cost.

One of Sonoma-Cutrer's earliest and most important "acquisitions" to this end was Bill Bonetti, who had shown such mastery of Chardonnay at Charles Krug in the early sixties and his own brand of gentle but firm managerial skill at Souverain since then. He joined Brice Jones in 1981 to help him switch his main focus from grape growing to wine making.

In 1981 the winery, and Sonoma-Cutrer's string of dazzling Chardonnays, was begun. Not for them the inherited tradition of rich, toasty, often fat California Chardonnay. Perhaps more than any other Americans, Bonetti and Jones threw themselves and their working capital into technological emulation of the burgundian model: letting individual vineyards express themselves through the grapes with minimum human intervention.

They produce three bottlings of Chardonnay: Russian River Ranches from three local vineyards, Cutrer from the vineyard surrounding the winery in the low hills west of Windsor and, the undisputed star, Les Pierres. This comes from a rocky 120 acres (48 hectares) of Carneros at the base of Sonoma Mountain 15 miles south of, and therefore cooler than, the Cutrer vineyard.

In the winery all has been dedicated, and much of it specially designed, to get the most delicate fruit flavours into the bottle. This begins in their vineyards, with specially designed shallow picking trays which leave the grapes as whole and cool as possible. The grapes then go into the extraordinary cooling tunnel which was so useful in the hot years of 1982 and 1983. It was custom built at great expense to get the grapes to about 45°F (7°C) so as minimise oxidation during fermentation. Then there are the carefully designed oscillating sorting tables (which could not remain unique to Sonoma-Cutrer forever).

Sonoma-Cutrer claim to have been the first to ferment all their Chardonnay in small French oak casks when they set out in 1981. Bill Bonetti really does seem to view his damp underground cellar full of wine fermenting or ageing undisturbed on the lees as a nursery full of barrel-shaped babies. Racking is minimal, lees contact minimal, quality maximal.

The other Sonoma-Cutrer Chardonnays age faster than Les Pierres. Accelerate by one year for the Cutrer vineyard bottling and two years for Russian River Ranches.

1981 Green-gold and paler than the 1982 or 1983. Not even a hint of age to the eye. Lovers of Hunter Valley whites would find something to enthuse about in the toasty bouquet. Real concentration of pure unadorned Chardonnay flavour with excellent length.

Weather and timing
Good quality vintage, low yield. Low rainfall (only about two thirds of the average 80-90"/20-23cm). Bud break about three weeks early. Hot, dry winds during spring concentrated the grapes by drying them. Early start to the summer; normal length growing season (203 days). Early harvest began Sept 12.

Quantity produced
750 cases of this inaugural vintage were released in 1983 at $174 a case and immediately sold out. (Les Pierres represents 20-25% of Sonoma-Cutrer's annual produc-tion and 1% of the total Sonoma County output.)

Other details
The winery was still under con-struction. A programme was initi-ated to convert the Les Pierres vineyard from a Pinot/Riesling/Chardonnay mix to almost exclu-sively Chardonnay. This was achieved by T-budding rather than replanting. The conversion was completed in 1984.

1982 Deep greenish gold. A golden treasure of a wine smelling of pears, honey and minerals. Ter-tiary aromas only just starting to develop. Quite fat but with such glorious acidity that the whole is balanced. The *Botrytis* should help to preserve it over the next few years.

Weather and timing
Very good quality vintage, good yield. El Niño – a shifting of ocean currents off South America that caused tropical storms along the

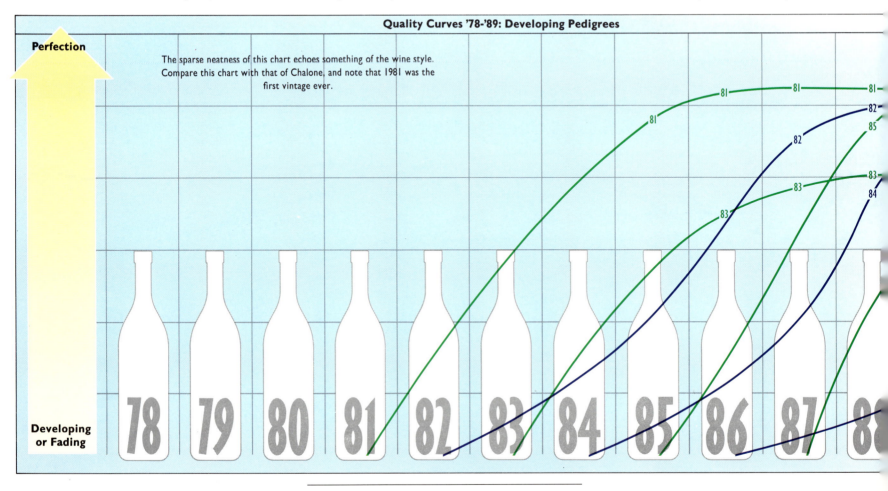

Quality Curves '78-'89: Developing Pedigrees

Perfection

The sparse neatness of this chart echoes something of the wine style. Compare this chart with that of Chalone, and note that 1981 was the first vintage ever.

Developing or Fading

78 79 80 81 82 83 84 85 86 87 88

American Pacific coast – dominated the weather. Above average rainfall. A cool spring meant that grapes were slow to ripen. Some *Botrytis*, mostly "noble rot". Very long growing season (226 days). High acidity levels: below average sugar levels. Late harvest began Oct 5.

Quantity produced

Production up to 2,000 cases, almost three times the 1981 level. Release price was $186 a case. 1988 price: $240.

Other details

The first phase of the winery was completed.

1983 Deep greenish gold. Very slightly vegetal note on Les Pierres' base of mineral flavours, most powerfully demonstrated on the 1986. Secondary aromas developing nicely into an integrated whole but already quite open. One of Les Pierres' less dazzling examples.

Weather and timing

Average vintage. El Niño disturbed the usual weather patterns for the second year in a row. More than twice the normal winter rainfall was followed by a wet spring and late bud break. Cool summer, early rains. 212-day growing season. Some *Botrytis*. Very high acidity levels. Harvest began Sept 22.

Quantity produced

More than a threefold increase in output to 7,500 cases released at $186 a case. 1988 price: $240.

Other details

Began construction of new barrel cellar.

1984 Pale with slightly lower acid and therefore less excitement than the 1985. Definitely a member of the family but one of the dumber and shorter ones. Like every other vintage, no suggestion of oak as a separate ingredient from the fruit.

Weather and timing

Very early vintage, excellent quality. Winter began early and wet and finished late and dry. Followed by a warm spring which led to an early bud break. Short growing season (193 days). Heat-wave in July and during the harvest, which began on Sept 8. Good sugar levels with lower than average acidity.

Quantity produced

A further increase in output to 10,000 cases released at $198 a case. 1988 price: $300.

Other details

Malolactic fermentation used for the first time in part of the wine.

1985 Deeper than the green-tinted pale gold that is the Sonoma-Cutrer norm. Relatively broad, open, evolved nose with hints of *crème brulée*. Easy to drink in 1988 but with great balance and sufficient acid to suggest future pleasures too.

Weather and timing

Exceptional vintage, average crop. Again an early, wet winter. Warm spring led to early bud break. Cool summer with hot spells at the end of June and July. Average-length growing season (207 days). Warm weather for the harvest (Sept 17). Good acidity levels.

Quantity produced

12,000 cases released at $210 a case. 1988 price: $300.

1986 Exceptionally powerful, almost aggressive, for this wine. Penetrating aroma reminiscent of burnt toast. Jagged and unresolved in Aug 1988 but promising much in two to three years.

Weather and timing

Excellent vintage, large crop. Foggy but dry winter. On Feb 11 torrential rains began (18"/457mm in the first storm alone) and lasted for two weeks – worst floods since 1964. Vines

undamaged. Warm spring brought an early bud break. Very long growing season (223 days). Cool, dry Aug. Early harvest began Sept 12.

Quantity produced

15,000 cases released at $234 a case.

Other details

Continuing experimentation with SO_2 levels and the use of wood.

1987 For wine-maker Bill Bonetti in 1988 this was the best vintage ever. A classic thoroughbred of well-knit flavours encompassing delicate green fruit and Chablis-like acid along with suggestions of honey and melon. Still smelled of attractive perfectly ripened fruit even after several months in bottle.

Weather and timing

Classic vintage, small yield. Dry winter, warm spring. Early flowering. Hot during set. Then a cool, relatively dry summer and

shorter than average growing season (199 days). Harvest began end Aug.

Quantity produced

Production stabilized at 15,000 cases. Release date: Sept 1989. Estimated release price: $300 a case.

1988 (Not tasted) According to the vineyard this wine appears to have good structure and intense flavour. Small berries and bunches led to below average yield but the quality was good with excellent sugar levels.

Weather and timing

Good quality vintage, below average yield. Dry winter and spring followed by late bud break. Warm, early spring led to early flowering. Apr, May and early June were wet and cool. Hot July. Early harvest in good, cool weather.

Quantity produced

15,000 cases. Release date: 1990.

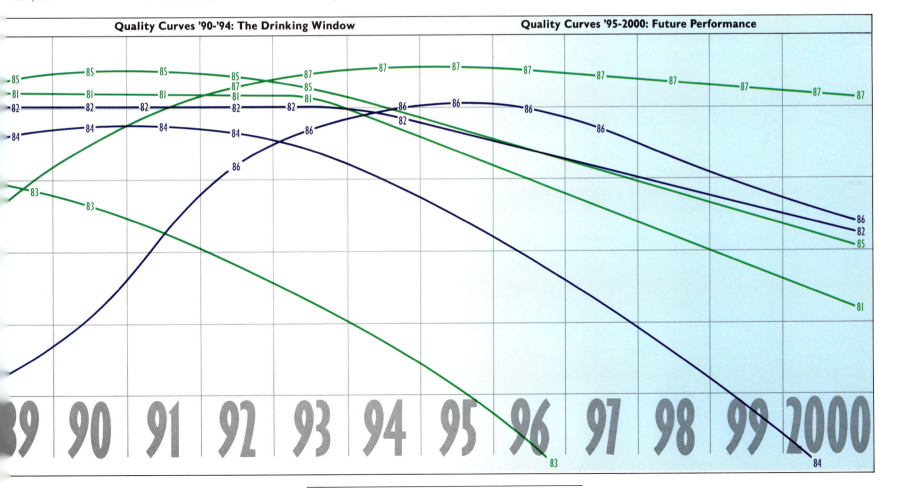

Quality Curves '90-'94: The Drinking Window

Quality Curves '95-2000: Future Performance

Saintsbury Pinot Noir

Perhaps one of the more salient features of this chart is the gap on the left hand side. Top quality California Pinot Noir is a relatively recent phenomenon with only the likes of Chalone and Hanzell able to boast vintages going back into the pre-history of the seventies. In bottles from wineries such as Saintsbury, Acacia and Château Bouchaine, and from wineries in warmer climes to the north who have regularly bought in Pinot from Carneros, this cool, fog-prone region between the Napa and Sonoma Valleys and the San Pablo Bay has shown itself an exciting source of top quality California Pinot Noir fruit. It is arguably the most consistent area of all producing admirably delicate, if not blockbusting, wines thanks to the Pacific Ocean influence.

Saintsbury's first vintage ever was 1981, when they produced one Pinot labelled Napa Valley, Rancho Carneros Vineyard (charted here as a regular bottling of Carneros Pinot) and another labelled Sonoma Valley. Most of Saintsbury's Pinot fruit is grown in the Napa side of Carneros. The Garnet name and concept emerged with the 1983 vintage. It consists of a blend of lighter, earlier-maturing lots which is bottled first and treated to less than 30 per cent new oak (as opposed to nearly 40 per cent for the superior Carneros bottling) and makes up about 40 per cent of Saintsbury's Pinot Noir production.

David Graves and Richard Ward, two of California wine's most attractively laid back characters, were the pair who had the audacity to launch a wine made from what was in the early eighties California's least fashionable grape variety.

They met as students in the early seventies. During the next decade they separately picked up practical experience at an impressive collection of wineries. By 1981 they had scraped together $1 million worth of investment from family and friends and by 1983 had completed their no-frills, barn-like winery on the flatland to the north of the San Pablo Bay. By 1988 they were embarking on a substantial expansion programme. This included buying their first vineyard, over 13 acres (five hectares) of Pinot Noir around the winery whose revolutionary divided canopy trellis is the object of much curiosity from visiting Burgundians.

Saintsbury's early Pinot Noirs were admired for their delicacy but dismissed as not being serious wines designed for the long term. Time has proved the doubters wrong and Saintsbury's reputation has evolved alongside their wines.

The early peaks in some vintages of Garnet at two or three years old signify what Richard Ward describes as Garnet's "bimodal period of drinking". This lighter blend can be delightful in exuberant youth and can then be cellared for a further three or four years during which the more complex bottle bouquet will develop. Only the Carneros bottlings and their 1981 and 1982 antecedents are charted here. Garnet is usually ready to drink about two years before the same vintage's Carneros.

1981 Napa Valley, Rancho Carneros Vineyard. (Made from California's Gamay Beaujolais clone of Pinot Noir). Lovely evolution of delicate red fruit flavours. Violets and raspberries on impressive nose. Good acid.

Sonoma Valley. Looks younger than the 1983. Simple, slightly jammy, almost dusty, nose. Sweet palate entry and good acid but duller and more astringent than the Napa 1981.

Weather and timing
Average vintage, light crop. Dry winter, early bud break. May heat-wave. Warm June-Sept. Early harvest Sept 10 and 15.

Quantity produced
Napa Valley: 800 cases released at $90 a case. Sonoma Valley: 1,050 cases at $96.

Other details
Rented space in local winery to make this debut vintage. 68% Pinot Noir, 32% Chardonnay.

1982 Carneros. Almost yellow-green rim. Old, verging on maderised, nose with medicinal notes of ripe, juicy fruit.

Sonoma Valley. Deep, almost murky colour with some orange. An odd, jammy note reminiscent of metal polish. The wine suffered a stuck fermentation in this difficult year. Apparently big in build but with marked acidity and nothing in the middle.

Weather and timing
Average vintage. El Niño – a shifting of ocean currents off South America which can disrupt normal weather along American Pacific coast – caused winter storms. Above average winter rainfall. Normal bud break and flowering. Cool growing season. Harvest began mid-Sept.

Quantity produced
Carneros: 1,875 cases released at $120 a case. Sonoma Valley: 2,025 cases at $96 a case.

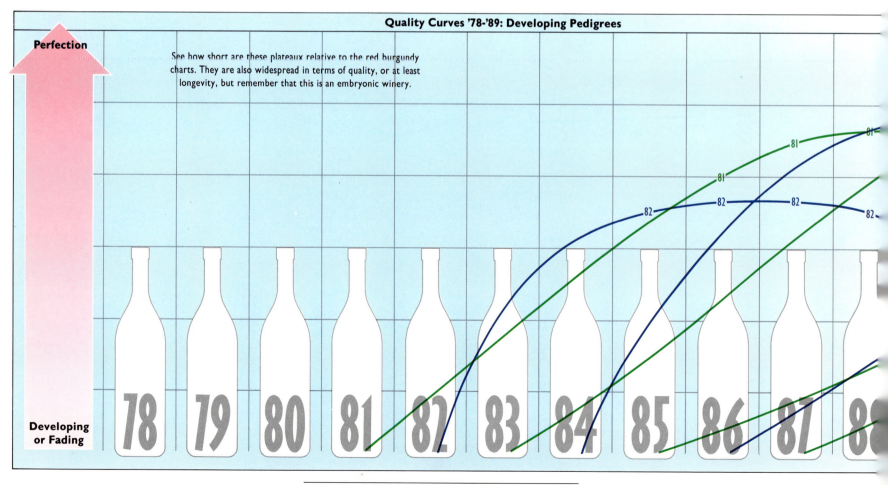

Quality Curves '78-'89: Developing Pedigrees

Perfection

See how short are these plateaux relative to the red burgundy charts. They are also widespread in terms of quality, or at least longevity, but remember that this is an embryonic winery.

Developing or Fading

78 79 80 81 82 83 84 85 86 87 88

Other details

Wines sold well in spite of talk about California "wine lake". Built temporary winery north of St Helena.

1983 Carneros. Garnet colour with some orange at rim. Lighter bouquet than Garnet 1983. Impressive, high extract, opulent palate with powerful stawberry fruit and a suggestion of white pepper. Ripe, long and still promising.

Garnet. Starting to age to the eye and nose. Simple, sweet nose then acidity on the palate. Hot and chewy. Good initial fruit but not enough bottle development.

Weather and timing

Average vintage. Second El Niño winter. Normal bud break mid-March. Good flowering. Showers during harvest, which began mid-Sept, caused some rot.

Quantity produced

Carneros: 1,950 cases released at $144 a case. Garnet: 2,300 cases at $96 a case.

Other details

Carneros appellation introduced in Aug. Began building own Carneros winery in July, completed Dec 1 so wine made outside. Added Lee Vineyard to Rancho Carneros. Chardonnay production 53% of total.

1984 Carneros. Dark, intense colour. Sweet, cough medicine notes, full-bodied and rich. Impressive balance for such a hot year. Toasty and certainly not subtle.

Garnet. Garnet-hued too. Powerful medicinal aroma. Fuller and heavier than 1985-1987 with high phenolics so seems more than a year younger than 1983. Big but slightly muscle-bound.

Weather and timing

Good vintage, very large crop. Dryish winter, early bud break, good flowering. Warm growing season. Harvest Sept 7-11; heat-wave stressed some vines so picked rapidly in early morning.

Quantity produced

Carneros: 2,600 cases released at $144 each. Garnet: 2,700 at $96 each.

Other details

Increased interest in American Pinot Noir (California and Oregon). Added De Soto Vineyard.

1985 Carneros. Ruby colour, muted nose. Lots of young fruit, fan of red fruit flavours and some astringency on the palate. Youthful. Less extract and more tannin than 1986.

Garnet. Well modulated colour to slight brick tinge at rim. Relatively simple, sweet, juicy nose. Lightweight but pure, neat and well balanced. An impressive fan of flavours at the end.

Weather and timing

High quality vintage, average crop. Normal winter rainfall (Oct-May 19"/480mm). Good flowering then cool, even in growing season. Showers mid-Sept aggravated rot problems; careful picking required during harvest Sept 16-21.

Quantity produced

Carneros: 3,300 cases released at $156 a case. Garnet: 2,900 cases at $96 a case.

Other details

French imports less competitive due to strengthening franc.

1986 Carneros. Penetrating and pretty floral aromas – candied violets? Ripe fruit on the middle palate with tannins nudging in later. Substantial, chewy, youthful and promises much for the future. Classic, vibrant young medium-weight Pinot.

Garnet. Mid-cherry. Powerfully rich aromas starting to knit together. Hint of cough drops. Some tannin. Chewy, bitter cherry flavour with good acid and impressively complex finish.

Weather and timing

Average vintage, moderate crop. Good drainage minimized effect of mid-Feb floods. Cool, foggy summer caused powdery mildew and rot. Careful harvest began Aug 27.

Quantity produced

Carneros: 4,800 cases released at $168 a case. Garnet: 3,800 cases at $96. Both wines sold out quickly.

1987 (Cask samples) Carneros. Lovely sweet raspberry fruit with some oak, plums and spice. Richness and opulent, concentrated fruit yet still delicate.

Garnet. Light crimson. Morello cherry aroma and lighter-bodied than the regular Pinot but vibrant, mouthfilling and opened out well in the glass.

Weather and timing

Best vintage yet, above average crop. Dry winter, early bud break, good flowering. Some powdery mildew. Harvest Aug 27 to Sept 10.

Quantity produced

Carneros: 8,300 cases. Estimated release price: $168 a case. Garnet: 5,100 cases. Estimated price: $108.

Other details

Total production: 28,000 cases. Now third largest Pinot Noir producer in Napa County.

1988 (Not tasted) "The Carneros is a rich, round wine with great promise. The Garnet is full with more extract than usual." (David Graves)

Weather and timing

Fine vintage, small crop. Dryish winter then early bud break. Cool, wet during flowering. Hot spells and fog in growing season. Harvest Aug 25 to Sept 10.

Quantity produced

Carneros: 10,000 cases. Estimated release price: $168-180 a case. Garnet: 6,000 cases. Estimated price: $108.

Other details

Cellar expansion.

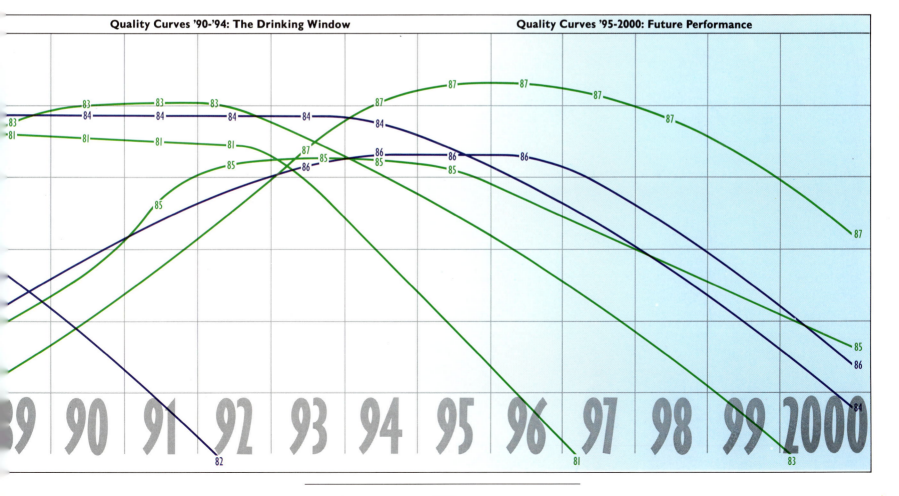

Ridge Monte Bello Cabernet Sauvignon

Apologies would be due for the inclusion in this book of two wines from the same winery were it not for the twin facts that Ridge's Geyserville Zinfandel and Monte Bello Cabernet Sauvignon come from two such disparate regions, and the latter wine represents such a distinctive prize for collectors of fine wine. (A third factor, it must be admitted, is the unparalleled single-mindedness of Ridge wine-maker Paul Draper, who was deaf to transatlantic and on-the-spot protestations that tasting and discussion be restricted to the Zinfandel.)

The Monte Bello vineyard effectively constitutes the home farm, as well as flagship for Ridge Vineyards, one of California's oldest wine outfits and certainly one of its most idiosyncratic. The vineyard, like the winery, is situated on an other-worldly ridge a cool 2,600 feet (800 metres) above the Pacific shoreline. In a region with an established reputation for "claret" it was already planted with Cabernet Sauvignon in 1880.

Today there are about 50 acres (20 hectares) of exceptionally venerable vines at Monte Bello, of which most are Cabernet Sauvignon although the final blend usually contains between four and 10 per cent Merlot. Yields are predictably low, about two tons per acre (five per hectare), and the flavours are concentrated accordingly.

Monte Bello is one of California's more dependably identifiable Cabernets, a wine that genuinely broadcasts its specific geographical origins, even if because of its location there are wide swings between remarkably cool and remarkably warm vintages.

Paul Draper has claimed that the style he is aiming for is Château Latour, but to many tasters coming upon this wine blind in a line-up of top Bordeaux growths, it is easier to confuse it with a Château Haut-Brion: it has an unashamed suggestion of dustiness and sun on warm bricks. Draper's slightly testy statement "We're *not* simply trying to convert sugar into alcohol in the most efficient way" is telling testimony to the character in these wines. He certainly doesn't claim to have a carbon copy bordeaux as his main objective, but he is proud that in some ways Ridge use more traditional techniques than many properties in Bordeaux. American oak has been the norm but the proportion of French cooperage has now crept up to 15 per cent.

The vintage variation entails keen selection. In each vintage, up to 40 per cent of the Monte Bello fruit is rejected for the Cabernet that bears its name. When the original boffins who established Ridge decided in 1986 to liquidate their investment, big corporations were automatically rejected as suitors. It was felt that this selection process would be the first casualty of a professional accounts department.

The wines are designed to be drinkable within five years but there is delightful evidence that some can still be giving pleasure at 25 years, an unusual feat in California.

Earlier vintages

The 1964 is still drinking beautifully now, as is the 1965. The 1967 is beginning to fade (Ridge admit the 1968 will never come round) while the hot year 1970 is still climbing and the cool year 1971 is complex and delightful but perhaps too delicate to hang on to. The 1972, 1973, 1974, 1975 and 1977 are all worth trying.

1978 A tribute to Ridge philosophy. Some yellow at the rim. Warm, sweet, mature bouquet of medium intensity. Hints of chocolate. Sweet on entry, counterbalanced by dry finish. Big, beefy and some tannins left with sufficient guts to evolve for many years. Fascinating, assertive yet charming, and long.

Weather and timing

Very good vintage, small crop. Warm growing season. Hot early Sept. Harvest Sept 30 to Oct 21.

Quantity produced

1,820 cases released at $360 a case (no selection – the entire production of the estate was bottled). Total California production: 159,000,000 cases.

Other details

Retraining of vines completed.

1979 None made.

Weather and timing

Fair vintage, small crop. Vines weakened by 1976-77 drought: bad mildew infection. Overripe grapes.

1980 Very promising. Exceptional combination of depth of colour and maturing rim. Attractive whole made up of several ingredients including a slightly herbaceous note. Mature and maturing wine whose luscious fruit almost masks what tannin remains. This should go on till 2005 or so. Long and flatteringly rich.

Weather and timing

Very good vintage, very large

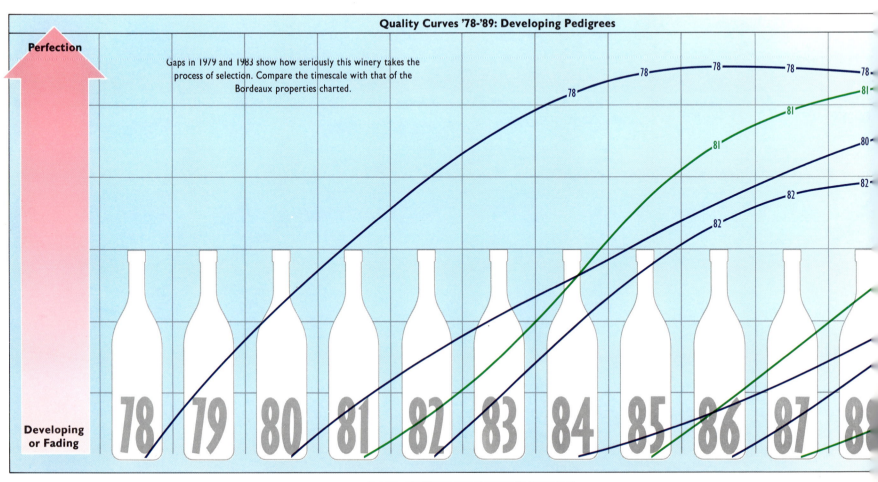

Quality Curves '78-'89: Developing Pedigrees

Perfection

Gaps in 1979 and 1983 show how seriously this winery takes the process of selection. Compare the timescale with that of the Bordeaux properties charted.

Developing or Fading

78 79 80 81 82 83 84 85 86 87 88

crop. Heavy winter rains. Late bud break. Cool growing season. Hot Sept. Lower vineyards harvested Oct 1-3; upper vineyards early Nov.

Quantity produced
2,923 cases released at $330 a case (no selection). Included grapes from Jimsomare vineyard. California: 199,000,000 cases.

Other details
Strong dollar: wine sold slowly. Reserve stock established.

1981 Exceptionally deep colour. Massive structure, slightly muted nose in 1988 but beautiful balance and sufficiently soft tannins to make the wine a drinkable proposition. Lovely rich red fruit flavours keep the palate delightfully distracted until the tannins gently make their presence felt at the end of the palate. This is the wine to drink now.

Weather and timing
Very good vintage, average crop.

Early spring with mixed weather during flowering and set. Warm Sept. Most exposed vines harvested Sept 19: main harvest Oct 3-29.

Quantity produced
2,500 cases released at $300 a case (10% selection). 1988 price: $720. California: 177,000,000 cases.

Other details
In spite of strong dollar, wine sold well. Some vines were hedged to increase exposure of grapes to the sun.

1982 Strong dusty mineral notes on the nose but the palate lacks real packed fruit intensity in the middle.

Weather and timing
Very good vintage, large crop. Excellent flowering. Heaviest set in over 20 years. Cool growing season. Slow to ripen. Harvest began Oct 16.

Quantity produced
4,200 cases released at $216 a case (limited selection). Sold slowly: small reserve. California: 216,000,000 cases.

Other details
Large yield and slow sales highlighted need for rigorous selection, especially in cool years.

1983 None made.

Weather and timing
Good vintage, small crop. Mixed weather during flowering. Cool growing season. Harvest Oct 15 to Nov 18.

1984 Intense ruby. Slightly murky, almost alcoholic indistinct nose with the sweet richness of butter icing. Then marked acidity on the palate. Not yet an integrated whole; much tannin still in evidence. Hot wine, again with mineral notes. Tastes more of old California vines than obvious Cabernet Sauvignon.

Weather and timing
Good vintage, normal crop. Fine for flowering and set. Warm growing season. Early harvest Sept 20 to Oct 10.

Quantity produced
3,000 cases released at $480 a case (30% selection). 1988 price: $720. California: 168,000,000 cases.

Other details
Leaf stripping introduced to increase grapes' exposure to sun. New French oak barrels used for first time.

1985 Medium crimson. Very attractive, confident, medium-weight meld of spice and minerals with discernibly ripe fruit. Comparatively austere for a Monte Bello. Surprising tannin level at the end of the palate. A wine to keep. Too classically structured to win any blind tastings.

Weather and timing
Great vintage, normal crop. Even flowering. Warm growing season. Harvest Sept 25 to Oct 7.

Quantity produced
2,250 cases released at $480 a case (45% selection). California: 174,000,000 cases.

1986 Relatively light and lightweight for Monte Bello. Sweet, simple aromas with marked acidity. Light tannins: just a little scrawny.

Weather and timing
Excellent vintage, above average crop. Good set, cool growing season. Harvest began Oct 7.

Quantity produced
2,162 cases released in 1989 at $480 a case (47% selection). California: 185,000,000 cases.

Other details
New vineyard manager, Fred Peterson.

1987 (Cask sample) Dense crimson. Relatively herbaceous aromas with spice and intensity underneath and a mineral undertow à la Haut-Brion. Mouthfilling, harmonious. Not massive but with impressively neat richness. Concentrated.

Weather and timing
Good vintage, very small crop. Warm Mar. Early flowering; cold winds and fog caused 70% crop loss. Cool growing season. Indian summer ripened grapes. Harvest Sept 22 to end Oct.

Quantity produced
800 cases to be released in 1990 (20% selection). California: 164,000,000 cases.

1988 (Not tasted) According to Paul Draper, one of the decade's finer vintages. Well balanced with complex flavours and a deep colour. Similar weight to 1981.

Weather and timing
Excellent vintage, below average crop. Early, warm spring followed by variable weather during flowering. Hot Sept. Late harvest Oct 4 to Nov 2.

Quantity produced
1,500-2,000 cases. Estimated release price: $600 a case. California: 170,000,000 cases.

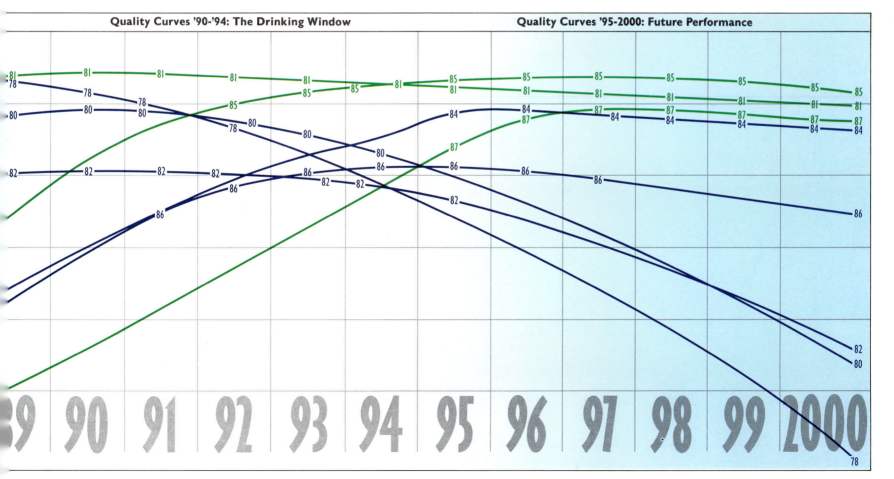

Quality Curves '90-'94: The Drinking Window   **Quality Curves '95-2000: Future Performance**

Chalone Chardonnay Reserve

The Chalone Vineyard, almost as high as its neighbour the post-volcanic Mount Chalone, nudges right up against the Pinnacles National Monument of sky-scraping crags. It is best approached by small plane – ideally that of Richard Graff, chairman of Chalone Inc, the only American premium wine producer to go public. Water, electricity and the telephone reached this unlikely mountain patch only in the late eighties. So dry were the vintages between 1983 and 1987 that they had finally to admit defeat in the dry farming battle and bought their own pipeline for carefully judged drip irrigation. Pests are kept at bay not just by these arid conditions, but by the isolated position of the vineyard.

Chalone is the antithesis of Napa's artful tourist attraction wineries. It is a collection of shacks and lean-tos which have grown organically in this improbable setting because vines planted here in 1919 (surely the least auspicious year to plant a vineyard in America) and 1946 proved that wine of exceptional character could be coaxed from the well-drained, decomposed granite and clay.

The 1970 plantings of Pinot Noir and Chardonnay form the basis of the winery's reputation, although about 60 acres (24 hectares) mainly of Chardonnay, representing a third of the winery's vineyard, were planted in 1986, 1987 and 1988. Chalone's output is still well under 20,000 cases.

Although the vines are cooled to some extent by the influence of the Pacific only 35 miles to the west, many grapes ripen by mid-August and the vintage is usually over by September. All but the Reserve Chardonnays need some added acid in most vintages. Uneven ripening can often mean three or four trawls through the vineyard, but this is less time-consuming than in many other vineyards as here no vine is more than 10 minutes away from the press.

Chalone blend press juice with free run right from the start, perhaps not surprising when total yields average scarcely two tons per acre (six per hectare), and after adding yeast run the must into small French oak, a third of it new for regular Chardonnay, a half new for regular Pinot and usually all their coveted Reserve bottlings. All bottling of Chalone wines was by hand until 1986, which may explain why bottle variation is more common here than elsewhere.

To those who understand them however, Chalone's Reserve Chardonnays represent a pinnacle of American white wine achievement. They exhibit unabashed individuality: relatively deep golden tints even in youth and an exuberance and muscle often missing in some of California's more conventional Chardonnays.

Wine-maker Michael Michaud admits, "We don't always get good write-ups because our wines are designed to be aged much more slowly than most other Chardonnays." He suggests opening these at five to eight years, but knows that some will happily last 15 and "ideally they should be drinkable for 20 years".

Earlier vintages
1969 "Lovely in 1987," (R H Graff). **1974** Still holding well.

1978 Stockholder's Reserve. This rich, toasty Chardonnay has held up well but is now fading into slightly overweight old age.

Weather and timing
Excellent vintage, small crop. Wet year (22"/560mm rain). Bud break in mid-Feb; hail in Apr before flowering. Bad powdery mildew infection. Warm summer: hot Aug. Late harvest began Oct 1.

Quantity produced
Bottled in 1980: 144 cases released at $300 a case. Sold out. Total estate production: 7,304 cases.

Other details
Malolactic fermentation and extended lees contact used for first time. Long ageing (16 months) in new burgundian barrels.

1979 Honeyed, low-key bouquet: fruit flavours have given way to bottle development. A relic with interest rather than an appetizing drink.

Weather and timing
Good vintage, normal crop. 13"/330mm rain. Bud break Mar 27. Clear, warm weather throughout growing season. Harvest began Sept 11.

Quantity produced
No Reserve wine: 3,728 cases released at $216 a case. Sold out. Total production: 10,983 cases.

1980 Reserve. Exceptionally deep apricot gold. Almost over-ripe aromas hinting at putrid tropical fruit, but excellent acid level. May never be subtle but is still extremely youthful. High extract, great length.

Weather and timing
Great vintage, small crop. Severe wind damage in late May. Clear during flowering, erratic temperatures in growing season, leading to very small grape clusters.

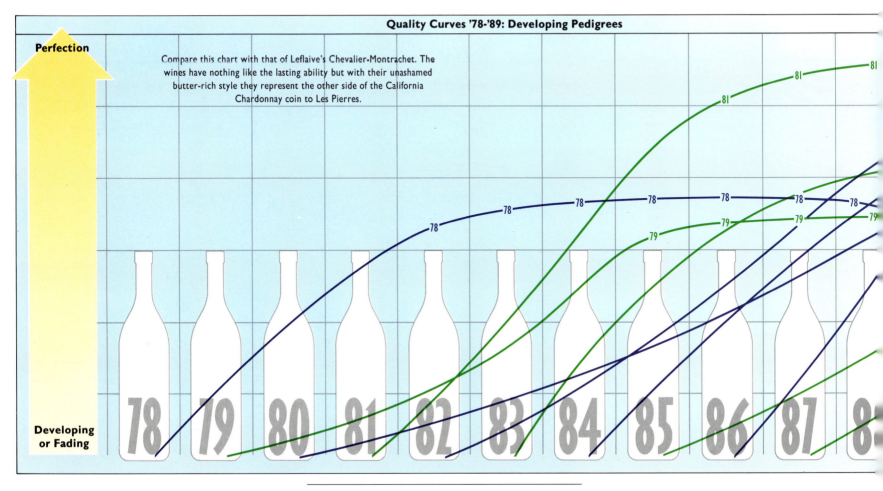

Quality Curves '78-'89: Developing Pedigrees

Perfection

Compare this chart with that of Leflaive's Chevalier-Montrachet. The wines have nothing like the lasting ability but with their unashamed butter-rich style they represent the other side of the California Chardonnay coin to Les Pierres.

Developing or Fading

78 79 80 81 82 83 84 85 86 87 8

Normal harvest began Sept 26.

Quantity produced

180 cases released at $264 a case. Sold out. Total production: 7,624 cases.

Other details

Very high alcohol content. SO₂ additions delayed until after first racking.

1981 Reserve. A mature, and maturing, classic. Resolved, creamy-rich aromas suggest honey and brown toast. Well balanced, harmonious whole with enormous punch and texture yet crisp enough to promise more.

Weather and timing

Good vintage, below average crop. Low rainfall (11"/280mm). Good weather from flowering to harvest, which began Aug 28.

Quantity produced

357 cases released at $264 a case. Total production: 10,569 cases.

1982 Reserve. Well developed toasty bouquet with life and character on the palate. Of all these wines, perhaps the most typical Chalone Chardonnay.

Weather and timing

Very good vintage, normal crop. Above average rainfall (16"/405mm). Warm during flowering. Harvest began on Sept 16.

Quantity produced

498 cases released at $300 a case. Total production: 11,474 cases.

1983 Reserve. Well-knit but slightly muted bouquet. Relatively shy and retiring wine: paler than most with an exceptional green tinge. Demonstrates the relationship between quantity and quality nicely. A pretty, delicate wine that can still open out in the glass, but unusual for Chalone.

Weather and timing

Fair vintage, large crop. 28"/710mm rain. Feb storms caused soil erosion. Rain after bud break, clear for flowering. Storms during harvest which began Sept 16.

Quantity produced

616 cases released at $300 a case. Sold out. Total production: 16,814 cases.

Other details

Wine-maker Peter Watson-Graff succeeded by Michael Michaud.

1984 Reserve. Meaty, savoury, well balanced. Lower acids than 1985 and 1987 but still holds plenty of promise. Not a blockbuster. Attractive notes of honeysuckle on the palate.

Weather and timing

Excellent vintage, very small crop. Dry year (13"/330mm rain) following wet one. Very warm for flowering, perfect growing season. Harvest began Aug 27.

Quantity produced

364 cases released at $300 a case. Sold out. Total production: 8,595 cases.

Other details

25th anniversary vintage. Longer, cooler fermentation introduced.

1985 Reserve. Creamy restraint in this taut young cocktail of tropical fruit flavours. Designed for the future: slight astringence but the promise of an explosion of secondary aromas in the nineties.

Weather and timing

Very good vintage, small crop. Second dry year in a row (9½"/240mm rain). Fair, cool through flowering. Very warm before harvest which began Sept 3.

Quantity produced

307 cases released at $336 a case. Sold out. Total production: 8,639 cases.

Other details

Some replanting of vines.

1986 Reserve. A different style from the Chalone norm with enticingly early opulence. Tastes more than a year older than 1987 and notably more developed than the 1985. The nose is pure Meursault; the palate classically built without promising the eventual power of the 1985. Like 1981 without the intensity.

Weather and timing

Excellent vintage, small yield. 14"/355mm rain. Hot for flowering. Hail storm in Mar removed 50% of flowers. Excellent growing season. Powdery mildew infection. Early harvest Aug 21 and 25.

Quantity produced

378 cases released at $336 each. Sold out in four days. Total production: 10,314 cases.

Other details

Mechanical bottling introduced. Some replanting of vines, mainly Chardonnay.

1987 Reserve. Some Musqué clone fruit from the new upper vineyard added a floral note to this dramatically styled wine. Lots of overtly opulent but still un-knit flavours. Apricot, subtle French oak, great power and extract yet sufficient acid to suggest a long future.

Weather and timing

Good vintage, very large crop. Localized drought (8"/205mm rain); adequate irrigation. Warm through flowering and for harvest which began Aug 24.

Quantity produced

727 cases. Release date: 1989. Estimated release price: $336 a case. Total production: 15,364 cases.

1988 *(Not tasted)* According to Richard Graff, this wine is full-bodied and has a rich, velvety texture. Although dry, there is a lingering fruitiness. Long finish.

Weather and timing

Good vintage, very large crop. Localized drought (9½"/240mm rain). Erratic flowering, mild growing season; hot for harvest which began Aug 24

Quantity produced

Approx. 650 cases. Release date: 1990. Total production: 17,500.

Other details

Systematic irrigation introduced.

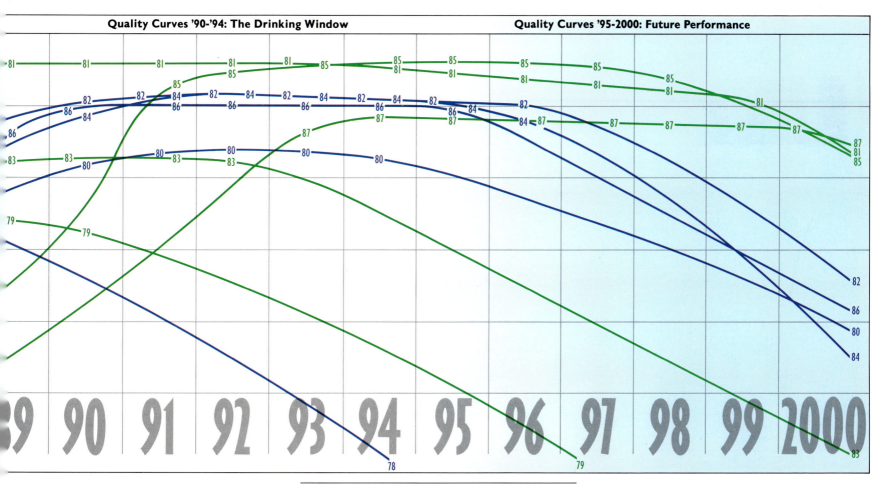

Quality Curves '90-'94: The Drinking Window

Quality Curves '95-2000: Future Performance

REST OF THE AMERICAS

Pines and vines, the image appearing on The Eyrie Vineyard labels, is also the State symbol of the nascent but ambitious Oregon wine industry.

There is little doubt that the Pacific Northwest, comprising Oregon, Washington and Idaho, qualifies as a new source of ageworthy wines. Vinifera vine cuttings were planted in Oregon and Idaho in the eighteenth century but it was not until the 1960s that the serious potential of the three states began to be realised.

In wine regions as new as this, the general rule – as in the other American states, New Zealand and South Africa for example – is that the most recent vintage is the best. This is because wine regions are so new and unfamiliar that vintage generalisations are difficult to make, and because the skills and techniques of grape growers and wine-makers improve so significantly and perceptibly each year. In the Pacific Northwest however there are wine regions where the climate is so variable that the weather can override this convenient rule.

Oregon, and in particular Oregon's most important vine-growing area the Willamette Valley in the cool northwest of the state, has one of the world's more dramatic and difficult climates for grape ripening. This, as the picture shows, is fir tree country, damp and green. A good year for Oregonian vine growers is one in which the sun manages to shine enough to ripen the grapes and the rain manages to hold off until the grapes are safely gathered (into the curious fruit bin fermenters, a David Lett-inspired expedient that nicely illustrates the small scale of the Oregon wine industry).

Such years have been 1988, 1987, 1985, 1983, 1982, 1979, 1978 and 1975. These last three were effectively part of the Oregon wine industry's pre-history when few wine-makers knew how to make the best of a really ripe vintage – how to avoid the problems of overripeness and hot fermentations. This is one area in which better understanding of the importance of pH has been vital, although most Oregon wine-makers only really got into gear with the 1985 vintage. Many earlier wines, especially Pinot Noirs, browned prematurely and lost their nerve during the fourth year.

The Eyrie Timechart, showing an impressive run of successes with a few rainy intermissions, is in this book to offer proof of Oregon's potential rather than to a provide an infallible guide to the quality of other Oregon wineries' early efforts. Adelsheim, Amity, Elk Cove, Knudsen-Erath, Ponzi and Sokol-Blosser are all now experienced and consistent enough to follow the vintage pattern as far back as the early eighties. Pinot Noirs from most producers and certainly from exciting newcomers such as Rex Hill and, the real new boys, Domaine Drouhin and Panther Creek, should conform to vintage patterns from the mid-eighties.

Oregon, usually, does not produce wines like those illustrated on Chart A (page 19). Even the simplest whites should stand up well to being drunk at three or even four years, although this is not (yet) a region for really ageworthy Chardonnays.

Mount Hood, snow-capped well into summer, dominates the vineyards of both Oregon and Washington whose respective climates differ dramatically. The vineyards near the coast have too much rain and those inland need artificial irrigation.

Washington's wineries are more protected from the vagaries of climate – with some artificial help from the huge circular irrigation systems that transform the local river water into "rain". This is badly needed by the Columbia Valley in the east-of-state wine country where summer days are hot and the nights cold enough to fix acids and grape flavour firmly into the wines.

Washington wines tend so far to be less subtle and more workmanlike than those produced immediately to the south in Oregon. Apart from the odd bottle of 1986 Botrytised Riesling and a handful of Cabernet and Merlots, most Washington wines have bloomed most conspicuously in youth. See Chart B on page 19 for the maturity pattern of most Washington wines, noting that 1983 was a particularly good vintage for Washington's most ageworthy Cabernets and Merlots such as Arbor Crest's Bacchus bottling.

Idaho, which effectively means Ste Chapelle winery, manages blockbusting Chardonnay that blooms for up to four years.

Of America's other wines, those made from vines other than viniferas, are surefire Chart A candidates. A host of genuinely exciting vinifera wines is now emerging from all over the United States but few have been around long enough to establish a track record. Long Island Chardonnays may well turn out to have some of the best ageing potential.

South American whites should be drunk young. The only reds with serious ageing potential so far are Cabernet Sauvignons from Chile. Most are at their best within four to five years of the vintage but some, such as Cousiño Macul's Antiguas Reservas, Los Vascos and Viña Linderos, can improve in bottle for eight years or even longer. Vintage variations are much slighter than elsewhere, the main variant being summer temperatures.

The Eyrie Vineyards Pinot Noir Reserve

Just before the vertical tasting that David Lett generously arranged for the purposes of this book, he gazed in wonder at the line-up of 16 wines. "I think I may break down and cry", he said without any suggestion of artifice, "because of all the effort I know I've put into these bottles."

David Lett is Oregon's most famous, most quoted but possibly most reclusive wine-maker. Although Davis-trained, he rejected the glitz of the Napa Valley and, after some thought, both the Douro Valley and the nascent vineyards of New Zealand's South Island. He planted his first *vinifera* vines in the Willamette Valley's now famous Dundee Hills back in 1966, when few of today's band of Oregon wine prospectors had a clue what *vinifera* meant.

The Eyrie Vineyards (so named because hawks nest in a particular tall fir on the modest Lett property) therefore has a uniquely long run of vintages of Oregon Pinot Noir. But its inclusion here is justified not just on this quantifiable basis but on the basis of the extraordinary quality coaxed by this novice grapegrower out of his Pinot Noir (and now Pinot Gris) vines. Eyrie Pinot Noir manages an impressively high success rate in achieving the subtlety and ageability that characterise the Pinots of Burgundy. (The wide variation between vintages is also convincingly burgundian.) Early vintages, such as the embryonic 1969 ("crushed in Jim's diaper pail",) the 1970 ("I was ashamed to call it Pinot Noir so I put Oregon Spring Wine on the label") and the others before 1974 when

Lett discovered the virtues of malolactic fermentation, are perhaps more interesting than great – though they are certainly a moving testimony to great enterprise and enormous risk.

In 1979, the 1975 vintage made from Lett's South Block vines did notably well at the famous Gault-Millau "wine olympics" in Paris. It was then that Lett felt vindicated and wine lovers started to seek out Oregon on the map. At the 1980 replay in Beaune the wine was beaten into second place by Drouhin's 1959 Chambolle Musigny – by just a fifth of a point.

Eyrie vines, mainly from the Swiss Wädenswil clone, are widely spaced but trained upright and managed by leaf-pulling and "absolutely no insecticide or herbicide". The grapes are picked at around 22 Brix, between the third week of September and the end of October, notably later than burgundy. The workmanlike winery in McMinnville is eight, not five, miles away and so forfeits Lett's right to use the term Estate Bottled on the label. There, all grapes are de-stemmed, chaptalization is avoided except in disastrous vintages, and all oak is French (now mainly *Tronçais*), new only when the Letts can afford it. As the tightly-managed Eyrie accounts have allowed, David Lett has experimented with the (fairly limited) range of different oaks and coopers available in Oregon – including some American oak which, he declares, "kills" his precious Pinot Noir.

Earlier vintages

David Lett is understandably fond of the vintages he made in the early 1970s but to the critical palate the acidity, unsoftened by malolactic fermentation before 1974, mars the often fading fruit. The **1972** is harmonious and at its peak but the spicy, confident **1974** is in a different league.

1975 South Block. Very subtle shades of garnet to brick. Rich, gamey, mature nose suggesting a stage beyond tertiary aromas. Great harmony and lovely feel in the mouth. Compelling and still lively with potential. One of the great non-burgundian Pinots.

Weather and timing

Great vintage, average crop. Perfect season. Wet July. Superb Aug. Dry Sept. Ripened well. Fine for harvest Oct 4-6.

Quantity produced

About 500 cases released at $108 a case. Oregon production: 45,400 cases.

Other details

A bottle fetched $325 at auction in 1988.

1976 A little too tannic for the fruit with a streak of acidity that seemed more mean than life-preserving. Still very youthful but recalls wines of the pre-malolactic era.

Weather and timing

Great vintage, average crop. Cool start to season. Good, late set. Second half of July warm and dry. Cool Aug-Oct; slow maturation. Harvest Oct 25-27.

Quantity produced

About 600 cases released at $108 a case. Oregon: 37,300 cases.

1977 Light ruby and muted bouquet. Some spice but a bit diffuse. A developed, paler version of the 1979. Not quite ripe.

Weather and timing

Good vintage, small crop. Cold,

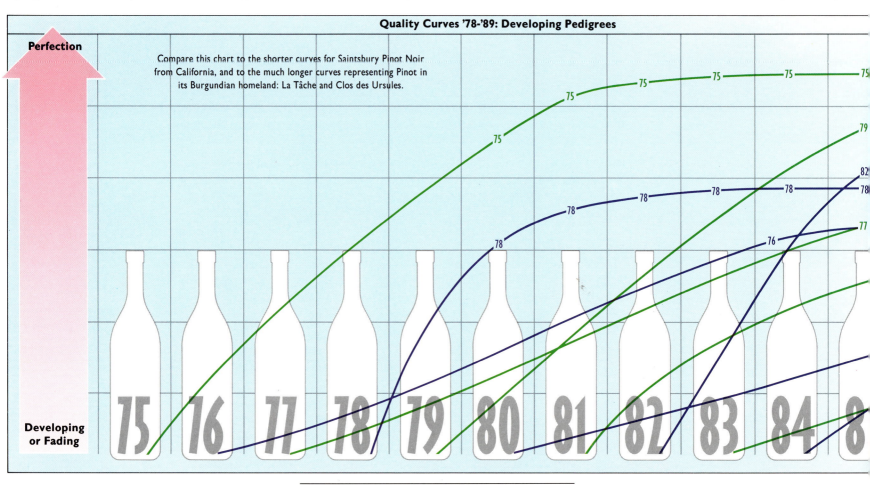

Quality Curves '78-'89: Developing Pedigrees

Perfection

Compare this chart to the shorter curves for Saintsbury Pinot Noir from California, and to the much longer curves representing Pinot in its Burgundian homeland: La Tâche and Clos des Ursules.

Developing or Fading

75 76 77 78 79 80 81 82 83 84 8

wet Mar. Poor flowering; late set. Wet, cool Sept. Harvest Oct 20-26.

Quantity produced
About 400 cases released at $90 a case. Oregon: 17,500 cases.

1978 The sort of wine the French would imagine as American Pinot Noir, and atypical for the Eyrie. Blockbusting stuff with lots of rather blowsy charm. Sweet, soft and easy.

Weather and timing
Poor vintage, small crop. Warm Mar; early bud break. Very wet Apr and May. Dry for flowering. Very hot July-Oct with some rain early Sept. Fast maturation. Harvest delayed because the pickers were late; very high sugar levels. Harvest Oct 9-12.

Quantity produced
25 cases. Not released. Oregon: 62,000 cases.

1979 A real vindicator. Light ruby with fox-tinged rim. Lovely,

rich, complex bouquet suggesting wintry warm smells such as roasted nutwood. Dried spice again. Pretty, charming with good balance and exciting length.

Weather and timing
Very good vintage, large crop. Cool Apr. Perfect for flowering. Hot July and Aug. Wet early Sept. Fine for harvest early Oct.

Quantity produced
1,200 cases released at $150 a case. Oregon: 77,000 cases.

1980 Best, deepest colour of all the 1980-1985 range. Relatively closed nose. Meaty, high acid and tannin. Almost more suggestive of Rhône than burgundy. Concentrated, dry, youthful but not very Pinot. Develops well in glass. Decant early.

Weather and timing
Exceptional vintage, small crop. Cool Apr. Volcanic ash showers in May from Mount St Helens left vines undamaged. Cool, wet June

delayed flowering. Average July-Sept. Downy mildew infection. Fine for harvest early Oct.

Quantity produced
300 cases released at $216 a case. Oregon: 109,000 cases.

1981 Looks quite youthful and, again, relatively closed nose, with some mintiness. The same astringence marks 1980. Simple backbone of acidity. David Lett thinks this will come into its own next century.

Weather and timing
Excellent vintage, very small crop. Cold Apr-June. Wet June. Warm, dry July; late flowering completed by July 17. Hot Aug. Cool, showery weather from late Sept. Wet for harvest early Oct.

Quantity produced
400 cases released at $300 a case. Oregon: 109,000 cases.

Other details
Grapes picked prematurely. Chaptalized for the first time.

1982 A pretty little thing. Looks 10 years older than 1983. Straightforward, soft, sweet smells suggesting licorice and an easy, attractive, fairly light-bodied attempt at fine Pinot from outside Burgundy. Definitely ready to drink by 1988 but the acidity should preserve it well.

Weather and timing
Very good vintage, above average crop. Wet, cool Apr. May and June perfect; good flowering. Warm summer. Harvest in by Oct 8.

Quantity produced
750 cases released at $180 a case. Oregon: 114,000 cases.

1983 Young concentrated crimson. Cold tea leaf aromas. In 1988 awkward and the opposite of charming. Tannic with slightly charred mineral edge. Opened out in the glass to more animal flavours.

Weather and timing
Outstanding vintage and above

average crop. Hot Apr. Excellent flowering. Warm, dry Aug then rain. Perfect maturation during Sept. Fine for harvest which ended Oct 13.

Quantity produced
800 cases released at $180 a case.

1984 Open, easy, light with tea/herbal aromas. Lighter-bodied than 1983 and much more approachable but there are some similarities. There are good reserves of acid and tannin even though this is obviously a dilute vintage.

Weather and timing
Good vintage, large crop. Wet Apr and May; mildew infection. Normal flowering. Fine July, cool Aug. Damp, cool, dull Oct; delayed picking in hope of improvement. Wet for harvest early Nov; no rot. Local nut driers used to dry fruit.

Quantity produced
1,400 cases released at $198 a case.

Other details
New de-stemming machine used for first time. Chaptalized.

1985 Jewel-like ruby. Headily perfumed. Still some primary fruit aromas but already layers of flavour reminiscent of tea, strawberries and spice. Most attractive herbal note. Clearly built to last with real structure and guts. It is clear that what lies deeper will power this wine into the next century, but the top layer is already dangerously seductive.

Weather and timing
Excellent vintage, average crop. Excellent flowering. Warm July, cool Aug. Good Sept and maturation. Harvest completed Oct 10.

Quantity produced
950 cases released at $456 a case. Oregon: 214,000 cases.

Other details
This vintage increased international recognition of Oregon wines.

AUSTRALIA & NEW ZEALAND

Lindemans' baking hot winery in the Hunter Valley, New South Wales, manages to produce white wines that can last 15 years and more.

A statistic much quoted in marketing departments of the Australian wine business is that over 90 per cent of all wine bought in Australia is consumed within 48 hours of purchase. Australian wine buyers are wine consumers rather than collectors; a small group of world-class connoisseurs may hoard bottles, but the climate there is inimical to this inherently anti-Australian activity. Domestic cellars are as rare as compliments down under and it is not unknown for an Australian wine fanatic to maintain at least one cellar in Britain where cold, damp and a supply of fine mature wine is assured.

Producers know that there is less chance in Australia than in any other country that bottles designed for the long term will see their third year. To be certain that their longer-term wines are drunk when they are mature, or at least broachable, producers have to keep them from reaching the shelves, and of course only the largest, longest-established companies can afford this luxury. Thus Penfolds release Grange Hermitage (page 150) only at five or six years, and Lindemans (page 158) lock up a significant proportion of their better wines to be released, sometimes in tranches, at up to 20 years old. Their still rich and lively 1965 Hunter River Burgundy 3110 (made, perversely, from Syrah) was first released in 1977, for example, and then several times subsequently. But smaller-scale producers of equally good and sometimes superior wines can rarely afford to slow down consumption – especially since they have, typically, been in business for less than a decade and are still busy counting the cents.

But it is not just their famously powerful thirst and an unsuitable cellaring environment that encourages Australians to drink the youngest wine available. The wines produced in Australia have improved so rapidly in the last few years that in many cases it really does make sense to choose the most recent vintage over even its immediate predecessor. It can mean the difference between, for example, a Chardonnay that was barrel-fermented or not (although the second option can in some cases be preferable) or enjoying a Sauvignon Blanc that has been spiked with aromatic fruit imported from New Zealand, a Pinot Noir that has benefited from summer crop thinning or a Cabernet Sauvignon fattened up with a judicious proportion of Merlot.

To benefit from the speed of recent changes in Australian wine however – all of them directed at making finer, better balanced wines that can stand the test of time – it is worth studying likely maturity patterns, and individual vintages. With the exception perhaps of the most ambitious whites, such as Petaluma, and the most tannic reds, such as Virgin Hills, the average Australian wine can be enjoyed almost as soon as it is released, but the proportion of wines that repay bottle ageing is growing.

Yarra Yering (page 156) is one of the oldest wineries now operating in Victoria's Yarra Valley, where it is cool enough even for champagne giants Moët & Chandon to have chosen to invest.

The vintages themselves may not have mattered much when grapes came exclusively from places where they could be expected to ripen, or even overripen. But now that so much of Australia's most exciting wine comes from areas deliberately chosen for their "cool" climates, the most modish attribute in an Australian vineyard, the vagaries of nature can be detected more clearly in the bottles.

To an Australian, a wine from just three vintages back is considered old. In very general terms, Australian wines used to age almost visibly, and certainly *much* faster than their European counterparts. But many of the wines made from the mid-eighties – especially Cabernet and Cabernet/Shiraz (Syrah) blends, Riesling and Semillon – now age at a slightly more seemly pace. Many Chardonnays however still seem built to last just long enough to ship them to the UK or US and give them a few months' shelf life.

Australia's cheapest blended jug wines from the irrigated interior are even faster-maturing. Exceptionally well made, they should be regarded as Chart A (page 19) wines par excellence, remembering that all southern hemisphere wines are six or seven months older than a northern hemisphere wine carrying the same vintage year. Australia's cheapest varietals are usually Chart B wines. The following comments refer, as usual, to the best examples that the country can produce.

The notion of what constitutes ideal weather conditions for an Australian grape harvest has been evolving almost as rapidly as the Australian wine map. Drought was the old bugbear, stressing the vines and often resulting in a small crop of grapes with high pHs and poor lasting abilities. Now that grapes are being planted higher and further south, growers have to cope with a host of new viticultural problems. Spring frosts destroyed Padthaway's 1988 crop in October 1987 and cold wet weather during flowering hit the Mornington Peninsula's 1987 vintage. Vines are prey to diseases and pests unknown in the hotter areas, such as the powdery mildew, light brown apple moth and perennial bird marauders that badly affected the 1987 Yarra crop.

And then there was the 1983 vintage during which drought, bushfires, floods, wasps and summer hail all played their part. In 1984 things calmed down for a generally cool year while 1985 yielded much-needed record quantities in most regions. 1986 was notable for some very good quality wines, but only a small proportion of them worth ageing.

Australia's most westerly fine wine region, Margaret River, is cooled, sometimes salted, by the Indian Ocean and can produce Chardonnays, Cabernets and even Pinots that develop complexity in bottle. Cabernets from the likes of Moss Wood, Vasse Felix, Cape Mentelle and Leeuwin can continue to evolve for almost a decade. Particularly good vintages for Margaret River and nearby Mount Barker have been 1986, 1984, 1982 and 1981.

South Australia, which enjoyed a run of cool dry years throughout the late eighties, is *the* wine state, producing three out of every five bottles of Australian wine. This accounts for the inclusion of so many South Australian Timecharts. Grange is there because it illustrates the limits of ageability of a distinctly Australian wine style, American oak-aged Barossa Shiraz. Few other South Australian Shiraz's have anything like Grange's staying power, but accelerating the Grange chart by two years for Penfolds Magill Estate and three for Bin 707 Cabernet Sauvignon should give a good idea of the keeping potential of these two great wines. Most other Australian Shiraz is at its best at two to four years. Notable exceptions are some of the great old bottlings of Lindemans Hunter River Burgundy (see above), some old Rothburys, and the much more modern, more rigorous Shiraz from the likes of Mount Langi Ghiran and Taltarni in Victoria and Cape Mentelle in Margaret River, which are focused on six to seven years from the vintage.

For the weather conditions affecting other Barossa wines and those produced in wine regions around Adelaide, such as Southern Vales and Langhorne Creek, see the vintage notes for Grange.

Although in the same state, Coonawarra is well over 200 miles from Barossa and experiences quite different weather, as examination of the Wynns (pages 152/3) shows. The somewhat variable longevity of Wynns Coonawarra Cabernets should reflect that of its peers but in two different periods: the lesser bottlings should last about as long as Wynns before 1985; top bottlings such as Cabernets from Bowen, Hollick, Katnook, Lindemans St George, Penfolds Bin 128 and Petaluma's red should age similarly to Wynns from 1985.

Coonawarra Shiraz matures in general a year before Coonawarra Cabernet while all but a handful of the whites are Chart B wines. The vineyards at nearby Padthaway are subject to very similar conditions although they are perhaps better known for Chart B-type whites and some longer-living Botrytised Rieslings.

South Australia's exciting dry Rieslings, specifically from Clare-Watervale, cry out for bottle age. Leo Buring and Orlando established the style of wonderfully mineral-scented, substantial, lemony Rieslings that last a decade or more; today the flag is carried by Petaluma, Mitchell and Jeffrey Grosset. Good vintages for Clare Riesling have been 1988, 1986, 1982, 1980, 1979 and 1978. For the weather conditions of Clare-Watervale and Eden Valley as well as Adelaide Hills, see those for Petaluma.

The Petaluma Timechart spells out vintage conditions for fruit grown in Clare and the fashionable, almost chilly, new wine region in the Adelaide Hills. For the moment, most Australian Chardonnay seems designed to be drunk as exuberant, fairly simple wine within three years of the vintage. Odd bottles with greater ambitions shine out and the quality-conscious producers of Australia's most opulent Chardonnay such as Rothbury, Evans Family and Rosemount of the Hunter Valley are beginning to set their sights on a more distant timescale. The grandfather of them all, Tyrrells Vat 47, turned in a 1977 that can still dazzle. But so far the only other Chardonnays with any sort of long-distance track record come from Cullens and Leeuwin of Margaret River, although there have been stunning bottles for at least the medium term from Petersons of the Lower Hunter, Montrose of Mudgee, Pipers Brook of Tasmania and Lillydale of the Yarra Valley in Victoria.

This book's only Victorian representative comes from the Yarra. The notes for Yarra Yering show what sort of climatological influences the likes of John Middleton at Mount Mary and James Halliday at Coldstream Hills have to contend with. Their reds are built on a similar timescale to Yarra Yering's, and their Chardonnays for drinking at two to six years.

In Victoria, pockets of cool but isolated vineyards produce ambitious medium-term wines which express the philosophies of the wine-maker more forcefully than any regional generality. All one can say about recent Victorian vintages is that in general 1988 and 1986 were extremely good, and 1987 was perhaps too sharp a reminder of how cool a cool climate can be. The Mornington Peninsula is a good example of a new area cool enough to produce fine Pinot Noir. Virgin Hills near Kyneton is a good if isolated example of an Australian wine, Cabernet-based in this case, deliberately made for ageing.

In the much hotter northeast of the state, Brown Brothers of Milawa have been planting vines ever

Petaluma (page 152) owns this vineyard in the Clare Valley nearly two hours' drive north of the winery itself. Clare has established a reputation for long-lasting whites, especially Rieslings.

higher to boost acid levels. Most of the valley vineyard is too hot for fine wine production but a great source of raw material for the wonderful sweet fortified wines of this region, Liqueur Muscats and Tokays (which are aged in cask, not bottle).

"The Hunter" is New South Wales' most famous wine region which is divided into two very different, and distant, halves. See the Lindemans notes for details of vintage variation in the Lower Hunter. The great majority of non-Semillon wines produced there are made for a shorter timespan. Most Chardonnays and Shiraz (also known as Hermitage) are designed to be drunk between two and six years of bottling.

Most of the rest of New South Wales's wine regions – the Upper Hunter, Mudgee and Cowra – can produce dazzling Chardonnays for the short- to medium-term. Perhaps the most famous is Rosemount's Roxburgh, which is at its best at about three years old. The Montrose Mudgee and Rothbury Cowra Chardonnays are built to a similar timescale: 1988 and 1987 were especially good for whites in the Upper Hunter.

It is an exceptional New South Wales red that musters all the components, particularly the pH, necessary for a long life. Rosemount buy in Cabernet from Coonawarra, for example, and the new Orange vineyards west of Sydney may have enough altitude to provide longevity.

Tasmania's viticultural problems are at the other end of the climatological spectrum. There are years when the grapes planted in the cooler sites simply will not set, or reach high enough sugar levels even for Roederer's sparkling wine. The harvest can be well into May, while the Lower Hunter has virtually finished by the end of January. Good years for the excellent Chardonnays and promising Pinot Noirs now emerging from Tasmania have been 1986, 1981 and 1980 and, with their elevated acid levels, they can be much better medium- to long-term bets than their mainland counterparts. Tasmanian wines can evolve real subtlety after three or four years in bottle, but only if the grapes were fully ripe.

The Château Hornsby wines of Alice Springs are made to be drunk very young, while the Shiraz of Queensland's Granite Belt has ageing potential for up to five years.

New Zealand bears little relation to Australia in wine terms, other than in the vaguest geographical sense. Wine-making expertise is evolving so rapidly that the youngest vintage is almost invariably the best. A handful of reds, such as those of Te Mata, Kumeu River, Stonyridge, C J Pask and Matua Valley are worth ageing for up to five years in bottle. Few whites improve after their fourth birthday although the best Chardonnays of Te Mata (again), Kumeu River, Nobilo and Cloudy Bay from 1988 onwards may manage to.

Penfolds Grange Hermitage

"Grange" is without doubt the most famous wine currently produced in the southern hemisphere. As befits all virtuosos, it is surrounded by controversy. Since Penfolds is by far the biggest Australian wine company, handling almost a third of each year's vintage, it can afford the luxury of corporate reticence with production details, but this isn't the only reason for the controversy. It also exists because the style of the wine itself encourages strong opinions from all sectors of the industry.

As one of its earliest detractors remarked, there are many ways in which Grange is a "very good dry port". More concentrated than any other table wine (and indeed even more intensely crimson in youth than the Taylor's port tasted for this book), Grange somehow, like an elephant on a trapeze, manages the trickiest balancing act of all. It is rich but not sweet, intoxicatingly heady (12.5 to 13 per cent alcohol) but not unduly alcoholic, extractive but not astringent, intense but not unappetising.

It is arguably, however, just too much of a good thing. With the gamey, chocolaty scents of fully ripe South Australian Shiraz and volatility hovering around 0.9 gm/lit, it attracts no shortage of critics.

Grange's many enthusiasts outside Australia wonder why it exists in such isolation, why no other wine company tries to emulate its brooding stature. The answer is not just that, to many of Australia's younger wine-makers, Grange represents the traditional, volatile, almost tonic side of Australian wine which is to be marvelled at rather than copied, but also that no company other than Penfolds could afford to make it. Like several other wines in this book, for example, new American oak is a key factor in its production.

It is also a selection of a selection of a selection. There is a panoply of other similarly styled, if lesser, Shiraz and Shiraz/Cabernet blends in the considerable Penfolds range, and these hint at what happens to those lots deemed not quite up to scratch for Grange Hermitage.

When Penfolds sent their wine-maker Max Schubert to visit Bordeaux in 1950 they could not have known how influential that visit would be. It inspired him, appropriately enough for this book, with "the idea of producing an Australian red capable of staying alive for a minimum of 20 years, and comparable with those produced in Bordeaux" Had South Australian Cabernet fruit been available in any quantity then, the resulting wine might have been quite different, but Max Schubert fashioned his mould-breaking "dry port" out of the grape Australia is still lucky enough to have as its staple red: Syrah, Shiraz or "Hermitage".

The source of the fruit has varied over the years. Much of it used to be supplied by the Magill vineyard by the eponymous Grange, a cottage belonging to the Penfold family. Today the 350-acre (140-hectare) Kalimna vineyard just north of Penfolds' Barossa headquarters is the prime source.

Earlier vintages

Grange is designed to evolve slowly over two if not three decades, being released a full six years after the vintage. All older vintages are worthy of respect although the 1957 and 1958 are lesser, non-oaked versions. Some of the most stunning older vintages include 1953, the 1955 which was just starting to fade in the late eighties, 1962, the 1966 which was at its peak at 20 years old, 1967 and 1971 (which was still climbing and heralded enjoyment throughout the nineties).

Quantity produced

Exact figures are not released by the owners, Penfolds.

1978 Looks much more than one year older than the 1979 but still shows textbook shading of a youngish maturing wine. Just starting to show what Grange can really do. Lovely, complete blend of very ripe pruney fruit with the structure of a rigorously oak-aged wine. Gorgeous stuff just this side of molasses. Ultra rich and very good. A big wine with tannis well covered by mellow fruit, and plenty of length.

Weather and timing

Good vintage, average crop. Hot Mar. Cool and windy during harvest which began early Feb.

Other details

Released at A$420 a case. Total Barossa production: 3,600,000 cases.

1979 Exceptionally deep colour for this age. Rather rustic, almost cheesy nose followed by enormously opulent fruit and spice on the palate. Much less developed than the 1978 with quite marked acid and tannin in late 1988. Still a bit of a brute (Penfolds maintained this was one of the worst bottles of 1979 they had seen).

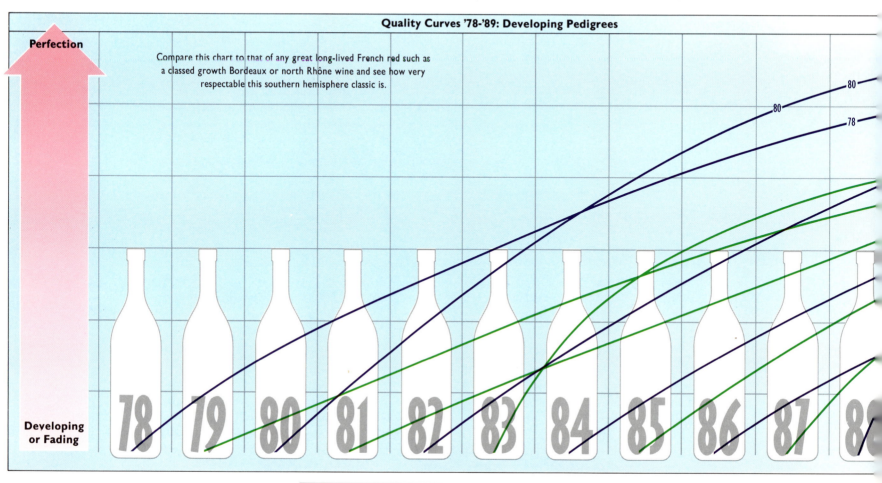

Quality Curves '78-'89: Developing Pedigrees

Perfection

Compare this chart to that of any great long-lived French red such as a classed growth Bordeaux or north Rhône wine and see how very respectable this southern hemisphere classic is.

Developing or Fading

78 79 80 81 82 83 84 85 86 87 88

Weather and timing

Fair vintage, average crop. Above average seasonal rainfall. Good for flowering and set. Warm growing season; healthy harvest.

Other details

Released at A$420 a case. Barossa: 3,600,000 cases.

1980 A highly successful vintage though it was one of the few wines in this line-up that didn't actually coat the inside of the glass. More directly, gorgeously aromatic than the 1981 tasting as though there were a seasoning of Cabernet fruit in the blend. Leafily scented. Seductive, velvety texture and lovely mouthfilling fruit. Very big and so ripe that the tannins, definitely there, are hardly perceptible.

Weather and timing

Exceptional vintage, average crop. Wet spring then dry; good yield. Mild growing season. Slow to ripen. Hot during harvest.

Other details

Released at A$480 a case. Barossa: 3,900,000 cases.

1981 Still unevolved. Almost porty first impression, especially to the eye, but followed by well integrated secondary flavours. Spicy prune-like fruit but with the rigour of oak ageing. Waiting patiently in the wings.

Weather and timing

Excellent vintage, below average crop. Wet, windy spring disrupted set. Mild, wet conditions slowed ripening: some disease. Good harvest.

Other details

Released at A$540 a case. Barossa: 3,600,000 cases.

1982 A renowned vintage, somewhat in the same style as 1983. Particularly sweet, almost overripe fruit with perceptible oak and not yet fully integrated.

Weather and timing

Exceptional vintage, above aver-age crop. Good set. Warm grow-ing season. Dry hot harvest.

Other details

Released at A$660 a case. Barossa: 4,900,000 cases.

1983 Exceptional colour and volatility. Very ripe; suggestion of prunes in armagnac. Big, rich, al-ready complex.

Weather and timing

Exceptional vintage, small crop. Drought. Very dry, hot spring; severe vine stress. Fair harvest.

Other details

Released at A$696 a case. Barossa: 2,600,000 cases.

1984 One of the chunkier Granges. Very deep colour coats the glass. Inky, rugged, with a suggestion of tea leaves and even French oak on the nose. Opulent on the palate with a broad range of ripe autumnal flavours. Big and less elegant than the 1985.

Weather and timing

Very good vintage, below average crop. Cool year. Wet winter and spring needed after drought of 1983. Fine summer. Good harvest.

Other details

Release date: late 1989. Barossa: 3,700,000 cases. No Magill fruit.

1985 One of the most inter-esting and distinctive Granges fashioned for a long life thanks to its especially good acidity. Less obviously Grange and a little more European in style. Very deep crimson with a wonderful floral top note in the bouquet. Rich, full, round and chewy on the palate. Definitely different.

Weather and timing

Very good vintage, large crop. Cool year. Mild, wet spring. Hot and dry for ripening. Some pow-dery mildew. Rain late Mar. Excel-lent harvest.

Other details

Barossa: 4,400,000 cases.

1986 Still relatively simple young Shiraz (not the same as young Syrah) fruit with few oak markings at two years old. Almost refined and even almost Bor-deaux-like, for heaven's sake! Less palate impact and less alcohol than most. Dry and relatively restrained.

Weather and timing

Exceptional vintage, small crop. Dry season. Good spring. Dry, hot growing season. Severe water stress. Hot during harvest.

Other details

Barossa: 3,900,000 cases.

1987 (Cask sample) Deep blackened crimson which coats the inside of the glass heavily. Very serious wine, almost magi-cally flavoured with spice and well-tamed ripe fruit. Gorgeous, serious stuff which should put on yet more flesh. Far from its opu-lent peak.

Weather and timing

Very good vintage, below average crop. Mild winter and spring. Hail storm late Oct damaged foliage and inflorescences. Cool, wet growing season. Warm Mar and excellent harvest.

Other details

Barossa: 3,100,000 cases.

1988 (Cask sample) A quite exceptional wine. Extraordinary port colour with vibrant shocking pink at the very edge. Some of the burnt rubber aromas of Syrah plus the wonderful warmth of fully ripe fruit and lots of unintegrated oak. Raw and vital; a baby rugby player. Gorgeous full, ripe stuff with a high level of remarkably soft tannins. Should last ex-tremely well.

Weather and timing

Excellent vintage, below average crop. Strong winds and hail storm disrupted set. Dry growing sea-son: vines stressed due to lack of water. Good harvest.

Other details

Barossa: 3,400,000 cases.

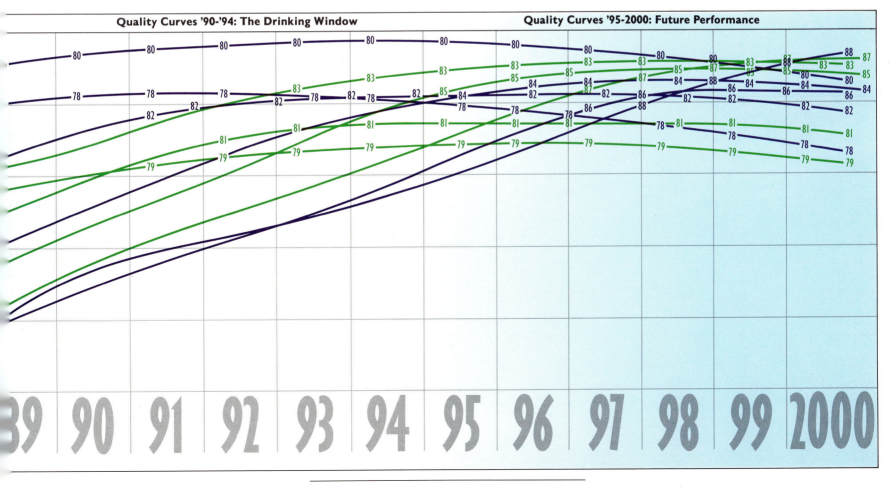

Petaluma Chardonnay

Australian Chardonnay is noted for its commercial success but not for its longevity. These two facts may be related. It is so easy to sell early-maturing, medium quality Australian Chardonnay that it can only be personal professional pride that spurs on those trying to produce something several notches above: a Chardonnay with a long, interesting life ahead of it.

The Tyrrell dynasty in the Hunter Valley laid the foundations for such a wine with their remarkable Vat 47 Chardonnay in 1973, a wine that was just hanging on to the vestiges of its glory in 1988. Australia had to wait until the 1977 vintage to see any other such Chardonnays among the debut wines of a new wine enterprise perched way up the Adelaide Hills.

Petaluma must be viewed as a freak, a scientific experiment posing as a winery and vineyards, and this is particularly true of the Petaluma way with Chardonnay. The analytical brain behind all the experimenting belongs to Brian Croser, who will probably still be known as Australian wine's young Turk in his eighties. His verdict on Petaluma's entire output of Chardonnay to date was that the top wines don't rate more than a potential seven out of 10, and the others only about five. A fan notably of Leflaive and Sonoma-Cutrer, Croser treads a solitary path, but claims that it will lead to the same end everyone else is rather more obviously seeking: top quality Australian Chardonnay. Unlike his rivals who are

more easily influenced by market fluctuations, he believes in changing only one variable at a time. Over the last decade he has been engaged in getting the fruit source right, as outlined below, arguably at the expense of the fullest expression of each vintage's potential.

In some cases Petaluma Chardonnay may end up being composed entirely of fruit grown at the Piccadilly winery but in other, cooler years, Croser may achieve the Australian ultimate here: fruit that cannot be sufficiently ripened for still wine (although it would be useful for his eponymous fizz).

Unlike any other wine-maker in the world, with the possible exception of some Asti producers, Croser refuses to be hurried by nature. After being picked the fruit is pressed, settled for three weeks, then the chilled clean juice stored until winter when he is ready to ferment it. Separate lots are carefully fermented in batches at almost unthinkably low temperatures and the wine is constructed at the tasting table. Croser claims that, along with Leeuwin and possibly Cullens of Margaret River, Petaluma is virtually alone in deliberately fashioning Australian Chardonnays for the long term. "Our company's reputation is built not on the current vintage but on our older bottles". And certainly Petaluma Chardonnays, unlike for example Rosemount's gloriously opulent Roxburgh, do not stand out in a line-up of young wines. But the proof, and evolution, of Croser's philosophy is evident in these wines.

Earlier vintages

1977 The first vintage. Preserved rather than evolved on the nose with relatively simple flavours. Perhaps the result of being treated too antiseptically, like a Riesling, in the winery.

1978 Another triumph of the embalmer's art, tasting far less mature than any other Australian counterpart but demonstrates Croser's concern that his wines can be too simple. Admirable rather than pleasurable.

Weather and timing
Very good vintage, above average crop. Early bud break Sept 13. Hot, dry growing season; rapid maturation. Harvest Feb 14.

Quantity produced
800 cases released at A$131 a case. Australian Chardonnay crop: 980 tons (1,000 tonnes).

Other details
All grapes from Cowra vineyard.

1979 Deep green/gold with powerful floral, almost exotic aromas that may owe too much to ethyl acetate, but an undertow of rich, ripe fruit.

Weather and timing
Fair vintage, large crop. Bud break Sept 20. Humid season. Rain in Feb. Late harvest Mar 15.

Quantity produced
1,100 cases released at A$139 a case. Chardonnay: 1,440 tons (1,500 tonnes).

Other details
100% Cowra fruit.

1980 A triumph. Much more restrained gold than either 1981 or 1982 with a subtle bouquet that repays study over several hours. Excellent balance and youthful structure on the palate. Arguably the most classic.

Weather and timing
Good vintage, above average crop. Slow start to cool, dry season. Harvest end Feb (Cowra) and

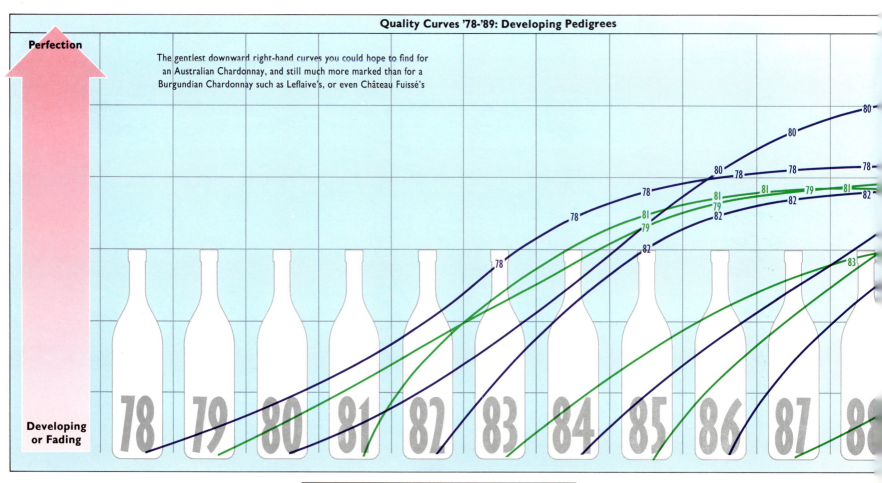

Quality Curves '78-'89: Developing Pedigrees

Perfection

The gentlest downward right-hand curves you could hope to find for an Australian Chardonnay, and still much more marked than for a Burgundian Chardonnay such as Leflaive's, or even Château Fuissé's

Developing or Fading

78 79 80 81 82 83 84 85 86 87 88

early Apr (Coonawarra).

Quantity produced

1,800 cases released at A$162 a case. Chardonnay: 1,860 tons (1,900 tonnes).

Other details

76% Cowra, 24% Coonawarra. 13% alcohol. Began skin contact.

1981 Very deep gamboge. Full, powerful savoury aromas. Big, perhaps too big, but with complexity and evolution. Intriguing herbal notes; only just enough acidity which tends to come in a whack on the finish. Reminiscent of some California wines of the same era.

Weather and timing

Fair vintage, below average crop. Very hot, dry season; high sugar levels, low acidity. Harvest one month early.

Quantity produced

1,800 cases released at A$177 a case. Chardonnay: 2,760 tons (2,800 tonnes).

Other details

50% Cowra, 50% Coonawarra.

1982 An oddity. Its partial malolactic gives it a different bouquet: more of an Australian white than a Petaluma Chardonnay. Deep gold with perceptible mineral elements. The palate is initially almost sweet though is saved by considerable but well-integrated acidity. Mellifluous.

Weather and timing

Very good vintage, above average crop. Average season. Dry and sunny harvest.

Quantity produced

2,500 cases released at A$187 a case. Chardonnay: 2,950 tons (3,000 tonnes).

Other details

70% Coonawarra, 30% Cowra. Lees contact and barrel fermentation introduced.

1983 Not one of the best vintages. Meaty, charred nose without the concentration of some of

its successors. Low-key with simple sweetness and obvious unintegrated acidity. Good long finish with intriguing elements.

Weather and timing

Poor vintage, below average crop. Very dry winter and spring. Severe frosts in Coonawarra and Clare. Hot, dry growing season. Bush fires. Wet during harvest.

Quantity produced

3,000 cases released at A$210 a case. Chardonnay: 4,570 tons (4,600 tonnes).

Other details

80% Coonawarra, 20% Clare. Rigorous selection introduced.

1984 An excitingly nervy specimen with toasted mineral flavours and perceptible oak. Unresolved with primary elements still in evidence but signs of real quality. The fruit was picked at 22.5 Brix and Croser feels that he may have slightly underdone this wine.

Weather and timing

Very good vintage, average crop. Cool, late season. Humid summer. Harvest early Mar (Clare) and early Apr (Coonawarra).

Quantity produced

5,000 cases released at A$271 a case. Chardonnay: 8,390 tons (8,500 tonnes).

Other details

50% Coonawarra, 50% Clare. 12.2% alcohol.

1985 Green/gold and a rich creamy, slightly vanillin nose with perhaps too little acidity. Full of melon and quince flavour.

Weather and timing

Very good vintage, average crop. Second cool, humid season in a row. Harvest mid-Mar (Clare), late Mar (Coonawarra) and mid-Apr (Piccadilly).

Quantity produced

7,000 cases released at A$271 a case. Chardonnay: 11,240 tons (11,500 tonnes).

Other details

45% Coonawarra, 45% Clare, 10% Piccadilly. 12.3% alcohol.

1986 Elegant and Puligny-like despite hints of tropical fruits. Definite smokiness with a lean, silky structure. Long, and showing signs of developing beautifully but early. Wonderful fan of savoury notes on the long finish.

Weather and timing

Excellent vintage, average crop. Cool season. Harvest mid-Mar.

Quantity produced

7,500 cases released at A$306 a case. Chardonnay: 17,170 tons (17,500 tonnes).

Other details

40% Coonawarra, 40% Clare, 20% Piccadilly.

1987 Extraordinarily promising. Green in among the light gold (a Petaluma hallmark). Smoky elements with some acacia blossom. Low-key and restrained just after bottling although compared with

the 1977 it seems redolent of tropical fruits. Delicacy with little evident oak. Good ripe fruit, lots of concentration and acid.

Weather and timing

Excellent vintage, below average crop. Cool season. Cold and wet during flowering in Piccadilly; poor set. Indian summer.

Quantity produced

8,000 cases released at A$325 a case. Chardonnay: 19,680 tons (20,000 tonnes).

1988 *(Not tasted)* Similar to 1987. Picked at 23.5 Brix. Not blended by Dec 1988 although this warm year yielded sufficient ripe Piccadilly fruit for the blend to be entirely from the home farm.

Weather and timing

Very good vintage, below average crop. Wet winter and spring. Poor set. Hail storm Oct 15. Long, dry summer.

Quantity produced

About 8,000 cases.

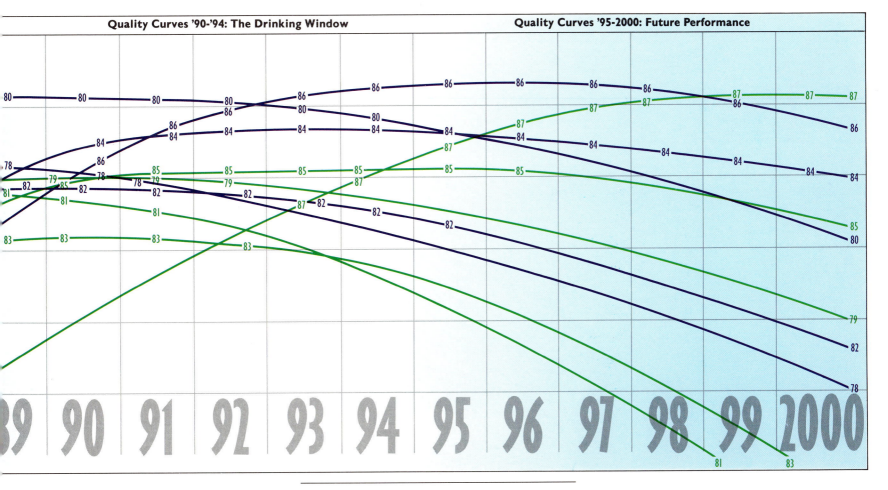

Quality Curves '90-'94: The Drinking Window

Quality Curves '95-2000: Future Performance

Wynns Coonawarra Estate Cabernet Sauvignon

A survey such as this should certainly include a Coonawarra Cabernet, one of Australia's few tried and tested combinations of soil, location and grape variety. What is by no means so clear-cut is which Coonawarra Cabernet to choose.

This isolated strip of extraordinary South Australian *terra rossa*, rich red loam that stretches a mere nine miles (15 km) down towards the Victorian coast, has for some reason failed to yield a single consistently triumphant wine-producing star. There are certainly new stars in the Coonawarra firmament, such as Hollick's and Bowen Estate, but their history is too short for the purposes of this book, while firms such as Mildara, Redman's and Rouge Home have a longer but chequered history. Perhaps the very isolation of the region, 250 miles (403 km) from Adelaide which is the nearest town of any size, has deterred the bigger companies that have invested so heavily in Coonawarra from keeping a firm grip on quality.

The biggest vineyard owners in Coonawarra are Wynns, whose catch-phrase is "The estate that made the Coonawarra famous". Certainly no wine region could have wished for a better marketeer than David Wynn. In 1951 he bought an old property in this area which was previously exploited only as an unacknowledged source of fine, claret-structured blending material. He immediately renamed it Wynns Coonawarra Estate, advertised the name Coonawarra far and wide and

commissioned the delightfully striking woodcut that continues to distinguish Wynns' labels to this day.

The company has since passed through the hands of Britain's largest brewer and is currently part of the giant Penfolds Australian wine conglomerate. This means that these wines are shipped up to the Penfolds giant wine terminal in the Barossa Valley for bottling. Since Wynns' initial heyday in the late fifties and early sixties, wine-making policy has been subject to something of a switchback, an educative example of what goes wrong when the market is allowed to dictate what the vineyard produces, as the chart and tasting notes show.

In the late seventies company policy was that even these Coonawarra Cabernets should be made "light" for early consumption. They were, for example, subjected to cold stabilization so that they would not be besmirched by the commercial inconvenience of sediment.

Since 1982 the wines have been made for maturity at five to 10 years and an exciting upturn in quality can be seen as wine-maker Peter Douglas' influence grew in the mid-eighties. An average of one in four casks are new and rather more than that are of Nevers oak rather than American. This is modern wine, all machine picked and fermented in Australia's pride, the giant Potter fermenters, for six to eight days. The results are variable, as can be seen here, but improving.

Earlier vintages

The golden era was from **1954 to 1965**. A bottle of 1954 has been known to dazzle 35 years on but bottle variation is now great. The **1976** won the coveted Jimmy Watson Trophy, but did not hold as well as it could have.

Quantity produced

Exact production figures are not released by the owners, Penfolds.

1978 Ordinary red wine as opposed to a vehicle for Cabernet splendour. More concentrated colour than 1979 but still light. Pleasant seasoning of mineral flavours but lightweight with definite acidity and rather jammy, simple fruit. Minimal tannin.

Weather and timing

Good vintage, below average crop. Frost during bud break reduced yield. Mild growing season. Cabernet Sauvignon harvest Mar 24–29. 11.9% alcohol.

Other details

New wine-maker, John Wade. South Australia (SE District) production: 1,600,000 cases.

1979 The greatest disappointment. Pale cherry red with no luminosity. Low-key nose. Sweet, simple charm but the acidity is starting to dominate. Fruit is fading and the finish is bitter and chewy. Valpolicella structure.

Weather and timing

Good vintage, average crop. Dry spring and summer; some low-lying vines were water-stressed. Poor set. Cool, mild growing season. Harvest Mar 15–22.

Other details

Refrigeration used during fermentation. Machine picking at night. SE District: 1,600,000 cases.

1980 Lightish but looks more youthful than 1981. Herbaceous; different from its successors. Fruit on the palate but a metallic taste overlays it. Acidity, and some

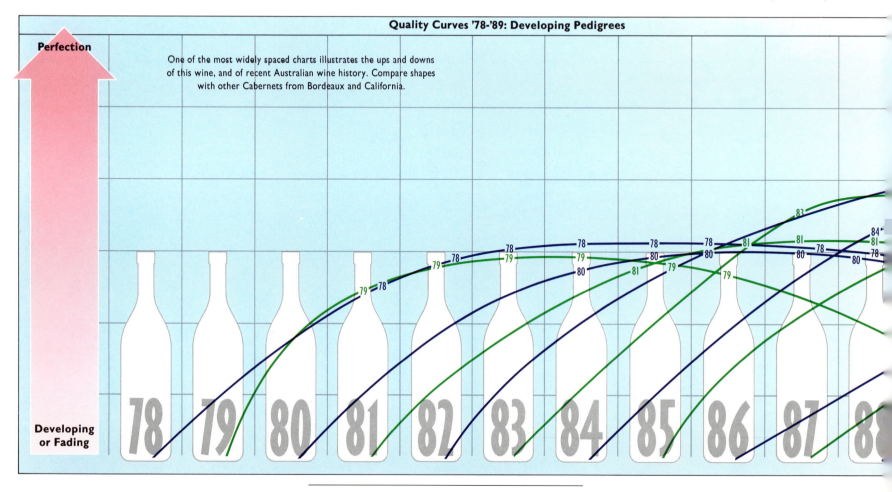

Quality Curves '78-'89: Developing Pedigrees

One of the most widely spaced charts illustrates the ups and downs of this wine, and of recent Australian wine history. Compare shapes with other Cabernets from Bordeaux and California.

Perfection

Developing or Fading

tannin, obvious. A note of bitterness, although highly regarded as a 1980 Coonawarra.

Weather and timing
Fair vintage, above average crop. Good set. Dry summer then fine and mild. Slow ripening. Excellent harvest Mar 21 to Apr 3.

Other details
Increased time on skins. Matured in puncheons (378 litres): 20% new American oak. SE District: 2,000,000 cases.

1981 Light red with pale brick rim. Fairly lightweight nose with some tobacco notes but some cardboard. Good full fruit flavours losing power but lively for a seven-year-old. Tannins retreating.

Weather and timing
Good vintage, average crop. Cool, overcast spring. Dry, hot mid-summer; some water stress, relieved by rain late Jan. Dry for start of harvest then dew which encouraged *Botrytis*.

Other details
SE District: 1,800,000 cases.

1982 Better quality. Good deep colour with dark ruby out to rim. Fuller, more ripe and intense than the 1983. Could perhaps do with a point more of 1983's acid. Gamey notes add interest. Good full, ripe palate attack followed by a thwack of tannin. Lively: will probably develop, but a slight note of bitterness on the finish.

Weather and timing
Exceptional vintage, average crop. Wet winter. Mild spring. Dry and sometimes hot summer. Good harvest.

Other details
New (1981) wine-making style continued; fruit picked later with enhanced tannin and colour extraction. 23% new oak. SE District: 2,400,000.

1983 Much lighter and duller than the 1984. An early developer with hints of cassis and spice:

Good fruit and tannins with acids that hint at greenness.

Weather and timing
Fair vintage, below average crop. Drought year; retarded growth and berry development. Severe frosts Sept and Oct; crop reduced. Mar heat-wave then rain. Widespread *Botrytis* and rot.

Other details
Increased time in barrel to compensate for poor crop. SE District: 1,700,000 cases.

1984 A highly regarded year although in late 1988 this wine seemed to have been overwhelmed by sheer power of unsubtle fruit. Notes of herbaceousness. Deep ruby. Little oak influence and no layers – just size.

Weather and timing
Very good vintage, above average crop. Wet winter and spring. Cool summer. Gale-force winds and hail storms in Nov caused damage. Heavy rain before harvest.

Other details
SE District: 2,300,000 cases.

1985 A half-way house between 1984 and 1986. Deep ruby and obvious, fully ripened (cf 1984) fruit. Stewed plums. A notch up from 1984 with more subtlety, layers of flavour and evidence of well-mannered oak. Without the complexity that the 1987 showed after less than two years, but in a similar style. Tannins at the end suggest this is not yet ready.

Weather and timing
Excellent vintage, large crop. Favourable spring; excellent set. Cool summer; slow ripening. Fine and mild for harvest.

Other details
New wine-maker, Peter Douglas. French hogsheads (228 litres) introduced. SE District: 3,000,000 cases.

1986 This is real wine! Very attractive purple meld of

Cabernet Sauvignon fruit and tobacco flavours. More vigorous and austere than 1987. Powerful cassis with oak overlay and hints of tea leaves. Relatively elegant. Lovely dry finish with high tannin level. Undeveloped, but real potential.

Weather and timing
Exceptional vintage, above average crop. Satisfactory set. Hot, dry summer; excellent ripening. Good harvest.

Other details
5% matured in new French hogsheads (228 litres), 20% new American oak. SE District: 2,700,000 cases.

1987 Less classical and more full-blooded than the 1988. Dark ruby. Sweet luscious mulberries on the nose with floral, blackcurrant high notes. Great power but very voluptuous. Less obvious tannins than the 1986 but should develop into an alluring and interesting wine. Good acid level.

Weather and timing
Good vintage, below average crop. Wet during flowering; poor set. Dry, cool summer. Early autumn frosts. Poor maturation. Late harvest.

Other details
25% new oak. SE District: 2,500,000 cases.

1988 (Cask sample) Very grown-up. Deep crimson (though not as deep as its Grange stablemate). Attractive well-mannered blend of medium-weight fruit and some oak. Spice and cigarbox flavours. Real class even in youth. Excellent structure: oak influence. Taut and concentrated. Should develop beautifully.

Weather and timing
Very good vintage, below average crop. Dry, mild season. Frosts Sept-Nov reduced crop. Poor set. Early harvest.

Other details
SE District: 1,600,000 cases.

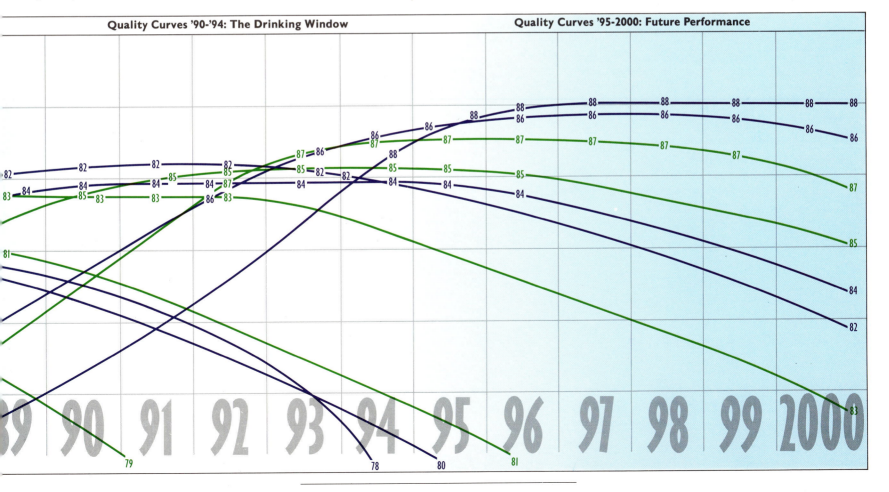

Yarra Yering Dry Red No 1

Examination of Yarra Yering wines as an entity distinct from Yarra Yering's founder and animating spirit is unthinkable. Dr Bailey Carrodus towers above his idiosyncratic Yarra Valley neighbours in his own particular blend of confident, educated idiosyncrasy.

Dr Carrodus is no redneck from the outback. A plant physiology don at All Souls' College, Oxford, he somehow retains an impeccable Oxford accent and the dress and manners of a particularly courtly English squire, together with an annoying, however little flaunted, grasp of most subjects known to man.

The winery is as unusual as the man. Lo-tech is an understatement. The total staff managing this workmanlike shed and Yarra Yering's unirrigated 40 acres (16 hectares) is three.

Grapes are picked into specially designed stackable black plastic buckets and poured through an antique crusher-destemmer into one of Bailey's extraordinary fermenters, which are basically stainless steel-lined tea chests on wheels. Should cooling be necessary, ice blocks are lowered into these unique fermentation vessels.

Fermentation lasts only between five and 10 days, although Bailey was for some time preoccupied with the question of the merits of maceration after a visit to Bordeaux during the 1988 vintage. The density of his Cabernets right out to the rim of the glass demonstrates eloquently why he has no need of extra anthocyanins. One suspects, though, he may be in the process of revising his laudable preoccupation with primary fruit flavours, which was his great concern when he set out in 1969 to produce Australia's finest fruit from a patch of the Yarra's most suitable vineyard land.

New oak, both hogsheads and *barriques*, is always French and increasingly Limousin. The proportion has risen dramatically since one third was new in 1978 and then a half from 1983. The 1989 vintage was the first to be treated entirely to new oak. The wine is not usually bottled until about two years after the vintage in late March, April or even May.

The hand-drawn labels and even the names of Yarra Yering's wines complete the picture, as unique as each of the eighteenth century samplers and Persian rugs in Bailey's thoughtfully designed house.

While Dry Red No 2 is based on Shiraz spiced with a little Mataro (also known as Mourvèdre) Yering's most famous wine is Dry Red No 1, which is about 80 per cent Cabernet fleshed out with Merlot and Malbec. In future vintages it will be likely to have its (always natural) acidity boosted by some Petit Verdot.

Older vintages had their detractors on the grounds of high volatility, but since the 1978 vintage it is widely accepted that the Carrodus philosophy is fully vindicated. He does not think even his first vintage 1973 is yet at its peak, although allows that all vintages prior to 1984 are "fit to use".

Earlier vintages

Yarra Yering No I made from the **1973 to 1977** vintages have, according to Australian wine critic James Halliday, "never been accepted by the mainstram of Australian opinion. I, like almost every other critic or judge, found them successively volatile." Dr Carrodus swears they will all recant one day.

1978 Still crimson. Looks younger and tastes more sophisticated than 1979. With some tannin still in evidence, this wine has all the complex balance and enticingly interwoven secondary and tertiary flavour elements of a top quality Bordeaux, perhaps a Graves, from the same vintage. Correct, rigorous and very dry.

Weather and timing

Good vintage, large crop. Cool, dry season. Good flowering. Shiraz failed to ripen. Late harvest in Apr.

Quantity produced

About 2,000 cases released at A$60 a case. Victoria production: 5,100,000 cases.

Other details

Dr Carrodus full-time at the vineyard for the first year.

1979 Looks mature although with no hint of yellow tones. Intriguing meld of mellow Cabernet family fruit flavours but slightly blowsy and full-blown on the initial palate, followed by high acid. I suspect it needs an Australian palate to appreciate it fully. Bailey thinks it is one of the best wines he has ever made.

Weather and timing

Average vintage, below average crop. Mild, wet season. Rain during flowering reduced crop. Downy mildew.

Quantity produced

About 2,000 cases released at A$72 a case. Victoria: 5,100,000 cases.

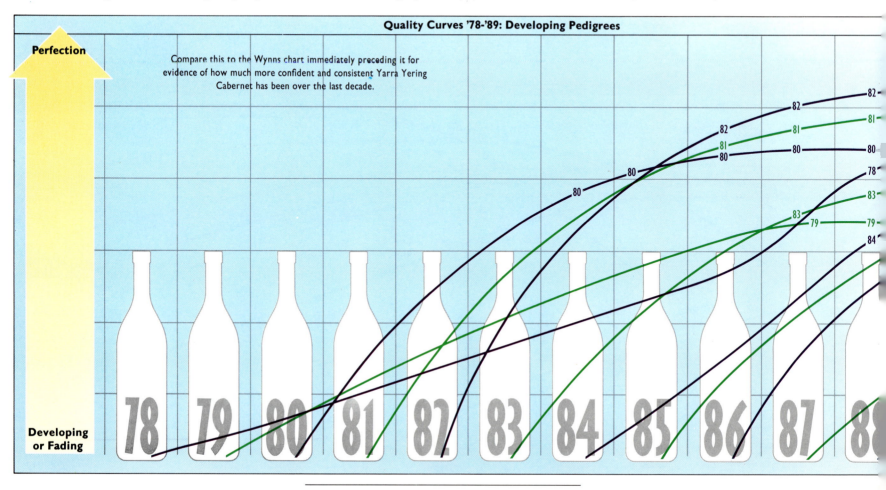

Quality Curves '78-'89: Developing Pedigrees

Perfection

Compare this to the Wynns chart immediately preceding it for evidence of how much more confident and consistent Yarra Yering Cabernet has been over the last decade.

Developing or Fading

78 79 80 81 82 83 84 85 86 87 88

Other details
Won Gold Medal at Victorian Export Awards.

1980 Good rich colour, deeper than 1981. Hot, rich, essences of old-fashioned Australian red. More Rhône than Bordeaux, this is what they might make of Cabernet Sauvignon planted on the hill of Hermitage. Slightly hot finish but easy to appreciate. Certainly "fit to use".

Weather and timing
Excellent vintage, below average crop. Almost ideal season. Good flowering. Warm, wet summer. Dry during Mar harvest.

Quantity produced
About 2,000 cases released at A$90 a case. Victoria: 5,700,000 cases.

1981 Looks much less concentrated than most but no signs of age. Low-key, mild, well-balanced blend of secondary Cabernet aromas. Refreshingly direct. Very attractive now with lovely spicy Merlot notes. Definitely ready but should continue to improve.

Weather and timing
Average vintage, large crop. Dry season. Good harvest.

Quantity produced
About 2,500 cases: A$84 a case. Victoria: 5,100,000 cases.

1982 Excellent deep crimson, browning at the rim. Very powerful, rich, plummy aromas. Notable but not obtrusive volatility with enticingly rich, broad evolved fruit and tobacco notes. Still sufficient acid and tannin to promise well. Opulent.

Weather and timing
Good vintage, above average crop. Good start to season; early bud break and wet spring. Cool, dry summer; slow ripening. Fine for harvest.

Quantity produced
About 2,000 cases: A$90 a case. Victoria: 4,500,000 cases.

Other details
Blend almost 100% Cabernet Sauvignon.

1983 Colour just starting to mature. Relatively evolved, very Bordeaux nose. Integrated secondary aromas but fairly lightweight and tart on the palate.

Weather and timing
Very good vintage, record crop. Dry winter. Warm, dry spring. Early flowering, excellent set. Summer drought: severe vine stress. Late harvest.

Quantity produced
About 3,500 cases released at A$96 a case. Victoria: 5,000,000 cases.

Other details
Most Yarra Valley vineyards produced a small crop, some failed completely.

1984 Deeply impressive colour. A descendant of the 1980 in style and weight. This should continue to be easy to enjoy, even though those looking for real complexity might find other vintages more satisfying.

Weather and timing
Exceptional vintage, large crop. Wet spring. Good set. Cool, moist growing season. Late harvest.

Quantity produced
About 3,500 cases: A$96 a case. Victoria: 6,500,000 cases.

1985 Deep crimson right out to the rim. Bouquet still developing but it is easy to see some Malbec plumminess among the warm mineral overtones. Good acid and tannin levels but this may not last as long as the 1986.

Weather and timing
Very good vintage, small crop. Cold, wet during flowering; crop reduced by half. Cool summer. Slow to ripen. Warm days and cool nights for harvest.

Quantity produced
About 1,500 cases: A$144 a case. Victoria: 7,500,000 cases.

Other details
Began replanting programme which increased the proportion of Pinot Noir and Merlot. Increased use of new oak.

1986 Very deep crimson. Sweet, almost chocolate-like nose, rich plumminess. Sweet and spicy bouquet followed by appetising acidity on the palate. Still youthful with some oak in evidence but more opulent than the 1987.

Weather and timing
Outstanding vintage, small crop. Cold, wet winter. Difficult, late flowering. Warm during growing season and for harvest.

Quantity produced
About 1,600 cases: A$168 a case. Victoria: 5,300,000 cases.

1987 (Cask sample) Intense plum red out to rim. Relatively aromatic. Tarry and intense with much higher acid than 1988. Very youthful, classically structured with marked tannin.

Weather and timing
Good vintage, above average crop. Cold, wet start but warm end to season. Late harvest.

Quantity produced
About 1,700 cases. Release date: 1989. Victoria: 5,200,000 cases.

1988 (Cask sample) Very deep crimson. Lots of full, if unsubtle, warm Cabernet Sauvignon. Still to take on a more rigorous structure. Fruit initially low in tannin: surprisingly low acid. Rather simple but with good balance and a neat, dry finish.

Weather and timing
Very good vintage, above average crop. Cool start to season. Poor flowering. Hot and dry for ripening. Very hot for harvest.

Quantity produced
About 1,800 cases. Release date: 1990. Victoria: 6,100,000 cases.

Other details
Unusually, had to cool Cabernet Sauvignon fermentation.

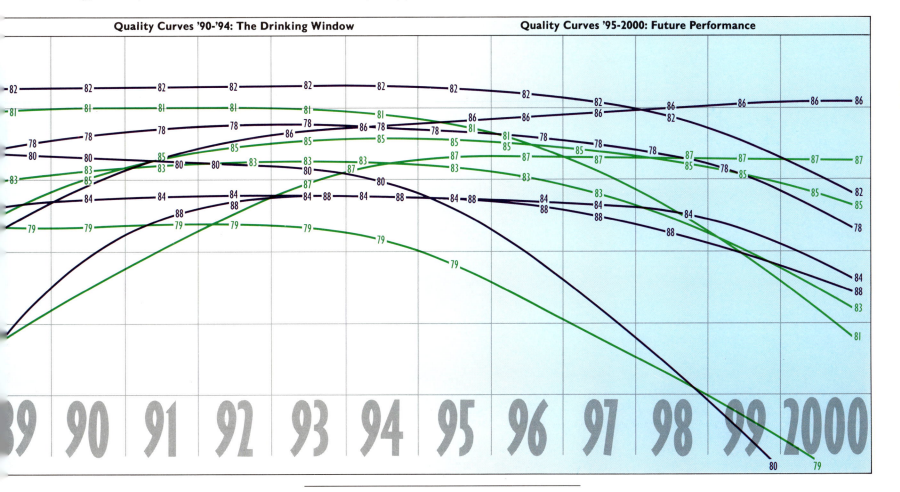

Quality Curves '90-'94: The Drinking Window

Quality Curves '95-2000: Future Performance

Lindemans Hunter Semillon

Before considering this wonder of the wine world, a nasty whirlpool of nomenclature has to be negotiated. The Semillon vine has flourished in the Hunter Valley, New South Wales' answer to Napa Valley, since the beginnings of the Australian wine industry when it was known as "Hunter River Riesling".

Throughout the last century wine merchants built up the reputations of bottlings whose styles were recognisable to a European-based culture. Thus Lindemans, whose New South Wales history is as distinguished as Penfolds' in South Australia, came to sell three different bottlings of the Semillon fruit that can make such dazzling dry whites in this historic wine region.

Their "Hunter River Chablis" is made substantially from the first, free-run juice. It has the most delicate structure, high acidity, and often the longest potential because of it. "Hunter River Riesling" tends to be a blend of the most aromatic lots with perhaps as much as 10 grams per litre of residual sugar. And the fullest-bodied lots, together with a high proportion of sturdy press wine, go to make "Hunter River White Burgundy".

The European authorities are unimpressed by Lindemans' arguments citing historical precedent. Outside Australia all these wines have to be sold simply as Hunter Valley Semillon and identified solely by their numbers. These four-digit numbers would present a challenge even to Second World War code-breakers but, in theory at least, they are fairly straightforward. The first two digits denote the year of bottling in consecutive numerical order, and the second two hold the key to the style of the wine: 75 for Chablis style, 55 for the Riesling type and 70 for the White Burgundy style. The suffix 76, 56 or 71 denotes a second bottling of one of the respective styles.

The extraordinary feature of these wines is their ability to age, from exuberantly fruity, fairly full young bottles to gamboge-tinted, toasty, mineral-laden bombs packed with explosive layers of complexity. But they are bizarre, wild colonial oddballs, quite unlike the stately dry white Graves which are perhaps their closest relatives in the wine world. Doubtless the lack of malolactic fermentation helps preserve them through what can be a dull middle age, as does the tartaric acid that is added to the juice of most years.

The Hunter Valley is plagued by high temperatures, habitual cloud cover, saltwater that prohibits irrigation, widely varying yields and an irregular rainfall that can bring terrible rot during the January/February vintage. Lindemans' accountants must argue annually that their 300 acres (120 hectares) of Hunter vineyard be sold off, but the company has luckily returned to the policy instituted in the early sixties of storing away the most successful vintages in order to release them (now internationally) in their grand old age as Lindemans Classics.

Earlier vintages

Quality here is at notable variance with vintage reputation. Even the Bin 4355 1968 was frisky at 20 years old (although the Bin 4370 was fading). Of the 1970s, the Bin 3875, the Chablis style, is perhaps the star although the 3855 Riesling type is also a gem in which the 8gm/litre residual sugar is no longer intrusive. This is a vintage of which the local Department of Agriculture said there was "no hope". As wine-maker Karl Stockhausen puts it, "the grapes were so rotten they had whiskers". 1971, 1975 and 1977 all produced some distinguished wines that will remain in their prime until at least the early nineties.

Most of the wines below are the White Burgundy style and will probably reach their peak two to three years before the Chablis and Riesling styles.

1978 Bin 5470. Deep gamboge. A bit subdued and flabby on the palate. Not one of the stars in late 1988.

Weather and timing
Fair vintage, average crop. Hot and dry first half of the season. Rain late Dec helped ripening. Early harvest began Feb 10.

Quantity produced
2,890 cases. Hunter Valley: 1,700,000 cases.

1979 Bin 5670. An exotic, very deep golden essence smelling powerfully of rum and rich lime cordial. At its peak with a gorgeously long tropical fruit finish and layers of tertiary flavours.

Weather and timing
Very good vintage, above average crop. Rain in spring and summer. Good flowering. Hot growing season. Harvest began Feb 14.

Quantity produced
5,440 cases. Hunter Valley: 1,700,000 cases.

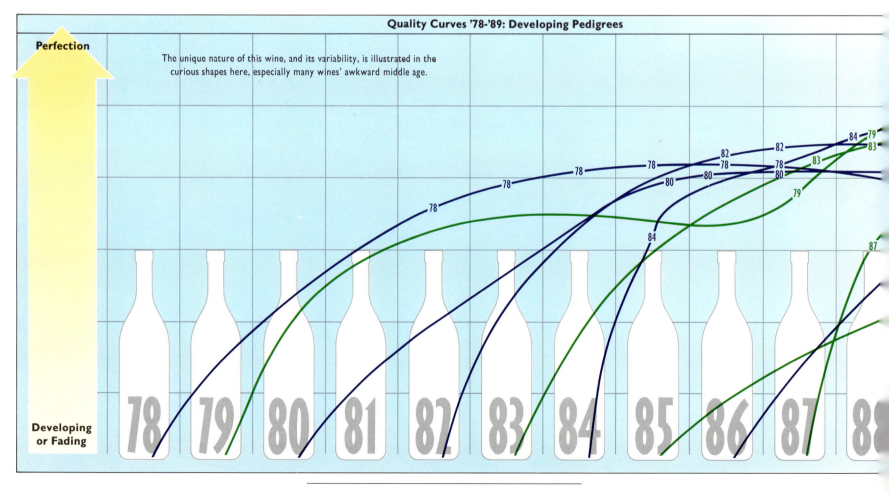

Quality Curves '78-'89: Developing Pedigrees

Perfection

The unique nature of this wine, and its variability, is illustrated in the curious shapes here, especially many wines' awkward middle age.

Developing or Fading

Other details

Abandoned old Sunshine vineyard for one at Broke.

1980 Bin 5771. Deep gold with toasty mineral notes. If anything a little simple but with good flattering ripeness initially followed up by refreshing lemon acidity.

Weather and timing

Very good vintage, below average crop. Dry, hot season. Harvest began Feb 4.

Quantity produced

1,330 cases. Hunter Valley: 1,100,000 cases.

1981 All sold out. In the late seventies and early eighties Lindemans suffered a crisis in their policy on reserves of superior wines and, some would say, in their wine-making.

Weather and timing

Good vintage, small crop. Second dry season in a row. Some rain in Dec. Early harvest began Jan 17.

Quantity produced

6,700 cases. Hunter Valley: 800,000 cases.

1982 Bin 6075. Pale gold, nutty, relatively forward, open bouquet. Powerful for a Chablis style, on the cusp of a White Burgundy style, and a relatively beefy early developer.

Weather and timing

Good vintage, below average crop. Good rains during spring and early summer. Warm growing season. Harvest began Feb 2.

Quantity produced

6,300 cases. Hunter Valley: 1,000,000 cases.

Other details

No oak.

1983 Bin 6275. Deep gold with notable acid but less concentrated, less obviously ripe fruit than most and a certain delicacy of structure. Perceptibly Chablis in style and well constituted for a fairly long if delicate life.

Weather and timing

Very good vintage, small crop. Wet during bud break. Hot growing season. Jan heatwave. Harvest began Feb 1.

Quantity produced

5,220 cases. Hunter Valley: 900,000 cases.

1984 Bin 6470. Lovely, developed, Hunter "burnt toast" nose. Strongly mineral, although without great concentration. Creamy if slightly light and vegetal in the Hunter context. Lovely for the early nineties but perhaps slightly too light for a very long life. Long, nutty finish.

Weather and timing

Fair vintage, average crop. Cool, wet season. Mildew and *Botrytis* outbreaks. Harvest began Feb 2.

Quantity produced

11,000 cases. Hunter Valley: 1,300,000 cases.

Other details

32% Verdelho. No oak.

1985 Bin 6670. Deep gold and a whiff of oxidation, perhaps because of the Chardonnay or new oak. Good acid if somewhat overripe fruit on the palate but at four years old this wine did not show the completeness of subsequent vintages. This may be the notorious middle-age phenomenon but this is an exceptional wine if only in its varietal make-up.

Weather and timing

Good vintage, above average crop. Wet, mild growing season. Hail storm Jan 28. Good harvest began Jan 29.

Quantity produced

3,200 cases. Hunter Valley: 1,100,000 cases.

Other details

40% Verdelho, 20% Chardonnay. New oak. 11.5% alcohol.

1986 Bin 6870. Savoury, meaty and confident. Mid-gold with slight fizz. Very citrus, lemon and lime peel, on the nose but with a great undertow of richness and a hint of toast already. Residual sugar perceptible. Very clean, lots of body and richness. Real balance and concentration with a lemon-like element in the flavour which may be due to the 20% Verdelho.

Weather and timing

Very good vintage, average crop. Excellent start to season; good growth. Long, cool, dry summer. Fine for harvest which began Feb 14.

Quantity produced

5,100 cases. Hunter Valley: 1,400,000 cases.

Other details

Gerry Sissingh succeeded Karl Stockhausen as wine-maker.

1987 Bin 7070. Comparatively light, even subdued. Light straw with a hint of Verdelho (15%) varnish. A different set of flavours from the 1988 with some early development of flowers and the Hunter mineral whiff. Well integrated fruit and acid already.

Weather and timing

Excellent vintage, average crop. Dry, cold winter. Wet Aug. Ideal growing season. Perfect during harvest which began Feb 9.

Quantity produced

6,200 cases. Hunter Valley: 1,300,000 cases.

Other details

Introduced burgundy bottle.

1988 Bin 7270. Very good acid and aromas of honey-flavoured fruit. Quite exotic, scented and floral, almost *musqué*. Lovely full, mouthfilling flavours.

Weather and timing

Good vintage, above average crop. Late start. Harvest began Feb 2: heavy rain mid-Feb.

Quantity produced

Not yet determined.

Other details

100% Semillon. Hunter Valley: 1,400,000 cases.

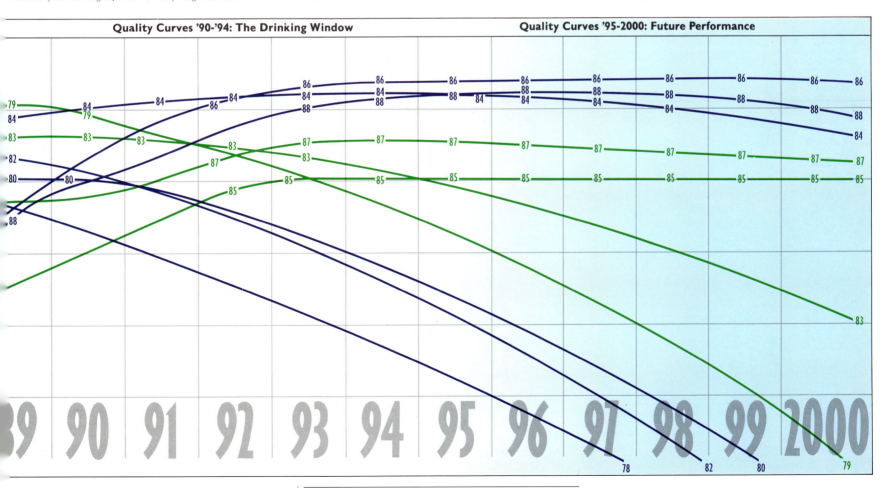

Quality Curves '90-'94: The Drinking Window   **Quality Curves '95-2000: Future Performance**

THE MATURITY INDEX

The Maturity Index differs in structure from the rest of the book: red wines are listed first, then white (beginning on p162) to allow easy comparison between the various possibilities. This allows you to choose red or white wines from your collection which are at an appropriate state of maturity. The vintages recommended reflect when the wine is at its peak: see the individual Timecharts for more detail.

See the notes above the Timecharts, headed Earlier Vintages, for details of vintages older than those charted.

RED WINES

WINE	PAGE	1989	1990	1991	1992	1993	1994	1995
BORDEAUX								
CH POTENSAC CRU BOURGEOIS, MEDOC	30	78, 80, 84	78, 84	78, 79, 81, 82, 84	78, 79, 81, 82, 83	74, 81, 82, 83	82, 83, 85, 86	82, 83, 85, 86
CH COS D'ESTOURNEL SECOND GROWTH, ST-ESTEPHE	32	78	78, 79, 80	78, 79, 80	78, 79, 80	78, 79, 80, 81, 82, 84	78, 79, 80, 81, 82, 83, 84	79, 80, 81, 82, 83, 84, 85
CH LYNCH-BAGES FIFTH GROWTH, PAUILLAC	34	78, 80, 81	78, 80, 81, 83	78, 80, 81, 83, 84	78, 80, 81, 82, 83, 84	78, 80, 81, 82, 83, 84, 85, 87	80, 81, 82, 85, 87	80, 82, 85, 87
CH GRUAUD LAROSE SECOND GROWTH, ST JULIEN	36	79, 80, 84	78, 79, 80, 81, 84	78, 79, 80, 81, 84	78, 79, 81, 85	78, 81, 85, 87	78, 83, 85, 87	78, 82, 85, 87
CH MARGAUX FIRST GROWTH, MARGAUX	38	79, 80	79, 80	79, 80, 84	79, 80, 84	79, 80, 81, 84	79, 81, 84, 85, 87	78, 79, 81, 85, 87
CH HAUT-BRION FIRST GROWTH, GRAVES	40	80, 81	78, 80, 81	78, 80, 81, 84	78, 79, 80, 81, 84	78, 79, 81, 82, 84	78, 79, 82, 84, 87	79, 82, 84, 87
CH PETRUS POMEROL	44	78, 80	78, 80, 84	78, 80, 84	78, 80, 84	78, 80, 81, 84	78, 79, 80, 81, 84, 87	79, 81, 83, 84, 87
CH CANON PREMIER GRAND CRU CLASSE, ST-EMILION	46	78	78, 80, 83	78, 80, 81, 83	78, 80, 81, 83	78, 79, 80, 81, 83	78, 79, 80, 81, 82, 83, 87	78, 79, 80, 81, 82, 83, 85, 87
CH MONBOUSQUET GRAND CRU, ST-EMILION	48	79, 80, 83	79, 80, 83	78, 80, 81, 83	78, 81, 83, 85	78, 81, 85, 86	78, 82, 85, 86	82, 85, 86
BURGUNDY								
LA TACHE, DOMAINE DE LA ROMANEE – CONTI GRAND CRU, COTE DE NUITS	58	78	78	78, 79, 80, 82	79, 80, 82	79, 80, 82	79, 80, 82	79, 80, 81, 82
BEAUNE VIGNES FRANCHES, CLOS DES URSULES, LOUIS JADOT PREMIER CRU, COTE DE BEAUNE	60	78, 80, 82, 84, 86	78, 80, 82, 84, 86	78, 80, 82, 84, 85	78, 80, 81, 82, 84, 85, 87	78, 79, 81, 82, 84, 85, 87	78, 79, 81, 82, 84, 85, 87	78, 79, 81, 85, 87
MORGON, JEAN DESCOMBES CRU BEAUJOLAIS	70	82, 84, 86, 87	82, 85, 86, 87	85, 86, 87, 88	85, 86, 85	85, 88	85, 88	
RHONE								
COTE ROTIE, COTES BRUNE ET BLONDE, GUIGAL COTE ROTIE	84	78, 80, 81, 82	78, 80, 81, 82	80, 81, 82, 84	79, 80, 81, 82, 84	79, 80, 81, 82, 83, 84	79, 80, 81, 82, 83, 84	79, 80, 81, 83, 84
HERMITAGE LA CHAPELLE, PAUL JABOULET AINE HERMITAGE	86	80, 81	80, 81	78, 79, 80	78, 79, 82, 84	78, 82, 84	78, 82, 86, 87	78, 82, 85, 86, 87

WINE	PAGE	1989	1990	1991	1992	1993	1994	1995
CH DE BEAUCASTEL, CHATEAUNEUF-DU-PAPE SOUTHERN RHONE	88	78, 80, 82, 84	78, 80, 81, 82, 84	78, 80, 81, 82, 84	78, 79, 80, 81, 82, 84, 85	78, 79, 80, 81, 82, 84, 85	78, 80, 81, 82, 83, 84, 85	78, 80, 81, 83, 85, 86
ITALY								
BARBARESCO, GAJA PIEDMONT	102	79, 80	79, 80, 81	79, 80, 81	79, 80, 81	79, 80, 81, 82	78, 79, 81, 82, 83	78, 81, 82, 83, 85
TIGNANELLO, ANTINORI NORTHERN TUSCANY	104	78, 80	80, 81, 82	80, 81, 82	80, 81, 82, 83	81, 82, 83	81, 82, 83	82, 85, 86
BRUNELLO DI MONTALCINO, IL POGGIONE SOUTHERN TUSCANY	106	79, 80, 81	78, 79, 80, 81, 82	78, 80, 81, 82	78, 80, 81, 82	78, 80, 81, 83, 86	80, 81, 83, 86, 87	83, 85, 86, 87, 88
AMARONE MAZZANO, MASI VENETO	110	75, 76, 79, 80	75, 76, 79, 80, 81	75, 76, 78, 79, 81, 83	75, 76, 78, 79, 81, 83	75, 76, 78, 79, 81, 83	75, 76, 78, 79, 81, 83	75, 76, 78, 79, 81, 83
SPAIN								
IMPERIAL RESERVA, CVNE RIOJA	114	78, 81	78, 81	78, 80, 81	78, 80, 81, 82	78, 80, 82, 85	78, 80, 82, 85	78, 80, 82, 85, 87
GRAN CORONAS, MAS LA PLANA, TORRES PENEDES CABERNET	116	78, 82	78, 82	78, 81	78, 81, 83, 85	81, 83, 85	81, 83, 85	81, 83, 85
PORTUGAL								
TAYLOR'S VINTAGE AND QUINTA DE VARGELLAS VINTAGE PORT	122	63, 75, 76	63, 66, 75, 76	63, 66, 70, 75, 76, 78	63, 66, 70, 75, 76, 78	63, 66, 70, 75, 76, 78	63, 66, 70, 75, 76, 78, 82, 84	63, 66, 70, 75, 76, 78, 80, 82, 84
CALIFORNIA								
RIDGE GEYSERVILLE ZINFANDEL CALIFORNIA ZINFANDEL	128	78, 80, 81	80, 81, 82, 84	80, 81, 82, 84	81, 82, 83, 84, 85, 86	81, 83, 84, 85, 86, 87	83, 85, 87	83, 85, 87
HEITZ MARTHA'S VINEYARD CABERNET SAUVIGNON SINGLE VINEYARD NAPA CABERNET	130	78, 79, 80	78, 79, 80, 81	78, 79, 80, 81, 83	78, 79, 80, 83, 84	79, 80, 83, 84	80, 83, 84	80, 83, 84
ROBERT MONDAVI CABERNET SAUVIGNON RESERVE/OPUS ONE OAKVILLE CABERNETS	132	78, 79, 82	78, 79, 80, 81, 82	78, 79, 80, 81, 82, 84, 85	79, 80, 81, 82, 84, 85	79, 80, 81, 83, 84, 85	80, 81, 83, 84, 85	83, 84, 85, 86
SAINTSBURY PINOT NOIR CARNEROS PINOT NOIR	136	81, 84	81, 83, 84	81, 83, 84	83, 84, 85	84, 85	85, 86, 87	86, 87
RIDGE MONTE BELLO CABERNET SAUVIGNON SANTA CRUZ CABERNET	138	81, 82	80, 81, 82	81, 82	81, 82	81, 85, 86	81, 85, 86	81, 84, 85, 86
REST OF THE AMERICAS								
THE EYRIE VINEYARDS PINOT NOIR RESERVE OREGON PINOT NOIR	144	78, 79, 82	78, 79, 81, 82, 84	78, 79, 81, 82, 84	79, 80, 81, 83, 86	80, 81, 83, 86	80, 81, 83, 86	80, 81, 83, 86, 87
AUSTRALIA								
PENFOLDS GRANGE HERMITAGE SOUTH AUSTRALIA SHIRAZ	150	78, 80	78, 80	78, 79, 80	78, 79, 80, 82	79, 80, 81, 82	79, 80, 81, 82	79, 80, 81, 82, 83
WYNNS COONAWARRA ESTATE CABERNET SAUVIGNON COONAWARRA CABERNET	154	82, 83	82, 83, 84	82, 83, 84, 85	84, 85	84, 85	84, 85, 87	85, 86, 87
YARRA YERING DRY RED No. 1 VICTORIA CABERNET	156	79, 80, 81, 82	78, 79, 80, 81, 82	78, 79, 80, 81, 82, 83, 84	78, 79, 81, 82, 83, 84	78, 81, 82, 83, 84, 85, 88	78, 82, 83, 84, 85, 86, 88	83, 84, 85, 86, 87, 88

WINE	PAGE	1989	1990	1991	1992	1993	1994	1995
WHITE WINES								
BORDEAUX								
CH D'YQUEM/YGREC* PREMIER GRAND CRU CLASSE, SAUTERNES	52	85*, 86*	76, 85*, 86*	76, 85*	76	76	76	76, 77, 80
BURGUNDY								
CHEVALIER-MONTRACHET, DOMAINE LEFLAIVE GRAND CRU, COTE DE BEAUNE	62	78, 79, 81, 82	78, 79, 81, 82	78, 82, 84	78, 84	78, 84, 87	78, 84, 87	
CHABLIS GRAND CRU, LES CLOS, RAVENEAU CHABLIS GRAND CRU	66	79, 82, 84	82, 84, 85	82, 84, 85	78, 81, 82, 84, 85	78, 81, 83	78, 81, 83, 87	78, 81, 83, 87
CH FUISSE, VIEILLES VIGNES, JEAN-JACQUES VINCENT MACONNAIS	68	78, 79, 81, 84	78, 79, 81, 84	78, 79, 81, 82, 84	78, 79, 81, 82, 84, 85	79, 81, 82, 84, 85, 87	82, 84, 85, 86, 87	82, 84, 86, 87
CHAMPAGNE								
ROEDERER CRISTAL CHAMPAGNE	74	75, 77, 79, 81	77, 79, 81	77, 81	77, 81, 82	77, 82	82, 83	82, 83
ALSACE & LOIRE								
RIESLING CLOS STE-HUNE, TRIMBACH ALSACE	80	75, 77, 79, 81, 82	75, 77, 79, 81, 82	75, 76, 77, 79, 81, 82	75, 76, 77, 78, 79, 81, 82	75, 76, 77, 79, 81, 82	75, 76, 77, 78, 81, 82, 83, 85	75, 76, 77, 78, 81, 83, 85
VOUVRAY, PRINCE PONIATOWSKI LOIRE CHENIN BLANC	82	78, 79	78, 79, 82	78, 81, 82, 83, 85, 87	81, 82, 83, 85, 87	81, 82, 83, 85, 86, 87	81, 83, 85, 86, 87, 88	81, 83, 84, 85, 86, 87, 88
GERMANY								
WEHLENER SONNENUHR, J J PRUM MIDDLE MOSEL	94	76, 77, 79	76, 77, 79, 82	76, 77, 79, 82, 83	75, 76, 79, 82, 83	75, 79, 80, 81, 83, 84, 85	75, 79, 80, 81, 83, 84, 85	75, 79, 80, 81, 83, 84, 85, 86
HATTENHEIMER MANNBERG, LANGWERTH VON SIMMERN RHEINGAU	96	78, 80, 81, 82	79, 81, 82, 84, 85	79, 82, 84, 85	79, 84, 85	79, 84, 85, 86	79, 85, 86, 87	79, 85, 86, 87
CALIFORNIA								
SONOMA-CUTRER CHARDONNAY LES PIERRES SONOMA CHARDONNAY	134	81, 82, 83, 84	81, 82, 84, 85	81, 82, 84, 85	81, 82, 85, 87	82, 85, 87	82, 86, 87	86, 87
CHALONE CHARDONNAY RESERVE CALIFORNIA CHARDONNAY	140	79, 81, 83	80, 81, 82, 83, 86	80, 81, 82, 83, 84, 86	80, 81, 82, 83, 84, 86	80, 81, 82, 84, 85, 86	81, 82, 84, 85, 86, 87	81, 82, 85, 86, 87
AUSTRALIA								
PETALUMA CHARDONNAY ADELAIDE HILLS CHARDONNAY	152	78, 79, 80, 81, 82, 83	78, 79, 80, 82, 83	79, 80, 82, 83, 85	80, 82, 83, 84, 85	80, 84, 85, 86	84, 85, 86	84, 85, 86
LINDEMANS HUNTER SEMILLON HUNTER VALLEY SEMILLON	158	79, 80, 82, 83	79, 80, 83, 84	83, 84	83, 84, 85	84, 85, 86, 87	84, 85, 86, 87, 88	84, 85, 86, 87, 88

THE WINE CROSS-REFERENCE INDEX

This index provides ageing data on over 550 wines, wine districts and countries, appellations and châteaux. Use the index to discover when to drink a wine not covered by a Timechart in this book. Many of the references are to specific Timecharts, with suggestions on how much to accelerate or retard the chart (see *How to Use The Timecharts*, page 20, for an explanation of this process) to apply the information to your bottle. Other references are to pages where you will find written advice on how to judge the ageing qualities of particular wines. The right-hand column of the Index suggests briefly when to drink the wines. The comments usually précis the detailed notes given in the text.

References to "A" and "B" are to the charts on page 19 which show the maturity curves of wines made for early consumption.

KEY "A" = Drink as young as possible. See chart A on p19   "B" = Drink within 2-3 years. See chart B on p19   (r) = red (w) = white
Aus = Australia; AVA = American Viticultural Area; Bdx = Bordeaux; Calif = California; Ch = Château; Dom = Domaine; Fr = France; Ger = Germany; Gra = Graves

KEY WORD	COUNTRY/REGION	CHART PAGE	TEXT PAGE	COMMENTARY
ADELAIDE HILLS	Australia		146	Cool climate wines worth ageing
AGLIANICO DEL VULTURE	Italy		109	Drink within 4-8 yrs
ALBANA DI ROMAGNA	Italy		109	B
ALELLA	Spain		118	Sweet whites can improve in bottle
ALENTEJO	Portugal		119	Some ageworthy reds
ALIGOTE	Burgundy, Fr		57	Drink within 2 yrs
ALOXE-CORTON	Burgundy, Fr		56	Côte de Beaune village: 4-15 yrs
ALSACE	France	80	76	B to 12 yrs
ALTO ADIGE	Italy		108	Mostly B
ALEXANDER VALLEY	AVA, Calif, USA	128	125	Ridge Geyserville chart shows this big area's class. Some ageworthy Chardonnays
AMARONE	Italy	110		Ageing mandatory
ANDERSON VALLEY	AVA, Calif, USA		125	Noted for sparkling wines. Still whites from good producers also age
ANJOU	France	82	77	A for Anjou Rosé to decades for late-picked whites
ANTINORI	Italy	104		
APREMONT	France		90	See Savoie; B
ARROYO SECO	AVA, Calif, USA		125	Good Riesling (can age); early-maturing Chardonnays
ASTI	Italy		100	A
AUSTRALIA			146	NB: Southern Hemisphere harvests 6 mths before Northern
AUSTRIA			124	Mostly B; some exceptions
AUXEY-DURESSES	Burgundy, Fr		55	Côte de Beaune village: up to 6 yrs
BADEN	Germany		98	Germany's earliest-maturing wines
BAIRRADA	Portugal		121	Good ageworthy reds
BANDOL	France		91	Ageing demanded for reds; pinks are B
BANYULS	France		91	Wide variety of styles; mostly ready once bottled
BARBARESCO	Italy	102	99	
BARDOLINO	Italy		108	Some A, typically B
BAROLO	Italy	102	99	
BAROSSA	Australia		148	Some of Australia's earliest-maturing wines
BARSAC	Bordeaux, Fr	52	50	May mature slightly faster than Sauternes
BASTOR-LAMONTAGNE, CH	Sauternes, Fr		51	Accelerate Yquem chart by at least 3 yrs

KEY WORD	COUNTRY/REGION	CHART PAGE	TEXT PAGE	COMMENTARY
BATAILLEY, CH	Pauillac, Bdx, Fr	34	28	Follow Lynch-Bages chart
BATARD-MONTRACHET	Burgundy, Fr	62	55	May not last quite as long as Chevalier
BEAUCASTEL, CH DE	Châteauneuf-du-Pape, Fr	88	79	
BEAUJOLAIS	Burgundy, Fr	70	65	Mostly B, but see p65 for exceptions
BEAUNE	Burgundy, Fr	60	55	Can make wine for long ageing, but very variable
BEERENAUSLESE	Germany		92	Indestructible
BELGRAVE, CH	St-Laurent, Bdx, Fr	36	28	Accelerate Gruaud Larose chart by 1 yr
BELLET AOC	Provence, Fr		91	Mostly B
BERGERAC	France		91	Whites are B, reds 3-6 yrs
BEYCHEVELLE, CH	St-Julien, Bdx, Fr	36	28	Accelerate Gruaud Larose chart by 1 yr
BIONDI-SANTI	Italy	106	101	
BLAYE	Bordeaux, Fr		54	Lighter clarets, 2-5 yrs
BOCA	Italy	102	100	At least 3 yrs ahead of Gaja, often different
BONNES MARES	Burgundy, Fr	58	55	Morey St Denis Grand Cru, Côte de Nuits
BONNEZEAUX	Loire, Fr	82	76	
BORDEAUX, AC (r)	France		54	B
BORDEAUX, AC (w)	France		54	B, sometimes A
BOURG, COTES DE	Bordeaux, Fr		54	Ready at 2 yrs
BOURGEUIL	France		90	Drink within 3 yrs. Exceptions: see p90
BOURGOGNE, AC	Burgundy, Fr		55	Mostly B but there are exceptions
BOYD-CANTENAC, CH	Cantenac-Margaux, Bdx, Fr	38	28	Accelerate Margaux chart by 2 yrs
BRAMATERRA	Italy	102	100	At least 3 yrs ahead of Gaja
BRANAIRE-DUCRU, CH	St-Julien, Bdx, Fr	36	28	Accelerate Gruaud Larose chart by 1 yr
BRANE-CANTENAC, CH	Cantenac-Margaux, Bdx, Fr	38	28	Accelerate Margaux chart by 2 yrs
BRICCO DEL DRAGO	Italy	102	100	At least 2 yrs ahead of Gaja
BRICCO DEL MANZONI	Italy	102	100	At least 2 yrs ahead of Gaja
BROUILLY	Burgundy, Fr	70	64	
BRUNELLO DI MONTALCINO	Italy	106	101	
BULGARIA			124	Whites now! Reds last up to 10 yrs, mainly best by 5
BURGUNDY			55, 64	Burgundies are notoriously unpredictable
BUZET	SW France		91	Worthy reds, drink at 3-6 yrs
CABARDES	SW France			2-5 yrs
CAHORS	SW France		91	Variable: 3-10 yrs
CAIRANNE	Rhône, Fr	88	79	Can age up to 4 yrs
CALIFORNIA	USA		125	Basic wines A up to marvels at 20 yrs
CALON-SEGUR, CH	St-Estèphe, Bdx, Fr	32	28	Accelerate Cos d'Estournel chart by 2 yrs
CAMENSAC, CH DE	St-Laurent, Bdx, Fr	36	28	Accelerate Gruaud Larose chart by 1 yr
CANON, CH	Canon-Fronsac, Bdx, Fr	44	54	Accelerate Petrus chart by 1 yr
CANON DE BREM, CH	Canon-Fronsac, Bdx, Fr	44	54	Accelerate Petrus chart by 1 yr
CANON-FRONSAC	Bordeaux, Fr	44	54	Accelerate Petrus chart by 2 yrs
CANTEMERLE, CH	Macau, Bdx, Fr	36	28	Accelerate Gruaud Larose chart by 1 yr

KEY WORD	COUNTRY/REGION	CHART PAGE	TEXT PAGE	COMMENTARY
CANTENAC	Bordeaux, Fr		28	
CANTENAC-BROWN, CH	Cantenac-Margaux, Bdx, Fr	38	28	Accelerate Margaux chart by 2 yrs
CARAMINO	Italy	102	100	At least 2 yrs ahead of Gaja, often different
CAREMA	Italy	102	100	At least 2 yrs ahead of Gaja, often different
CARINENA	Spain		118	Mostly B
CARMIGNANO	Italy	104	100	
CARNEROS, LOS	AVA, Calif, USA	136	127	See Saintsbury chart for conditions & vintages, & for Pinot
CARSO	Italy		108	Mostly B, but Terrano del Carso can last longer
CASTEL DEL MONTE	Italy		109	5-8 yrs
CENTRAL COAST	California, USA		126	Cheapest are B; best up to 10 yrs
CHALK HILL	AVA, Calif, USA		125	Mostly B
CHABLIS	Burgundy, Fr	66	64	Varies according to status & producer
CHALON, CH	Jura, Fr		90	Leave as long as possible
CHALONE	California, USA	140	125	Chalone is the sole winery in this AVA
CHAMBERTIN	Burgundy, Fr	58	56	Capable of long ageing from good producer
CHAMBOLLE-MUSIGNY	Burgundy, Fr	58	56	Côte de Nuits village: 5-12 yrs
CHAMPAGNE	France	74	72	
CHANTEGRIVE, CH (r)	Graves, Bdx, Fr		28, 54	Accelerate Haut-Brion chart by 3 yrs
CHANTEGRIVE, CH (w)	Graves, Bdx, Fr		54	
CHASSAGNE-MONTRACHET	Burgundy, Fr	58	57	Generally earlier-maturing than Puligny
ChATEAUNEUF-DU-PAPE	Rhône, Fr	88	79	Wide variations
CHENAS	Burgundy, Fr	70	64	
CHEVAL BLANC, CH	St-Emilion, Bdx, Fr	44	42	Petrus chart (p44) is a better guide than Canon chart (p46)
CHEVALIER-MONTRACHET	Burgundy, Fr	62	57	None will last longer than Leflaive's
CHIANTI	Italy	104	101	Wide variations according to status & producer: B to 10 yrs
CHILE	S America		143	Whites mostly B; reds up to 10 yrs
CHINON	Loire, Fr		90	Drink within 3 yrs. Exceptions: see p90
CHIROUBLES	Burgundy, Fr	70	64	
CIRO	Italy		109	Red repays ageing up to 7 yrs
CLARET, see Bordeaux AC (r)				
CLARE-WATERVALE	S Australia		148	Some Rieslings worth ageing 5 yrs
CLEAR LAKE	AVA, Calif, USA		125	Cabernet Sauvignon does well, but no clear track record yet
CLERC-MILON, CH	Pauillac, Bdx, Fr	34	28	Follow Lynch-Bages chart
CLIMENS, CH	Sauternes, Bdx, Fr	52	51	Accelerate Yquem chart by 3 yrs
CLOS DES LAMBRAYS	Burgundy, Fr	58	55	Côte de Nuits *Grand Cru*
CLOS DU MARQUIS	St-Julien, Bdx, Fr	36	54	Accelerate Gruaud Larose chart by 3 yrs
CLOS DES MOUCHES (BEAUNE)	Burgundy, Fr	60	55	Red earlier-maturing than Clos des Ursules, white as Puligny
CLOS DE LA ROCHE	Burgundy, Fr	58	56	Côte de Nuits *Grand Cru*
CLOS ST-DENIS	Burgundy, Fr	58	56	Côte de Nuits *Grand Cru*
CLOS STE-HUNE	Alsace, Fr	80	76	
CLOS ST JACQUES	Burgundy, Fr	58	56	Côte de Nuits *Premier Cru*

KEY WORD	COUNTRY/REGION	CHART PAGE	TEXT PAGE	COMMENTARY
CLOS DE TART	Burgundy, Fr	58	56	Côte de Nuits *Grand Cru*
CLOS DE VOUGEOT	Burgundy, Fr	58	55	Can make wine for long ageing, but rarely as long as La Tâche
COLARES	Portugal		121	These need 12 yrs plus
COLLI ORIENTALI DEL FRIULI	Italy		108	Mainly B
COLLIOURE	Roussillon, Fr		91	B to 8 yrs
COLUMBIA VALLEY	Washington, USA		143	Improving every yr
CONDRIEU	Rhône, Fr		78	Time brings interest but not necessarily improvement
COONAWARRA	S Australia	154	148	Variable but ageworthy reds; whites: B
CORBIERES	Rousillon, Fr		91	Mainly B but there are noble exceptions
CORNAS	Rhône, Fr	86	78	Follow Hermitage chart
CORSICA	France	58	91	B to 5 yrs
CORTON	Burgundy, Fr	58	56	Côte de Beaune *Grand Cru* (r)
CORTON-CHARLEMAGNE	Burgundy, Fr	62	56	Côte de Beaune *Grand Cru* (w) can last as long as Chevalier
COS D'ESTOURNEL, CH	St-Estèphe, Bdx, Fr	32	28	
COS LABORY, CH	St-Estèphe, Bdx, Fr	32	38	Accelerate Cos d'Estournel chart by 2 yrs
COTE DE BEAUNE	Burgundy, Fr	60	55	Typically mature at 3-6 yrs
COTE DE BEAUNE-VILLAGES	Burgundy, Fr		55	Typically mature at 3-6 yrs
COTE DE BROUILLY	Burgundy, Fr	70	64	Can last longer than Brouilly
COTE CHALONNAISE	Burgundy, Fr		64	Most whites ready at 2-3 yrs; reds 3-5 yrs
COTE ROTIE	Rhône, Fr	84	78	
COTEAUX D'AIX-EN-PROVENCE	Rhône, Fr		91	Longevity increasing every yr
COTEAUX CHAMPENOIS	Champagne, Fr		90	B
COTEAUX DU LAYON	Loire, Fr	82	76	Can go on & on, but variable
COTEAUX DU TRICASTIN	Rhône, Fr		91	Chart B, sometimes up to 4 yrs
COTES DE BERGERAC	SW France		91	Sweet whites can last 5 yrs
COTES DE BOURG	Bordeaux, Fr		54	Lightish, variable reds
COTES DE CASTILLON	Bordeaux, Fr		54	Rustic Bordeaux reds up to 6 yrs
COTES DE DURAS	SW France		90	Usually leaner & earlier than Bergerac
COTES DE FRANCS	Bordeaux, Fr		54	Bumpkin but improving Bordeaux reds: up to 6 yrs
COTES DU FRONTONNAIS	SW France		91	Light Toulouse reds: 2-5 yrs
COTES DU LUBERON	Rhône, Fr		90	Variable; mainly B
COTES DE LA MALEPERE	Roussillon, Fr		91	Drink within 3-5 yrs
COTES DE MONTRAVEL	SW France		91	Sweet whites can last up to 6 yrs
COTES DE NUITS-VILLAGES	Burgundy, Fr		55	Typically mature at 3-6 yrs
COTES DE PROVENCE	Provence, Fr		91	More worthy of ageing each yr
COTES DU RHONE	Rhône, Fr	88	79	Drink most at 2-3 yrs
COTES DU RHONE-VILLAGES	Rhône, Fr	88	79	Drink most at 3-5 yrs
COTES DE ROUSSILLON-VILLAGES	Roussillon, Fr		91	Drink at 3-5 yrs although some are B
COTES DE ST MONT	SW France		90	Mainly B
COTES DU VENTOUX	Rhône, Fr	88	90	Variable: reds mainly B, rosés even A
COTES DU VIVARAIS	Rhône, Fr		90	Mainly B

KEY WORD	COUNTRY/REGION	CHART PAGE	TEXT PAGE	COMMENTARY
COULEE DE SERRANT	Loire, Fr		77	These demand long ageing
COUTET, CH	Barsac, Bdx, Fr	52	51	Accelerate Yquem chart by 3 yrs
COWRA	New South Wales, Aus	152	149	Fast-maturing Chardonnay
CRIOTS-BATARD-MONTRACHET	Burgundy, Fr	62		See Bâtard-Montrachet
CROIZET-BAGES, CH	Pauillac, Bdx, Fr	34	28	Follow Lynch-Bages chart
CROZES-HERMITAGE	Rhône, Fr	86	78	Mostly ready in 3 yrs but Thalabert can last more than 5 yrs
CVNE	Rioja, Spain	114	112	
DAO	Portugal		121	Reds usually best at 6-12 yrs; whites often prematurely aged
DAUZAC, CH	Labarde-Margaux, Bdx, Fr	38	28	Accelerate Margaux chart by 2 yrs
DE FIEUZAL, CH (r)	Graves, Bdx, Fr	40	28	Accelerate Haut-Brion chart by 2 yrs
DE FIEUZAL, CH (w)	Graves, Bdx, Fr		54	B; recent vintages more ageworthy
DESCOMBES, JEAN	Burgundy, Fr	70	64	
DESMIRAIL, CH	Margaux, Bdx, Fr	38	28	Accelerate Margaux chart by 2 yrs
DOISY-DAENE, CH	Barsac, Bdx, Fr	52	51	Accelerate Yquem chart by 3 yrs
DOMAINE DE CHEVALIER (r)	Graves, Bdx, Fr	40	29	See Haut-Brion chart
DOMAINE DE CHEVALIER (w)	Graves, Bdx, Fr		54	One of Bordeaux's longest-living dry whites: up to 15 yrs
DOURO	Portugal		121	Ageworthy reds best within 4-10 yrs
DRY CREEK VALLEY	AVA, Calif, USA	128	126	Cabernet, Sauvignon Blanc & Zinfandel: all can age well
DUCRU-BEAUCAILLOU, CH	St-Julien, Bdx, Fr	36	28	Accelerate Gruaud Larose chart by 1 yr
DUHART-MILON-ROTHSCHILD, CH	Pauillac, Bdx, Fr	34	28	Follow Lynch-Bages chart
DURFORT-VIVENS, CH	Margaux, Bdx, Fr	38	28	Accelerate Margaux chart by 2 yrs
ECHEZEAUX	Burgundy, Fr	58	56	Côte de Nuits *Grand Cru*: can make wine for long ageing
EDEN VALLEY	Australia		148	Some ageable whites
EDNA VALLEY	AVA, Calif, USA		125	Cool conditions make ageworthy Chardonnays & sparkling wine
EISWEIN	Germany		92	Longevity controversial but usually much less than Trockenbeerenauslese
EMERALD REISLING	California, USA		125	California grape, drink young. B, sometimes A
EMILIA-ROMAGNA	Italy		109	Lots of A & some B
ENGLAND			124	Up to 4 yrs in bottle can soften
ENTRE-DEUX-MERS	Bordeaux, Fr		54	White A, some Bs
EYRIE VINEYARDS	Oregon, USA	144	142	
FARA	Italy	102	100	At least 3 yrs ahead of Gaja, often different
FARGUES, CH DE	Sauternes, Bdx, Fr	52	51	Accelerate Yquem chart by 3 yrs
FAUGERES	France		91	Mainly B but some demand longer
FERRIERE, CH	Margaux, Bdx, Fr	38	28	Accelerate Margaux chart by 2 yrs
FIANO DI AVELLINO	Italy		109	Extraordinary white can take 15 yrs
FIGEAC	St-Emilion, Bdx, Fr	44	42	Petrus chart (p44) is a better guide than Canon (p46)
FITOU	Roussillon, Fr		91	Some of the region's most robust reds
FIXIN	Burgundy, Fr		55	Typically mature at 3-6 yrs
FLEURIE	Burgundy, Fr	70	65	Domaine bottlings follow Morgon chart
FORTS DE LATOUR, LES	Pauillac, Bdx, Fr	34	54	Released only when judged broachable
FRANCIACORTA	Italy		108	Best at 3-5 yrs

KEY WORD	COUNTRY/REGION	CHART PAGE	TEXT PAGE	COMMENTARY
FRANKEN	Germany		98	Whites can last surprisingly well
FRIULI-VENEZIA-GIULIA	Italy		108	Mostly B
FRONSAC	Bordeaux, Fr	44	54	Accelerate Petrus chart by 2 yrs
FUISSE, CH	Burgundy, Fr	68	64	
GAILLAC	SW France		91	Sweet whites & the very best reds can be aged
GAJA	Italy	102	99	Even the Chardonnay needs ageing
GALICIA	Spain		118	Definitely A
GARRAFEIRA	Portugal		121	Usually mature when exported
GATTINARA	Italy	102	100	2 yrs ahead of Gaja but often different
GEVREY-CHAMBERTIN	Burgundy, Fr		56	Côte de Nuits: can make wine for long ageing
GEYSERVILLE	California, USA	128	126	Good for ageworthy Zinfandels
GHEMME	Italy	102	100	Some B, otherwise 2 yrs ahead of Gaja
GIGONDAS	Rhône, Fr	88	79	Accelerate Beaucastel chart by 3 yrs
GILETTE, CH	Sauternes, Bdx, Fr		50	Sold only when ready to drink
GISCOURS, CH	Labarde-Margaux, Bdx, Fr	38	28	Accelerate Margaux chart by 2 yrs
GIVRY	Burgundy, Fr	60	64	Drink at 3-5 yrs
GRAND-PUY DUCASSE, CH	Pauillac, Bdx, Fr	34	28	Follow Lynch-Bages chart
GRAND-PUY-LACOSTE, CH	Pauillac, Bdx, Fr	34	28	Follow Lynch-Bages chart
GRAVES	Bordeaux, Fr	40	28	Wide variation including some ageworthy whites
GRAVES DE VAYRES	Bordeaux, Fr		54	A or B
GREECE			124	Reds need 2-4 yrs in bottle; otherwise A
GRILLET, CH	Rhône, Fr		79	They last, but don't necessarily improve after 5 yrs
GRUAUD-LAROSE, CH	St-Julien, Bdx, Fr	36	28	
GRUMELLO	Italy		109	Drink at 3-5 yrs
GUENOC VALLEY	AVA, Calif, USA		125	One-winery AVA. See Clear Lake
GUIGAL	Rhône, Fr	84	78	
GUIRAUD, CH	Sauternes, Bdx, Fr	52	51	Accelerate Yquem chart by 3 yrs
HATTENHEIMER MANNBERG	Germany	96	92	
HAUT BATAILLEY, CH	Pauillac, Bdx, Fr	34	28	Follow Lynch-Bages chart
HAUT MONTRAVEL	France		91	
HAUT POITOU	Loire, Fr		90	Allow 1 yr in bottle to soften
HAUT-BAGES LIBERAL, CH	Pauillac, Bdx, Fr	34	28	Follow Lynch-Bages chart
HAUT-BRION, CH	Pessac, Gra, Bdx, Fr	40	28	
HAUT-BRION BLANC	Pessac, Gra, Bdx, Fr		54	Drink at 5-6 yrs
HAUTES COTES DE BEAUNE	Burgundy, Fr		55	Typically mature at 3-6 yrs; some Bs
HAUTES COTES DE NUITS	Burgundy, Fr		55	Typically mature at 3-6 yrs; some Bs
HAUT-MEDOC	Bordeaux, Fr		28	Follow Potensac chart for best examples
HEITZ	California, USA	130	125	
HERMITAGE	Rhône, Fr	86	78	Whites mainly B
HOWELL MOUNTAIN	AVA, Calif, USA		125	Cabernet Sauvignon & Zinfandel. No clear ageing track record
HUNGARY			124	Whites and most reds are usually at or past their best once exported

KEY WORD	COUNTRY/REGION	CHART PAGE	TEXT PAGE	COMMENTARY
HUNTER VALLEY	New South Wales, Aus	158	148, 149	Very variable
IDAHO	USA		142	Longevity not high on the current agenda
INFERNO	Italy		109	Drink at 3-5 yrs
IRANCY	Burgundy, Fr		90	
IROULEGUY AOC	SW France		91	Mainly 3-5 yrs
ISSAN, CH D'	Cantenac-Margaux, Bdx, Fr	38	28	Accelerate Margaux chart by 2 yrs
JABOULET AINE, PAUL	Rhône, Fr	86	78	
JADOT, LOUIS	Burgundy, Fr	60	56	
JEREZ	Spain		118	Sold when ready. Drink Fino & Manzanilla soon
JULIENAS	Burgundy, Fr	70	65	Domaine bottlings follow Morgon chart
JUMILLA	Spain		118	Usually ready to drink once exported
JURA	France		90	Vin Jaune needs 15 yrs in bottle; most others B to 6 yrs
JURANCON	SW France		91	Admirably long lifespan
KIRWAN, CH	Cantenac-Margaux, Bdx, Fr	38	28	Accelerate Margaux chart by 2 yrs
KNIGHTS VALLEY	AVA, Calif, USA		125	Between northern Napa & Sonoma. Late harvest Riesling excellent
LADOIX-SERRIGNY	Burgundy, Fr	60	55	Typically mature at 3-6 yrs
LAFAURIE-PEYRAGUEY, CH	Sauternes, Bdx, Fr	52	51	Matures about 3 yrs ahead of Yquem
LAFITE-ROTHSCHILD, CH	Pauillac, Bdx, Fr	34	28	Retard Lynch-Bages chart by 3 yrs
LAFLEUR	Pomerol, Bdx, Fr	44	42	Ages as Petrus
LAFON-ROCHET, CH	St-Estèphe, Bdx, Fr	32	28	Accelerate Cos d'Estournel chart by 2 yrs
LAGRANGE, CH	St-Julien, Bdx, Fr	36	29	Accelerate Gruaud Larose chart by 1 yr
LAGUNE, CH LA	Ludon, Bdx, Fr	38	28	Accelerate Margaux chart by 2 yrs
LALANDE DE POMEROL	Bordeaux, Fr	44	43	Country cousins to Petrus
LAMOTHE-GUIGNARD, CH	Sauternes, Bdx, Fr	52	51	Accelerate Yquem chart by 3 yrs
LANDWEIN	Germany		92	Mainly A; some B
LANGHORNE CREEK	Australia		148	Many reds ready by 2 yrs
LANGOA-BARTON, CH	St-Julien, Bdx, Fr	36	28	Accelerate Gruaud Larose chart by 1 yr
LASCOMBES, CH	Margaux, Bdx, Fr	38	28	Accelerate Margaux chart by 2 yrs
LATOUR, CH	Pauillac, Bdx, Fr	34	28	Retard Lynch-Bages chart by 4-5 yrs
LAVILLE-HAUT-BRION, CH	Graves, Bdx, Fr		54	Pre-1983: see p54
LEBANON			124	Only reds (chiefly Musar) repay ageing
LEFLAIVE, DOMAINE	Burgundy, Fr	62	57	
LEON	Spain		118	Reds can evolve perceptibly up to 5 yrs
LEOVILLE-BARTON, CH	St-Julien, Bdx, Fr	36	28	A good long-term bet
LEOVILLE-LAS CASES, CH	St-Julien, Bdx, Fr	36	28	The slowest, most concentrated Léoville
LEOVILLE-POYFERRE, CH	St-Julien, Bdx, Fr	36	28	The most variable Léoville
LESSONA	Italy	102	100	About 2 yrs ahead of Gaja, often different
LIEBFRAUMILCH	Germany		98	A
LIQUEUR MUSCAT/TOKAY	Australia		146	Ready when bottled
LIRAC	Rhone, Fr	88	79	Rosés mainly B; reds as Châteauneuf
LIVERMORE VALLEY	AVA, Calif, USA		125	Whites, especially Sauvignon Blanc, can be worth 3-5 yrs ageing

KEY WORD	COUNTRY/REGION	CHART PAGE	TEXT PAGE	COMMENTARY
LOMBARDY	Italy		108	Some reds last for 3-6 yrs
LONG ISLAND	USA		143	Some Chardonnays can repay bottle age
LOUPIAC	Bordeaux, Fr	52	50	Way ahead of Yquem
LOUVIERE, CH LA (r)	Graves, Bdx, Fr	40	28	Accelerate Haut-Brion chart by 3 yrs
LOUVIERE, CH LA (w)	Graves, Bdx, Fr	54		B
LOWER HUNTER	New South Wales, Aus		149	See Lindemans chart notes (p158/9) for weather
LUSSAC-ST-EMILION	Bordeaux, Fr		43	Accelerate Monbousquet chart by 2 yrs
LUXEMBOURG			124	Many B, but some benefit from bottle ageing
LYNCH-BAGES, CH	Pauillac, Bdx, Fr	34		
LYNCH-MOUSSAS, CH	Pauillac, Bdx, Fr	34	28	Follow Lynch-Bages chart
McDOWELL VALLEY	AVA, Calif, USA		125	Single winery area. Syrah is made to age, as is Cabernet Sauvignon
MACON (r)	Burgundy, Fr		64	B
MACON (w)	Burgundy, Fr	68	64	Mainly B; a very few are worth keeping longer
MADEIRA	Portugal		121	Usually ready to drink when sold; last indefinitely
MADIRAN	SW France		91	One of Gascony's longest-livers
MALAGA	Spain		118	Bottled when ready to drink
MALARTIC-LAGRAVIERE, CH (r)	Graves, Bdx, Fr	40	28	Accelerate Haut-Brion chart by 2 yrs
MALARTIC-LAGRAVIERE, CH (w)	Graves, Bdx, Fr	54		Can repay ageing
MALESCOT ST-EXUPERY, CH	Margaux, Bdx, Fr	38	28	Accelerate Margaux chart by 2 yrs
MANCHA, LA	Spain		118	Whites A; reds B
MARCHE	Italy		109	Mainly A & B, some exceptions
MARCHES DE BRETAGNE	France			Reds & whites mainly A
MARGARET RIVER	W Australia		148	Some of Australia's best cellar candidates
MARGAUX	Bordeaux, Fr	38	28	The famous Margaux bouquet demands time
MARGAUX, CH	Margaux, Bdx, Fr	38	28	
MARQUIS D'ALESME BECKER, CH	Margaux, Bdx, Fr	38	28	Accelerate Margaux chart by 2 yrs
MARQUIS-DE-TERME, CH	Margaux, Bdx, Fr	38	28	Accelerate Margaux chart by 2 yrs
MARSALA	Italy		109	Most are ready to drink when bottled
MARSANNAY	Burgundy, Fr		55	Typically mature at 3-6 yrs
MARTHA'S VINEYARD	Napa, Calif, USA	130		
MAS DE DAUMAS GASSAC	France		90	Needs at least 10 yrs
MASI	Italy	110	108	
MAURY	France		91	Most are ready to drink when bottled
MAZERIS, CH	Canon-Fronsac, Bdx, Fr	44	54	Accelerate Petrus chart by 1 yr
MEDOC	Bordeaux, Fr	30	28	Highest concentration of cellar candidates in the world
MENDOCINO	AVA, Calif, USA		125	Warm region. Whites mostly A; reds mostly early-maturing: B to 4 yrs
MENETOU-SALON	Loire, Fr		90	Mostly B
MERCUREY	Burgundy, Fr	60	64	Drink most at 3-5 yrs
MEURSAULT	Burgundy, Fr	64	55	Usually develop slightly ahead of Pulignys
MILAWA	Australia		148	Some light & ageworthy reds are bottled here
MINERVOIS	The Midi, Fr		91	Each vintage brings wines which last longer

KEY WORD	COUNTRY/REGION	CHART PAGE	TEXT PAGE	COMMENTARY
MISSION HAUT-BRION, CH LA	Graves, Bdx, Fr	40	29	Can take longer than Haut-Brion
MONBAZILLAC	France		91	Some can last 15 yrs & more
MONBOUSQUET, CH	France	48	42	
MONDAVI, ROBERT	Napa, Calif, USA	132	125	Huge output varies from A to 12-yr wines
MONTAGNE-ST-EMILION	Bordeaux, Fr		43	Accelerate Monbousquet chart by 2 yrs
MONTAGNY	Burgundy, Fr	62	64	Drink at 2-3 yrs
MONTALCINO	Italy	106	100	See Brunello chart
MONTEPULCIANO, VINO NOBILE DE	Italy	106	101	
MONTEPULCIANO D'ABRUZZO	Italy		109	Flexible: drink between 2 & 6 yrs
MONTEREY	AVA, Calif, USA	140	125	Wide variation in conditions but see Chalone chart for outline
MONTILLA	Spain			Ready when bottled. Drink light, dry ones fast
MONTLOUIS	Loire, Fr	82	76	The best demand ageing
MONTRACHET	Burgundy, Fr	62	57	A variable appellation
MONTROSE, CH	St-Estèphe, Bdx, Fr	32	28	Follows similar pattern to Cos d'Estournel
MORELLINO DI SCANSANO	Italy		101	Drink at 3-5 yrs
MOREY ST-DENIS	Burgundy, Fr	58	56	Côte de Nuits village: 4-15 yrs
MORGON	Burgundy, Fr	70	65	
MORNINGTON PENINSULA	Australia		147	Developing; some ageworthy reds & whites
MOSCATEL DE SETUBAL	Portugal		121	Most are ready to drink
MOSCATO	Italy		100	Drink sparkling versions as young as possible. Liqueur versions will age
MOSEL-SAAR-RUWER	Germany	94	92	From A for Tafelwein to decades
MOULIN A VENT	Burgundy, Fr	70	65	Domaine bottlings follow Morgon chart
MOULIN-PEY-LABRIE, CH	Canon-Fronsac, Fr	44	54	Accelerate Petrus chart by 1 yr
MOULIS	Bordeaux, Fr		28	Some good cellar candidates
MOUNT BARKER	W Australia		148	Can develop well in bottle
MOUTON ROTHSCHILD, CH	Pauillac, Bdx, Fr	34	28	Retard Lynch-Bages chart by 3 yrs
MOUTON-BARONNE-PHILIPPE, CH	Pauillac, Bdx, Fr	34	28	Follow Lynch-Bages chart
MUDGEE	New South Wales, Aus		149	Chardonnays living longer
MUSAR, CH	Lebanon		124	Ageing required & rewarded for reds
MUSCADET	Loire, Fr		90	B, sometimes A
MUSCAT	France		90	Vin Doux Naturel ; most are bottled when ready
MUSIGNY	Burgundy, Fr	58	55	Côte de Nuits Grand Cru
NAHE	Germany		98	Some delightful whites for 3-8 yrs
NAIRAC, CH	Sauternes, Bdx, Fr	52	51	Accelerate Yquem chart by 3 yrs
NAPA VALLEY	AVA, Calif, USA	130, 132	125	For Cabernet Sauvignon see Heitz & Mondavi charts. Chardonnays age approximately as Sonoma (page 134)
NAVARRA	Spain		118	Rosados B; reds mainly ready within 5 yrs
NEBBIOLO	Italy	102	100	Mostly B; but see p100 for exceptions
NEW ZEALAND			149	Recent vintages last best; some reds still collapse
NORTH AFRICA			124	Some reds clearly keep
NOUVEAU	France		90	Drink now, although the decline can be quite slow

KEY WORD	COUNTRY/REGION	CHART PAGE	TEXT PAGE	COMMENTARY
NOVELLO	Italy		100	Drink now!
NUITS-ST-GEORGES	Burgundy, Fr		56	Emphatically *the* Côte de Nuits town: 5-12 yrs
OLTREPO PAVESE	Italy		108	Fizz & some medium-term reds
OPUS ONE	Napa, Calif, USA	132	126	
OREGON	USA	144	142	Lifespans increasing every yr
ORVIETO	Italy		109	Mainly B, Bigi longer
PACHERENC DU VIC BILH	SW France		91	Can last & develop splendidly
PADTHAWAY	Australia		148	Wide variation; mostly B, even A
PALETTE	France		91	Long ageing demanded
PALMER, CH	Cantenac-Margaux, Bdx, Fr	38	28	Accelerate Margaux chart by 2 yrs
PASO ROBLES	AVA, Calif, USA		125	Solid, ageworthy Zinfandels (3-7 yrs) recently; Sauvignon Blanc is B
PAUILLAC	Bordeaux, Fr	34	28	Use Lynch-Bages chart for classed (except 1st) growths
PAVILLON BLANC DU CH MARGAUX	Margaux, Bdx, Fr	38	54	
PAVILLON ROUGE DU CH MARGAUX	Margaux, Bdx, Fr	38	54	Accelerate Margaux chart by 3 yrs
PECHARMANT	SW France		91	A to B
PEDESCLAUX, CH	Pauillac, Bdx, Fr	34	28	Follow Lynch-Bages chart
PENAFIEL	Spain		118	Some very serious, ageable reds
PENEDES	Spain	116	112	Whites & rosados B, reds longer
PENFOLDS GRANGE HERMITAGE	Australia	150	146	
PERNAND-VERGELESSES	Burgundy, Fr	60	55	Typically mature at 3-6 yrs, Côte de Beaune village
PESQUERA	Spain	116	118	
PETALUMA	Australia	152	148	
PETRUS, CH	Pomerol, Bdx, Fr	44	42	
PICHON-LALANDE, CH	Pauillac, Bdx, Fr	34	28	Compare Lynch-Bages chart but can last 10 yrs longer
PICHON-LONGUEVILLE BARON, CH	Pauillac, Bdx, Fr	34	28	Compare Lynch-Bages chart but can last 10 yrs longer
PICOLIT	Italy		108	Mainly ready to drink when sold, some 5 yrs
PIEDMONT, PIEMONTE	Italy	102	99	A great source of ageworthy red
PINEAU DES CHARENTES	France			Ready when bottled
POMEROL	Bordeaux, Fr	44	42	A good source of ageworthy red
POMMARD	Burgundy, Fr	60	56	Côte de Beaune village: 4-15 yrs
PONTET-CANET, CH	Pauillac, Bdx, Fr	34	28	Follow Lynch-Bages chart
PORT	Portugal	122	119	Ready to drink except for vintage & single *quinta* crusted ports
POTENSAC, CH	Médoc, Bdx, Fr	30	28	
POTTER VALLEY	AVA, Calif, USA		125	White wine country: B
POUGET, CH	Cantenac-Margaux, Bdx, Fr	38	28	Accelerate Margaux chart by 2 yrs
POUILLY-FUISSE	Burgundy, Fr	68	64	Accelerate Fuissé chart by 2 yrs
POUILLY-FUME	Loire, Fr		90	Mostly B, but the best endure
PREMIERES COTES DE BLAYE	Bordeaux, Fr		54	Ready at 2 yrs
PREMIERES COTES DE BORDEAUX	Bordeaux, Fr		54	Most ready at 2-3 yrs
PRIEURE-LICHINE, CH	Cantenac-Margaux, Bdx, Fr	38	28	Accelerate Margaux chart by 2 yrs
PRIMEUR	France		90	Drink now, although the decline is quite slow

KEY WORD	COUNTRY/REGION	CHART PAGE	TEXT PAGE	COMMENTARY
PRINCE PONIATOWSKI	Loire, Fr	82	76	
PRUM, J J	Germany	94	92	
PUISSEGUIN-ST-EMILION	Bordeaux, Fr	48	43	Accelerate Monbousquet chart by 2 yrs
PULIGNY-MONTRACHET	Burgundy, Fr	62	57	White village wines yrs ahead of Chevalier
QUARTS DE CHAUME	Loire, Fr	82	76	See Vouvray chart
QUEENSLAND	Australia		149	Some robust reds
QUINCY	Loire, Fr		90	B
QUINTA DE VARGELLAS	Portugal	122	120	
RABOSO	Italy		108	Long ageing demanded
RASTEAU (r) & VIN DOUX NATUREL	Rhône, Fr		79	Reds can age up to 4 yrs, but Vin Doux Naturel is ready to drink
RAUSAN-SEGLA, CH	Margaux, Bdx, Fr	38	28	Accelerate Margaux chart by 2 yrs
RAUZAN-GASSIES, CH	Margaux, Bdx, Fr	38	28	Accelerate Margaux chart by 2 yrs
RAVENEAU, FRANÇOIS	Chablis, Fr	66	64	
RAYMOND-LAFON, CH	Sauternes, Bdx, Fr	52	51	Accelerate Yquem chart by 3 yrs
RAYNE-VIGNEAU, CH	Sauternes, Bdx, Fr	52	51	Accelerate Yquem chart by 3 yrs
RECIOTO DELLA VALPOLICELLA	Italy	110	108	Accelerate Mazzano chart by 3 yrs
RECIOTO DI SOAVE	Italy	110	108	
REGELEALI	Italy		109	Rosso del Conte is worth a decade's cellaring
REGNIE	Burgundy, Fr	70	64	
RESERVE DE LA COMTESSE	Pauillac, Bdx, Fr	34	54	Accelerate Lynch-Bages chart by 3 yrs
REUILLY	Loire, Fr		90	B
RHEINGAU	Germany	96	92	Relatively consistent Riesling region
RHEINHESSEN	Germany		98	From Tafelwein & Liebfraumilch (A) to long-term sweet wines
RHEINPFALZ	Germany		98	Sturdy wines worth keeping
RIBERA DEL DUERO	Spain		118	Ageing demanded
RIBOLLA	Italy		108	B to 5 yrs
RICHEBOURG	Burgundy, Fr	58	55	Côte de Nuits *Grand Cru*
RIDGE VINEYARDS	California, USA	138	126	
RIEUSSEC, CH	Sauternes, Bdx, Fr	52	51	Accelerate Yquem chart by 3 yrs
RIOJA	Spain	114	112	Most can be drunk once released
RIVESALTES	France		91	Most bottled when ready
ROEDERER CRISTAL	Champagne, Fr	74	73	
ROMANEE, LA	Burgundy, Fr	58	55	Côte de Nuits *Grand Cru*
ROMANEE-CONTI, DOM DE LA	Burgundy, Fr	58	56	
ROMANEE-ST-VIVANT	Burgundy, Fr	58	55	Côte de Nuits *Grand Cru*
ROMANIA			124	Mainly A whites & B reds
ROSETTE	France		91	Sweet whites worth a good 5 yrs in bottle
ROSSO CONERO	Italy		109	Up to 4 yrs but mainly B
ROSSO DI MONTALCINO	Italy	106	101	Drink well ahead of Brunello
ROSSO PICENO	Italy		108	B
RUEDA	Spain		118	Whites mainly B

KEY WORD	COUNTRY/REGION	CHART PAGE	TEXT PAGE	COMMENTARY
RULLY	Burgundy, Fr	68	64	Drink at 2-3 yrs
RUSSIAN RIVER VALLEY	AVA, Calif, USA		125	Chardonnays and Gewurztraminers can age well from good producers
RUTHERFORD	Napa Valley, Calif, USA	130, 132	126	See Martha's Vineyard and Mondavi charts
SAAR-RUWER	Germany	94	92	Marvellously long-lived
ST AUBIN	Burgundy, Fr		55	Typically mature at 3-6 yrs
ST NICOLAS DE BOURGEUIL	Loire, Fr		90	Drink within 3 yrs. Exceptions: see p90
ST-CHINIAN	France		91	B & up to 5 yrs
STE-CROIX-DU-MONT	Bordeaux, Fr	52	51	Yquem chart gives relative quality of vintages; otherwise mainly B
ST-EMILION	Bordeaux, Fr	48	42	Very variable indeed
ST-ESTEPHE	Bordeaux, Fr	32	28	Almost invariably for long ageing
ST-GEORGES-ST-EMILION	Bordeaux, Fr	48	42	Accelerate Monbousquet chart by 2 yrs
ST-JOSEPH	Rhône, Fr	84, 86	78	Variable but only reds worth ageing
ST-JULIEN	Bordeaux, Fr	36	28	Classic & all repay bottle age
ST-PERAY	Rhône, Fr		78	Drink young
ST-PIERRE, CH	St-Julien, Bdx, Fr	36	28	Accelerate Gruaud Larose chart by 1 yr
ST-POURÇAIN-SUR-SIOULE	Loire, Fr		90	Allow 1 yr in bottle
SAINTSBURY	California, USA	136	127	
ST-VERAN	Burgundy, Fr	68	64	Mostly B
SALINAS VALLEY	California, USA		125	See Monterey
SAN LUIS OBISPO	California, USA		127	From B to 8 yrs
SANCERRE	Loire, Fr		90	Archetypally B, but the best endure
SANTA BARBARA	California, USA		127	Cool, good Zinfandel and Chardonnay. From B upwards
SANTA CLARA	California, USA		125	See Ridge Montebello for conditions & vintages
SANTA CRUZ	California, USA	138	126	Some of California's best cellar candidates
SANTA MADDALENA	Italy		109	B, sometimes A
SANTA MARIA VALLEY	AVA, Calif, USA		125	Very cool source of good Chardonnay
SANTA YNEZ VALLEY	AVA, Calif, USA		125	Sauvignon Blancs from good producers worth 3 yrs' ageing. Also Chardonnay
SANTENAY	Burgundy, Fr	60	55	Typically mature at 3-6 yrs
SASSELLA	Italy		108	Drink at 3-5 yrs
SASSICAIA	Italy	104	101	Only tangentially related to Tignanello. All coastal Cabernet
SAUMUR	Loire, Fr		77, 90	Some A, most B
SAUSSIGNAC	France		91	Sweet whites worth ageing
SAUTERNES	Bordeaux, Fr	52	50	From B to Yquem
SAUVIGNON DE ST BRIS	Burgundy, Fr		90	B, never longer
SAVENNIERES	Loire, Fr		76	One of the world's longest-lasting dry whites
SAVIGNY-LES-BEAUNE	Burgundy, Fr	60	55	Typically mature at 3-6 yrs
SAVOIE	France		90	Drink whites young, reds at 3-6 yrs
SCHIOPPETTINO	Italy		108	B to 4 yrs
SETUBAL	Portugal		121	Usually ready to drink when sold
SHERRY	Spain			Sold when ready. Drink Fino & Manzanilla soon
SIMMERN, LANGWERTH VON	Rheingau, Ger	96	92	

KEY WORD	COUNTRY/REGION	CHART PAGE	TEXT PAGE	COMMENTARY
IZZANO	Italy	102	100	3 yrs ahead of Gaja, often different
OAVE	Italy		108	A, sometimes B; see p108 for exceptions
ONOMA	California, USA	134	126	Variable; some good developers. See Sonoma Cutrer chart for conditions
ONOMA-CUTRER	California, USA	134	126	
OUTH AMERICA			143	Mainly B, some A & some very ageworthy reds
OUTHERN VALES	Australia		148	See Grange notes (p150) for weather details
PANNA	Italy	102	100	At least 2 yrs ahead of Gaja
TAG'S LEAP	AVA, California, USA	130	125	Cabernet can age well (10 yrs plus). See Heitz chart
UDUIRAUT, CH	Sauternes, Bdx, Fr	52	51	Accelerate Yquem chart by 3 yrs
WITZERLAND			124	Mostly A & B
ABLE WINE			18	Drink now!
ACHE, LA	Burgundy, Fr	58	56	
AFELWEIN	Germany		92	Drink now!
ALBOT, CH	St-Julien, Bdx, Fr	36	28	Accelerate Gruaud Larose chart by 1 yr
ASMANIA	Australia		149	Most wines designed for bottle age
AURASI	Italy		109	Repays ageing 10 yrs
AYLOR	Portugal	122	120	
AZZELENGHE	Italy		108	B to 5 yrs
EROLDEGO	Italy		108	B
ERTRE, CH DU	Arsac-Margaux, Bdx, Fr	38	28	Accelerate Margaux chart by 2 yrs
HIEULEY, CH	Entre-Deux-Mers, Bdx, Fr		54	B
IGNANELLO	Italy	104	101	
OKAJI	Hungary		124	Depends on style & sweetness
ORGIANO (RUBESCO DI)	Italy		109	Many stand the test of time
ORO	Spain		118	Reds mostly best at 3-6 yrs
ORRES	Spain	116	113	See p113 for Torres wines other than Mas la Plana
OUR CARNET, CH LA	St-Laurent, Bdx, Fr	34	28	Accelerate Lynch-Bages chart by 2 yrs
OURAINE	Loire, Fr	82	77	Sauvignon is mostly A; for Chenins see Vouvray chart
REBBIANO D'ABRUZZO	Italy		109	Only Valentini's is worth ageing
RENTINO-ALTO ADIGE	Loire, Fr		108	Mostly B
RIMBACH	Alsace, Fr	80	76	
ROCKENBEERENAUSLESE	Germany		92	Can last almost indefinitely
ROTANOY, CH	Pomerol, Bdx, Fr	44	42	Ages as Petrus
USCANY	Italy		100	For whites see p101
MBRIA	Italy	104	109	Cross-refer reds to Tignanello chart
PPER HUNTER	New South Wales, Aus		149	Mostly B still
TIEL-REQUENA	Spain		118	B to 4 yrs
ACQUEYRAS	Rhône, Fr	88	79	Can age up to 4 yrs
ALBUENA	Spain		118	
ALDEPEÑAS	Spain		118	Some reds can last up to 8 yrs
ALGELLA	Italy		109	Drink at 3-5 yrs

KEY WORD	COUNTRY/REGION	CHART PAGE	TEXT PAGE	COMMENTARY
VALPOLICELLA	Italy		108	A, but some single vineyard wines up to 5 yrs
VALTELLINA	Italy		108	Drink at 3-5 yrs; some Bs
VEGA SICILIA	Spain		118	
VENEGAZZU	Italy		108	May develop for up to 7 yrs
VENETO	Italy		108	Most are B, but see p108 for exceptions
VERDUZZO	Italy		108	Mainly B
VERNACCIA DI SAN GIMIGNANO	Italy		101	Still mainly B but some are worth cellaring
VICTORIA	Australia		148	Some of Australia's most ageable wines
VIN DE PAYS	France		90	Whites mainly A; reds mainly B, sometimes A, see Mas de Daumas Gassac
VIN DE TABLE	France		90	A
VINCENT, JEAN-JACQUES	Burgundy, Fr	68	55	
VINHO VERDE	Portugal		121	Mainly A
VINO DA TAVOLA	Italy		101	Expensive Tuscan VDT: see p101, otherwise A
VOLNAY	Burgundy, Fr		55	Côte de Beaune village: can make wine for long ageing, 4-12 yrs
VOSNE-ROMANEE	Burgundy, Fr	58	55	Côte de Nuits village: can make wine for long ageing, 6-15 yrs
VOUGEOT	Burgundy, Fr	58	55	Côte de Nuits village: can make wine for long ageing, 5-15 yrs
VOUVRAY	Loire, Fr	82	76	
WASHINGTON	USA		142	Mainly B, some A
WEHLENER SONNENUHR	Mosel, Ger	94	93	
WHITE ZINFANDEL	California		126	A
WILLAMETTE VALLEY	Oregon, USA	144	142	Chardonnay & Pinot Gris age faster than Pinot Noir
WYNNS	Australia	154	148	
YARRA YERING	Australia	156	148	
YARRA VALLEY	Australia	156	147	
YECLA	Spain		118	Some reds worth serious ageing
YORK MOUNTAIN	AVA, Calif, USA		125	See Paso Robles
YQUEM, CH D'	Sauternes, Bdx, Fr	52	50	
YUGOSLAVIA			124	Mainly A whites but some reds repay 5 yrs
ZINFANDEL	California	128	126	Styles vary widely. See Ridge chart

Diagram artwork by Radius.

PICTURE CREDITS

8: Jean Daniel Sudres/Scope; 10: Michel Guillard/Scope; 11(top): TMB/Photo: Kim Sayer; 11(bottom): Jaques Guillard/Scope; 12: Adam Woolfitt/Susan Griggs Agency; 13: Michel Guillard/Scope; 14: Colin Maher – QED/Visionbank/England Scene; 15: Michel Guillard/Scope; 16: Michel Guillard/Scope; 18: Michel Guillard/Scope; 23: Michel Guillard/Scope; 24: Michel Guillard/Scope; 25: Michel Guillard/Scope; 28: Michel Guillard/Scope; 29: P Somelet/Diaf; 42: Michel Guillard/Scope; 43: Kerth Klaus/Zefa; 50: Michel Guillard/Scope; 51: Michel Guillard/Scope; 55: Jaques Guillard/Scope; 57: Jean-Luc Barde/Scope; 64: Michael Busselle; 65(left): Henri Veiller/Explorer; 65(right): Jaques Guillard/Scope; 73: Jaques Guillard/Scope; 76: Jaques Guillard/Scope; 77: Michael Busselle; 78: Jaques Guillard/Scope; 79: Jaques Guillard/Scope; 93: Hans Wolf/The Image Bank; 99: John Sims; 100: John Sims; 113: Kiernan/Landscape Only; 119: V Wentzel/Zefa; 120: John Heseltine; 125: Michael Freeman; 127: Jim Patton/Chalone; 142: Chris Bennion/The Eyrie Vineyards; 143: F Petersen/Zefa; 146: Patrick Eagar; 147: Patrick Eagar; 149: Jean-Paul Ferrero/Visionbank/England Scene; 160-176: MB/Photo: Alistair Laidlaw